Ravi and Marcia have combined practical research in the "real world" with visionary thinking. I recommend this book to anyone trying to better serve customers, suppliers, and employees.
> —Chuck Williams, Chief Technology Officer
> Pfizer, Inc.

In their back-to-basics approach, Kalakota and Robinson demonstrate how managers can thrive by providing excellent multi-channel services on the front end by taking a cross-enterprise perspective.
> —Frances X. Frei, Assistant Professor, Technology and Operations Management
> Harvard Business School

After a time of ERP, SCM and CRM implementations, e-business initiatives, and m-business projects, enterprises now have to get real value out of these investments. The "services blueprints" described in this book show how all those initiatives can be aligned so that they deliver the desired ROI. It's a great roadmap from vision to reality.
> —Dr. Mathias Kirchmer, CEO
> IDS Scheer, Inc.

Digitization represents a staggering opportunity for most businesses. How to execute effectively continues to plague most executives. The authors once again present a superbly researched work, with an insightful framework.
> —Peter McNally, Managing Director
> Cyberstarts Inc.

Services Blueprint: Roadmap for Execution *gives technology officers, tasked with the challenging responsibility of using technology to save money, increase revenue and profit an in-depth and information rich analysis of how Web Services should be used as a technology foundation for better business processes in their company*
> —Ramon Ray, Editor and Analyst
> Smallbiztechnology.com

Poignant case studies make this book terrific for benchmarking how well you're marrying Web Service technology and organization to digitize any aspect of your business—from product development to customer service.
> —Andrew Ellicott, Technology Director
> Infinity Pharmaceuticals, Inc.

Essential reading for anyone considering digitization.
> —Jeff Gainer, Principal Consultant
> Darwin Partners

Addison-Wesley Information Technology Series
Capers Jones and David S. Linthicum, Consulting Editors

The information technology (IT) industry is in the public eye now more than ever before because of a number of major issues in which software technology and national policies are closely related. As the use of software expands, there is a continuing need for business and software professionals to stay current with the state of the art in software methodologies and technologies. The goal of the **Addison-Wesley Information Technology Series** is to cover any and all topics that affect the IT community. These books illustrate and explore how information technology can be aligned with business practices to achieve business goals and support business imperatives. Addison-Wesley has created this innovative series to empower you with the benefits of the industry experts' experience.

For more information point your browser to http://www.awprofessional.com/itseries

Sid Adelman, Larissa Terpeluk Moss, *Data Warehouse Project Management.* ISBN: 0-201-61635-1

Sid Adelman, Joyce Bischoff, Jill Dyché, Douglas Hackney, Sean Ivoghli, Chuck Kelley, David Marco, Larissa Moss, and Clay Rehm, *Impossible Data Warehouse Situations: Solutions from the Experts.* ISBN: 0-201-76033-9

Wayne Applehans, Alden Globe, and Greg Laugero, *Managing Knowledge: A Practical Web-Based Approach.* ISBN: 0-201-43315-X

David Leon Clark, *Enterprise Security: The Manager's Defense Guide.* ISBN: 0-201-71972-X

Frank P. Coyle, *XML, Web Services, and the Data Revolution.* ISBN: 0-201-77641-3

Kevin Dick, *XML, Second Edition: A Manager's Guide.* ISBN: 0-201-77006-7

Jill Dyché, *e-Data: Turning Data into Information with Data Warehousing.* ISBN: 0-201-65780-5

Jill Dyché, *The CRM Handbook: A Business Guide to Customer Relationship Management.* ISBN: 0-201-73062-6

Patricia L. Ferdinandi, *A Requirements Pattern: Succeeding in the Internet Economy.* ISBN: 0-201-73826-0

David Garmus and David Herron, *Function Point Analysis: Measurement Practices for Successful Software Projects.* ISBN: 0-201-69944-3

John Harney, *Application Service Providers (ASPs): A Manager's Guide.* ISBN: 0-201-72659-9

International Function Point Users Group, *IT Measurement: Practical Advice from the Experts.* ISBN: 0-201-74158-X

Capers Jones, *Software Assessments, Benchmarks, and Best Practices.* ISBN: 0-201-48542-7

Ravi Kalakota and Marcia Robinson, *e-Business 2.0: Roadmap for Success.* ISBN: 0-201-72165-1

Ravi Kalakota and Marcia Robinson, *Services Blueprint: Roadmap for Execution.* ISBN: 0-321-15039-2

Greg Laugero and Alden Globe, *Enterprise Content Services: Connecting Information and Profitability.* ISBN: 0-201-73016-2

David S. Linthicum, *Enterprise Application Integration.* ISBN: 0-201-61583-5

David S. Linthicum, *B2B Application Integration: e-Business-Enable Your Enterprise.* ISBN: 0-201-70936-8

Sergio Lozinsky, *Enterprise-Wide Software Solutions: Integration Strategies and Practices.* ISBN: 0-201-30971-8

Anne Thomas Manes, *Web Services: A Manager's Guide.* ISBN: 0-321-18577-3

Larissa T. Moss and Shaku Atre, *Business Intelligence Roadmap: The Complete Project Lifecycle for Decision-Support Applications.* ISBN: 0-201-78420-3

Bud Porter-Roth, *Request for Proposal: A Guide to Effective RFP Development.* ISBN: 0-201-77575-1

Ronald G. Ross, *Principles of the Business Rule Approach.* ISBN: 0-201-78893-4

Karl E. Wiegers, *Peer Reviews in Software: A Practical Guide.* ISBN: 0-201-73485-0

Ralph R. Young, *Effective Requirements Practices.* ISBN: 0-201-70912-0

Bill Zoellick, *CyberRegs: A Business Guide to Web Property, Privacy, and Patents.* ISBN: 0-201-72230-5

Services Blueprint
Roadmap for Execution

Ravi Kalakota and Marcia Robinson

✦✦ Addison-Wesley

Boston • San Francisco • New York • Toronto
Montreal • London • Munich • Paris • Madrid • Capetown
Sydney • Tokyo • Singapore • Mexico City

The publisher offers discounts on this book when ordered in quantity for bulk purchases and special sales. For more information, please contact:

U.S. Corporate and Government Sales
(800) 382-3419
corpsales@pearsontechgroup.com

For sales outside of the U.S., please contact:
International Sales
(317) 581-3793
international@pearsontechgroup.com

Visit Addison-Wesley on the Web: www.awprofessional.com

Library of Congress Cataloging-in-Publication Data
Kalakota, Ravi.
    Services blueprint : a roadmap for execution / Ravi Kalakota, Marcia Robinson.
        p. cm. — (Addison-Wesley information technology series)
    Includes bibliographical references and index.
    ISBN 0-321-15039-2 (alk. paper)
        1. Service industries—Management. 2. Service industries—Automation.
    3. Service industries—Management—Case studies. 4. Service industries—
    Automation—Case studies. I. Robinson, Marcia, 1964– II. Title. III. Series.
    HD9980.5.K355 2004
    658—dc21   2003049594

Pearson Education
Rights and Contracts Department
75 Arlington Street, Suite 300
Boston, MA 02116
Fax: (617) 848-7047

ISBN 0-321-15039-2
Text printed on recycled paper
1 2 3 4 5 6 7 8 9 10 — CRS — 0706050403
First printing, June 2003

To Lynn Lorenc, a fabulous friend
Thank you for your unwavering support and encouragement

Contents

Foreword   xvii

Preface   xxi

      E-Commerce, E-Business, Now Services   xxii

      The Need for a Services Blueprint   xxiv

    The Focus of This Book   xxv

      The Audience for This Book   xxvi

      The Organization of This Book   xxvi

    Acknowledgments   xxviii

PART I   THE NEED FOR DIGITIZATION   1

CHAPTER ONE   FROM E-BUSINESS TO SERVICES: WHY AND WHY NOW?   3

What to Expect   3

Introduction   3

Services Is the Mega-Trend   5

    Technology Payoff and ROI Trends   6

    Process Configuration and Flexibility Trends   8

    Multi-Channel and Cross-Enterprise Trends   9

    Improving Application Integration Trends   11

    Aligning Inside-Out and Outside-In Process Trends   12

The Need for a Services Blueprint   14

    Focal Points   15

    The Blueprint as an Execution Differentiator   16

Three Categories of Blueprints 17
Digitization at General Electric (GE) 19
WorkOut—Globalization 19
Six Sigma—Improving Manufacturing and Service Quality 20
Services—Converting Products into Solutions 20
Digitization—Increasing Productivity and Profitability 21
Digitization Themes at GE 21
Digitization at Wal-Mart 22
Wal-Mart—A Brief History 22
Wal-Mart's Blueprint for Digitization 23
Wal-Mart Differentiator—Effective Localized Store Management 24
Wal-Mart Differentiator—Logistics Management 24
Wal-Mart Differentiator—Information Technology Execution 26
Wal-Mart versus Kmart—A Blueprint Comparison 27
Digitization Execution Is a Senior Management Issue 28
Seven Points to Ponder 30

Chapter Two FOCAL POINTS OF DIGITIZATION 33

What to Expect 33
Introduction 33
Easy To Do Business With (ETDBW) 35
Customer-Centric Integration—Back-End Office Synchronization 37
Low Cost—Streamlined Supply Chains 39
Lowest Overhead—Business Process Outsourcing 42
Zero-Defect Quality—Supplier Relationship Management 43
Productivity Multiplier—Employee Portals 44
Fast Service—Fast Fulfillment 46
Product Innovation—Shrinking Product Lifecycles 47
Evolving Business Model—Changing Customer Priorities 49
Real-Time Business—Synchronized with the Market 51
Seven Points to Ponder 53

Chapter Three SERVICE PLATFORMS:
ENABLERS OF DIGITIZATION 55

What to Expect 55
Introduction 55

Focal Points and Portals—A Symbiotic Relationship   57
   Enterprise Portals Need Business Process Management (BPM)   58
   What Does a Service Platform Look Like?   59
New Trends in Enterprise Applications—Portal Infrastructure   61
   The Evolution of Enterprise Portals   61
   The Next Step in Portal Evolution—Controlling the Chaos   62
   Aligning Business Flexibility Needs with Portal Infrastructure   63
   Modularity and Composition—Concepts for Managing
      Complexity   65
   Modularity and Composition in Manufacturing—Product
      Platforms   66
Service Platforms—Making Complexity Manageable   68
   From Fragmented Portals to Service Platforms   68
   The Composite Process Layer—Enabling Business Process
      Management   69
   Exploring the Integration Layer—Web Services Architecture   71
   Putting Everything Together—SAP's xApps   76
Creating Value—Different Types of Service Platforms   78
Seven Points to Ponder   80

PART II   **EXAMPLES OF SERVICE BLUEPRINTS   83**

CHAPTER FOUR   MULTI-CHANNEL BLUEPRINT: CREATING
NEW CUSTOMER EXPERIENCES   85

What to Expect   85
Introduction   86
   From Uni-Channel to Multi-Channel—The Financial Services
      Industry   86
Evolution of Multi-Channel CRM   88
   Tele-Channel—From Telesales to Customer Interaction Centers   88
   Brick-and-Mortar Channel—Evolution of Face-to-Face Interaction   91
   Online Self-Service Channel—From Web Sites to E-Service   91
Long-Term Trends Shaping Customer-Centric Requirements   92
   Self-Service Customers—Are You Ready?   92
   Synchronizing Customer Interactions   93

New Cross-Channel Experiences—Line Busters   94

Outsourcing Call Centers and E-Mail Contact   96

Different Services for Different Customers—Real-Time Analytics   97

Creating Multi-Channel Blueprints   98

Customer-Centric Focal Point—Easy To Do Business With   100

The Services Layer—Enabling Composite Processes   101

The Business Process Management Layer—Translating Services into
Processes   104

Integrating Enterprise Applications—Linking Processes via Integration
Layers   105

Multi-Channel CRM Service Platforms—The Vendor's Perspective   108

JC Penney—Product Returns in a Multi-Channel Setting   109

Multi-Channel Forward Fulfillment Process   111

The Product Returns Process   112

Seven Points to Ponder   114

CHAPTER FIVE   SPEND MANAGEMENT BLUEPRINT:
ENABLING SUPPLIER MANAGEMENT
SERVICES   117

What to Expect   117

Introduction   117

Evolution of Procurement   119

The Boom-Bust Cycle of E-Procurement   120

E-Procurement—From a Technology Focus to a Process Focus   120

Long-Term Trends Shaping Spend Management   123

Continuous Cost Reduction—Nonstop CFO Focus   123

Procurement Transparency   124

Global Sourcing as a "Need-to-Have" Capability   125

Faster, Smoother, and More Flexible Integration Is Necessary   127

Self-Service Desktop Procurement—Better Process Automation   128

Spend Analysis—Monitoring and Controlling Contracts   129

Creating Spend Management Blueprints   130

Spend Management Focal Point   131

The Services Layer—Enabling Composite Processes   132

The Business Process Management Layer—Translating Services into
Processes   136

Integrating Enterprise Applications—Mapping Processes into
Applications   137
Spend Management Platforms—The Vendor's Perspective   138
Service Parts Procurement—An Emerging Service Platform   141
Why Focus on Service Parts Management?   142
Defining the Business Problem   143
Procurement as a Key Part of Service Management   144
Seven Points to Ponder   145

CHAPTER SIX   SUPPLY CHAIN BLUEPRINT:
CREATING AN ADAPTIVE ENTERPRISE   147

What to Expect   147
Introduction   148
Evolution of Supply Chain Management   149
Trends in Supply Chain Management   153
Low-Cost Manufacturing—Outsourcing   153
Matching Supply and Demand in a Volatile Environment   154
Collaboration—Maximizing Utilization of Assets   155
New Forms of Differentiation—Reverse Logistics   156
Adaptive Supply Chains—Monitor, Alert, and Act   157
Supply Chain Blueprint   158
Where Are We Today?   159
Supply Chain Focal Point—Fast Service   161
The Supply Chain Services Layer—Enabling Composite
Processes   163
The Business Process Management Layer—Translating Services into
Processes   166
Integrating Enterprise Applications—Mapping Processes into
Applications   167
SCM Service Platforms—The Vendor's Perspective   168
Eastman Chemical—Creating a Logistics Service Platform   170
Growing Focus on Supply Chain Efficiency in the Chemical
Industry   170
Supply Chain Technology—A Competitive Weapon for Eastman   171
Cendian—A 4PL Service Platform for the Chemical Industry   173
Seven Points to Ponder   175

CHAPTER SEVEN EMPLOYEE-CENTRIC BLUEPRINT:
ENABLING HUMAN CAPITAL
MANAGEMENT   177

What to Expect   177
Introduction   177
Evolution of HR Digitization—Processes versus Platforms   180
    Process Perspective—Types of HR Process Digitization   180
    Technology Perspective—Evolution of Employee Service Platforms   182
Long-Term Trends Shaping Employee-Centric Investments   184
    Cost Reduction Trend—HR Process Outsourcing   185
    Organizational Structure Trend—Mergers, Acquisitions, and
        Divestitures   186
    Demographics Trend—Changing Workforce Needs   187
    Regulatory Trend—Complexity and Changing Regulatory
        Environment   188
    Employee Alignment Trend—Sync Employees with Corporate
        Objectives   189
    Benefits Management Trend—Provide Flexibility   190
People, Processes, and Technology—Creating New HR Services
    Blueprints   191
    Defining the HR Focal Point   193
    The HR Services Layer—Enabling Composite Processes   195
    The Business Process Management Layer—Translating HR Services into
        Processes   197
    Enterprise Applications—Mapping HR Processes into Applications   198
Employee Service Platforms—The Vendor's Perspective   200
General Motors Case Study—Ease of Self-Service   202
    Business Challenges Facing GM Human Resources   202
    Focal Point—Increasing Employee Productivity   203
    The Employee-Centric Solution—mySocrates   204
    GM and Labor Productivity   205
Seven Points to Ponder   206

CHAPTER TWELVE THE DISCIPLINE OF EXECUTION:
A TALE OF TWO COMPANIES   315

What to Expect   315
Introduction   315
The Mergers and Acquisitions Strategy   316
    The Amazing Saga of AT&T   317
    Diversifying from Long-Distance Only to Soup-to-Nuts Services   318
    Blur of Deals—Understanding the Strategic Shifts   319
    Breaking up AT&T, Again   320
    Key Lessons Learned from AT&T—Chasing a Moving Target   320
IBM's Digitization Journey   322
    Change of Leadership   322
    Phase 1—Simplification   323
    Phase 2—Digitizing IBM Internally   324
    Phase 3—Customer-Centric Process Transformation   325
    Phase 4—Consultative Solution Selling   326
    Transformation Management—The Blueprint Team   327
    Key Lessons Learned from IBM's Transformation—Hitting a Moving
        Target   329
Services Transformation—Management Is Essential   329
    The Roadmap for Services Digitization   329
    Guiding and Coordinating Large-Scale Digitization   330
    The Discipline to Implement   331
A Final Thought—Services Digitization Is Inevitable   332

Endnotes   335
Index   343

Measure 275

Analyze 277

Improve and Implement via Service Platforms 279

Control and Learn 280

Workforce Changes—New Job Design 281

Seven Points to Ponder 284

CHAPTER ELEVEN MAKING DIGITIZATION HAPPEN:
MICRO-LEVEL TECHNOLOGY
BLUEPRINT 287

What to Expect 287

Introduction 287

Short-Term IT Decisions versus Long-Term IT Decisions 288

Princeton University—Digitizing Education 289

The Web—A Core Part of the Digital Education Experience 290

Serving the Digital Student—Portals and Service Platforms 291

Micro-Level Blueprint Planning Models 292

One Project at a Time 294

What Is Our Data Model? 295

Fixing the Data Model Problems—Iterative Development 296

What Is Our Enterprise Applications Model? 296

The Portfolio Method of Application Investment 298

Single Vendor versus Best-of-Breed 299

Drawbacks of the Portfolio Method 300

What Is Our Portal Strategy? 301

Investing in Portals 303

Implementing Portal Blueprints 304

What Is Our Infrastructure Model? 304

Business Process Outsourcing Demands a Federated Model 305

Putting Everything Together 307

The Need for Federated IT Architecture—The Transformation of
Georgia-Pacific 308

From a Building Products Company to a Consumer Products
Company 309

Spin-offs and Divestitures—Reshaping the Company 310

The Execution Challenge 311

Seven Points to Ponder 312

PART III   CREATING A SERVICES BLUEPRINT   237

CHAPTER NINE   VISION TO EXECUTION:
                THE BLUEPRINT METHODOLOGY   239

What to Expect   239
Welcome to the Company, Mr. VP   239
Your Challenge Is Not Strategy, but Execution   241
Do You Have a Unified Blueprint to Manage Enterprise-Wide Execution?   243
    Macro-Level—Creating an Operating Strategy Using a Balanced
        Scorecard   246
    Meso-Level—Creating a Process Strategy with Six Sigma   247
    Micro-Level—Creating a Technology Strategy   249
How Are You Going to Coordinate the Macro-, Meso-, and Micro-Levels?   251
Coordination: You Need to Create a Blueprint Management Office   253
    Structure of the Blueprint Management Office   254
    What Power Does the BMO Have?   256
    Staff the BMO with Service Thinkers   257
    Example of a BMO Project—Supply Chain Digitization   258
Seven Points to Ponder   260

CHAPTER TEN   THE ANALYSIS AND DESIGN OF NEW
               SERVICES: MESO-LEVEL BLUEPRINT   263

What to Expect   263
Moving from Strategy to Process Design   263
    Evolving to Brick and Click—New Multi-Channel Government
        Services   264
    Evolving to Cross-Enterprise—New Order-to-Cash Services   265
    The Growing Importance of Service Analysis and Design   266
Picking a Meso-Level Change Management Methodology   267
    Picking a Performance Improvement Method   268
Six Sigma—Dominant Performance Improvement Method   269
    Six Sigma's Momentum   270
    Six Sigma = Culture Change   271
    Criticism of Six Sigma   272
Steps for Service Digitization   273
    Define   273

CHAPTER EIGHT PRODUCT INNOVATION BLUEPRINT: ENABLING PRODUCT LIFECYCLE MANAGEMENT 209

What to Expect 209
Introduction 209
The Evolution of PLM 212
Long-Term Trends Shaping PLM 214
  Accelerated New Product Design 215
  Emphasis on Time to Market and Quality 216
  Expanding Health, Safety, and Environmental Regulations 217
  Custom-Configured Products 218
  Engineering Digital Products 219
  Accelerated Online Product Launches 220
People, Processes, and Applications—Creating PLM Blueprints 220
  PLM Focal Point—Accelerated Product Innovation 222
  The PLM Services Layer—Enabling Composite Processes 222
  The Business Process Management Layer—Translating PLM Services into
    Processes 224
  Integrating Enterprise Applications—Mapping Processes into
    Applications 226
PLM Service Platforms—The Vendor's Perspective 228
Nike Footwear—A PLM Case Study 230
  Evolution of Athletic Footwear Design 231
  The Mold Process—Computer-Aided Engineering 231
  The Next Generation of Design—Design for the Environment 232
The New York Times—Creating Digital Products 232
  Next Generation of Online Advertising—Impressions via Sessions 234
  Going Beyond Surround Sessions—Site Sessions 234
  New Products from Old Material—Archive Packaging 235
  Digital Product Lifecycle Management—The New Frontier 235
Seven Points to Ponder 236

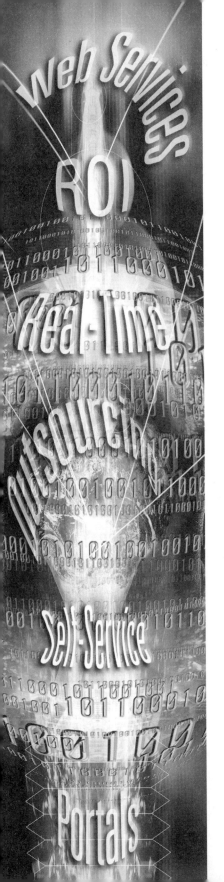

Foreword

All too many managers are looking for "the next big thing," and all too many academics and consultants are prepared to satisfy their hunger by offering a "revolutionary" nostrum on technology or management. The authors of this book, however, are a welcome exception. Not that their ideas don't have currency; the notion of viewing organizations as a collection of services is certainly fresh, as are their up-to-date perspectives on Web Services and other new technologies. Yet the authors have the wisdom and modesty to acknowledge the importance of previously discussed ideas.

What is particularly refreshing about the book is its appeal to managers to practice time-honored virtues in a contemporary technological context. These virtues include process design and improvement, a focus on execution, and continual implementation of technologies and management approaches even when they are not particularly fashionable.

This may sound unexceptional, but think of how many organizations reacted to the e-commerce movement. Certainly many were slow to jump on the bandwagon before it became a full-fledged trend. In the late 1990s, virtually every company decided that it must have a Web presence and the ability to accept online orders. Some implemented these capabilities earlier than they needed to, but that was not the primary problem. The real tragedies were that many firms did not implement these capabilities in an integrated fashion, and that they virtu-ally stopped aggressively pursuing e-commerce when the Internet bubble burst around 2001. Evidence of the lack of e-commerce integration comes from Inter-national Data Corporation, which estimates that only 10% of e-commerce sites are connected to the back-end transaction sites within their companies.

The integration isn't likely to happen soon, given the retreat from e-commerce and IT investment in general. Worldwide spending on IT declined in 2002 for the first year in decades. Most companies are focusing only on the most problematic aspects of IT, and few are investing in the IT-enabled future of their businesses. They are taking a "bulimic" approach to IT—binging on it when times are good, and purging themselves of it when the economics become more difficult.

It doesn't have to be this way. Kalakota and Robinson describe a small num-ber of companies that aren't driven to IT by fad and fashion, but rather by the prospect of long-term competitive advantage. These organizations—including the giants General Electric, Intel, Wal-Mart, and a few firms, such as Eastman Chemical—weren't necessarily the first in their industries to embrace IT, but they are the most loyal and persistent adopters. They view economic downturns as an opportunity to gain share. While other companies cut back on IT investments, these firms "double down," expanding their commitments to technology and to efficient, IT-enabled business processes. This is one of the reasons why large, suc-cessful companies became and stayed profitable.

The need for ongoing digitization, however, is only one focus of this book. Two other key movements of the past several decades are integrated in a highly complementary fashion. The shift to a customer-oriented services focus, and the importance of process improvement and innovation, are also treated in detail. Interestingly, some of the same companies that are pursuing continuous digitiza-tion are also long-term advocates of service and process orientations. GE, for example, has had a formal, well-structured initiative to move into services (from what were once primarily manufacturing business units) for over seven years, and its Six Sigma process improvement initiative and WorkOut program have been in place for many years as well.

Although each of the components is familiar, together these three emphases comprise a truly new idea. That firms should continuously digitize their processes, redesign and optimize them, and bundle those activities into services for internal and external consumption has never really been stated in such a clear, cogent fashion. Kalakota and Robinson also provide insights about the specific content of processes—for example, that any customer-facing processes should be addressed from the beginning with a "multi-channel" orientation. The fact that

Web sites and call centers exist as important ways to reach customers should not be ignored, for example, when thinking about sales force automation.

The authors also don't stop at bright, "academic" ideas. Much of their writing focuses on how these ideas can be better executed. Just as organizations embrace one topic at the expense of another, our business society typically vacillates between the embrace of ideas and a strong orientation to execution. We are now in an execution phase—as evidenced by the difficult times for consultants, business conference providers, executive education units in business schools, and other branches of the "idea industry." The notable success of the book *Execution* by Bossidy and Charan is another piece of evidence. Interest in ideas will undoubtedly pick up, but what organizations obviously need is both ideas and execution. Most business books tend to slight the latter topic, but this tome is replete with both ideas and execution-oriented content.

I view the purpose of a foreword as getting the unconvinced potential reader to buy the book and read major chunks of it. I hope I've succeeded in that objective. If you work in business and have any inkling that technology and efficient, effective processes have a role in your success, then you need to go further into this volume. If you believe that services and service levels are critical to your success with customers, you need to read more. Even if you are totally convinced of these ideas, you'll find plenty of case studies and smaller examples to buttress your opinions. If you've read this far, you're probably in at least one of these categories—so take the plunge!

Thomas H. Davenport
Director, Accenture Institute for Strategic Change
President's Chaired Professor in Information
Technology and Management
Babson College

Preface

This book was seeded in a moment of tension. We were engaged in a project with a Fortune 500 firm aimed at designing new online and multi-channel services that leveraged existing e-business investments. In particular, the project was focused on the issues of translating the business imperatives "One Face to the Customer" and "Easy To Do Business With" into cross-enterprise services and delivered via portals. It was clear to us that in order to execute the plan and build a unified customer portal, the different e-business initiatives across the firm needed to be aligned. Its fragmented approach would not be sufficient to get the firm to where the leadership wanted to go.

As we presented our findings, the grumbling and arguments began. "Wait a minute. We might be serving the same customer, but we are a complex conglomerate with multiple business units, each with different operating targets and incentive structures. In some business units, the e-business initiatives are more advanced than in others. We don't want to be held back by the slower moving units; so, each business unit should launch its own e-business effort. At this very moment, we have ten different Siebel CRM implementations in progress with multiple consulting firms. We don't think that an integrated approach to support a unified customer-facing portal or consistent user experience will work in our company."

It was an uncomfortable moment as we looked out at the audience and realized that the notion of creating a cross-enterprise service platform to support customized user experiences delivered via enterprise portals is a novel concept for many managers. Although increased user demand for online and multi-channel services is straining the business processes and systems of most firms, managers are not aware of the structural problems they have to deal with. Political fiefdoms need to be breached. Cross-enterprise processes need to be architected. New infrastructures need to be deployed. Incentives need to be realigned.

The bottom line: Top management wants to leverage technology to deliver consistent, high-quality customer, employee, supplier, and partner experiences across channels and divisions. Current practices are not going to get them there. Leading companies, such as Intel, Wal-Mart, GE, Boeing, IBM, UPS, and American Express, are moving quickly to fix the problems by deploying new service platforms to create competitive differentiation. They are beginning to understand that new cross-enterprise and multi-channel services will set them apart.

What are the leading companies doing differently? As we did more research on best-practice service platforms, we realized that the state of the art in integration strategies was subtly changing. The traditional view of integration is tying together back-office processes and applications (often labeled Enterprise Application Integration). The emerging view of integration is a flexible composition of processes, applications, and infrastructure (broadly labeled e-Services or Web Services). Whatever the terminology, a services-driven architecture forms the foundation of enterprise portals.

Clearly, the game has changed. The challenge facing management is no longer: What enterprise applications do we invest in? The new question confronting many companies is: Now that I have enterprise applications, how can I leverage the company's investment in them? How do I invest in and create a blueprint of service platforms that can deliver integrated services through the various customer, employee, supplier, and manager portals? What do I need to do to differentiate the company in terms of services? These business questions form the framework for this book.

E-Commerce, E-Business, Now Services

Users don't care about technology; they care about services and their effective delivery. The broader market is already anticipating the movement to service platforms. Simply look at the announcements by various vendors: IBM (WebSphere and e-business on demand), Sun Microsystems (Sun ONE and Services on Demand), Microsoft (.NET Application Servers), SAP (NetWeaver and xApps), Siebel (UAN), PeopleSoft (AppConnect), and BEA (WebLogic).

Our research indicates that three out of four venture investments are earmarked for enabling services, rather than content or enterprise applications. Millions of dollars are being spent trying to market service platforms with fuzzy explanations of what it really means. So, what are these new service platforms and who needs them? How do you use them to create services? What strategy tools and methods are appropriate and in what context?

Answers to these questions will shape the blueprint of digitization in the next decade. Some specific business and technology trends driving the need for services blueprints are:

- **Business Process Management Trends.** Inside-out processes are complementing outside-in services. Companies are not limiting themselves to thinking about process management or automation; instead, they are thinking about digitizing the entire set of composite processes (for example, order-to-cash) that deliver value in the form of a service. This "service enablement" trend is new and has huge implications for companies.

- **ROI/Value Trends.** Investing in technology is getting much harder. The commoditization cycle times are short, industry consolidations are occurring more frequently, and the timeline for technology investments is shrinking. As a result, the challenge for management is not spending money but extracting an ROI. In a high-growth market you can get away with implementing monolithic, proprietary, closed applications and architectures. A cost-focused economy forces a little bit of "show me the money" technological pragmatism.

- **Application Integration Trends.** Applications need to be integrated into cohesive services. If you look at most large companies, they may have hundreds of uncoordinated integration initiatives, all with different objectives. This is not a good situation, as increasingly, Web applications tend to be cross-enterprise types of applications with complex workflows.

- **Infrastructure Trends.** The way software is built is changing. In the last decade we have seen three structural migrations—mainframe to client/server (2-tier) to Web applications (3-tier) to Web Services (multi-tier). Services Oriented Architectures are gaining momentum as companies struggle with the age-old issues of extending, scaling, maintaining, and integrating applications.

- **Macroeconomic Trends.** The structure of the twenty-first century organization is difficult to understand and even more difficult to plan for. A volatile mix is triggering changes: growing globalization, productivity and efficiency pressures, shrinking product lifecycles, and evolving technology. As the complexity increases, managers are struggling with issues of how to create effective service platforms to support a changing business environment.

All these trends argue for a "big picture" services blueprint at the enterprise level that can conceptualize, communicate, and coordinate these diverse needs.

The Need for a Services Blueprint

As business processes increasingly become digitized, the role of management is changing from technology users to the reluctant "architects of services blueprints." They need answers to strategic questions such as:

- What kind of platform will be most effective in supporting online self-service customers?

- In a converging world of service channels—bricks, clicks, and mobile—how should firms organize, strategize, and invest?

- What is the systematic model for planning the next generation of cross-enterprise processes? What mistakes and obstacles should managers avoid?

- How can companies make smarter investments in integration capable of binding different channels, devices, and applications?

Scratch the surface of almost any major business issue and you will find the blueprint theme—the unifying umbrella for integrating diverse legacy and emerging technology initiatives. This is especially true in firms that are attempting to bring about tighter brick-and-click, or with the introduction of mobile technology, brick-click-and-mobile cross-channel process integration.

The concepts of multi-channel services and service platforms are now entering the corporate technology lexicon, with the Internet becoming the delivery mechanism for a whole range of services. A big myth of e-business is that first movers have a better chance of locking out their competition. The truth is that technology provides only a temporary advantage. User requirements constantly evolve, and just because you are first doesn't mean you'll stay there. When a company's services are functional, elegant in their design, fairly priced, and a pleasure to use, the company will be successful. It will grow in the good times, weather the bad times, and make the difficult transition from one generation of technology to the next.

The Focus of This Book

The die is cast. Digitization is beginning to accelerate: e-commerce → e-business → services. Applications are evolving in parallel to support digitization inside company walls: enterprise applications → Web portals → service platforms. Service platforms are the foundation for implementing business initiatives ranging from consolidation to merger integration. They are essential for supporting cross-enterprise process imperatives such as cost reduction, new experience design, and innovation.

Managers are not interested in the nuts and bolts of technology that the various vendors are pushing. However, they are interested in the big picture and the value derived from technology investments. We understand this dilemma and present a balanced perspective of what managers need to know to make effective technology decisions. We are writing both to challenge the dominant orthodoxy of current piecemeal strategies and to address three critical issues:

- How to plan in an economy where differentiation is achieved not through products but through technology-enabled services.

- How to translate business imperatives into better technology execution.

- How to organize the changes Web Services have wrought on the business process and application landscape.

Since most firms operate on some form of a digital backbone, managers need a better grasp of the changing nature of enterprise applications and infrastructure. They must understand that unless their firms create an effective services strategy, they are likely to be left behind.

At a more detailed level, our goal is to thoroughly explain the set of complex choices that executing a service platform strategy entails. In order to make these choices with less than perfect information, managers need to understand: What exactly is a service platform? How should managers go about investing in supporting infrastructure? What is the blueprint for making these multi-million dollar platform decisions? Who are some best-practice firms we can learn from? These are some of the questions that we address in the ensuing pages. We also present a variety of case studies of companies deploying service platforms that show services in action.

The Audience for This Book

Any executive, line of business manager, project manager, consultant, or student involved with managing or implementing business applications, or interested in learning more about them should read this book. Although it will certainly be of interest to those directly engaged in strategic planning activities, it targets a much broader audience.

We approach the topic of services from a business angle, not a technical one. Currently, when managers look at the enterprise software landscape, all they hear is EAI, BPM, XML, LDAP, UDDI, SOAP—a tangle of tools and standards. It often takes a Ph.D. or an army of consultants to sort through the chaos. It is time to make it simpler for managers who are investing in platforms and infrastructure.

At present, that need is unmet. This book fills that gap by:

- Presenting a senior manager's perspective on the important digitization issues.

- Providing business insight into the new cross-enterprise platforms.

- Developing a blueprint that helps companies maneuver the services minefield.

We wrote this book to give managers and corporate strategists a better handle on their role in IT oversight and management. In the space of a few years, platform and infrastructure management have leaped from the back office to the boardroom, and most managers are ill-equipped to understand this subject. Nor is it easy for them to attain this understanding when they are surrounded by buzzwords rather than conceptual clarity.

The Organization of This Book

The book is organized into three separate sections, the first of which introduces and defines the services blueprint concept. In Chapter 1, we present the five compelling business reasons fueling the move towards services and outline the different categories of services blueprints—process improvement, strategic transformation, and business transformation. The chapter ends with two interesting case studies, General Electric and Wal-Mart, that illustrate the critical role of execution in achieving consistent results.

Chapter 2 builds on the formula Services Blueprint = Focal Point + Service Platform. We present our finding that companies that execute effectively tend to have focal points that prevent distractions. Ten different focal points are illustrated, including Easy To Do Business With, Low Price, Fast Service, Lowest Overhead (via business process outsourcing), and Real-Time Business. Each focal point is illustrated using real-world business examples.

Chapter 3 addresses the question: What does it take to execute against a focal point? The answer and the topic of the chapter are service platforms. We also present the three critical elements of the service platform—enterprise portals, composite processes, and the integration layer—and study some existing examples of service platforms.

In the second section, we dive into the specifics of the different services blueprints: multi-channel customer-facing, spend management, supply chain management, employee-facing productivity, and product lifecycle management.

In each of these chapters, we give a brief history of the area (for example, CRM, SCM) and present several long-term trends and emerging business requirements shaping the field. We then deconstruct the blueprint and show what the different layers are and how they come together to create business value. Each chapter concludes with a best-practice case that gives the previous discussion a practical context. The different cases include JC Penney, Eastman Chemical, General Motors, Nike, and New York Times Digital.

The final section focuses on execution, or how to put a services blueprint together. Chapter 9 centers on the macro-level blueprint. The questions addressed in this chapter are issues confronting executives: Why do good strategies produce bad results? For results, how should their efforts be organized? How should the strategy (for example, Balanced Scorecard), process (for example, Six Sigma), and applications (for example, IT Portfolio) be linked?

We continue on to the meso-level process blueprint in Chapter 10, which discusses how to analyze and design new services. Services are built from processes; so, at the core of any service is the notion of process analysis, design, and improvement. The most widely used technique for process thinking is Six Sigma. We introduce the reader to Six Sigma, which we think is a useful and underutilized technique in services digitization.

Chapter 11 talks about the micro-level technology blueprint. Despite the downturn in the economy, leading firms are undertaking a large replacement cycle—migrating from enterprise applications to cross-enterprise service platforms. To help readers understand the infrastructure evolution, we explain the relevant concepts of enterprise data models, application portfolio models, portal infrastructure, and federated architecture and bring them to life in the Princeton University and Georgia-Pacific case studies.

Finally, Chapter 12 presents the challenge of business transformation. How do you go about reinventing your business? To illustrate this point, we wrote two intriguing and contrasting case studies on AT&T and IBM. The point that we emphasize is how companies can fail or succeed in their business transformation efforts based on the quality of strategy and execution. We conclude the book with some final thoughts that summarize its key points.

Acknowledgments

Much of the thinking in this book has been shaped by our discussions and research with our clients and friends, in particular, Shirish Netke, Peter Zencke, Daniel Beringer, Lutz Heuser, Dan Panteleo, Tom Davenport, Chuck Williams, Frances Frei, Nagesh Vempaty, Ralph Olivia, Nirmal Pal, Arvind Rangaswamy, and Richard Welke. Special thanks to Roger Mowen, Terry Begley, Susan Armstrong, and Annette Giaudrone at Eastman Chemical for taking the time to help with the case study.

Thank you so much to our editor Mary O'Brien. Your support and encouragement over the years has been greatly appreciated. To the many other people at Addison-Wesley who made this book possible, especially Brenda Mulligan, Jacquelyn Doucette, and Brooke Booth, thank you for all your hard work. Many thanks to our reviewers, Capers Jones, David Linthicum, David Taylor, Andrew Ellicott, Jeff Gainer, Ramon Ray, and Thomas A. Smith who took time to read through the initial proposal and manuscript.

To Pavan Gundepudi, Allison Loudermilk, and Brandon Doty, thank you for your contributions. We appreciate the long hours that made this book much better.

To our family and friends who have supported us throughout the writing of this book, in particular, Bill and Judy Robinson.

Finally, to our readers throughout the world, thank you! We appreciate your support and feedback through the years. We tried hard to put together a book that you will enjoy reading.

Ravi Kalakota
ravi@ebstrategy.com

Marcia Robinson
marcia@ebstrategy.com

www.ebstrategy.com

PART I

The Need for Digitization

CHAPTER ONE

From E-Business to Services: Why and Why Now?

What to Expect

Today, the state of the art in business technology is moving from the pioneering efforts of e-business to a more complex theme of services digitization. Services digitization is the ongoing transformation of paper-based transactions into new integrated multi-channel processes. Services digitization may seem like just another "hot fad." Peering closer, however, you will find a significant difference: Digitization does not center on technology, but rather on capturing value through improved productivity and performance. Digitization gives every company the ability to reallocate their resources totally.

In this chapter, we set the stage for the rest of the book. We begin by looking at the five business, technology, and management trends that are causing the migration from e-business to services. We then show that services digitization is a concrete strategy that leading companies are executing against using the concept of a services blueprint. We illustrate the logic behind a services blueprint with two in-depth best-practice case studies of GE and Wal-Mart.

Introduction

We are often asked the questions: Is e-business over now that the dot-com bubble burst? Are we going back to the old ways of doing business? We don't think so. The changes set in motion by the Internet are irreversible and will take time to diffuse through organizations. Migrating from old to new ways of conducting business is a continuous, open-ended process. It's not a journey your company can opt out of if you hope to remain competitive.

The transformation of twenty-first century business is under way. At the heart of this wide-ranging transformation is the use of technology to digitize complex services. Some firms like Intel are well into this journey. Intel's mission is to be a worldwide, 100 percent e-corporation. This five-year effort began in 1999 with Intel selling products online, shooting to more than $1 billion in online sales per month within the first year. Since then, Intel's digitization efforts have expanded, and Web-based services are the preferred method for operating and conducting business with its customers, suppliers, and employees worldwide.[1]

Other firms are doing the same. They are systematically creating new services by rewiring and integrating existing business processes. Consider the following examples:

- GE is saving billions of dollars by improving and digitizing various sales, general, and administrative (SG&A) processes while some of its competitors flounder. Is GE's strategy of moving back-office services (call centers, payment processing) to India and China dramatically lowering overhead costs?

- HSBC Holdings PLC, a Hong Kong-based financial services firm, is thriving and buying U.S. banks while its peers lay off thousands. Do its sophisticated global financial operations, linked by advanced network technology, allow it to keep costs under control?

- Southwest Airlines is able to control its operating costs, despite all the turbulence in the airline sector, while competitors struggle and declare bankruptcy. Has Southwest's strategy of continuously digitizing core spend management and customer-facing processes separated it from the rest?

- Eastman Chemical is able to digitize its supply network and lower raw material costs while its peers in the chemical industry suffer from high costs. Is the lack of effective supply chain management one of the root causes leading to the poor performance of its peers?

- Amazon.com is thriving by becoming the online service channel for big retailers like Circuit City, Target, Office Depot, Toys "R" Us, and Nordstrom. Are the retailers implicitly acknowledging that Amazon.com can digitize processes (order-to-return, target-to-engage) better than they online?

What makes some companies so much better at new services design and digitizing business processes than their competitors? What business trends are they seeing that others are not able to perceive? How are they leveraging technology? What unique process, application, and infrastructure capabilities are they developing? These are the questions that form the basis of this book. Are they relevant? Well, just look around you. Market leaders in every industry are quietly incorporating as much digital technology into their products, processes, and services as possible. These firms are beginning to see financial results—better operating margins and lower costs—with the added plus of real-time interaction with the customer.

Clearly, the nature of competition is morphing, but how and why some firms are better at evolving into digital companies is not fully understood. What *is* known is that the macroeconomic transformations taking place are real and profound. Due to customer pressure, organizations are transitioning to a multichannel—brick, Web, mobile, and tele—services economy. However, there are many emerging perspectives on services. Some view it as a technology issue (Web Services). Some view it as an online process issue (e-services). Some view it from the customer perspective (value). All these views are relevant and pertinent. We need a framework—a services blueprint—that ties all of these viewpoints together. Not having a clear services blueprint invariably leads to suboptimal decisions that waste time and resources.

Before we talk about the services blueprint, how can we be sure that the trends are pointing toward services? This is an important issue, as it lays the foundation for the rest of the book.

Services Is the Mega-Trend

If you open a technology magazine or listen to any vendor presentation, you will read or hear the following: E-Business on Demand, Services on Demand, Business Process Management, Composite Applications, xApps, Real-Time Enterprise, Enterprise Application Integration, Web Services, and Adaptive Supply Chains.

What do all these buzzwords have in common? If you look closely you will find that they are all part of the services digitization mega-trend. The impetus for services digitization lies at the convergence of five core trends taking place in business.

- Technology Payoff and ROI—How can new value be created by leveraging existing technology investments?

- Process Configuration and Flexibility—How can technology help reconfigure operational processes and improve flexibility through business process outsourcing?

- Cross-Enterprise and Multi-Channel Business—How can companies move from uni-channel, single business unit solutions to cross-enterprise, multi-channel solutions?

- Improving Application Integration—How can applications be integrated more quickly and cheaply to create a real-time environment?

- Aligning Outside-In and Inside-Out—How can the inside-out process perspective (customer management, supply chain) be balanced with an outside-in services view (Easy To Do Business With, one face to the customer)?

Each of these trends, by itself, is important. Combined, they present the emerging picture that is services digitization.

Technology Payoff and ROI Trends

Companies don't want to hear about innovation, vision, or possibilities anymore. They want results, return on investment (ROI), and better execution.

In December 2002, McDonald's posted its first quarterly loss in 47 years. To turn things around, the board got rid of the CEO and installed a new management team. The team promptly started examining various money draining initiatives as they related to near-term financial benefits and restaurant profitability. The team zeroed in on technology spending in an effort to save "tens of millions" of dollars.

In particular, the focus was on an ambitious project called Innovate. Innovate was envisioned as a global real-time network that would link fast-food restaurants, headquarters, and suppliers of McDonald's. The long-term business objective was to create a digital environment to share consumer demand data and procurement information and to reduce paperwork. The initial installation of the network was scheduled for late 2003 beginning in Canada and France. The United States portion of its business was to be linked by 2005.[2]

McDonald's decided to kill the Innovate project because it was taking too long to realize an ROI. Millions of dollars had already been spent on Innovate, and tens of millions more would have been required before completion.

McDonald's is not unique. Tough business conditions and the need to focus on fewer priorities have inspired a backlash against mega-technology projects. The backlash has resulted in tech investments being placed under the ROI microscope. Many CEOs and CFOs are questioning whether they are getting results for the money spent. This introspection is forcing companies to refocus their energy on what customers care about. Some are going back to the basics; others are accelerating digitization initiatives to support and streamline business processes better.

Clearly, a shift in thinking is taking place among senior management, line of business users, IT departments, and mainstream technology vendors. They have come to the realization that technology is only part of the solution. Merely implementing technology applications and infrastructure doesn't amount to productivity or payoff. Business processes, change management, and incentives are key to wringing value out of technology investments. Common sense, you might say. But common sense is quite uncommon and often overlooked in search of the quick fix. So begins a new chapter in information technology.

As the technology love affair turns cautious, back-to-basics process thinking is taking center stage again. Evidence of this trend can seen in Table 1.1, which captures the evolution of business process transformation. We think that current digitization must be understood against the background of the past.

Table 1.1: Historical Perspective: Changing Process Priorities (Innovation)

Time Period	Focus	Method
1970s	Quality	Total Quality Management, Zero Defects, Statistical Process Control
1980s	Lean Manufacturing	Just-In-Time, Zero Inventory, Kanban, Computer Integrated Manufacturing
Early 1990s	Process Improvement	Vendor Managed Inventory, System Outsourcing, Customer Satisfaction, Enterprise Resource Planning, Lean Thinking
Mid- to Late 1990s	Process Reengineering	Business Process Reengineering, Six Sigma
Late 1990s to 2002	Transaction-Centric— Digitization of Tasks and Simple Processes	E-Commerce, E-Business, Collaborative Commerce (B2B), Customer Relationship Management
2003 onward	Services-Centric— Digitization of Cross-Enterprise Processes	End-to-End Supply Chain Enablement, Business Process Outsourcing, Business Process Management

Process Configuration and Flexibility Trends

Driven by the constant need to cut costs and gain flexibility, business processes are being reconfigured or outsourced.

The need for process flexibility is not a new trend. The trend has been evident for the last two decades. First, in blue-collar factory automation, on the heels of industrial robotics, came computers with intelligent shopfloor automation software. Second, in white-collar administration, spreadsheets and enterprise applications like ERP took hold. Networking facilitated by high-bandwidth fiber optics and other telecom innovations set the stage for mind-blowing innovation. Finally, the Internet, Web, and mobile computing came along and enabled a global productivity boom, resulting in technology innovations that are constantly laying the foundation for renovating industrial-age processes.

At the macro level, factors that caused this process redesign flux include customers, competition, (de)regulation, growth via mergers and acquisitions (M&A), divestitures, and internal reorganization. At the micro level, process instability was caused by the huge investment in factory automation technology, the demand for more real-time information, and tighter collaboration among business partners. Regardless of why companies redesigned processes, improving productivity—in manufacturing, sales, and supply chain—was the goal.

More recently, evidence of the dramatic process changes brought forth by the Internet is beginning to show up everywhere. Consider business process outsourcing. Service jobs such as call centers, billing, and claims processing, the mainstay of the United States, British, French, and other developed economies for the past 20 years, are moving. These jobs, courtesy of the Internet, are set to follow manufacturing jobs by emigrating to China, India, the Philippines, and other low-wage countries. We are witnessing in services exactly what happened in manufacturing 15 years ago. Whatever can get done in a more cost-effective location will be relocated.

Besides outsourcing, organizations are reconfiguring processes wherever possible to drive productivity higher. Even if various discrete parts of the business are operating at peak performance, too often the end-to-end business processes are not. That is because many processes—with customers, suppliers, and employees—remain largely disjointed, linked by a hodgepodge of information flows—telephone calls, faxes, e-mail, spreadsheets, and FedEx packages. Connecting and improving broken processes have taken on broader urgency due to the velocity and volatility of modern business.

Multi-Channel and Cross-Enterprise Trends

In some firms, processes are moving from a single channel to a multi-channel focus. In others, processes are moving from department to cross-enterprise. Both are fairly significant trends.

Most of the current e-business thinking is centered on uni-channel automation and single business unit applications. Unfortunately, customers don't think or act this way; they want flexibility. In other words, they want efficient and effective hybrid combinations, that is, new service designs that weave brick, click, call center, and mobile channels. They also want the service designs to span internal and external boundaries. For instance, when you call Delta Airlines, they offer internal transactions such as travel reservations but also external services such as car rentals and hotel reservations.

Consider the service problem facing retailers. Most have invested heavily in Web sites and digitized significant portions of the end-to-end processes (order-to-return). However, when the customer behavior changes from uni-channel (Web site) to multi-channel (Web site, retail store, and call center), the carefully crafted end-to-end process that worked well for a single channel breaks down completely. Let's look at a simple variant: The customer buys online but returns offline at a store and gets her account credited immediately. This simple action can wreak havoc with finely tuned back-office processes, such as inventory management, financials, and reverse logistics, which have been optimized for a single channel or business unit.

As the business environment changes, so must the underlying processes. Unfortunately, organizations tend to ignore process problems until it's too late. This primarily occurs because management regards process design as a low-level activity tied to the application implementation process. As a result, most management teams tend to trivialize end-to-end process design and pay a big price downstream. The numerous first-generation e-business projects that have been discontinued or minimally adopted prove our point.

All is not lost, however. Cutting-edge organizations are adopting new ways of attacking process transformation problems. These organizations see digitization as a complex combination of multi-channel process thinking, cross-enterprise integration, and business technology. This thinking increasingly shapes enterprise application innovation.

Process transformation has three interrelated dimensions:

- Changing Type of Process Interactions—new multi-channel processes are evolving from traditional uni-channel processes.

- Changing Scope of Process Integration—processes are expanding from business unit-centric to cross-enterprise and inter-enterprise.

- Changing Degree of Process Digitization—processes and transactions are evolving from manual to automated.

Figure 1.1 displays the process transformation. *Where does your corporation lie?* The nonstop management decision problem is to align all three dimensions continuously with customer, employee, or supply chain priorities. Optimizing only two dimensions, as is frequently done, often leads to poor choices that cause problems in the long run.

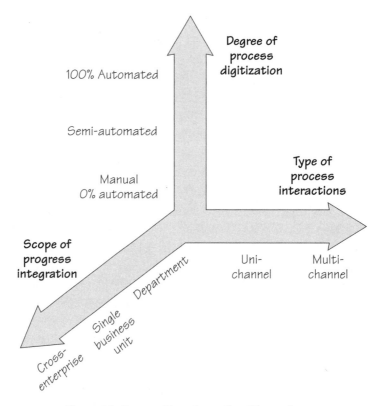

Figure 1.1: Process Transformation Dimensions

Improving Application Integration Trends

There are significant changes taking place in the way applications and supporting infrastructure are integrated. These changes are taking place under the broad umbrella of service platforms, Services Oriented Architecture (SOA), and Web Services. The corporate world is migrating from a bottom-up integration model to a top-down service integration model that leverages multiple underlying enterprise application components.

SAP, PeopleSoft, Oracle, IBM, Microsoft, Sun, and BEA have grasped this development and are racing to address the issues of change with a new breed of cross-application service platforms called xApps, Services on Demand, and E-Business on Demand. Service platforms are emerging as the foundation on which process digitization will actually occur. (See Chapter 3 for more details on service platforms.)

Leading companies have seen this service platform trend and have been creating proprietary versions for several years. FedEx, the world's largest express shipper, has been developing a Fast Service service platform. The company's complex cross-channel, multi-enterprise service platform allows it to outperform its competition in the business of door-to-door delivery of small packages and just-in-time delivery of high-value components. In order to build a service platform similar to FedEx, companies need to invest in a Services Oriented Architecture. Examples of SOA products are SunONE from Sun Microsystems, NetWeaver from SAP, and WebSphere from IBM.

An analogy should give you a better idea how everything fits together. A car (a service platform) has large components (chassis, powertrain, electronics, and climate). The chassis (SOA) in turn is made up of subcomponents (driveline system, steering system, and braking system). These subcomponents are further made up of sub-subcomponents. The braking system is made up of brake hubs, brake rotors, and catalytic converters. These, too, can be decomposed further. You get a picture of the complexity involved here.

Similarly, the underlying foundation for all these SOAs is the fledgling field of Web Services. Web Services enable different applications to be integrated without the hassle of custom coding. In addition, Web Services are not reliant on one vendor or programming language. They allow businesses to share data with each other and customers while keeping IT systems secure behind a firewall.

Web Services are often misunderstood. They are not a fad; they are a model of computing and integration that helps solve the challenges of multi-channel and cross-enterprise process integration. The business driver of Web Services is simple: As business requirements shift, companies are trying to keep pace and are demanding greater productivity, less risk, and higher returns from their software investments. They are also desperately trying to leverage their existing multimillion dollar investments in applications. Clearly, organizations everywhere are looking for standardized ways to integrate information assets.

A simple analogy for Web Services is the euro, the standard currency of the European Union. Prior to the euro, incredible inefficiency existed due to the need to change currencies every time a border was crossed. With the euro standardized across the Union, barriers to trade and cross-border movement have been lifted. Productivity has been boosted because a pile of paperwork tracking currency exchange has been eliminated. Similarly, without Web Services, the scale and scope of digitization will be constrained due to fragmented applications and infrastructure.

Web Services and SOA are closely intertwined with process thinking. Without process thinking, Web Services and SOA are not very effective. While this should be obvious, it is not widely accepted. We have found very little process thinking preceding Web Services adoption in organizations or vendors. If this does not change, the service platforms developed using Web Services will fail miserably.

Aligning Inside-Out and Outside-In Process Trends

Consider the following customer request: We want you to become Easy To Do Business With (ETDBW). A successful ETDBW digitization project starts with the recognition that the focus is not technology, but understanding customer priorities and aligning internal processes accordingly. So the key questions are: What new services do we need to design to become ETDBW? What channels (brick, click, tele, and mobile) do we need to synchronize?

Consider the internal management request: We want to lower the cost of serving the customer, increase the productivity of agents in our call centers, and increase customer loyalty. So the key questions are: How do we segment our customers? What applications do we need to integrate internally?

There are two viewpoints of digitization that are battling each other in the real world:

- **Customer-Centric**—outside-in design of cross-channel and cross-enterprise workflows driven by a superior understanding of what the customer really wants.

- **Process-Centric**—inside-out design of application integration to support workflows driven by what managers think the customer wants.

Design from the customer perspective is the problem that most customer-facing groups (strategy and marketing) are wrestling with. Process integration from the efficiency and productivity standpoint is the problem most internal-facing groups (operations and human resources) are grappling with.

While both viewpoints are necessary, the applications and infrastructure needed to support them tend to be different. Therein lies the problem. It is very difficult to leverage the investments in applications and infrastructure made to support the process-centric view in the customer-centric context. While this looks rather trivial, it is very hard to do. Why? Because most enterprise applications, which support internal processes in corporations, are fragmented and are not integrated. Significant investments have to be made in integrating applications to rectify the problem.

Now imagine a situation where there are twenty different customer-facing projects, each with its own customized integration model. The business outcome: severe structural problems in the organization's process foundation—applications, infrastructure, and people—as it struggles to keep up with changing corporate and customer priorities. Avoiding these structural problems, which in turn are driving up business risk, is job number one for management.

One way to avoid the inside-out and outside-in alignment problems is to have a clear focal point (for example, Every Day Low Price) and align the processes accordingly. For instance, Wal-Mart over the years has succeeded in executing its Every Day Low Price focal point while its competitors—KMart, Ames, and other discount retailers—have faltered. Wal-Mart's ability to focus and digitize the supply chain and logistics processes effectively allowed the company to slash prices and outperform its competition. We think that Wal-Mart's ability to align all its investments to create value around a focal point is a key long-term differentiator.

As Figure 1.2 shows, customers care about value. Line of business and IT departments tend to care about processes. Services represent the convergence of customer priorities, business priorities, and technology capabilities. Not aligning the three carefully can lead to problems. Operationally speaking, creating new services requires an outside-in (external) perspective on customers' interaction with the service and an inside-out (internal) perspective on existing capabilities and applications.

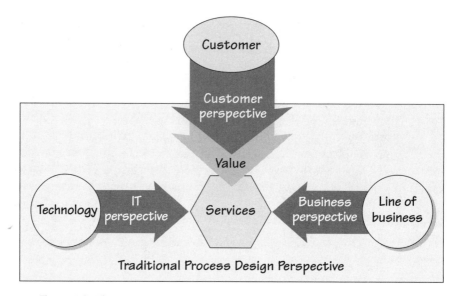

Figure 1.2: The New Process Thinking—Taking the Customer's Perspective

The Need for a Services Blueprint

We began the book by asking: Is e-business dead? We took you on a journey into some of the converging trends that are shaping the next wave of technology investments. We hope that you are now convinced that the state of the art in business technology is clearly centered on services digitization.

To understand the magnitude of the task that lies ahead, ask yourself the following questions: *How many processes do you have? What percentage have you digitized?* Most managers are taken aback by these questions. Take a moment and count all the critical business processes associated with ordering, fulfillment, payment, billing, employee benefits, sales, marketing, and customer service. In your opinion, what percentage of these processes is completely and effectively digitized? Is it 10 percent, 30 percent, 50 percent, or more? Our research indicates that the average is between 20 and 30 percent—higher for Global 2000 companies, lower for small- and medium-sized businesses (SMBs).

Clearly, after five decades of technology investments, the journey toward digitization of business processes is still in its infancy. To write its obituary as some in the media did after the dot-com collapse is somewhat premature. Process digitization is a multi-year marathon that will require tremendous endurance. Some companies have this endurance; most don't. The most challenging questions confronting business leaders and managers are not "What processes do we digitize?"

or "How do we digitize?" but "What is our focal point that ties together our ongoing process digitization efforts?"

Focal Points

What focal point is guiding your digitization investments? Focal points define what your business is all about. Market leaders have crisp focal points to direct their digitization efforts. Consider the following examples:

- **Easy To Do Business With**—Why did Staples, the office products superstore, succeed in executing its Easy To Do Business With strategy while others faltered? Did Staples' ability to create a technology-based service blueprint effectively allow the company to implement an integrated multi-channel strategy linking office supply stores, e-commerce, catalog operations, and contract stationery businesses?

- **Low Cost**—Why did Dell succeed in executing its build-to-order, customer self-service strategy while Compaq, AST, Packard Bell, Micron PC, and Gateway faltered? Did Dell's ability to improve continually an operational blueprint allow the company to digitize its low-cost supply chain and undercut prices?

- **Zero-Defect Quality**—Why did Toyota succeed in extending its market share in a down economy? How is it able to align changing customer priorities with its production process? Did Toyota's ability to digitize the design process allow it to take a new car from design to production in less than a year (compared with as many as three years for its competitors)?

There is a common ingredient shared by each example that is critical for success. That is the ability to focus digitization initiative. Everything that Staples does—customer-facing, employee-facing, supplier-facing—needs to support its Easy To Do Business With focal point. Unfortunately, very few companies have such clear direction in their digitization efforts.

Having a distinct focal point differentiates market leaders. These companies consistently execute a focused business strategy using technology as an enabler. These businesses stand out not only because of their superior talent for seeing the big picture and for sensing shifting customer priorities, but because they implement technology day in and day out to create customer value.

Why can't competitors copy market leaders? The answer is remarkably simple. Competitors take a piecemeal approach to technology innovation. They do well at finding and assessing new ideas, only to run into a shortage of people and skills during execution. Often the managers charged with execution are simply too busy addressing immediate urgent tasks to implement capably new ideas that will bear fruit tomorrow. Success is mostly a function of execution.[3] *Does your firm have a focal point that shapes the services blueprint, which in turn drives execution?*

The Blueprint as an Execution Differentiator

What is Dell Computer's services blueprint? Thousands of pages have been written about Dell Computer's direct-to-consumer business model. Many consulting firms have analyzed it for their clients. Yet, no competitor has replicated it with the same efficiency. So, a focal point is necessary but not sufficient. Steady execution over a long period of time is critical to success. Few executives dispute that.

Execution is the science of turning multi-million dollar application and infrastructure investments into results. This is proving to be much harder than expected. Consider the following data: More than $300 billion is spent on software application initiatives in the United States every year.[4] Unfortunately, only 17 percent of those initiatives finish on time, on budget, at acceptable performance levels, and at full scope. A whopping 50 percent of initiatives miss targets—they are late, overspent, and have reduced features and functionality. Even more appalling is that the remaining 33 percent are canceled.[5] This means that more than $100 billion per year is flushed down the drain because of poor execution. Poof! It's gone.

Another way to interpret the data is to say that 83 percent of all technology initiatives get into trouble. What is keeping businesses from executing better? This is becoming a core question as post-dot-com firms transition from the glitz of strategy to the nitty-gritty of execution. Poor execution cannot be hidden anymore. It is estimated that companies implement at most 20 percent of their stated technology strategy. The dire straits of technology execution have been visible for some time, but companies were able to gloss over their problems in the frenzy of the dot-com era. That tactic has been exhausted.

So what differentiates the doers from the talkers? The big differentiator we found is the market leaders' ability to digitize systematically and continually complex business processes such as supply chains or employee self-service. The business processes that get digitized are selected based on a focal point.

Market leaders don't deviate too much from their core focal point. A focal point such as Low Cost or Zero-Defect Quality is usually the steadfast guiding principle that anchors their execution efforts. These focal points are not generic branding messages or vision statements, instead they help focus ordinary products, processes, and services into solutions or value-added experiences that people want.

The essence of a crisp focal point is knowing what customers want. Bad things happen to good companies when companies don't execute according to customers' immediate priorities. The visible result is a steady erosion of companies' revenues, profits, and market value. Just look at the plight of the telecommunications industry. Former heavyweights, such as Lucent Technologies, Nortel Networks, and Alcatel, tumbled as troubled telecomm customers, such as World-Com, KPN, Frontier, and Qwest, slashed capital spending in an attempt to remain solvent. After a job-shedding spree and other draconian cutbacks in every cost category imaginable, these firms don't have much room to maneuver. Can you think of the focal point of these companies? Do you think these companies had a clear blueprint?

Effectively digitizing processes to cut costs and stay competitive is a priority as firms restructure for the future. A growing vanguard consisting of Siemens, Nike, Kraft Foods, Nestlé, and 3M appears to understand the rules of the new battle being fought. These companies know they must relentlessly refine processes to withstand the multiple shock waves that followed the incredible prosperity of the 1990s. The best method for refining is to digitize ever-expanding processes and embed them into a service infrastructure to ensure survival and gain sizeable leads over competition.

Three Categories of Blueprints

Services digitization hinges on clear focal points and superb execution. There are three different categories of blueprints in play today—process improvement, strategic improvement, and business transformation (see Figure 1.3). The categories are based on the scale and scope of impact you want to make on the organization.

A blueprint falls into the process improvement category if companies are in mature markets and face relatively low uncertainty. These companies are mostly attempting to move the ball forward. In executing process improvement, a company must focus doggedly on conventional measures like capacity utilization or throughput and on such basics as creating operational efficiencies through improving administrative tasks. This is a conservative approach—call it hitting singles instead of swinging for the fences. Companies that have executed systematically on process improvement, such as Siemens, Kodak, and Alcoa, have steadily cut costs and raised productivity.

Objective	Example	Description
Process Improvement	GE Honeywell Caterpillar	• Reducing hand-off costs and rework • Reducing process variation using Six Sigma • Transaction cost reduction—using technology to shorten end-to-end processing time • Business process outsourcing—fixing specific errors • Improving customer satisfaction
Strategic Improvement	Wal-Mart Dell Intel Cisco	• Replacing manual processes with digital processes wherever possible • Enhancing logistic and supply chain efficiencies • Increase customer focus—Web-enabling strategic operations • Cycle time reduction—decreasing time to market
Business Transformation	IBM AT&T Vivendi	• Rewiring the industry—changing the rules of the game • Creating a new customer focus—from product-centric to customer-centric • Abandoning old ways of doing business • Major culture change required among all participants

Figure 1.3: Three Categories of Execution

Strategic improvement occurs when firms attempt to grow into new areas by introducing additional products and services or streamline end-to-end processes by enhancing the linkages with customers and suppliers. When executing strategic improvement, a company generally focuses on measures such as increasing customer service and leveraging new business opportunities. Companies like Carrefour, Tesco, and Intel have embarked on strategic improvement and ultimately have dominated their competition.

Digitization related to business transformation is high risk. In executing this, a company (such as Amazon.com or Yahoo!) uses so-called "disruptive innovation" to change the rules of the game in a particular industry by creating new customer niches, channels, or cost economics. Due to uncertainty in the economy, transformational strategies that pave the way for the future are often based on inadequate information.

Transformation strategies may work for some start-ups. In a large corporation, however, it is very risky and has a high failure rate. Few corporations attempting business transformation have succeeded. Most dot-com companies that were talking revolution were intent on executing transformation strategies. Few survived—a testament to the fact that revolutions tend to be bloody. Companies like Vivendi Universal under Jean Messier, Ford under Jacques Nasser, and AT&T under Michael Armstrong were all attempting transformation strategies. These companies are in the midst of retrenching from their visionary strategies. In contrast, IBM appears to be a successful example of business transformation.

It's tempting, of course, to say, "I want to accomplish all of them!"—process improvement, strategic improvement, and business transformation. Don't. It takes vastly different skills to execute each. Identifying which one is your primary driver for digitization efforts is a very important first step. Your technology foundation depends on it.

Digitization at General Electric (GE)

More than any other institution, GE has mastered the art of digitizing while conducting business. GE is a 124-year-old diversified technology, manufacturing, and services company, committed to achieving leadership in each of its key businesses. GE's multi-business success comes from its competitive corporate culture, shared strategic priorities, and ability to find new and more efficient ways to run the business.

To reach and maintain the leadership position, GE's ongoing growth and strategy is focused on four key initiatives: WorkOut, Six Sigma, Services, and Digitization.

WorkOut—Globalization

WorkOut, the oldest initiative at GE (going back to the early 1980s), has become so ingrained in GE's culture that it's less of an "initiative" now and has simply become the way the firm operates. Globalization began as a search for new markets for GE's products and services. This quickly expanded to include finding the most competitive sources of finished products, components, and raw materials. When the globalization initiative began, the company derived more than 80 percent of revenues within the United States; today, more than 40 percent of GE's revenues are generated outside the United States. GE is a truly global company, always strengthening its international presence with new local operations, acquisitions, and joint ventures.

Six Sigma—Improving Manufacturing and Service Quality

During the 1990s, many companies utilized Six Sigma to eliminate process variability and optimize quality. Six Sigma—virtually defect-free processes, products, and services (3.4 defects per million)—takes its name from the Greek letter "sigma," which is used in statistics to indicate standard deviation. GE uses Six Sigma to help distinguish between work that is absolutely necessary versus work that is nice to do but not critical to quality.

Through this quality methodology, GE claims that it has been able to develop and deliver much-improved products and services. Six Sigma builds on the old quality principle that employees often have the best ideas about what tasks can be simplified or eliminated. It is estimated that GE has trained more than 100,000 people in Six Sigma and completed 500,000 projects.[6] Six Sigma has helped changed GE's focus from inside to outside, namely to the customer. This change in perspective has undoubtedly helped improve products and services in new ways. (For more information on Six Sigma, see Chapter 10.)

Services—Converting Products into Solutions

In parallel to the Six Sigma efforts, GE is transforming itself from an engineering company into a services firm. In some areas, it is going even further by moving from services to total solutions (that is, providing products, services, and financing). What's more, GE is focusing on creating service platforms to support high-tech products and equipment. For instance, part of GE's medical strategy is to provide services for a digitized hospital that has no paper files, no traditional nurses' stations, and no medical records department. Instead, all the information about a patient is available on computers and kiosks located strategically throughout the hospital. Critical information like diagnostic images and medication are available instantly. That means less time tracking and documenting patient information, and more time for patient care.

By developing leading-edge technology and then driving it back into the installed base of equipment, GE is aiming to increase its customers' productivity. For customers, this enables them to become more competitive at lower investment costs. For GE, this has created a rapidly expanding services business, which is expected to grow substantially for decades to come.

Digitization—Increasing Productivity and Profitability

GE is using Six Sigma to evaluate all the work it does and to shed, streamline, or simplify tasks that aren't critical. The logical next step of Six Sigma is process digitization. The digitization goal: to utilize Internet-based workflows wherever possible to eliminate process friction and streamline the operations of GE. The digitized GE expects to have smaller administrative "back rooms," reduced waste, and faster decision making.

Its financial goal is expanded productivity and profitability. It has invested $10 billion in IT since 1998 to make digitization a vital part of the company. GE is reserving spending for all sides of the business—from the "make" side of internal process digitization, to the "buy" side of sourcing and procurement, to the "sell" side of customer transactions and service.[7] Anything to do with customers and growing revenues is receiving digitization priority.

Digitization is a "game changer" for GE because it improves the competitive position. Consider how Internet and Web technology are allowing GE to reallocate back-office processes. At GE, 60 percent of the resources are in the front office—customer facing, manufacturing, selling, and accounting. The other 40 percent of the resources is in the back office—billing, receivables, and call centers. GE plans to take out $10 billion of its SG&A costs by 2005. Simply optimizing the working capital situation—faster recovery of receivables, reduction of liabilities, and reduction of inventories—would produce an ROI in the billions range as a direct result of GE's digitization effort.[8]

Digitization Themes at GE

At GE, digitization is the conduit through which globalization, Six Sigma, and product services strategies are shaping a leaner conglomerate. The purpose of digitization at GE is to implement corporate strategies that can be distilled into seven themes:

1. Make yourself Easy To Do Business With—present one face to the customer.

2. Develop a process enterprise—integrate around the customer.

3. Create an outside-in service focus, rather than an inside-out product view.

4. Anticipate customers' needs through services—build value around how the product is used.

5. Integrate virtually, not vertically, using flexible business process outsourcing.

6. Make the business agile—do less planning and more "sense and respond" to uncertain economic events.

7. Include measurement as part of management, not accounting—utilize digital cockpits (a report where managers can view an aggregate of customized company statistics) to monitor, act, and control events.

Once formulated, these enterprise-level themes must be converted into business processes, which are then mapped into applications and systems. All this must be done more quickly and cheaply than ever before. Translating an organization's strategic objectives into processes and applications that in turn drive operational results is the critical role of management.

Digitization at Wal-Mart

Wal-Mart has relentlessly pursued the Every Day Low Price (EDLP) focal point in its quest to become the world's largest retailer.[9] Process digitization based on the cornerstone EDLP focal point is a core part of its strategy.

Wal-Mart—A Brief History

Wal-Mart was born in 1945 when Sam Walton opened a Ben Franklin variety store in Newport, Arkansas. In 1946, his brother, James Walton, opened a similar store in Versailles, Missouri. In 1962, the first Wal-Mart Discount City, a no-frills discount store, opened its doors. In 1984, Wal-Mart created the first three SAM'S CLUBs, and in 1988, the first Wal-Mart Supercenter, a format that combines a supermarket with a general merchandise discount store, was unveiled.

Due to its aggressive acquisition strategy, customers from many countries can now appreciate the benefits of Wal-Mart's relentless focus on ELDP. In 1992, Wal-Mart went global with a joint venture (50 percent interest) in Mexico with Cifra. Since 1992, Wal-Mart's international presence has continued to thrive.[10]

- In 1996, Wal-Mart entered China with a Supercenter and a SAM'S CLUB in Shenzhen. By 2003, Wal-Mart had opened 20 units and employed more than 10,000 associates.

- To enter Germany, Wal-Mart bought the 21-store Wertkauf hypermarket chain in 1997. In 1999, Wal-Mart bought 74 Interspar hypermarkets from Spar Handels AG, a unit of the French retailing conglomerate Intermarche.

- In 2000, Wal-Mart purchased ASDA Group PLC, the third-largest retailer in the United Kingdom (229 U.K. stores) for $11 billion.

- In 2002, Wal-Mart bought 6.1 percent of The Seiyu Ltd., a Japanese chain, for $46 million.

The company has changed considerably and now forms almost 2 percent of the U.S. economy. Each week over 100 million customers, tempted by rock-bottom prices, traipse through the stores where they can buy diverse products and services, do their banking, get their eyes checked, or have the oil changed in their car—truly a one-stop shopping experience.

Wal-Mart's Blueprint for Digitization

Wal-Mart's blueprint for process digitization is illustrated in Figure 1.4. This blueprint captures four different layers:

1. Customer—the Every Day Low Price strategy for creating sustainable value and differentiation from the customer's perspective.

2. Business Services—the strategic priorities for various business processes, which enable low cost leadership, differentiation, and execution focus. They include expertise in store management, logistics, and supply chain management. Sales are primarily on a self-service, cash-and-carry basis, with the objective of maximizing sales volume and inventory turnover while minimizing expenses.

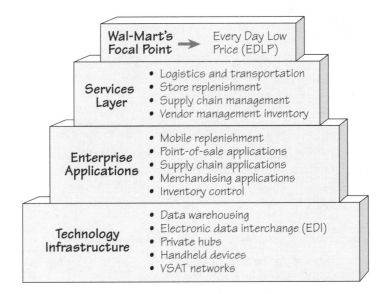

Figure 1.4: Blueprint for Wal-Mart's Digitization

3. Enterprise Application Infrastructure—the layer that helps digitize and integrate business processes tasks into streamlined information flows.

4. Technology Infrastructure—the foundation that supports the various applications across diversified store formats and geographic locations.

Of these, the customer's perspective is the most important. The ability to offer value and service continuously to customers largely determines Wal-Mart's top position within the retail industry. Wal-Mart employs many programs designed to meet the competitive pressures within the industry. These include Every Day Low Price, Low Price—Always, Item Merchandising, Store-Within-a-Store, Price Rollbacks, and Store of the Community.

Wal-Mart has core competencies and size advantages that allow it to fulfill the promise of Every Day Low Price. They include expertise in store management, logistics, and information technology. Let's look at each in detail.

Wal-Mart Differentiator—Effective Localized Store Management

Wal-Mart discount stores are mammoth. Many Supercenters, the larger cousins of the discount stores, have 500 associates and more than $100 million in annual sales, almost the size of a midsize business. A wide range of merchandise is sold and is grouped under 40 different departments.

Although Wal-Mart stores are ubiquitous, each one is different. Every Wal-Mart store is tailored for its community, which is no easy task. To keep customer-service levels high and sales increasing, Wal-Mart encourages associates to think creatively about how they merchandise and stock products.

One way that associates hone their merchant skills is through the VPI (Volume Producing Item) contest. VPI provides a store-level opportunity for associates to showcase their ability to promote items they think can be top sellers. Associates choose the VPI item, order it, design an eye-catching display, conduct promotional activities, and track and report sales progress. The goal of VPI: finding creative ways to turn products with potential into big sellers.[11]

Given the size of Wal-Mart, decentralized store management is extremely important. The managers who are closest to the action know what is important in their locale.

Wal-Mart Differentiator—Logistics Management

The processes for which Wal-Mart has set the best-practices standard are distribution and supply chain management (see Figure 1.5).

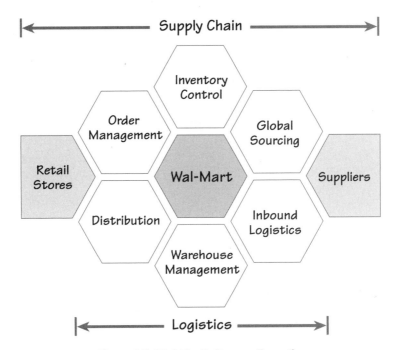

Figure 1.5: Wal-Mart's Process Expertise

The company's distribution network spans the globe. A total of 84 percent of Wal-Mart Discount Stores' and Supercenters' purchased merchandise was shipped from Wal-Mart's 72 distribution centers. Of these, 32 are general merchandise distribution centers, 20 are grocery distribution centers, eight are clothing distribution centers, and nine are specialty distribution centers. The specialty distribution centers ship items such as jewelry, tires, and optical supplies. The balance of merchandise purchased is shipped directly to the stores from suppliers.[12]

A key part of supply chain management is "global sourcing." Over the last few years, Wal-Mart has improved the quality of its goods—as well as its supply logistics and retail prices—by acquiring certain products for all of its stores around the world from a single source. To support global sourcing, Wal-Mart operates three import distribution centers in the United States and a total of 35 international distribution facilities.

Wal-Mart also controls logistics costs by having its own private fleet of trucks. This enables customized, cost-efficient delivery to stores, accommodation for peak seasonal periods, night deliveries, and accelerated delivery.

Wal-Mart Differentiator—Information Technology Execution

Using technology to simplify processes, eliminate waste, and analyze and react to more meaningful information has been the execution focus of Wal-Mart. Thus far, technology has aided in Wal-Mart reducing its operating and SG&A expenses as a percentage of sales to less than 15 percent.

Technology is the catalyst that enabled Wal-Mart to wring efficiencies out of processes that are unmatched by leading companies in other industries. Take, for instance, the replenishment problem. At any given moment, a typical Wal-Mart Discount Store has more than 70,000 standard items in stock. Every one of them has to be identified, ordered, inventoried, and replenished. A typical Supercenter is even tougher to stock since it carries more than 20,000 additional grocery items, many perishable. These have to be reordered frequently, sometimes even daily.

How does technology enable this? Since 1996, Wal-Mart has been using handheld computers linked to in-store servers by a radio-frequency network. It's a high-tech conduit to an internal inventory system. These handhelds help keep track of real-time information for the inventory on hand, deliveries, and back-up merchandise in stock at distribution centers. Mobile computing has enabled Wal-Mart to have higher quality sales and inventory information. As a result, suggested ordering quantities on many items are available to associates in real time to assist them in the task of keeping stores replenished and items in stock.

Across all of its formats, Wal-Mart is one of the most effective users of technology. Some other impressive technological feats include:

- In the 1980s, using satellite communications to link stores to headquarters for Just-In-Time inventory management (the first major retailer to do so).

- In the early 1990s, building the Retail Link system, which provides sales data—by item, store, and day—to vendor partners. This information saves suppliers time and expense in planning their production and distribution, which translates to lower merchandise costs.

- In the mid-1990s, utilizing an item locator system that allows associates to scan an item and electronically check on its availability in other area stores.

- In the late 1990s, creating the New Retail Link Private Hub, which allows more than 10,000 Wal-Mart suppliers to log into a Web portal, peruse databases, and find out which store sold how much of its products. With a latency of a mere six hours from transaction to analysis, Wal-Mart is using the Web to provide real-time information not only to stores and corporate managers, but to vendors as well.

The value of technology shows up in a crisis. An article in the *Wall Street Journal* on September 18, 2001, described how Wal-Mart used its Data Warehouse (built on NCR's Teradata technology) to understand its customers' changing buying patterns the week after the World Trade Center attacks. On the morning of the attacks, stores were desolate. By that Tuesday evening, customers stockpiled guns, ammunition, bottled water, and gasoline containers. On Wednesday, sales of flags shot up, causing a shortage and triggering orders to restock the flag inventory. By Friday, the number of customers in the stores returned to normal, but the average number of purchases declined. Based on predictive analysis, some stores were able to foresee a sharp increase in sales by the fifth day. As a result, they increased staffing by 20 percent for the weekend and stocked up on items that customers normally buy. This paid off as sales increased by 25 percent that weekend compared with the same weekend a year earlier.

Data-driven merchandising means that Wal-Mart shelves are hardly ever empty. The financial result: some of the highest sales per square foot of floor space in the retail world.

Other retailers, such as Lowe's (a home improvement store for the do-it-yourself consumer) are copying Wal-Mart's model. LowesLink gives vendors secure access to daily sales data—down to the SKU level—on the products they supply. The system also allows vendors to add item information to the database. Ultimately, Lowe's wants its vendors to control inventory levels in individual stores based on what's selling. Long-range purchasing forecasts (90 days to six months) will be e-mailed to vendors who can use the data to improve fill rates, lead times, and production efficiency.

So, if Lowe's could copy Wal-Mart's Retail Link, why couldn't Kmart?

Wal-Mart versus Kmart—A Blueprint Comparison

For more than three decades, Wal-Mart has demonstrated the willingness to embrace technology both in-house and with its suppliers. Competitors did not follow until it was too late.

Let's contrast Wal-Mart to Kmart. Kmart sprang from a pair of five-and-ten-cent stores, called Kresge's, in Memphis and Detroit, established in 1897 by Sebastian Kresge, a traveling hardware salesman. In 1962, Kresge's entered the large-scale discount retail market with the construction of the first Kmart outside

Detroit. With success, the company expanded aggressively and began selling home improvement supplies, office supplies, and sporting goods.

When Charles C. Conaway became Kmart's CEO in May 2000, he announced a massive $1.4 billion investment in technology in an attempt to make up for past neglect. The subsequent supply chain troubles were well documented. Lack of supply chain integration resulted in expensive advertising snafus where consumers could not buy the advertised specials because they were not on store shelves. Kmart could not effectively fix the supply chain problems, and it took a $195 million write-off in 2000.[13] Why the mismatch between effort and result?

In the long run, every business at its core is an information business. Wal-Mart embraced this trend in the late 1970s, while Kmart tried half-heartedly. The difference between Wal-Mart and Kmart was technology savvy and a pragmatic supply chain blueprint that took years to polish. In 1997, Wal-Mart had an annual technology and communication budget of $500 million and an information systems staff of 1,200. Kmart, on the other hand, had four CIOs in four years—no stability, no consistent strategy.

The Kmart example illustrates the challenges of execution. Blueprints—focal point, processes, applications, and technology—need to evolve in tandem with the corporate vision. Modern business is a study in perpetual motion—expansion, cost-cutting, mergers, acquisitions, divestitures, turnarounds, and bankruptcy. Organizations are in a constant state of flux as they reshape themselves to meet the demands of investors and customers. The companies that are built to last are those that change on all fronts: customer, data, and process.

Digitization Execution Is a Senior Management Issue

Services Blueprint = Focal Point + Services + Processes + Applications. If any one of these is missing or not in sync, the digitization effort will either fail or deliver less than expected ROI. As a result, all forays into digitization have to be carefully planned and managed. *Whose job is it to oversee digitization in your company?* Most people respond that it is the CEO's job, but it is really not. Most CEOs don't have the time or expertise to manage the digitization of processes. If digitization is considered important, then the CIO needs to step up to the plate.

The CIO function is changing and becoming more and more process oriented. It is hard to see how any modern corporation can operate without some sort of digitized foundation in critical functions, such as invoicing, billing, payroll, inventory, and customer service. As a result, the annual spending on technology infrastructure and applications worldwide—1.5 to 3.5 percent of revenues across most industries—is growing and is estimated to be around $1 trillion.[14]

Blueprint execution has moved up the agenda as companies demand better return on investment. Yet technology execution is not well understood or even taught. As far as we know, no university teaches a course on the basics of execution—the art of getting things done, surprisingly, given that execution is a fundamental managerial skill.

A few years ago, innovation was lauded, and execution was considered a foregone conclusion. We encountered few senior managers interested in the details of technology execution, let alone acquiring a superior understanding of it. However, the economic downturn of 2001–2002 changed everything. All eyes have turned to execution, as "nice-to-have" projects are replaced by "need-to-have" initiatives. Also, with the digitization of enterprise-wide supply chains and customer interactions, the locus of technology-enabled value creation shifted from transactions to complex processes. As a result, technology-enabled execution has inched its way to the top of management's agenda.

Not paying attention to execution issues can prove very costly. Consider the problems at Agilent Technologies, a testing equipment and chip maker, which resulted in roughly a $105 million revenue shortfall and $70 million in reduced operating profit. In June 2002, the former division of Hewlett-Packard began to roll out the first phase of its corporate-wide initiative, Project Everest, which included migrating 2,200 legacy systems to an Oracle ERP platform. This complex implementation covered more than 50 percent of the volume and virtually all of Agilent's financial processes, as well as functions such as order handling and shipping. Although the company had spent nearly 18 months working with roughly 100 consultants to install the program, integrating financial and operational data turned out to be more difficult than anticipated. It had to spend an additional $35 million in programming costs to cover the unexpected hitches in implementation and rollout.[15]

The case of Agilent Technologies is not an anomaly. Enterprise applications are so intertwined with day-to-day business operations that executives have no choice but to understand them. As technology implementations get bigger, managing them is getting harder. After paying lip service to technology, senior management and corporate boards are taking a closer look at technology investments and the link between planning and execution.

In a changing economy, every corporate board wants to make sure that technology investments result in business benefits. Executives recognize that they need to understand better the process digitization principles and tools that will allow them to create organizations superior to those of their competitors.

Seven Points to Ponder

> Now this is not the end.
> It is not even the beginning of the end.
> But it is, perhaps, the end of the beginning.
> —*Winston Churchill, 1942*

E-business has not taken its last breath—far from it. As these words are written, more companies worldwide are scrutinizing their businesses to determine what services or processes can be digitized. Timing is critical. Market leaders in various industries accepted the need for process digitization years ago and have been embracing it as a proven method for improving their business processes. The transition from process automation to digitized services has begun.

Critical points to remember regarding digitization: It's not just about technology; it is also about processes and execution. Managing digitization, from vision to implementation, is where you will either succeed or fail.

We spotlight seven points for you to ponder while you digest the chapter:

1. The current business environment has been described in terms of "chaos," "revolution," or simply "change." There is a clear pattern that can be gleaned from the turmoil: nonstop digitization of business processes.

2. Services digitization builds on the efforts of e-business and e-commerce. Digitization is the outcome of the nonstop business need to be more customer-driven and process-centric.

3. A successful digitization effort is one in which the company treats technology not as a sole solution, but as an enabler for innovating, improving, and integrating business processes. Process digitization has three dimensions: the type of interactions (uni- versus multi-channel), the scope of integration (business unit versus cross-enterprise), and the degree of digitization (manual to real time).

4. Good companies have a clear focal point; mediocre ones don't. Managers should devote themselves to determining a focal point to anchor

ongoing digitization efforts. Align digitization projects with your strategy, such as being Easy To Do Business With or offering an Every Day Low Price.

5. A focal point by itself is not enough. Digitization cannot be accomplished or managed without a blueprint that supports the focal point. Blueprints translate an organization's strategic objectives into process and applications that, in turn, drive operational results.

6. Three different blueprints—process improvement, strategic improvement, and business transformation—exist based on the scale of impact you want to make. Before going ahead with a digitization project, determine which blueprint is appropriate for you.

7. Finally, be patient. As the GE and Wal-Mart case studies show, process digitization is not a quick fix. You must successfully execute one project at a time. A digitization project draws resources from many distinct areas of a company. Overseeing and coordinating a digitization project at all times is exceedingly important.

Services are the new currency of business. Offering the fastest service, the best value, or the highest-quality product need not be a pipe dream. Services digitization is the vehicle through which your company can think on its feet and respond to customers with lightning speed. If that sounds relevant to you, read on.

CHAPTER TWO

Focal Points of Digitization

What to Expect

Where to focus? Therein lies the catch. Companies often try to do too many conflicting things at the same time with a limited set of resources. In other words, there is no focus! The current crop of digitization strategies may be too diffuse for effective execution.

A clear focal point clarifies the age-old questions: Who is the customer? What does the customer value? What initiatives do we need to create that value? In this chapter, we discuss ten basic focal points that anchor digitization initiatives and the business issues that drive them. Once you understand the focal points, the next step is applying them to your business.

Introduction

In Chapter 1, we discussed digitization and defined the Services Blueprint as Focal Point + Service Platforms. Our argument is simple: Implementing digitization without clear focal points leads to suboptimal results. But what exactly is a focal point? Focal points provide strategic clarity. For instance, Dell Computer's focal point is to be the leading direct computer systems company, bar none. Now contrast this to Hewlett Packard's focal point, which is to deliver vital technology for business and life.

Companies with well-defined focal points tend to out-execute their peers who may be trying to do too many disconnected initiatives at once. GE is a great example of a firm that believes in clear focal points. It is quite amazing how the entire GE organization works toward one goal: WorkOut in the 1980s, Six Sigma in the 1990s, and Digitization in the 2000s. Focal points guide execution by setting up the long-term target. Without a target, internal projects and day-to-day execution become exceptionally difficult to coordinate and complete. The result is a poor return on investment or even failure.

We strongly believe that focal points must guide the entire, complex, digitization execution process; without them, investments in sophisticated enterprise applications and technology infrastructure are not effective. Unfortunately, many firms are digitizing without clear focal points. This is similar to leading an army into battle with no map, no plan, no logistical support, no way to keep everyone informed, no scouting reports to assess and update progress, and no navigational instruments. That would be sheer madness, yet that's how many companies handle the journey to digitization.

In this chapter, we look at the characteristics and objectives of ten generic focal points that firms are racing to implement using digitization. These ten strategies are

1. Easy To Do Business With—Walking in the customers' shoes and eliminating hassles by integrating channels.

2. Customer-Centric Integration—Integrating internal applications and infrastructure to allow a shift from product silos to customers.

3. Low Cost—Offering customers an Every Day Low Price by creating low-cost or low-inventory supply chains.

4. Lowest Overhead—Minimizing overhead in areas such as human resources, logistics, and contact centers either via consolidation or outsourcing.

5. Zero-Defect Quality—Producing premium quality goods and services with very few defects.

6. Productivity Multiplier—Maximizing employee productivity using technology such as self-service portals or mobile computing.

7. Fast Service—Promising customers the fastest service by constantly speeding up the delivery and fulfillment of commodity products.

8. Product Innovation—Enabling product innovation so that companies may leap from laggard to fast follower or market leader.

9. Evolving Business Model—Edging into new businesses or markets (particularly relevant for companies that have customers with changing needs).

10. Real-Time Business—Responding and adapting in real time to market and customer demands.

Let's delve into each one of these focal points and examine the business requirements that anchor each. In the subsequent chapters, we will drill further down into the implementation details.

Easy To Do Business With (ETDBW)

Marshall Field, founder of the 100-year-old department store that bears his name, coined a golden rule for retailers: "Give the lady what she wants. The customer is always right." Today, customers want their business interactions (such as order-to-fulfillment) to be problem free.

Organizations do not want to be labeled "awkward to do business with." Unfortunately, most are. The problem is often out of their control. The underlying processes that support delivery of services to customers generally are built on top of inflexible applications. The result: unpleasant experiences and unhappy customers.

To rectify the situation, companies are moving to ETDBW focal points. This focal point yields three options: 1) Develop new services customized for the channel of usage on top of new infrastructure (very expensive); 2) Digitize existing services with an eye on customer priorities by integrating existing applications (moderately expensive); or 3) Do nothing (the cheapest option in the short term, but liable to put the firm out of business in the long term). In the dot-com heyday, organizations were picking the first option. With tighter resources, organizations are picking the less risky second option—multi-channel integration.

Channel integration is not a new problem. Toll-free 1-800 numbers, drive-through convenience retailing, 24/7 ATMs, and online "do-it-yourself" portals were all innovations that arose to support different customers' needs. Figure 2.1 illustrates the evolving customer needs of the past four decades: functionality, cost, quality, time, and customer service. In the past, technology was used to optimize one or two variables (say functionality and cost). Now the expectations are different. An average customer wants her channel interactions to be faster, better, cheaper, and feature-rich. Optimizing services across all these variables puts an incredible amount of stress on existing operations. As a result, ETDBW focal points are gaining visibility in management circles.

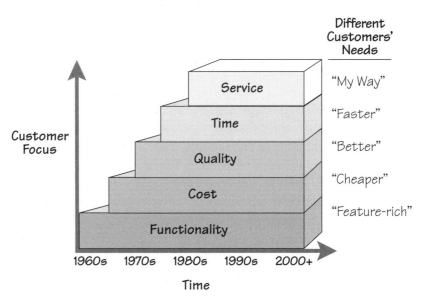

Figure 2.1: Evolving Customer Expectations

One aspect of ETDBW is the uncharted territory of multi-channel (brick, click, call center, and mobile handheld devices) customer experiences. ETDBW in a multi-channel environment means orchestrating experiences through integrated business processes that make interacting with the company painless, inexpensive, fast, and fun for self-service customers. It means accepting orders when and where the customer wants to place them; making it easy to check the status of an order with three clicks; addressing a question or complaint in the first call; billing customers accurately and in a timely fashion; and streamlining the return process if customers are not happy with the product.

Turn your attention to the financial services industry. Research has repeatedly shown that consumers desire ease of use and simplicity when managing their finances. TD Waterhouse, a financial services firm, even developed a national print and broadcast ad campaign titled "How Easy Is This," as part of a $165 million marketing initiative.[1] Marketing campaigns aside, implementing an ETDBW focal point is quite tricky for most financial companies and involves complex business process design that spans a number of back-end applications housed in various departments—credit card, mortgage, brokerage, checking, and savings accounts.

Now consider Lands' End, the direct merchant of classically styled apparel and home furnishings that often is mentioned as an ETDBW retailer. The focal point of Lands' End is to make it easy, informative, and fun to shop using either its catalog or its Web site. Landsend.com has become an ETDBW standard in the industry, with its huge array of merchandise, interactive shopping aids, and customer-friendly navigation and graphics.

Good ETDBW ideas come from watching and listening to customers. ETDBW strategies must better understand what customers expect when they interact with the company (that is, their experience requirements) and work to align the service delivery infrastructure with those expectations—easier said than done. An ETDBW solution is not a quick fix that can be splashed on like a new coat of paint over the multiple channels that customers use. It requires rethinking and retooling the end-to-end processes, applications, and infrastructure from the customer's vantage point.

> The bottom line: ETDBW digitization initiatives intend to improve the overall customer experience. A majority of companies have first-generation ETDBW projects in progress under the banner of customer relationship management (CRM). Their goal was to create a 360-degree customer view. The successful ones are now evolving into second-generation initiatives that endeavor to improve further the customer experience at all service touch points, including direct marketing, call centers, branches, and the Internet.

Customer-Centric Integration—Back-End Office Synchronization

Having a customer focus equates to giving the customers what they want when they want it consistently. To achieve a customer focus, companies must look at the problems both outside-in and inside-out. The outside-in approach is captured in the Easy To Do Business With multi-channel focal point. The inside-out approach is captured in the Customer-Centric Integration focal point.

The Customer-Centric Integration focal point is less ambitious than the ETDBW focal point. It is uni-channel and focuses on the need to integrate the back-office applications based on customer need. The health-care industry illustrates this point well. More than 150,000 patients pass through the doors of Oregon Health & Sciences University (OHSU), a teaching hospital. Two hundred different software applications are used to admit, track, and bill patients. Many of those applications cannot communicate with each other—the result: poor quality of service. If a patient sees a urologist who refers him to an endocrinologist, the records often don't show up on time in that department.[2]

Patient-centric data integration is a worldwide problem in the health-care industry. The goal of hospitals' integration efforts is to be personalized and efficient. Enabling both simultaneously is the essence of the customer-centric focal point. This is not easy to achieve when service firms are squeezed between customization and standardization.

Inside-out corporate strategies tend to oscillate from being product-centric to process-centric or from process-centric to customer-centric, depending on which organizational form will boost the bottom line. Hewlett-Packard, for instance, went the first route and consolidated 83 independent product lines into 17 product categories, with the goal of reducing redundant overhead and channeling the savings into R&D and sales. While these shifts often look good in PowerPoint, executing them is extremely painful for everyone in the company.

Why are these shifts so hard to do? All successful executives will tell you that they build their business around customers. In the beginning, customers were the focus of everything because the company's survival depended on it. As the organization matures and becomes more successful, attention invariably shifts from the customer to processes. Internal issues begin to compete for management's time, and customers fade to the periphery. Efficiency becomes the number one issue, resulting in millions spent on rigid software applications.

When an organization such as OHSU tries to move from being process-centric to customer-centric, the internal structure becomes a powerful inhibitor. The way companies have dealt with complexity is to reengineer and automate. In the last decade, it was widely assumed that large enterprise applications like ERP and CRM were going to eliminate layers of bureaucracy and make the transition to becoming customer-centric easier. Despite billions of investments, there is no evidence to back this assumption.

In theory, converting to a customer-centric approach appears doable. That is, if companies stand still they might have a chance. However, using mergers and acquisitions as a technique for growth muddies the waters and has created environments with overlapping applications, lost institutional knowledge, and fragmented architectures. Often, the trickle-down effect of bigger companies gobbling up others is poor customer service and incorrect billing.

Poor billing practices are not hard to find. Just look at your phone bill. It is very hard to get a correct statement from your telephone company anymore, and even worse, many times the problem is not fixed in the next billing cycle. How can companies survive when customer service is this poor? Unfortunately for all, the problem is worsening in many industries, such as telecom. Management of various companies went on buying binges and paid very little attention to billing and customer service application integration. Now the ability of those organizations to create service architectures that can meet simple customer needs is being curtailed precisely when the need for service is greatest.

> The bottom line: The Customer-Centric Integration focal point is being widely implemented as a growing number of companies struggle to improve service in existing channels. Even the best-managed companies, in spite of their attention to customers and continual investments in new service technology, have become highly susceptible to service quality problems.

Low Cost—Streamlined Supply Chains

To stimulate demand, prices have to be cut. Falling prices, or price deflation, create the need for low-cost manufacturing and retailing. They may be a benefit for consumers, but for companies in a mature industry facing stiff competition, these declines are a major hurdle to achieving earnings targets. Companies must reduce prices, introduce less expensive products, or cut production costs to meet profit goals and hold their ground against price-cutting competitors.

The high-tech industry is replete with examples of companies that perished due to focal points not optimized for continuously declining prices. In the consumer high-tech industry, it used to take an average of ten years for the price of a product to drop from $1,000 to $100. Now it takes 18 months. Economists label this phenomenon rapid price erosion.

Managing rapid price erosion in a supply chain requires a sophisticated blueprint that coordinates the actions linked along the supply chain. When producing a product or service of dependable quality, the company has to be both the volume and low-cost manufacturing leader across its entire product line. This position is achieved through a range of processes that take full advantage of the low-cost economics—decreased margins, product bundles, and high volumes.

The best example of a Low Cost focal point is Dell Computer, which is decimating competition in the low-margin desktop, server, and peripheral industry. Dell's initial focus has been on direct sales, volume, and commoditization. Its customers—consumers, small businesses, and large enterprises—demand a minimum acceptable quality level. Otherwise, they care about two things—low price for good performance and buying from a company that is easy to do business with.

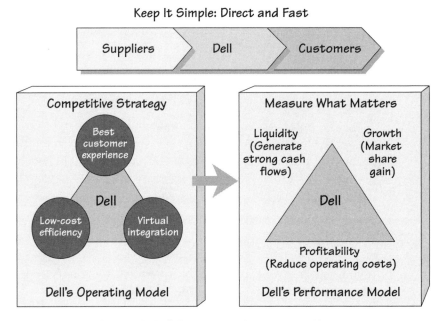

Figure 2.2: Dell Computer's Strategy at a Glance

To support its customers' needs, Dell created a high-level strategy comprised of a unique customer experience, low-cost efficiency, and virtual integration with suppliers. These focal points in turn drive performance—liquidity (ability to generate strong cash flows), growth (ability to gain market share), and profitability. Figure 2.2 illustrates Dell's strategy at a glance. At the end of the day, performance is what matters.

To keep customers happy, Dell and other high-tech companies constantly reorganize and optimize their supply chains and manufacturing around customers' priorities. The goal is to innovate with new product designs and simultaneously lower costs along the chain to give customers the lowest possible price.

The partial explanation for Dell's success is its use of low-cost suppliers and outsourced production. More than 90 percent of its revenues come from items that Dell designs and manufactures with partners (a concept it calls virtual integration). Effectively converting designs into individual products manufactured by third-party contractors, transforming them into end-user solutions, and then selling directly to customers is the end-to-end scope of build-to-order digitization. The digitization economics are interesting: Dell's operating expense-to-sales ratio is less than 10 percent, whereas most of its competitors' ratios are more than 20 percent.[3] The result is a very different cost structure.

Commoditizing or standardizing a product is fantastic for customers because lower costs mean lower prices. That's where Dell's business model shines. Aligning its supply chain with dropping component prices is a key element of Dell's game plan. The other critical process digitization elements include a fast-moving supply chain, a low-cost online sales channel, and minimal overhead.

Dell's execution is also impressive. The company's strategy has changed considerably in the last five years. It has moved into a market known as non-desktop computing—Intel servers, storage, networking, and peripherals. It is building a large professional and management services group to capture a lion's share of the $800 billion dollar IT market. As a result, Dell has evolved from a desktop company in the early '90s to a broad, international company that is supplying solutions and services for the entire enterprise. To support the new company strategy, Dell must accomplish three goals: 1) diversify its product portfolio so the company can weather unexpected economic turbulence, 2) take a long-term view of the company's market, and 3) improve processes regularly to smooth out the peaks and valleys while keeping Dell on track to satisfy customer goals.

Dell has to be very careful in changing its focal point. History has not been kind to high-tech companies that didn't align their execution to changing focal points. Look at the challenges Gateway Computer is having. During 1997–2001, Gateway's management moved from its direct-to-customer model to a hybrid—direct-to-customer and retail. In a short period, Gateway opened over 270 retail stores. The company envisioned these stores as places to configure low-priced PCs where customers could get great service. The problem with the model was that they still had to wait to receive their PCs. Customers didn't see any value in going into a store and not being able to walk out with a PC. In moving from a "pure low-cost" producer model to "high-touch + low-cost" model, Gateway lost valuable ground. It lost the momentum it had with the direct-to-customer model. Losses mounted due to price competition and dwindling market share, in which the change in focal point played a primary role. Gateway's founder, Ted Waitt, is trying hard to right the ship, but a hybrid model that resonates with customers is proving to be quite challenging. The moral of this example: Changing focal points is dangerous business. Proceed with caution.

The bottom line: The Low Cost focal point is a continuing challenge for many companies. Although benefits are reaped by customers through low prices, companies facing competition must streamline their supply chains to cut production costs.

Lowest Overhead—Business Process Outsourcing

Intense competition precludes companies from raising prices. On a perpetual journey to improve profits, companies are taking a hard look at overhead-reducing alternatives, especially business process outsourcing (BPO). A growing list of functions are ripe for outsourcing—purchasing and disbursement, order entry, billing and collection, human resources administration, cash and investment management, tax compliance, internal auditing, payroll, and call centers.

The lowest overhead focal point is usually found in slow growth or mature industries, where once profitable businesses—airlines, agriculture, insurance, telecommunications, and retailing—reached a point of diminishing profitability. To boost the balance sheet and save money, companies are scrutinizing their non-revenue generating functions. They are evaluating which functions they are good at and which they are not so good at. After this analysis, many companies decide to outsource various processes and departments.

This outsourcing trend is most evident in administrative services where human resources, billing, internal auditing, payment processing, and other finance functions are candidates for outsourcing. The core approach is the same: Scattered operations are pulled together into mega-service centers, which then serve all of a company's business units. These service centers can be centralized in-house or sent outside the company to a third-party provider. Many companies are choosing the latter for reasons of flexibility or agility. In the era of globalization, small and multi-national corporations alike can quickly outsource production to new suppliers, relocate a plant from Mexico to China, or move a customer service center from the United States to India to exploit the cheapest labor.

The insurance industry is actively pursuing low-overhead solutions for claims processing. With more than 1,500 U.S. companies selling some form of property and casualty insurance (P&C), the direct, written-premiums market size exceeds $280 billion. Over 120 million P&C claims are submitted every year. Statistics are staggering: The P&C claims industry annually spends over $23 billion in labor costs on an estimated 150,000 claims professionals and more than 300,000 supporting personnel.[4] Reducing the cost of simple, low-complexity claims origination and policy-servicing processes is a priority for insurance firms. As their comfort level increases, insurance companies are outsourcing more complex claims settlement, risk analysis, and underwriting processes.

Supply chain management and distribution, as well as logistics, are other areas where outsourcing is very common. Take the transportation logistics industry. In the past, trucking companies thought of their service narrowly—moving product from point A to point B. Today, truckers have expanded their scope and redefined their service to offer more complex, just-in-time delivery, warehousing, and inventory management. This has given rise to a new branch of logistics called 3PL—third-party logistics. Ryder, Menlo Logistics, UPS, and FedEx are examples of 3PLs. The entire sector is focused on solving customer problems.

Moving goods forward is one issue. Moving them back when they are returned is a whole different one. The reverse logistics industry that handles returns processing is another area where outsourcing solutions are prevalent. For many retailers, even large national chains with hundreds of mall stores, the cost of returns management is exorbitant. For a specialty retail chain with 25 to 500 stores, returns management, if not properly managed, can severely hurt the bottom line. By outsourcing to a 3PL specialist, the cost of the returns process is spread over numerous retailers.

> The bottom line: We expect the Lowest Overhead focal point to gain traction especially around outsourcing. However, outsourcing is challenging to implement. The execution challenges of outsourcing have nothing to do with features, quality, or price, but reflect the fact that conducting business across organizational boundaries is complex and problematic when the necessary processes, applications, and infrastructure are not in place. Often firms make the mistake of jumping to outsourcing contracts without thinking of the ramifications for their processes—the result: less-than-expected ROI.

Zero-Defect Quality—Supplier Relationship Management

Affluent customers are willing to pay a premium price for a product with star quality. They don't hesitate to reach into their wallets for superior quality, craftsmanship, customer service, performance, design, and brand. Proof of this lies in the success of BMW, Tiffany & Co, Nike, Porsche, and Harley-Davidson. These companies are pursuing a Zero-Defect Quality focal point.

Turn your attention to Lexus, the luxury division of Toyota Motor Company. Driven by a passion to improve continuously, the division has reached a level of quality that is unrivalled by its peers. Lexus designs automobiles that leave no wish unfulfilled. Its philosophy is that the perfection of the whole lies in the quality of the details. For Lexus, one satisfied customer is worth more than $500,000 in lifetime purchases and referrals.

The credit card industry has also followed this route by instituting exclusive platinum card programs to create unique experiences and provide exceptional service to upscale customers. For instance, users of the Platinum MasterCard, which is designed for frequent business or leisure travelers, are offered bonuses such as insurance benefits, rewards, and special offers negotiated with a range of upmarket suppliers. Customers can avail themselves of concierge services, travel reservations, and event ticketing. If they want to hire a car, charter a jet, or play a round of golf, MasterCard partners can arrange that, too. A single premium customer with ruffled feathers translates into significant revenue loss; therefore, creating a digitization strategy for managing supplier relationships and quality is a necessity.

For the commercial and military aircraft manufacturing industry, there is no choice about pursuing zero-defect quality. Boeing Integrated Defense Systems, one of the world's largest space and defense businesses, falls into this category. Headquartered in St. Louis, Boeing Integrated Defense Systems is a $23 billion business that supplies systems solutions to global military, government, and commercial customers. It is also a leading provider of intelligence, surveillance, and reconnaissance equipment.

Suppliers account for more than half the cost of Boeing's products. How well more than 12,000 suppliers do their jobs directly affects how well Boeing does its job. Accordingly, the company developed a preferred supplier certification program that enables it to identify and recognize high-performing suppliers. For instance, Northrop Grumman's electronics systems division, which met the standards for gold certification, had to deliver all parts and reports—in one case, more than 2,500 items—on time with zero defects over 12 months.[5]

> The bottom line: Managing supplier relationships and quality with a Zero-Defect focal point is becoming a requirement at many manufacturing companies. Any measures taken to work toward zero-defect quality seem wise, especially in the case of the airline industry.

Productivity Multiplier—Employee Portals

Alan Mulally, president of Boeing Commercial Airplanes, estimates that about 30 percent of the cost of developing a new airplane is rework. This means that one of every three people working on a Boeing project spends all of his time redoing what two other people did wrong in the first place. That's a huge productivity waste. The long-term goal is to digitize processes and reduce costly parts defects, scrap, and rework that ratchet up the expense of a commercial jetliner.

The productivity rate in many industries keeps growing robustly. Since 1995, productivity in the United States has been rising by 2.5 percent annually, far greater than the 1.0 to 1.5 percent rates that prevailed in most of the 1980s and early 1990s. In 2002, in a slow economy, productivity actually went up 3.0 percent. According to Alan Greenspan, chairman of the U.S. Federal Reserve, much of the productivity increase can be attributed to the infusion of high-tech products and applications in business. Information technology has enabled the tightening of the supply chain, and, in his view, made U.S. business more competitive and productive.[6]

Without the productivity rise, companies could not compete. Not surprisingly, there is growing demand for productivity multiplier digitization initiatives. When added to and employed by an organization, they dramatically increase the potential performance of employees, managers, and contractors.

Productivity multiplier initiatives are appearing in the form of employee Web portals. These portals are easy-to-use information gateways that provide a customizable window into scattered databases and business processes. The role of the worker determines what he sees when looking through that portal.

A typical employee Web portal addresses four distinct needs:

1. **Inform**—Employees, as well as suppliers and partners, can access basic information (employee directories) and key data (customer databases, enterprise management systems such as SAP and PeopleSoft) that allow them to perform their jobs and make intelligent decisions.

2. **Integrate** — New hires, contractors, and employees assigned to new projects are brought up to speed and can begin working on corporate applications as soon as possible.

3. **Connect** — Employees working on the road, at home, or in a satellite office can remotely access confidential information.

4. **Enable**—The workforce can find and manage personal information without the help of a human resource professional.

Employee portals are still young, but this has not discouraged several large companies from adopting the concept to improve the productivity of HR professionals. Before these portals were deployed, some HR personnel estimated that up to 75 percent of their time was spent on administrative tasks rather than more value-added work.

The bottom line: The Productivity Multiplier focal point's objective is to digitize processes and give managers and employees the ability to monitor transactions themselves. The tangible outcomes are greatly reduced paperwork, more consistent and efficient processes, improved data integrity, and reduced process cycle time.

Fast Service—Fast Fulfillment

Customers prize speed, and digitization is making the world even faster. Lower productivity work practices are being eliminated or digitized. We see this pattern in end-to-end order fulfillment (home grocery delivery), service management (government and health-care services), and different facets of employee self-service.

The goal is to deliver service to customers in minutes or hours, compared to today's standard of days or weeks. Let's look at Express Scripts, a company developing a Fast Service focal point for digitizing benefits interaction in the health-care industry. Based in Missouri, Express Scripts is one of the largest U.S. administrators of pharmacy benefits for health insurance plans, health maintenance organizations (HMOs), self-insured companies, unions, and government plans.

Express Scripts touches millions of lives a day, even though few of the beneficiaries know it. Express Scripts and others, like MedcoHealth Solutions, contract with both the health-care providers (e.g., AllState, Cigna, and Humana) and the pharmacy chains (e.g., CVS, Walgreens, and Eckerd). When a prescription is filled, the pharmacy chain is reimbursed by Express Scripts, which in turn charges the costs, plus an administrative fee, to the health-care provider. The company also dispenses prescription drugs through its mail pharmacy services. The company's ongoing effort to remove paper from complex processes has led to the development of a digital prescription network that connects all the players in the pharmacy process.[7]

How does this process work? First, a patient walks into a pharmacy and hands her prescription and insurance card to the pharmacist. Once the pharmacist swipes the card and identifies the benefits provider, the Express Scripts Pharmacy Benefits Management's (PBM) computer system kicks in. Each card carries a multi-digit code, which identifies the member and provides access to patient data and insurance coverage information. Express Scripts uses the code to determine eligibility, whether the drug is covered, if a less costly alternative is available, and the copayment amount.

Within seconds, every prescription goes through 140 steps of clinical and eligibility evaluation before any medication is dispensed. This interchange not only builds a repository of drug utilization and clinical data, but allows the company to consolidate claims and manage its cash. Express Scripts collects money from the insurers and in turn pays the pharmacies in bulk.

To reduce costs further, Express Scripts is slowly migrating the fulfillment of prescriptions from brick-and-mortar pharmacies to a click-and-brick mail-order model. The old model of counting out pills from behind a drugstore counter is giving way to warehouses with miles of conveyor belts and robots. Computers, optical scanners, and robotics have transformed the process of dispensing medications. Pharmacists supervise the process, but it is the robots that fill and label tens of millions of prescription bottles.[8]

Digitization at Express Scripts is not merely technology for its own sake; it's about serving customers quickly, creating new value propositions, improving productivity, and increasing profits. The results are impressive. In 2001, Express Scripts handled one in six prescriptions filled in the United States—a whopping 294 million retail pharmacy claims and 20.5 million mail claims, contributing to revenues of $9.3 billion.

> The bottom line: Express Scripts and other Fast Service companies like FedEx are attempting to differentiate themselves and meet changing expectations (total service fulfillment, speed, reliability, responsiveness, ease of use, timeliness, customization, and privacy).

Product Innovation—Shrinking Product Lifecycles

Competition is the essence of a market economy. For everything from cell phones to toilet paper, competition results in nonstop, Darwinian pressure to develop a continual stream of innovative products.

The Product Innovation focal point centers on four different business issues:

1. Companies need to produce new, customized products. In many industries, technology has shifted power to the buyers who are gaining control and learning how to exercise it. One response to buyer power by marketing departments is to adopt the concept of mass customization blindly (for some if

not all products). Mass customization, which sounds good in theory, wreaks havoc with fulfillment processes. It increases the number of products and services offered, and customizing them increases cost.

2. Companies need to collaborate internally on product development and quickly share product-related information across their organizations and value chains. A tremendous amount of information is generated during the product development process and throughout its lifecycle. A single shareable resource is needed to capture, aggregate, and manage product information from many sources, making it easy for people outside of engineering to add value to the development process.

3. Companies need to coordinate and control production across multiple plants in multiple locations. Offshore development in high-tech industries has become widespread. Offshore outsourcing is being increasingly implemented as part of an overall strategy to create a global mix of available resources and services. The combination of lower costs and reasonable quality represents a strategic weapon.

4. Suppliers need to accelerate strategic sourcing and integrate supplier management business processes earlier in the product lifecycle. Companies must communicate in real time with component parts suppliers and contract manufacturers. The objective is to streamline interactions between buyers and suppliers by transmitting standard purchasing documents electronically and allowing users to collaborate using a single Web-based model.

One strategy taking shape to support all of these issues is product lifecycle management (PLM). PLM is directed at helping companies manage, track, and control products, projects, and assets. Many perceive PLM as a coordinating strategy focused on delivering personalized products constructed from modules designed and built around the globe.

Every product goes through a lifecycle—idea, prototype, engineering, launch, and maintenance. This product lifecycle presents three challenges:

1. New product development—because all products get obsolete, a company must be proficient at developing new products to replace aging ones.

2. Product evolution strategies—companies must be good at adapting their product designs in the face of changing tastes, technologies, and competition.

3. Product customization strategies—companies must be adept at reacting to varied customization requests from customers.

The bottom line: Companies have to get better at developing and managing new and existing products. With pressure to develop products faster and faster, companies must make sure that speeding up the product lifecycle does not affect product quality. In industries facing increasingly shorter product lifecycles, the goal is not just to create products faster, but to make them better and of higher quality.

Evolving Business Model—Changing Customer Priorities

In some industries, customer priorities are changing faster than ever before. The number one job for management is to understand the direction and velocity of changing customer needs and to diversify accordingly. In this context, digitization must support the diversification strategy.

To illustrate the Evolving Business Model focal point and the issues it brings up, let's study McDonald's. McDonald's, one of the world's best-known brand names, serves 45 million customers daily through outlets located where customers work, play, and live. The company operates and licenses more than 30,000 outlets in about 121 countries.[9] The business has grown steadily by catering to the trend of fast food—burger, fries, and soft drinks—at low prices. The focal point: fast food at reasonable prices.

However, as the fast-food market gets saturated, growth has been hard to come by. In 2003, the company reported its first quarterly loss since going public 47 years earlier. Profit margins are being pressured by higher labor costs and "dollar menus." To find the next area for growth, McDonald's is being forced to address two trends: 1) healthier menus that are replacing artery-clogging foods and 2) casual dining experiences. The focal point is shifting, creating execution challenges.

The focal point that made McDonald's a growth engine is under siege as health-conscious consumers search for less fattening alternatives. Wendy's and Subway have responded with garden salads and low-fat sandwiches. McDonald's is reacting slowly with a series of copycat initiatives that are not groundbreaking.

Since 1998, McDonald's has tried a number of tactics in its core fast-food business to put some sizzle back into its sales. New kitchens were set up, a switch from ready-and-waiting to made-for-you products was completed, a bevy of new products was added, new drive-thrus were installed, updated technology was implemented, and quality, service, and cleanliness were emphasized more. But creating and moving to a new focal point are not proving to be easy for the Golden Arches.

In parallel, the casual dining sector is gaining market share from fast-food chains as an older population favors dining in full-service restaurants over fast-food concepts. Moreover, an emerging category of competitors that includes sandwich shops such as Panera Bread and Cosi are giving fast-food eaters more options. This departure from fast food is expected to continue as the population ages. With this trend in mind, McDonald's is branching out with a multi-pronged acquisition strategy to bring new restaurant concepts under its Partner Brand division: Boston Market, Chipotle Mexican Grill, Pret a Manger, and Donatos Pizza (see Figure 2.3).

McDonald's is at a crossroads. The company is experiencing the problem of shifting customer tastes firsthand. This is forcing McDonald's to diversify from

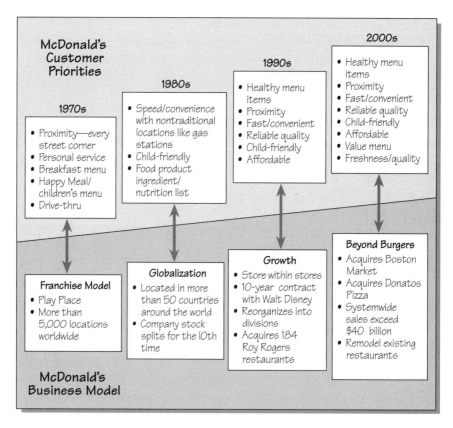

Figure 2.3: McDonald's Evolving Business Strategy

the slow-growth $105 billion fast-food industry to more rapidly growing "fast-casual" franchises. It must step out of its comfort zone and develop new fast-casual dining concepts. As a result, managers face a combination of greater complexity and less time for executing strategy. Tougher decisions have to be made at all levels of the company, despite incomplete information and less time to get it right. Diversification for McDonald's can range from extending a basic product line to acquiring and integrating completely unrelated businesses. It can be achieved through internal product research and development, the purchase of new product ideas or technology, or the acquisition of companies.

McDonald's is not alone. This diversification crisis plagues many companies: Coca-Cola's challenge—soda and bottled water; IBM's—outsourced technology services and management consulting; the Gap's—fashion fads and customer life-cycle strategy; and Starbucks'—coffee on-the-go and a sit-down café experience. Each of these transitions is not a simple add-on but a significant strategy change—people, processes, technology, and applications. To meet the challenge of unpredictable customer priorities, managers must ask: What is driving the changes? What processes in my industry will be affected and have to change? What short-term and long-term adjustments do I need to make to the enterprise applications to be prepared for where the customer is going?

> The bottom line: Companies facing the Evolving Business Model focal point need to create customer demand quickly for their new products. Whatever strategy that was used in the past is no longer working. They need to embrace digitization both to cut business model extension costs and to reach new customers.

Real-Time Business—Synchronized with the Market

A factory in London is destroyed by fire. Within 30 minutes, suppliers in China and shipping agents in Hong Kong adjust accordingly. A freak typhoon causes massive flight cancellations in Singapore. Within 60 minutes, ripple effects are felt throughout the world. Thousands of flights are rerouted and stranded passengers rebooked. The ability to deal with unexpected events is real-time business.

In industries such as toys, fashion apparel, and consumer electronics, forecasting demand and managing inventory is notoriously difficult because of new product introductions and highly fickle consumer demand. As a result, stockouts of hot items occur frequently. With an unprecedented number and variety of products on the market, how does management prevent stockouts? By synchronizing supply with market demand.

Better integration between supply and demand is critical. If a company is operating in a low-margin business, not matching supply and demand correctly can be disastrous. Firms must operate as real-time businesses whose processes are integrated end-to-end across the company as well as with key partners, suppliers, and customers. Not doing so means that businesses cannot speedily respond to customer demand, market opportunities, or external threats.

The Internet is the foundation for real-time information flow. It has given companies the power to put business processes online and connect them. Slowly but surely, market leaders such as Intel are moving to a real-time model. Under the old pencil-and-paper model, Intel used to take 45 days to reconfigure factories worldwide in response to demand changes. With its digitization strategy, the company can take constantly changing demand information reflected in product sales and realign the manufacturing network almost overnight.[10]

Companies historically have carried excess inventory, as they didn't have adequate information about what was happening upstream or downstream. As a result, there has been enormous attention paid to replacing inventory with real-time information. Pioneering companies like Wal-Mart, DaimlerChrysler, Toyota, FedEx, and UPS have committed to adopting and carrying out real-time strategies under the banner of adaptive supply chain management. These strategies have caused culture shocks that are still reverberating throughout their ranks, their partners, and even their customers.

While the rationale for real time is clear, its corresponding blueprint is not. Today's demand for delivery of just the right product, in the right place, at the right time, and at the right cost creates challenges for managers crafting new real-time processes. This is especially difficult for those firms whose processes run on a batch model where information is queued and distributed in intervals of 6, 12, or 24 hours.

> The bottom line: If Real-Time Business is your focal point, you need to execute carefully. Instead of making drastic changes by moving from batch to real time, companies need to take incremental steps by laying an application infrastructure that can use more up-to-date information to remove delays progressively and execute critical end-to-end business processes. It is important to work real-time digitization into your business, one step at a time.

Seven Points to Ponder

> To think that the new economy is over is like somebody in
> London in 1830 saying the entire industrial revolution is over
> because some textile manufacturers in Manchester went broke.
> —*Alvin Toffler, author of* Future Shock

In this post-dot-com era, management at all levels faces a different mandate—deliver results. Grandiose vision, glamour, and glitz are out. Focus and execution are in. The most challenging question confronting business leaders is no longer "Should we invest in technology?" It's "How can we make or save money with digitization?" and "Given limited resources, what digitization initiatives should become our priorities?"

Focused digitization initiatives will separate the winners from the losers. Over the last decade, companies have been constructing huge, complex information structures with tight integration as their blueprint. The temptation to adopt new technologies, like the Internet, with little thought as to how they will fit with existing processes has resulted in mounting maintenance, integration, and support costs, not to mention headaches. To avoid the loss of concentration, a well-defined focal point is an absolute necessity.

You likely are thinking about which focal point is right for your organization. We offer you seven points to ponder while you have your thinking cap on.

1. Often, corporate strategies are too vague for digitization. They need to be distilled into clear focal points. This is what market leaders do. Selecting and defining a focal point—Best Value, Zero-Defect Quality, or Fast Service—is the first step in digitization. *What is your company's focal point(s)?*

2. Ten different objectives for digitization crystallized during our research. All should benefit from three mega-trends: 1) an ongoing technology revolution that is redefining productivity, 2) the globalization of the world's economy, and 3) consumers that relentlessly seek better value. *Are any or all of these trends affecting your company?*

3. Focal points set a destination. Moving toward it is the whole point of execution. To reach the destination, you need a blueprint that defines the direction and priorities of information technology and bridges them to the focal point. *Does your company have a clear set of blueprints?*

4. Our research indicates that firms with a crisp focal point can improve the overall quality of their execution with no additional resources. All they need is the discipline to execute and the determination to persist until results are achieved. *Does your firm zigzag or maintain a steady course?*

5. Focal points typically don't change, but underlying processes and technology do. In an era of volatile stock prices and sudden shifts in strategies, businesses can adapt to change only if they continuously align their processes and technology. *Does your firm update its processes to account for business turbulence?*

6. In the past, a digitized company was one that allowed the buying and selling of most products online. Now the idea is much larger. Companies are developing focal points that encapsulate everything involved in an organization's business: customers, employees, factories, suppliers, and partners. *What is the scope of your focal point?*

7. Choosing not to digitize is slow death. Eventually, consumers will not patronize companies that don't offer them whatever it is they seek, such as the best value, high quality, fast service, or low price.

"The only certainty is uncertainty," said the Roman scholar Pliny the Elder. Two thousand years later, he is still right. Despite the uncertain landscape, corporate management must still chart a course for moving forward with digitization. Digitizing your company does not have to be an arduous task, however, thanks to focal points and the evolving service platform technologies, which we discuss in the next chapter.

CHAPTER THREE

Service Platforms: Enablers of Digitization

What to Expect

Now that you've seen how digitization focal points could shape your company's initiatives, it's time to deconstruct the execution process. Focal points have to be mapped into multi-channel user interactions, real-time business processes, enterprise applications, and infrastructure, all of which collectively fall under the banner of service platforms. This leads to a simplified equation: Services Blueprint = Focal Points + Service Platforms. Focal points provide strategic clarity, and service platforms provide the technical foundation.

In this chapter, we describe the concepts behind service platforms: What is a service platform? How are service platforms, portals, and enterprise applications related? What is the business case for investing in service platforms? What are the different types of service platforms? We also discuss modularity, which is the key concept behind service platforms and other emerging developments in enterprise applications, such as Services Oriented Architectures and Web Services.

Introduction

How are innovative organizations in business-to-business (Intel and Cisco), business-to-consumer (Dell, Yahoo!, or eBay), business-to-employee (General Motors), government-to-citizen (the Singapore Government), and university-to-student (London Business School) related?

In their respective niches, all were among the first to execute services blueprints. As we explained earlier, a Services Blueprint = Focal Point + Service Platform. Focal points set the strategic agenda, and service platforms provide the technical foundation. Having spent the previous chapter exploring focal points, we now turn to service platforms.

To explain the concept of a service platform, consider the Easy To Do Business With focal point. The ETDBW focal point is composed of services. What does this mean? When you visit an e-commerce portal as a customer, you expect integrated services that deliver on the ETDBW objective. These services include log in, catalog, ordering, and payment. Customers don't care what behind-the-scenes applications are providing these services; they simply want a seamless experience. The service platform acts as the hub that integrates the different services and provides a consistent experience for the customer. The purpose of the service platform is to hide the complexity and integrate different enterprise applications.

The race is on in multiple industries to build service platforms that enable better creation and delivery of end-to-end services across multiple channels. For instance, when self-service customers visit a multi-channel retailer like Dell, Lands' End, or Tesco, they expect end-to-end integrated processes (order-to-delivery). They don't really care about the applications, internal divisions, or third-party partners who are providing the individual steps of the service (catalog, shopping basket, order entry, payment processing, warehousing, shipping, and customer service). The same is true when the customer calls the call center and speaks to a customer service representative (CSR). CSRs have to interact with the same services as he enters the customer information into a Web portal. The customer self-service and CSR portal applications have a very similar functionality. Both of these portal applications interact with the same service platform. Until recently, most companies would have separate service platforms dedicated to each channel. With recent advancements in software technology, like Web Services, the need to have channel-specific strategies should diminish considerably going forward. This in turn, should save a significant amount of money for organizations, as they will not have to spend funds on channel-specific integration.

So, what is the definition of a service platform? A service platform integrates multiple applications from various departments, business units, or partners to deliver a seamless experience for the customer, employee, manager, or supplier.

Hiding the back-end complexity and creating a business process management plan plus an application integration layer that ties the various pieces together is the essence of the service platform.

It is becoming evident that services digitization is most powerful when it is engineered on integrated service platforms. Services digitization has progressed quickly and dramatically. In five short years, businesses have created a new genre of online processes. These processes evolved from simple task automation, like order entry, to large-scale composite processes, such as order-to-fulfillment, which support strategic digitization focal points.

Companies implementing digitization have switched tactics in recent years and are approaching it outside-in, that is, "walk in the customer's shoes" and create services aligned with what the customer wants, as opposed to inside-out, that is, "what is good for the company is good for customers." This shift is forcing parallel changes from an internal applications mind-set to an external services mind-set. Evidence of this paradigm shift is mounting, indicated by the rapid diffusion of enterprise portals. Service delivery through enterprise portals is becoming part-and-parcel of certain industries.

Focal Points and Portals—A Symbiotic Relationship

Look carefully at the focal points of the previous chapter and you will see a common thread. All entailed assembling new services and delivering them through portals. Enabling customer, supplier, or employee services through a portal is not a luxury anymore; it is a way of doing business.

The trend toward services delivery via portals is clear in the travel, car rental, and lodging industries, which are digitizing faster than others. Customers are gravitating toward companies that are capable of delivering integrated services. Companies like Expedia, Travelocity, Orbitz, hotels.com, and lastminute.com, have helped change the way leisure and business travelers plan and book travel. These companies have created service platforms that provide the inventory, booking tools, fulfillment, itinerary change management, and customer support that customers crave.

The objective is to make sure that customers don't fall through the cracks that are often created by poor hand-offs (e.g., between the booking and billing processes). Thanks to these service platforms, consumers are in the driver's seat when it comes to purchasing hotel rooms and airline tickets. Savvy travelers are aware that there are always rooms available at decent prices, and they are making hotel and flight reservations much closer to their departure dates. This change in consumer behavior is wreaking havoc on finely tuned yield/revenue management systems.

The financial services industry has also begun to accept that service platforms are a must for competitive reasons. The SuperMontage trading platform developed by the Nasdaq stock market is one example. Representing an investment of more than $100 million, the SuperMontage trading platform took around two years to develop. Nasdaq is hoping that SuperMontage will help it to regain the market share it has lost to the electronic communications networks (ECNs) like Instinet and Island by offering investors a faster and more transparent means of trading and settlement.[1]

Clearly, multiple industries are buzzing over the need to deliver integrated services. We are in the early stages of conceptualizing this new area. Before we go any further, however, let's state something up front: Service platforms are not cheap to build, deploy, or enhance. For instance, we estimate that between 1994 and 2002, Amazon.com invested more than $2 billion in its service platform—the portal, process, and underlying integration layer. This remarkable platform is capable of serving 40 million retail consumers, 600,000 store associates, and a growing number of retailers.[2] Amazon.com has created a powerful barrier to entry for competition. No wonder other retailers are outsourcing online customer interaction to Amazon.com.

Focal points → portals → service platforms → enterprise applications—the logical connection between strategy, processes, and technology is surfacing. Despite the cost, the design and implementation of service platforms are rapidly becoming central elements of every multi-channel or cross-enterprise strategy.

Enterprise Portals Need Business Process Management (BPM)

Portals by themselves don't create value. They are merely windows into various processes. The value creation is actually done by a behind-the-scenes service platform that assembles, integrates, and delivers services to the customer via the portal interface. How does this work in the real world?

Consider the order-to-delivery service. Getting an order and taking it all the way through to delivery are the staples of consumer-facing service platforms. This service has many smaller processes; the first is getting the order. This begins with marketing campaigns, lead generation, salesforce automation, and order entry—the territory of customer relationship management (CRM). Then the order flows into applications such as order management, planning, and manufacturing—the territory of enterprise resource planning (ERP). Then the order goes off to warehousing, logistics, and billing—the territory of supply chain management (SCM). If you have a problem with the bill or want to return the product, you enter the territory of customer service and call centers.

Following the order from beginning to end—this is the way companies operate, but that's not the way they have traditionally deployed enterprise applications. Companies have automated little fragments of the entire order-to-delivery process using various functional applications such as CRM, ERP, or SCM. As companies look for more leverage and value capture from technology investments, they are shifting their focus from process fragments (centered on functions) to integrated cross-enterprise processes (cutting across functions).

As the Internet became a dominant channel, creating online service platforms quickly became a new differentiator. On the online side, Amazon.com and eBay are perhaps the most well-known and advanced service platforms. Both are evolving into merchant platforms capable of carrying out their own transactions, as well as the transactions of other retailers. Amazon.com and eBay illustrate a new breed of service platforms capable of linking and synchronizing online and offline processes.

The trajectory of innovation is becoming clear. Multi-channel and cross-enterprise service platforms are the emerging foundation for integrating and digitizing end-to-end processes. They support companies that intend to become more customer-centric and less function-centric. The emerging service platform is the quintessential process environment, rich with customer, business, and transaction information. Translating customers' needs into business objectives, business objectives into processes, and processes into interactions is the role of service platforms.

What Does a Service Platform Look Like?

Figure 3.1 presents a high-level view of a service platform. The three layers are

1. The multi-channel interaction layer (i.e., Web portals, mobile handhelds, call center interfaces, in-store interfaces),

2. The composite process layer (i.e., order-to-cash, target-to-engage), and

3. The integration layer (i.e., security, identity management, and integration services).

The multi-channel interaction layer is the portal layer, the window through which a customer, supplier, employee, manager, or auditor interacts with services. The portal by itself is rather useless. The value is in the services that are

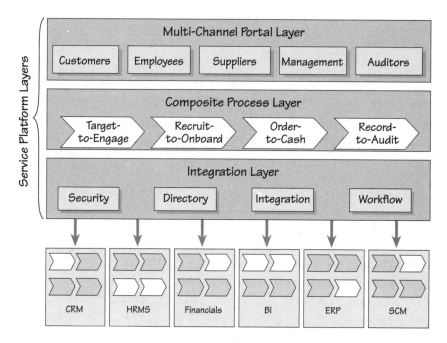

Existing Enterprise Applications

Figure 3.1: The Three Layers of Service Platforms

delivered through it. Service delivery through portals customized by channel—brick, Web, mobile, and call centers—is the way business will be done in the future.

Services are created and assembled in the composite process layer, a relatively new development in business computing. This layer is where the context and intelligence resides. It captures the unique characteristics of the workflow—how a company relates to its customers, suppliers, and employees. The composite process layer coordinates the integration of multiple applications and delivers their functionality to users via multiple portals. The composite process layer is really an intelligent layer that understands the channel and type of service request and triggers the next steps accordingly.

The integration layer enables the secure integration of the various front-office and back-office applications. This layer enables services integration, provisioning, and assembly by taking functionality from multiple applications, including CRM, ERP, and others. The goal is to leverage and reuse existing applications, not to buy new ones; this way companies don't waste money building the same functionality repeatedly.

However, all three layers are simply the means to the end. The end goal is to support digitization focal points. As a result, we need a much better understanding of how to create, deploy, maintain, and enhance cross-enterprise processes that can run on top of the integration layer.

New Trends in Enterprise Applications—Portal Infrastructure

As we move from enterprise portals based only on the Web channel to multi-channel enterprise portals, some interesting dynamics are beginning to play out. The primary driver for service platform investments is the underlying need to change the execution paradigm.

The first-generation enterprise portal models in many organizations were developed inside-out, or focused on automating processes. This type of thinking has to change in a multi-channel setting where the services have to be customized to the channel and the customer segment. In other words, multi-channel portals call for an outside-in paradigm, that is, "provide what the user wants in the channel of choice." This shift in perspective is forcing parallel changes from an enterprise applications mind-set to a service platform mind-set.

To develop the business case for a service platform, it is useful to trace the evolution of enterprise portals, the management issues, and the emerging business needs. We conclude this section by providing a short overview of modularity that provides a good framework for thinking about how to organize portal fragmentation issues.

The Evolution of Enterprise Portals

The demand for continuous improvement—both in terms of productivity and efficiency—is altering the genetic composition of business applications. From stand-alone programs to packaged applications, from packaged applications to enterprise portals, the evolution has been gradual.

- **Stand-Alone Programs.** Software development has evolved from an art based largely on trial and error to a more structured production based on concrete specifications. This resulted in the design of stand-alone software applications (e.g., accounting) that solved some particular problem. Usually the end product was visualized beforehand and the maximum number of potential users was known well in advance.

- **Packaged Applications.** After solving the same problem many times, software developers saw an opportunity to package applications that could satisfy a similar need across many organizations. Designing a range of software programs for a suite of applications (e.g., ERP) enabled a whole new set of interesting possibilities. These application suites—PeopleSoft, J.D. Edwards, SAP, Siebel, and Microsoft—share common elements and interfaces. The arrival of robust, packaged portal solutions has fundamentally changed the way applications are created, deployed, and interacted with.

- **Enterprise Portals.** The Internet dramatically expanded the pool of potential users. Establishing an entry point for accessing an organization's most important services—information and processes—took on a new urgency. Portals bring together structured and unstructured data, organizational knowledge, and transactions from multiple packaged software systems that exist in the organization. The goal is to combine the most important information, applications, and Internet-based services into well-defined, secure user interfaces.

Enterprise portals are the next generation of enterprise applications. The enterprise portal market just took off in recent years. The result is that companies have too many Web sites that masquerade as portals, many of which overlap. Many organizations are beginning to consolidate their myriad Web sites into a handful of enterprise portals.

The movement toward a consolidation of enterprise portals is fueling the need for modular service platforms. For instance, companies creating employee self-service portals to conduct operations worldwide want a single service platform that drives all portals. Similarly, companies creating customer self-service portals want to consolidate the multiple customer Web sites into a few points of access powered by a single service platform for all the electronic information and services.

Clearly, the long-term trend is service platforms that can power multiple enterprise portals across different channels—brick, Web, mobile handhelds, and call centers. Let's explore the trend of multi-channel portal infrastructure further to understand better the business issues shaping the need for service platforms.

The Next Step in Portal Evolution—Controlling the Chaos

In a few short years, portals have influenced how companies service external and internal users. From internal sharing of resources to customer transactions and real-time collaboration with partners, portals have been deployed widely in today's business landscape.

Time-to-value is one reason why portals have been rapidly adopted. Faced with the prospect of multi-year ERP and CRM projects, executives in the Internet boom began breaking down monolithic initiatives into discrete, fast-payback pilots in areas such as supplier, reseller, and customer portals. The executives wanted to reach different user segments with customized portals. While there was tremendous growth in portals, each had a different architecture and infrastructure. The catch phrase driving the portal growth is anyone, anywhere, anytime, and any device.

Every boom is followed by a cooling-off period. Not surprisingly, the portal revolution is experiencing growing pains. Take, for instance, the fragmentation problem. Within a single company there may be more than a hundred different portals, deployed by as many vendors, performing different tasks for different departments, and aimed at disparate user segments. Often, these portals are built on dissimilar platforms and integrate different back-end applications. It isn't hard to see that value is leaking out of the processes due to disconnected "stovepipe" portals and silos of information.

In many organizations, the situation has become unmanageable. Portals exist in isolation, unable to work with each other or the company as a whole. This is a huge headache for companies that need to share portal resources across the enterprise in a way that leverages their current investments and avoids having to build an entirely new system-wide portal network from scratch.

As the number of portals grows unchecked, integration costs escalate, and services become extremely fragmented and ineffective. The expected value and realized value are not even close (see Table 3.1). Deciding whether to centralize the portal infrastructure is the burning issue for organizations under pressure to achieve greater economies of scale from multi-million dollar technology investments.

Aligning Business Flexibility Needs with Portal Infrastructure

Consider the following business scenario: At a large financial services company, executives are always starting up small, new initiatives, trying out different strategies in the market, seeing what works and what doesn't, shutting down the things that don't work, and scaling up the things that do. Thus, at any moment, this company is trying out a variety of new services in the marketplace and testing various hypotheses about corporate strategy.

This experimentation approach allows the financial company's services to adjust constantly to changing customer priorities. In order to accommodate this

Table 3.1: The Trouble with Portals

Expected ROI of Portals	Realized ROI of Portals
• Increase efficiency through automation • Ability to adapt as needed	• Proprietary approaches have increased complexity
• Shorten delivery time for new services	• Point solutions and disconnected product suites jeopardize business results
• Foster innovation through customized understanding of business, customers, and core processes	• Complex deployments like business-to-business portals freeze current and new services • ROI is unclear
Increase value while reducing total cost of ownership	**Value is not increasing—integration costs are**

method of doing business, the company's underlying building blocks—processes, applications, and infrastructure—must enable new end-to-end processes. The building blocks must be capable of being rearranged in new ways and not be fixed in place. If they are not put together systematically, a negative ROI is inevitable.

The unpredictable nature of business demands a flexible services architecture. The need for an ever-increasing number of services has become one of the drivers of escalating costs for many digitization efforts. The managerial challenge becomes balancing low-cost service creation with acceptable levels of service and time to market. The ability to be responsive to the market and yet be internally efficient and stable in terms of resource requirements is the essence of the problem. Service platforms are the solution.

In parallel to business flexibility issues, companies are struggling with fragmentation. Until recently, organizations created their own portal solutions by buying and assembling separate best-of-breed components that were not always compatible. This is akin to people buying car components and assembling their own cars, which would lead to cars having different parts and not being built to a standard. Thus, when things broke down, repair and maintenance would become very costly.

This is exactly the reason why many organizations are rolling up hundreds of disparate portal initiatives under the enterprise architecture approach. As noted earlier, portals and Web sites have exploded unchecked, causing development, support, and integration costs to spiral out of control. Having hundreds of stand-alone portals is inefficient in terms of people, money, and time. Also, fragmentation inhibits organizations from modifying their customer-facing processes to accommodate changing market and competitive conditions.

Many partial solutions have come to market in an attempt to address the need for a portal foundation. No single approach has addressed all the necessary aspects—until now. Service platforms are emerging to solve the flexibility and fragmentation problem. Leading-edge companies are moving away from autonomously run portal operations to more efficient, user-focused service platforms.

Before we get into the detailed structure of service platforms, it is necessary to understand the concepts of modularity that are shaping the future of application design. Modularity enables a "Lego®-like building block" structure that facilitates efficient assembly of services. Modularity and composition are beginning to make their impact on the business applications industry.

Modularity and Composition—Concepts for Managing Complexity

Controlling complexity is not a new challenge. In a 1962 paper entitled "The Architecture of Complexity," Herb Simon, who later received the 1978 Nobel Prize for Economics, discussed what he had learned about the structure of complex systems. In the paper, Simon explained the need for hierarchy and modularity as core design elements in dealing with complexity.

Simon illustrated the need for modularity by offering a parable about two imaginary watchmakers named Hora and Tempus. Both were highly regarded in the community, and the phones in their workshops rang frequently with new orders. However, Hora prospered, while Tempus became poorer. What was the reason?

According to this story, the difference between them lay in the design of their watches. Each design involved 1,000 parts, but the similarity ended there. Tempus's watches were assembled one component at a time. Hora's watches were organized into subassemblies of ten parts each. Hora would combine ten subassemblies into larger subassemblies, and these in turn could be combined to make a complete watch.

The difference between the two watchmakers' process designs became crucial in the larger context of their business. Customers would call them constantly and interrupt their work. Whenever the phone rang, they were forced to abandon their current assembly. These interruptions did not bother Hora, who lost at most whatever subassembly he happened to be working on. Tempus, on the other hand, lost an entire watch. Since he didn't use modular subassemblies, the unfinished watch would fall apart into its elementary parts. Because interruptions were common, Hora would complete many more watches than Tempus, whose business suffered in terms of productivity.

Hora used building blocks to manage complexity effectively; Tempus didn't. The same pattern is repeating in corporations as they build next-generation portal applications. Some are constructing each portal from scratch like Tempus. Others swear that modularity, integration, and application architectures are requisite for a new technological platform to carry out service customization and delivery through portals.

Modularity and Composition in Manufacturing—Product Platforms

The IT industry can learn from the evolution of product development in the manufacturing sector. In the early days, production was based on the notion of master craftsmen. Everything was handcrafted with appropriate materials, tools, and skills. The Industrial Revolution changed the old system of production, replacing hand tools with the main instruments of machinery and mechanization for production. In the 1920s, Henry Ford introduced mass production, which used interchangeable parts, specialized machines, process focus, and division of labor. One of the precepts of mass production is producing standardized products for homogeneous markets.

Mass production methods are limiting in the volatile marketplace where customers' priorities change frequently. Customers can no longer be lumped into well-defined market segments or homogeneous groups; they need to be treated as individuals (segments of one) with different needs. This emphasis on the individual has introduced the concept of mass customization, in which configuration and customization replace standardized products. The need for product configuration customization increases complexity, cost, and development time.

Engineers found a way around these problems: Develop the product platform carefully, and then use different modules to provide product variety. A product platform is a collection of the common elements implemented across a range of products.[3] For instance, in the computer industry, PCs and servers are composed of components such as microprocessors, memory chips, monitors, keyboards, and disk drives, all of which can be customized in a variety of ways to meet customer demand. Breaking down PCs and servers this way allows companies to add or delete quickly features of existing products to address certain market segments or to develop new capabilities without having to develop a whole new product. Examples include IBM's ThinkPad, Dell's Latitude, and HP's LaserJet.

A well-defined product platform has a common core technology, shares a set of basic components, and requires similar manufacturing processes. Product platforms are now deemed essential to support any customization strategy. Research done in the areas of mass customization, concurrent engineering, design for product variety, and design of product families supports this viewpoint.

In the early 1970s, managers at Black & Decker began a program called "Double Insulation" to replace entire older lines of products. The goal was to redesign the product line and develop a variety of products by studying commonality, reuse, and standardization. The most frequently found component in all power tools is the universal motor. Black & Decker used standardization to produce the entire range of power tools from a single line of motors. Standardization was also used for bearings, switches, cord sets, cartons, and fasteners. The result of this consistency was that new designs did not have to be invented from scratch, but rather were developed using components that were already standardized. Black & Decker's power tools division launched one new product every week for several years after adopting platform thinking in its power tools division.[4]

Sony Electronics is considered a leader in leveraging product platforms. In 1979, Sony introduced the Walkman with a variety of intensive strategy. It built its models with common platforms and standardization, and used modular design to provide variety. Sony has since continued this tradition with digital cameras, camcorders, and its VAIO personal computers. Sony's management understood that in order to achieve consumer acceptance, full interoperability between various devices, applications, services, and networks had to be achieved. The strategy is simple: Use a common product platform, but target diverse market segments with different models.[5]

Whirlpool, the appliance manufacturer, is using product platforms to create a "world washer" that can be sold in European and U.S. markets. Whirlpool designed new washing machines by first developing a basic robust platform and then offering variants of it by using a limited number of add and drop modules. The outcome of this effort: a front-loading washer platform that could be customized for different markets. In the United States, the result was the Duet, a front-loader introduced in fall 2001 with 10–15 percent more capacity than a top-loader. In summer 2002, Europe got the Dreamspace, a front-loading washer with slightly different sizing, styling, and spin and wash cycles than the Duet. Same platform, different configurations.[6]

The subject of product platforms is central to the auto industry as well. Every year the cost of building a car is less due to common platforms and modular components. The logic is simple: Every time a new car is introduced, it must be built on a platform and assembled at a plant. Platforms and plants are very expensive to design, build, or modify. This leads to the strategy of developing common platforms for similar class cars. Ford was the first to adopt this strategy. In 1994, Ford announced a focus on common platforms for its North American and European vehicles. GM followed suit. GM's goal was to design seven passenger-car architectures worldwide by varying wheelbase, width, and windshield placement within a platform. For the new Accord, Honda developed new models for the Americas, Asia, and Europe using flexible platforms and similar components.

Product platforms are a well-established engineering concept. Their use in fields ranging from automobiles, construction, and consumer electronics to aircrafts and medical equipment has been documented extensively. The trend of standardization in IT service platforms is very similar to the product platform trend in manufacturing.

Service Platforms—Making Complexity Manageable

Service platforms are conceptually very similar to manufacturing's product platforms. They are defined as reusable foundations for delivering services. One service platform will enable multiple portals to function. Each of these portals reuses common functionality with the goal of streamlining business processes through self-service and eliminating work.

In the previous section, we presented the business case for service platforms. In this section, we delve into the high-level structure of service platforms presented earlier in the chapter. In particular, we focus on the composite process and integration layers.

From Fragmented Portals to Service Platforms

The U.S. Air Force has taken the value of service platforms to heart and developed an Air Force One Network strategy. The objective: to create a service platform to serve all 1.2 million U.S. Air Force personnel, consolidate information and applications, and provide users with access to everything. This system ranges from personnel data to front-line combat intelligence from 28,000 legacy information systems and more than 1,500 Air Force Web sites and intranets.

The first portal initiative is My.AF, the Air Force portal that will give users single-point network access to hundreds of information resources and services. In the case of My.AF, many labor-intensive support processes are being transferred to this self-service portal accessible through a browser. One of the first self-service applications was virtual-Military Personnel Flight (vMPF), a secure Web-based link to each Air Force member's personnel records. Once an account has been activated, members can view personnel records and conduct transactions from any computer with Internet capability, whether they are at work, at home, or on temporary duty.

Why is the Air Force making this happen? First, it is ensuring that it is extracting value out of existing assets and organizational infrastructure. Second, the Air Force is taking the friction out of multi-department processes. Both of these objectives can be met with a service platform.

The Air Force example illustrates that it makes good business sense to tie the customer to the process rather than the underlying application. For customer-responsive solutions, it's essential to integrate applications in a transparent manner and shield the customer from internal processes. The logic behind this is that firms should manage their different customer-facing services through the concept of composite processes (order-to-cash), not as portfolios of unrelated applications.

Service platforms are necessary to accomplish the following business goals:

- Enable flexibility and change to keep pace with new cross-application processes that have to be deployed progressively faster.

- Protect organizations' application investments and harness them as their customers' needs change.

- Reduce integration costs and reduce interoperability risk on the road to a multi-channel service model.

These business requirements are accelerating service platform innovation. Over the next few years, we expect to see some jaw-dropping service platform innovations make their way into mainstream business.

Figure 3.2 illustrates the different elements—portal layer, composite processes layer, and integration layer—of the service platform architecture. Although this figure appears complicated, it is critical that you understand how the different elements interrelate. Since we have covered the portal layer in detail, let's turn our attention to the composite process layer.

The Composite Process Layer—Enabling Business Process Management

Users care about services. They really don't care what is behind the scenes. When developing services, companies must give a lot of thought to the design of the supporting composite processes.

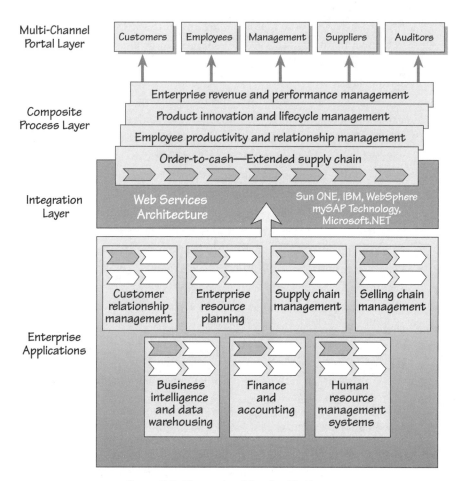

Figure 3.2: Elements of Service Platforms

Composite processes, which by necessity span multiple applications, enterprise divisions, people, and trading partners, are probably the raison d'etre of service platforms. Examples of composite processes are a 360-degree view of the customer, order management and fulfillment, inventory visibility in the supply chain, customer claims processing, order-to-cash processes, and straight-through processing (in financial markets).

Consider the following order-to-cash scenario: Customers can place their own orders, check on the status, and make payments whenever they desire through the Web. Sounds simple, but this is a big deal. Before this integrated customer self-service scenario happens, firms have to integrate their various underlying applications so that a customer query made through the portal is routed through a CRM system, which is able to find out manufacturing details from the ERP system, credit details from the finance system, and delivery data from the SCM system.

For most companies, the next step in the digitization journey is setting these composite processes in motion. Composite processes represent a new form of business integration, service-level integration, that seeks to enable firms to build flexible, responsive, composite applications quickly, usually exploiting an underlying and preexisting software infrastructure.

Various marketing terms are being batted around to describe the concept of service-level integration. For instance, SAP has developed its own marketing term to describe the new breed of cross-applications: xApps. Siebel has countered with its version of a cross-application framework: Universal Application Network (UAN).

What is common to xApps and UAN? They are both built on a Web Services architecture layer. Unfortunately, Web Services has become a rather vague and muddied term. Different vendors, authors, and magazines are using it to describe completely different things. It is being used as a synonym for an Internet standard, system-to-system integration technique, and services architecture. Let's go into more detail to understand fully what Web Services means.

Exploring the Integration Layer—Web Services Architecture

Every decade or so, business applications go through a wrenching metamorphosis that alters their foundation. In the late 1980s, ERP changed the business application landscape. In the 1990s, the Web drastically revolutionized the structure of enterprise applications. In the 2000s, Web Services based on XML technology is considered the disruptive force.

The vision behind Web Services is the same everywhere. Existing and future applications (back-end) have to support flexible business transactions and processes (front-end). Currently, the front end and back end are tightly coupled; if one changes, the other has to be rewritten, which costs a lot of money. To solve this problem, software engineers devised a method to decouple the front end from the back end. This allows both to change without the whole application having to be redone each time. This flexibility is very valuable.

Modularity is the central theme in enabling this "Internet is one giant distributed computer" vision. Organizations want modularity in order to combine application components in a "plug-and-play" model to create more user-centric solutions. Some companies also want to be free to buy modular components from different vendors and combine them with components from third-party firms to provide a more customized experience.

We expect that even big existing applications will be restructured into large modular components. Whether it's using tool kits like WebSphere or Sun ONE, the theory is that applications will evolve as a series of loosely coupled components, as opposed to big chunks of monolithic code. To make this vision a reality, several critical pieces of the Web Services architecture have to come together:

- The low-level XML Web Services—core software technology,

- The medium-level integration services—enterprise application integration,

- The high-level Services Oriented Architecture—business process support.

XML Web Services—Enabling the "Internet Is the Computer" Vision

Everything starts with XML. The Web changed how users interacted with applications. XML is extending this vision and is changing how applications communicate and interoperate with other applications.

A core XML innovation is providing a universal data format that allows data to be adapted or transformed. The logic behind this is simple: If your data and documents are in French and my data and documents are in Spanish, then it becomes quite difficult for us to share information. Now imagine the difficulty of building business processes that require a piece of data from the French side and a piece from the Spanish side to be integrated with an English document and presented to a customer in one Web page. The way around this complexity is create a structure that alleviates the translation problem.

This is exactly what XML does. XML is turning the way programmers build and use data and documents inside out. Table 3.2 shows the potential impact of XML in contrast to other major innovations.

Simply put, Web Services are XML data standards along with communication standards.[7] Businesses adopting the Web Services standards will be able to create "plug-and-play" software applications or make them available for communication with other applications of authorized, trusted trading partners.[8] As the software industry adopts XML standards for data description and communication over the Internet, the promise of "wiring together" distributed systems is becoming a reality.

While very important, XML is really the first step in the value chain. The complete value chain is as follows: XML standards enable low-level Web Services—data standards, communication standards, and security. Low-level Web Services

Table 3.2: XML and Web Services Relationship

Technology Innovation	Technology Foundation	Business Value
Morse Code	Telegram	Standardize Communication
Dial Tone	Telephone	Connect Society
Modem Code	Fax	Standardize Communication
SMTP	E-Mail	Standardize Communication
TCP/IP	Internet	Standardize Networking
HTTP/HTML	World Wide Web	Web and E-commerce
XML	Web Services	Digitize Processes

enable Services Oriented Architecture (SOA)—integration servers, directories, and portal servers. SOA enables cross-enterprise processes (order-to-cash). Cross-enterprise processes are the foundation of every digitization initiative.

Integration Services

Integration innovation is in full swing. Vendors are racing to create new Enterprise Application Integration (EAI) tool kits that are built on XML. These tool kits include messaging backbones, integration brokers, EDI connectors, object request brokers, and transaction monitors. The business objective is to reduce the cost of first-time integration and subsequent maintenance.

Consider this scenario: General Motors has more than 5,000 applications, and integrating them is a nonstop problem. GM is not unique; every large or medium-size organization faces the same problem. It is estimated that more than 60 percent of every digitization project budget is spent on integration costs—software, consulting, and salaries. This is a significant "integration tax" on organizations. Reducing the cost and pain of integration and allowing flexible changes based on business needs are the essence of EAI.

Why has EAI received significant attention in recent years? It permits different applications from different sources to talk to each other without the pain of custom programming. Integration with proprietary methods has proven to be cost-prohibitive. Why is this the case? Every time a change needs to be made to the customer-facing process, much time and money are spent rewiring and testing the connections to the various back-end applications. Here's a fact for you: For every dollar a company spends buying application software, it will spend $5–$10 on consultants to make it all work together.

Application integration is moving from being a low-level issue to a critical managerial issue. Portal-driven integration and transparency are recurring nightmares for many organizations as they struggle to integrate applications and get the right information to the right people in real time. The primary reason is that most organizations have between 20 and 5,000 applications that they may have to stitch together. The odds are high that application integration will become a boardroom issue as the overall business performance deteriorates due to poor integration.

Maintenance- and upgrade-related issues are beginning to take center stage as organizations that deployed the first-generation Web portals begin planning the next version. Many are in for a shock as they realize that existing portals are mostly supported by primitive integration architectures—point-to-point or rigid portal-to-application—that were homegrown and cumbersome to build and maintain. In many cases, the underlying integration infrastructure will have to be rearchitected to solve business problems such as excessive hand-offs between applications and frustrated users.

To lower the cost of integration, the newer-generation XML-based EAI is being engineered under the banner of business process management (BPM) tool kits. These tool kits create low-level connections between various applications and coordinate transactions that span those systems. The intent is to facilitate standard cross-application and cross-enterprise integration and transparency. Another goal is future-proofing the architecture by enabling upgrades and changes. Companies competing in this BPM market include Tibco, Vitria, Savvion, Fuego, and webMethods.

Services Oriented Architecture (SOA)

It is not enough to have multiple Web Services scattered all over the place. You need a framework that can pull everything together and make everything talk to each other. Different marketing labels are being used to describe these new frameworks: Portal Foundation Services, Processware, and Services Oriented Architecture (SOA). They are all pretty much talking about the same thing: a new set of components that helps firms build coherent service platforms.

Essentially, every SOA is a set of building blocks (e-mail servers, directory servers, identity management) that enable the creation of multi-device and multi-channel information services. The business value of SOAs is to help solve the IT challenge of integrating fragmented middleware products to run composite processes. This is achieved by providing one platform that can replace many separate point products from multiple vendors.

Table 3.3: Service Platform and SOA Relationship

Vendor	Services Oriented Architecture	Technology
IBM	E-Business on Demand	WebSphere
Sun Microsystems	Services on Demand	Sun ONE
SAP AG	Enterprise Services Architecture (ESA)	NetWeaver
PeopleSoft	Real-Time Enterprise	AppConnect
Microsoft	.NET	.NET Enterprise Servers
Oracle	Dynamic Web Services	Oracle9i Application Server
BEA Systems	WebLogic Workshop	WebLogic Platform

As Table 3.3 illustrates, vendors are racing to provide the SOA components necessary to build the different types of service platforms models. All these vendors want to become the dominant industry standard and have everyone use their tools, languages, and technology, thereby assuring themselves a revenue stream for perpetuity.

Each of these SOA models has a common structure (see Figure 3.3). The generic elements of an SOA are security services, user-centric portal services, management services and integration, and infrastructure services. Capturing, modeling, storing, and appropriately invoking business processes from multiple applications are the challenges that lie at the heart of the SOA.

How does all this work? Consider the case of British Airways (BA), which has vowed to achieve 50 percent of its bookings over the Internet. That promise is dependent on BA.com, an aggregator portal that gives customers a single view of the "look-to-book" process—booking, ticketing, flight information, and customer relationship services. In order to provide a single view to the customer, the BA portal is built on BEA Systems' WebLogic, which links the various operational systems used to run and monitor business on a day-to-day basis.[9]

From a business perspective, what value does BEA's WebLogic (a typical SOA) add? The WebLogic layer saves money by leveraging existing CRM, ERP, financials, human resources (HR), supply chain, and procurement applications; it does not replace them. For instance, the BA portal had to integrate many underlying applications that support the marketing and selling activities of the airline, which are often large-scale and complex. Detailed information for all Executive Club members is held in a corporate database surrounded with sophisticated analytical tools, which support BA's expertise in relationship marketing

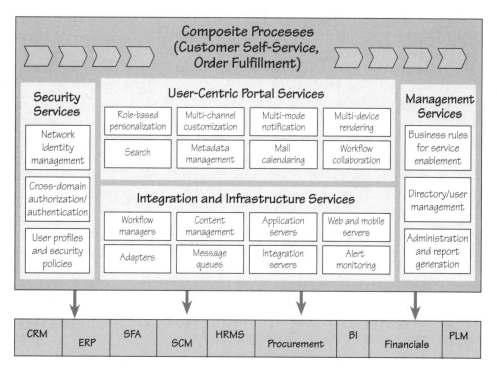

Figure 3.3: Generic Elements of an SOA

and revenue management. BA must integrate all those systems to unlock and extract their embedded value.

British Airways is not unique. Every organization has a similar need. Now that the market has largely accepted the need for SOAs, vendors are fighting tooth and nail to provide the underlying service platform. The IT organization has the unenviable task of deciding which architecture to choose, for example, .NET, Sun ONE, or WebSphere.[10] Picking an SOA requires addressing challenging questions: How can existing investments in various back-office applications be integrated to provide transparency? How should the core functionality be isolated from the cosmetic?

Putting Everything Together—SAP's xApps

To illustrate a complete service platform—composite processes, Services Oriented Architecture, and Web Services technology—it is useful to look an example from SAP. Why did we pick SAP? Because of its installed base of enterprise applications, the company has a significant influence on what organizations are going to deploy in the next decade.

SAP is anticipating that to solve emerging cross-enterprise and multi-channel business problems, its customers will move from enterprise applications to service platforms. SAP's version of a service platform consists of

- Composite Process Layer—xApps (Extended Applications)

- Services Oriented Architecture Layer—Enterprise Service Architecture

- Web Services Technology—NetWeaver

xApps are composite applications. They aim to "bring it all together" by building on existing applications within and across enterprise boundaries and creating value by delivering adaptable cross-functional business processes. Examples of prepackaged xApps include new product launches, mergers and acquisitions (M&A), and resource and program management. An organization like Nestlé would buy an M&A xApp and customize it to its environment.

The point of xApps is to enable complex cross-enterprise workflows. For instance, a company wants to order aluminum. This workflow needs pricing, availability, delivery schedules, terms and conditions, insurance, logistics, and credit, that is, all that is involved in a multi-step workflow with multiple vendors, from the logistics company to the insurance company to the credit company to the contract lawyers. Using xApps makes this possible.

The xApps service platform, built on Web Services standards, unifies multiple disparate systems within and across businesses. The underlying design principles of xApps are

- Cross-Functionality—runs across multiple existing applications and databases, driving end-to-end processes across functional, organizational, and technical silos.

- Integrated Functionality—synchronizes with existing business processes (embedded in ERP, for instance), allowing a flexible workflow structure across heterogeneous systems.

- Configurable—allows an enterprise to assess, refine, and adapt its business processes in line with business opportunities.[11]

Instead of restricting itself to selling enterprise applications only, SAP is moving into the area of cross-enterprise integrated solutions. What does the revenue model look like? Let's say SAP sells packaged business processes at around a 17 percent maintenance fee a year. So, if a corporation buys ten million dollars' worth of licenses, it has to pay a $1.7 million maintenance fee every year to receive new versions and upgrades. xApps could be a lucrative long-term business model for SAP. Clearly, composite processes built on service platforms are not theory anymore.[12]

Creating Value—Different Types of Service Platforms

The concept of a service platform, no matter how innovative, is rather useless without the specific business context. It is simply a means to the end, which is creating value and delivering it via portals. So, how are organizations putting service platforms to use? Creative usage of service platforms is evident in eight different areas (see Figure 3.4):

1. **Customer-Facing Service Platforms.** These allow organizations to move from the first-generation CRM capability—automating the transaction process (placing an order and checking order status)—to the second-generation capability—enabling the entire portfolio of multi-channel and cross-enterprise customer interaction (presales, ordering, fulfillment, and payment). The transition to multi-channel customer interaction involves significant process change and substantial investments in reconfigurable processes.

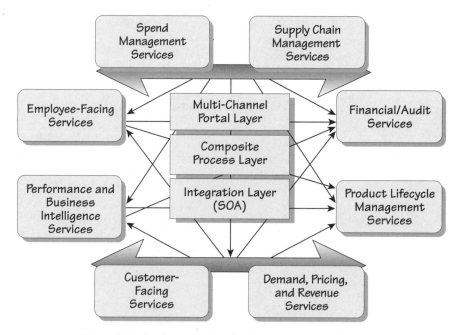

Figure 3.4: Moving from Applications to Service Platforms

2. **Demand, Pricing, and Revenue Service Platforms.** These allow firms with reseller channels and large salesforces to quote, bid, contract, and bill customers better. These are typically firms that don't have customers who service themselves. Various pricing, promotion, and discounting structures have to be managed and coordinated carefully to support the salesforce.

3. **Employee-Facing Service Platforms.** These guide companies move from the transaction automation application stage that they are currently in to a harder-to-implement and higher value employee self-service stage of "human capital management." The focus is on productivity tools and information to ensure that strategic functions such as learning and compensation affect workforce behavior and improve the bottom line.

4. **Supply Chain Management Service Platforms.** These enable the integration of all the critical functions in a supply chain, in moving order information, in goods, and in payments. Streamlining the order-to-delivery process is the focus of supply chain management platforms. The goal is constantly to lower costs, reduce inventory levels, manage global supply chains, and improve service levels.

5. **Spend Management Service Platforms.** These are focused on managing different types of costs—direct and indirect materials, maintenance, repair, and operations (MRO), as well as services spending. Traditionally centered on isolated functions such as purchasing, sourcing, procurement, or requisitioning, the processes have become increasingly fragmented. Purchasing organizations are responding to this problem by taking a more process-oriented approach. Enabling these processes is the objective of the spend management service platform.

6. **Product Lifecycle Management (PLM) Service Platforms.** These support the new product lifecycle of design to launch. Competition is forcing companies to innovate more quickly. As the products go from novelty to commodity faster, companies have to innovate and create new products to stimulate demand. The need for innovation is driving the interest in integrating cross-application processes around customer needs management, collaborative product design, product data management, direct materials sourcing, and new product introduction.

7. **Financial/Audit Service Platforms.** These involve creating a single and complete source of the truth about the financial health of the organization for the

CFO's team whenever they need it. This also involves supporting critical areas like traditional financial (A/R, A/P, and GL entries), real-time close, and regulatory reporting.

8. **Performance and Business Intelligence Service Platforms.** These involve aggregating data from multiple business systems and providing tools to analyze the business performance data in myriad ways. The data is converted into information about the business to support its decision-making and reporting needs. Managers are looking for the right answers and patterns within the mountains of underutilized—and potentially valuable—data.

The shift from enterprise applications to service platforms is significant and real. We think this structural shift will take years to play out. The good news is that the first step of the shift is already complete: Managers and decision makers are beginning to grasp the importance of a services-oriented model.

However, building up the requisite integration and application infrastructure to produce a services-oriented model is no small feat. You can't buy your way into it, or just go out and hire a bevy of consultants. You need to harness a range of disciplines. Layering one kind of expertise on top of another won't work either. This isn't just filling up two beakers, one labeled "customer" and the other labeled "technology" and mixing them. It takes years and a lot of knowledge to be able to mix those elements properly. Careful long-term planning will be critical.

In the next five chapters, we illustrate the inner workings of five service platforms. We picked these five because they are the most commonly implemented.

Seven Points to Ponder

> We are not retreating—we are advancing in another direction.
> —*General Douglas MacArthur (1880–1964)*

The invention of the steam engine in the latter part of the eighteenth century gave an enormous impetus to the Industrial Revolution. Similarly, the development of enterprise portals has accelerated the entire area of digitization. The next step in the digitization journey is beginning to take shape with the emergence of an improved engine—the service platform.

This brings us to the equation structuring our discussion: Services Blueprint = Focal Point + Service Platform. A focal point defines your strategy, and a service platform provides the underlying processes and technology. Service platforms—why, when, where, what, and how—was the subject covered in this chapter.

Why is there a growing buzz around service platforms? Because digitization initiatives by nature are cross-enterprise. As a result, they must be designed with the understanding that companies will not throw away diverse ERP, CRM, and other existing homegrown systems found throughout the enterprise. With service platforms, companies are attempting to put a foundation in place that will maximize a corporatewide return on assets: employees, knowledge, products, business relationships, and applications. Enterprise architects and business strategists will be talking about nothing else for the next few years.

To be successful in the long run, CIOs must constantly align focal points and service platform execution. *Which of the following objectives would you like to accomplish with service platforms?*

1. Drastically reduce the time needed to formulate and execute digitization initiatives.

2. Identify and exploit innovative opportunities through better collaboration within and outside the enterprise.

3. Quickly respond to new customer priorities or business realities with highly adaptable business processes.

4. Implement corporatewide initiatives by cutting across formerly isolated business units and vertical hierarchies.

5. Leverage existing investments in enterprise software.

6. Reduce the escalating costs of application integration.

7. Deliver services over a variety of channels (brick, Web, and wireless) to a variety of devices (PC, handhelds, and mobile phones) and a broad set of users.

If you responded that you would like to achieve one or more of these objectives, then service platforms are inevitable in your organization. The increasingly volatile business world demands that corporations innovate, execute, and refine their application strategies in a more rapid-fire fashion. If continuous innovation and change are business requirements, then service platforms fall into the category of "need to have." Let's look at how service platforms are transforming the way companies interact with their customers.

PART II

Examples of
Service Blueprints

CHAPTER FOUR

Multi-Channel Blueprint: Creating New Customer Experiences

What to Expect

Many companies are losing sight of the customer's perspective in the transition to a multi-channel model. To compensate, they are investing heavily in leading-edge technology that does not make it any easier for the customer to do business with them. We think that more technology is not the answer; better multi-channel process design is.

Organizations face many challenges as they move from the stable brick-and-mortar world to a self-service world supported by multi-channel services. To understand the magnitude of the problem, take a minute to look at your firm from the customer's perspective. What do you see? Do you see disjointed processes fragmented by channels (brick and mortar, call centers, Web portals, e-mail)? Or are your services coordinated across the channels?

In this chapter, we address two questions: 1) What kind of blueprint is required to satisfy the self-service customer? and 2) What multi-channel process designs are necessary to make this type of customer happy? We begin by focusing on the business problems and long-term trends that are shaping multi-channel customer relationship management (CRM) investments. We explore how the concept of service platforms is quietly inspiring the next wave of CRM solutions. We conclude with a best-practice case study on JC Penney that illustrates an interesting reverse CRM issue: how to manage product returns in a multi-channel retail setting.

Introduction

E-services, self-service portals, e-CRM, e-selling, contact centers, interaction centers, customer analytics, one-to-one, customer-centric, relationship marketing, and customer focused—what do all these buzzwords have in common?

All are synonymous with the digitization focal point Easy To Do Business With (ETDBW). In order to become ETDBW, companies have invested billions in the last decade in CRM applications. Many have been disillusioned with the results. In some cases, companies have succeeded in alienating customers and causing their satisfaction to plummet. What went wrong? Why didn't the promises of CRM materialize as planned?

CRM, despite good intentions when deployed, didn't actually center on customers, relationships, or management. It morphed into technological buzzwords and unrealistic expectations. There was too much technology (features and functionality) and not enough process thinking. Why did so many companies fall into this trap? Often when companies rely on emerging technologies to attract and serve customers, they mistakenly think that more technology results in better service. In fact, the opposite is true. More than features and functions, customers value simplicity, consistency, and well-integrated processes.

Somewhere along the road to technological Utopia, we forgot the basics of customer satisfaction. We forgot that the average customer does not care about the technical razzle-dazzle or sophistication behind the scenes. She cares about solving her problems with one phone call (once and done). She cares about the exorbitant amount of time she is on hold. She cares about getting billed correctly. She cares about being given consistent information at the various interaction points—store, Web site, call center, and catalog.

If a process or service does not connect with the basic needs and values of the customer, it will fail, regardless of technological sophistication. Fortunately, some companies realize this and are working hard to fix these multi-channel service design problems. The others, sadly, are preparing to file for bankruptcy.

From Uni-Channel to Multi-Channel— The Financial Services Industry

Let's look at a few common service problems that customers encounter in the financial services industry. In the 1990s, deregulation changed the financial services industry forever by removing the barriers that prohibited retail banking, investment banking, brokerages, and insurance from entering each other's markets. At the same time, nontraditional players such as retailers (Sears and Target) and manufacturers (Ford, GM, and GE) entered the credit card and mortgage services industry, all are competing for the same pool of customers. To differentiate themselves and "bind" the customer, companies were offering new products faster than ever before.

In parallel to the market structure changes, there have been significant service channel changes. First, the conventional "brick" face-to-face branches and ATMs were augmented by new "tele" call centers. The Internet changed the dynamics with "click" Web portals and became a growing channel of choice. The looming prospect of mobile interaction further complicates the service design. So, in a relatively short period, the structure in financial services has gone from a uni-channel to a multi-channel model. Coordinating the channels regardless of the product lines (checking accounts, mortgages, credit cards, and debit cards) to address customers' needs is a nontrivial business problem. We illustrate the multi-channel integration and synchronization problem in Figure 4.1.

The problem is hard enough without adding another variable—mergers and acquisitions. The merger mania that swept through the global financial services

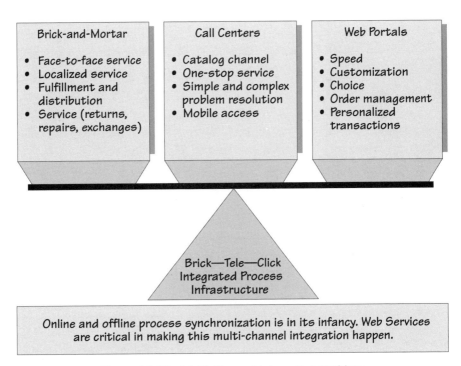

Figure 4.1: The Multi-Channel Integration Problem

industry created a loosely integrated collection of business units. The outcome: a lack of channel, product, and business unit integration resulting in tremendous service variation and customer frustration. For instance, Bank One Corporation found that it was conducting business 24 different ways in 24 different markets. If a customer moved from one part of the country to another, it was easier to close the account and reopen it in the new location than to transfer it. Or, if the customer had problems with a statement, she would get different answers depending on which channel she interacted with. To combat these service quality issues, the company launched a series of initiatives aimed at combining operations and systems and centralizing various staff and line functions.

The financial services industry example clearly shows that we are in a multi-channel economy and one that, courtesy of the Internet, is increasingly interactive. Now that we have established the case for multi-channel services, we will examine the challenge of execution. Let's begin by looking at the evolution of multi-channel CRM.

Evolution of Multi-Channel CRM

Finding, targeting, supporting, and retaining customers are core themes of customer service. The way that companies carry out these activities has changed considerably over the last three decades. Next-generation self-service platforms are the combined offspring of the three dominant channels—brick, tele, and click. Figure 4.2 illustrates the evolution of these channels.

Today, firms are racing to understand and create unique cross-channel experiences that reduce costs of service and increase sales. To understand better where we are going, it is useful to know where we came from. Let's look at the brief evolution of these channels. This will help set the stage for the multi-channel discussion later in this chapter.

Tele-Channel—From Telesales to Customer Interaction Centers

During the last decade, the call center, an integral part of customer service, has expanded from a simple phone operation to a full-service interaction center capable of handling all customer queries via any communication channel—telephone, e-mail, fax, mail, and the Web.

In the late 1970s, the state of the art was outbound telesales. The technology was primitive—an outbound tele-services representative (TSR) would have three basic tools: 1) a rotary-dial phone, 2) a stack of 3"×5" index cards, and 3) a pencil. Prospective leads were picked from phone books, and each agent cold-called a

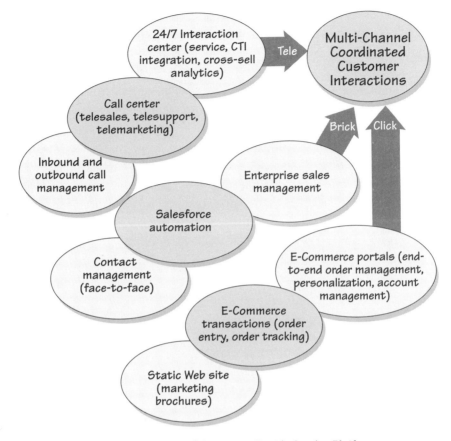

Figure 4.2: Evolution of Customer-Centric Service Platforms

range of people. Agent burnout and turnover were high, and the process was time-consuming and inefficient. Some relief came with predictive and preview dialers; TSRs no longer had to dial manually and could make more calls per hour. In fact, predictive and preview dialing are estimated to have increased outbound productivity by 300 percent, an event that created the call center industry.[1]

The big challenge in the early 1980s was blending inbound and outbound calls. Initially, companies had designated inbound agents and outbound agents. They soon realized that this didn't make sense for several reasons: Agents dedicated to one mode were underutilized, and time and resource management became difficult. Following a TV commercial or direct mail campaign, inbound calls might spike by several hundred percent. Days later, when inbound calls dropped off, the previously swamped agents would have nothing to do, while the outbound agents were busy dialing out offering new discounts to customers.

It became apparent that inbound calling and outbound calling needed to be managed jointly. For all these reasons, blended call centers, staffed by universal agents (who could handle both inbound and outbound calls) and powered by automatic call distributors, mushroomed. Inbound and outbound duties were shifted based on need, which helped to spread the work among all agents and minimize downtime. This further increased productivity and fueled the demand for more call center automation.

Initially, many call centers were set up as low-cost solutions to provide basic customer service and support. They were equipped to handle order entry, information services, and customer dispatch. The economies of scale led businesses to build large, centralized call centers that covered wide territories. For mass marketing business objectives, these centers were the most efficient way to deliver basic customer service and sales. Travel and hotels, media, banks, insurance, credit card and telecom companies, utilities, and retailers used them.

However, as niche segments grew, the mass marketing techniques practiced by these call centers became less effective. Process integration was a problem. Agents, lacking access to customer-specific information, repeated the same script to every customer. The result: Customers complained of unsatisfactory encounters. A built-in conflict existed between the economies of scale and individual customer attention. It wasn't enough to reduce the costs of call center functions if you couldn't also improve customer satisfaction. In many cases, customers began to migrate rapidly to companies with better customer service.

In the mid-1990s, computer telephony integration (CTI) gave companies the ability to combine the power of the computer with the telephone. Businesses began concentrating on the heart of the matter: the relationship between the agent and the customer. The objective was once and done, that is, complete the process during a single call. CTI, initially based on client/server architectures and Windows-based PCs, allowed better integration between the data and voice environments—putting more information on the desktop to empower agents. This helped the agent foster better relationships with customers.

In the 2000s, the trend in call center technology is multi-channel interaction centers. These are service platforms that allow firms to integrate service, sales, and marketing efforts. This transformation stemmed from the business requirement to turn what has traditionally been a cost center into a revenue center. Each customer interaction is an opportunity to cross-sell and up-sell. The obstacle has not been just the unified software applications, but people—creating a universal agent capable of sales, marketing, and service.

So, contrary to the hype, call centers will remain a key element of CRM. In fact, they are going to be more prevalent given the broad use of mobile phones.

Brick-and-Mortar Channel—Evolution of Face-to-Face Interaction

The traditional CRM channel is face-to-face interaction. The technology behind face-to-face service has also developed considerably in the last decade. For instance, in the banking industry, teller systems have evolved in four stages: 1) mainframe consoles, 2) DOS-based front ends, 3) Windows–based front ends, and now, 4) Internet browser–based interfaces. The objective was to increase tellers' productivity.

Face-to-face selling has also evolved considerably with new technological tools. The first generation of sales force automation (SFA) was DOS-based database applications that allowed a salesperson to store addresses, phone numbers, and related information about customers in a searchable database. Many early SFA products ran on portable computers that were under 15 pounds and were able to fit in a briefcase. The advent of laptops and Windows created a boom in SFA applications. These applications helped salespeople pull together contact management, sales forecasting, and opportunity management tools in one application.

Field support applications, which cover postsales customer support, also went through a makeover similar to that of the SFA applications. Mobile technologies have created a quantum improvement in what the next-generation field support applications can and will do.

To enable better face-to-face interaction, significant investments in CRM applications have been made. In the 1990s, companies were very busy using various software applications to automate customer interaction disciplines: customer service, sales, quality, marketing, field support, and internal help desks. These software applications typically provided a separate silo for each of these internal business functions, suffered from limited functionality, and were difficult to integrate.

Large organizations were able to overcome some of these limitations by investing in highly customized packaged applications, which were costly to create and maintain. This trend continues in the 2000s but the focus is shifting to small and midsize businesses (SMBs). We expect that it will take at least a decade to implement CRM in the SMB market.

Online Self-Service Channel—From Web Sites to E-Service

The online channel began to take hold in 1995 with "brochureware" Web sites that were a combination of corporations' annual reports and product information.

From advertising to retailing to providing information, the corporate marketing groups began taking their well-worn ways of doing business and desperately trying to fit them to the Web.

Brochureware soon gave way to e-commerce transactions. E-commerce transactions evolved into self-service portals that provide presale, sale, and post-sale support. With enhanced broadband access and technological improvements, it is conceivable that in three to five years, online self-service will become the primary channel in certain industries. From rather humble beginnings, online self-service has become a dominant customer interaction channel in a short period.

Although self-service has gained considerable momentum, the other channels are not going away. Companies have to understand how to blend different channels. Many don't have processes in place to determine the value proposition from their multi-channel customers' perspective. Most tend to have strong biases about what they think the customer should have versus what the customer really wants. Building the multi-channel value proposition from the customer's perspective is today's challenge. Several other trends are also shaping the way companies are reacting to the multi-channel opportunity.

Long-Term Trends Shaping Customer-Centric Requirements

Value, speed, lower cost, consistency, simplicity, enjoyment, long-term relationships, and mobility—multi-channel customers want them all. How does an organization design and implement a multi-channel service blueprint that delivers these requirements?

In this section, we look at the long-term trends driving the transition from uni-channel to multi-channel CRM. Before designing a blueprint, it is vital to understand which dimensions of service are the most important in a self-service environment. What do customers want today and in the future? How much are they willing to change their behavior? These two questions shape the multi-channel service platform.

Self-Service Customers—Are You Ready?

The emergence of self-service is a big deal and growing rapidly in many industries. In 75 years, no marketing innovation has stirred up as much controversy or revamped as many strategies as self-service. Today, self-service Web sites are accepted as part of most companies' overall service strategy.

Many consumers' first experience with self-service was in the form of the automated teller machine (ATM) or the self-service gas station. The revolution really started in 1916 when Clarence Saunders opened the first Piggly Wiggly grocery store and introduced a novel approach to market research. In trying to figure out exactly what customers wanted, he came up with an idea: make customers choose from an array of products on the shelf and put their choices in their own shopping baskets.[2]

The idea took hold during the Great Depression of 1929 when supermarkets adopted self-service to save labor. Economics soon forced retailers with personalized service to the new marketing strategy. Self-service not only cut costs, it increased revenues. And retailers happily discovered "impulse buying," a profitable behavior of self-service customers.

In the gas station business, self-service began in May 1947 at Urich Oil station in Los Angeles, California. The signs read: "Save 5¢." "Serve Yourself." "Why Pay More?" This marked the transformation of gas marketing. During the early days of self-service gas, there was considerable resistance to the idea. The naysayers said, "Self-service is a passing phase." It wasn't. Self-service not only helped spark gasoline price wars in the 1960s, it also caused major oil companies to redesign their stations totally. They reluctantly realized that a sizeable number of people in certain markets wanted self-service. About 1 percent of the U.S. gasoline market was self-service in 1969; by 1975, the ratio had climbed to 35 percent. By 1982, it had soared to 72 percent. By 2000, it was 99 percent.[3]

> The bottom line: Web-based self-service is in its infancy. It took 22 years for self-service gasoline to reach 1 percent penetration. Compared to that statistic, online self-service retailing is growing quite rapidly (in only seven years, online sales account for 2.5 percent of the retail industry totals).[4] Self-service capability means that businesses can service more customers with fewer workers. This trend bodes well for long-term productivity growth.

Synchronizing Customer Interactions

Jane Smith is a new breed of customer. She is what retailers call a "multi-channel shopper." She shops online, from catalogs, and at department stores.

Multi-channel customers want companies to stitch together and synchronize their customer channels. The trend is seamless interplay among all customer channels (customer service, field service, the Web, marketing, and sales) in order to create a consistent and easy-to-use experience. Companies that offer multi-channel experiences are separating themselves from the pack. JC Penney found that shoppers who bought in all three of its channels—stores, catalogs, and online—spent more than $800 a year on average (as compared to those who shopped in one channel and spent $200 or less).[5]

Even grocery stores are rebelling against their uni-channel past. Today, traditional retailers like Tesco, Safeway, and Albertsons with well-established brands, purchasing power, and existing distribution infrastructure are bringing the multi-channel grocery model back to life. Retailers now recognize that, far from being a threat to stores, well-designed Web portals build brand loyalty and increase sales. Contrast the multi-channel approach to the online uni-channel grocers like Webvan, HomeGrocer.com, Pets.com, and Kozmo.com.

History has repeatedly shown that stand-alone channel strategies don't succeed in any industry. Yet we always ignore history and proclaim that our situations are radically new and out of its reach. Take, for instance, the banking industry. Between 1998 and 2002, banks spent billions trying to create standalone, Internet-only operations designed to exploit what was seen as the Web's low-distribution costs. Bank One opened and closed Wingspanbank, Bank of America abandoned its effort to build loans.com into a stand-alone Web site, and Citigroup yanked finance.com and citi f/i not long after their launches.

In the financial services industry, the realization that customers are multi-channel—as likely to drop in at the brick-and-mortar branch as they are to log on to the Internet—is spurring renewed investment in branches. Large banks are spending millions to revamp and upgrade the service technology in their branch networks after trying and failing to get customers to adopt Internet banking only.

> The bottom line: Stand-alone channels are out. Coordinated transactions are in. Multi-channel shoppers are forcing firms to refine their Web sites, connect their catalogs to their online portals, and modify their processes at brick-and-mortar locations. As a result, the left hand knows better what the right hand is doing.

New Cross-Channel Experiences—Line Busters

It is one thing to integrate channels and coordinate existing processes; it is a whole different thing to create entirely new blended service experiences. What do we mean by this? The transaction may start online, but it is completed offline. The transaction may start in the call center but is completed at a self-service kiosk.

Consider the following example: in retail, Wal-Mart is leading the way in developing new cross-channel experiences. Customers can send digital photos to be developed via Walmart.com and then pick up the prints at a local store. Alternatively, they can drop off film at a store and have the digital photos e-mailed to them. Customers who are less interested in film and more interested in, say, tires can order those online too, and make a date to have them installed at a Wal-Mart tire center. The transaction moves smoothly from one channel to another.

Cross-channel experiences are driving the trend toward self-service kiosks (line busters) that are an alternative to standing in line. An interesting variation of this is to start the process online and continue the process at a kiosk. Southwest Airlines, for example, has teamed with IBM's Global Services to offer self-service check-in kiosks at major airports. Improving the airport experience is critical for airlines as their customers continuously seek convenience and speed. Southwest and IBM have built a multi-channel service platform that seamlessly links the online process (southwest.com) with the airport kiosk process.

New cross-channel experiences like those at Southwest are aimed at eliminating service queues. How does the cross-channel process work? The customer books his electronic ticket online. On the day of travel, the customer with (ticketless) e-reservations may use kiosks (in English or Spanish) simply by swiping a credit card or Southwest frequent flyer card to start the check-in process. The system can print a boarding pass, baggage tags, travel itinerary, or receipt, and even add the customer's frequent flyer account number.

A cross-channel service requires a heavy investment in the back-office applications. As the service interface changes, so must the back-office processes. These have to be rapidly upgraded or integrated. Customers from any channel value visibility during a multi-stage process like order management (select, buy, pay, ship, receive, and return). They want to know what is happening with their order. The Internet has further shaped customer expectations by enabling visibility into the process—giving the customer the perception of empowerment and control.

Companies that understand this basic customer need have done well. The package tracking application pioneered by FedEx is truly one of the biggest customer-centric innovations in order management. Frederick W. Smith, founder and CEO, made a prophetic statement in 1979: "Information about the package will soon be just as important as the delivery of that package."[6] This ranks as one of the most insightful statements about technology uttered in the past 35 years. This statement is the slogan for the shift from an Industrial Age to an Information Age mind-set.

Today's organizations recognize that they must become cross-channel process fanatics to achieve differentiation. No one enjoys waiting in line or being on hold; therefore, companies that try to eliminate these annoyances will have happier customers.

> The bottom line: Too much to do, too little time sums up a significant segment of customers. For many, time is the new currency: People would rather spend money than waste precious time. Technology has to help reduce the time people spend waiting in line. As a result, we are seeing a cross-channel trend in sectors such as retail, airline, and hotel self-service.

Outsourcing Call Centers and E-Mail Contact

So far the trends that we talked about were related to new customer experiences. Now let's shift gears and focus on cost reduction trends. How can companies cut the cost of key customer servicing events and transactions, while coping with the new customer communication channels?

Many companies are wrestling with this question as they attempt to reduce customer service costs. The answer is outsourcing key communication channels like voice, e-mail, and real-time chat.

Call center outsourcing is quite common. Take the case of UPS, the logistics company, which has an outsourcing deal with APAC Teleservices. Its process flow looks like this: A customer or prospect calls the UPS toll-free 800 number to request information, place an order, or obtain assistance. Once the call is received, it is routed to the right APAC customer service representative (CSR).

How does this happen? APAC utilizes automated call distributors to identify each inbound call by its 800 number and route the call to a CSR trained for the client's program. Simultaneously, with receipt of the call, the CSR's computer screen flashes the customer, product, and service information relevant to it. APAC then reports the information and results captured during the call to UPS for order processing, fulfillment, and database management.

Aside from calling, customers can also request service from companies via e-mail or on a real-time chat with a call center representative. If the customer e-mails, she expects a reply within a few hours. Consumer sites like Amazon.com or Expedia.com, which deal with millions of customers, are bombarded by service e-mails. Answering each one might take ten minutes. When you multiply processing-time-per–e-mail by the number of e-mails per month, you are looking at a considerable amount of time and money. To keep these e-mail response costs under control, some companies are moving them offshore. For example, Amazon.com has an e-mail contact center in India operated by Daksh, a New Delhi–based call center outsourcer. Several U.S. and U.K. banks are following suit.

As companies continue concentrating on efficiency and cost savings, developed countries will outsource a larger array of labor-intensive tasks (first-level service calls and e-mail management) to low-wage markets.

> The bottom line: The trend toward customer service outsourcing is very strong. While the economics make sense, caution must be exercised to make sure that the processes survive the hand-offs.

Different Services for Different Customers—Real-Time Analytics

Every large organization handles tens of thousands of customer inquiries a day across all channels—face-to-face, telephone, e-mail, and the Web. Traditionally, customer information enters the organization from each of these channels, yet they remain independent, and the information is rarely consolidated. Without comprehensive "360-degree customer views" or "customer memories," organizations find it difficult to deliver consistent levels of service and identify opportunities to cross-sell additional products and services.

Customers do not want status quo service. Loyal ones want firms to recognize and appreciate them. Imagine the following: Allison Park is a British Airways customer who flies more than 100,000 miles a year. Allison has a simple request—treat her special. She wants British Airways to acknowledge that she is a loyal customer by creating a check-in, boarding, and in-transit process that would treat her differently than people who fly infrequently. Allison Park is not unique. Customers who have long-term or multi-product relationships with companies want recognition and acknowledgment that they are special.

To understand and differentiate between customers, there is a growing online trend, especially among the market leaders, toward using real-time customer analytics. How does this work? Say Brandon is logged on to a retailer's Web site; his customer profile and purchase history are analyzed in real time to calculate a customer score. The score can be used to generate a special offer on certain products or a discount to be applied to the next purchase. In marketing terms, this is called score-based cross-selling.

A simpler way of differentiating based on customer score and profile is already implemented in various call center software packages. Applications like

PeopleSoft, Siebel, or SAP automatically identify the customer by an account code that the caller is prompted to enter on her touchpad. Based on the customer's score and service issue, she is routed to the agent with the best skills and knowledge to handle her inquiry.

> The bottom line: Customers want their histories with organizations to be recognized; thus, companies should have complete customer records easily accessible. Having a 360-degree view of the customer is a major trend.

Creating Multi-Channel Blueprints

Envisioning the ideal end state is often the easy part of self-service strategies. The hard part is everything in between, or managing the transition to the new blueprint. One glance at the wreckage left from first-generation customer-centric portal applications proves our point. The list of companies that implemented CRM applications over the past few years is long. Many of these "one-face-to-the-customer" portals are now gathering dust as companies look for better and simpler ways to do business with their customers.

What went wrong? The technology was too far ahead of the day-to-day realities of many organizations. Most haphazardly built Web portals without considering how the portal would work across several channels, including Web sites, call centers, and retail outlets. The technology vision was sound, but the process and channel integration visions were flawed. Is your firm taking a "let's hope it works" approach to CRM?

Not every corporation made this mistake. The more experienced firms, such as Dow Chemical, the chemical giant, spent considerable time reengineering internal processes before taking a phased approach to implementation. Dow spent an estimated $50 million to buy Siebel CRM software licenses in 1995—knowing that years would pass before it would be ready to implement the technology. In fact, it was nearly four years before the company carried out its plan because it was busy making sure that the business processes were in place. In 1999, Dow finally rolled out its "One Face to the Customer" CRM strategy by first digitizing call centers, inside sales, and customer service. The next step is to reengineer the entire order management process.[7]

Most organizations don't have the luxury of being methodical like Dow or have the $50 million to invest. So, what is the right approach to digitizing customer-facing interactions? The simple answer is to put yourself in the customer's shoes and identify where the different processes are breaking down. Some organizations do this, but few do this on an ongoing basis. Over the years, we have realized that most organizations—from executives to front-line workers—don't really understand what their customers have to go through in order to do business with the company. Without a detailed understanding of the current customer experience, it is impossible to architect a new multi-channel blueprint.

Assuming that you are among the few who have a good understanding of the current customer experience, how do you go about creating a multi-channel blueprint? Figure 4.3 shows the high-level schematic of a multi-channel blueprint. The first step in designing any new multi-channel service is to distinguish between the value, the form and function, the experience, and the outcomes of a service. This is the role of the focal point.

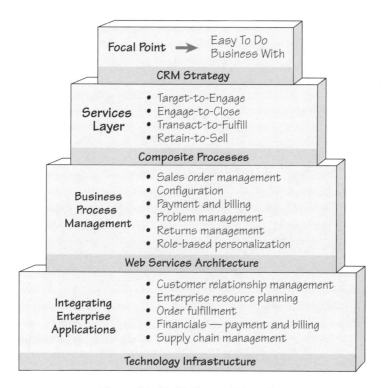

Figure 4.3: Multi-Channel Blueprint

Customer-Centric Focal Point—Easy To Do Business With

Being Easy To Do Business With (ETDBW) can separate companies from their rivals. The concrete way to accomplish this is to create an integrated customer-centric service platform that gives customers the ability to move seamlessly from the Web to the call center to the face-to-face channels. The platform should give customers the choice to execute transactions online or through the call center and provide them with a person who could assist them at any time.

Why has executing ETDBW proven to be difficult for many companies? The primary reason is the absence of a well-defined focal point for execution. Without one, companies attempt to solve too many issues simultaneously with scarce resources. To create a focus, managers should first answer the following questions: Who are my priority customers? What do my customers want and need? How can I best meet those needs?

What are some of the companies with the sharpest focus? In the retail industry, the obvious choice is Amazon.com. While other retailers have pulled back in hesitation from the online channel, Amazon.com has evolved into a sophisticated multi-channel retailer. It is interacting with customers using Web portals, call centers, e-mail contact centers, and catalogs. Through kiosks placed strategically in its various partners' stores, Amazon.com even has a significant presence in the brick-and-mortar channel.

The multi-channel blueprint of Amazon.com is the way business will be conducted in the future. The proof is not only in the millions of customers who spend their money everyday on the site, but in the growing number of retailers (Toys "R" Us, Circuit City, Target, Office Depot, and Nordstrom) who are outsourcing their online channel interaction to Amazon.com. In a relatively short period, it has built a lucrative new outsourcing business selling new and used goods online on behalf of other merchants. Amazon.com collects commissions on those third-party sales without the risks and cost of owning inventory. This new business is an amazing accomplishment and an open acknowledgment by major retailers that they cannot service the customer online any cheaper, better, or more efficiently than Amazon.com.

Figure 4.4 shows the strategy map that illustrates the ETDBW focal point.[8] This map has three perspectives: 1) financial, 2) customer, and 3) service. The customer expects an easy-to-use experience, continuous low prices, more choices, no stockouts, accurate fulfillment, and excellent customer service (once and done). The customer perspective is enabled by the service perspective. Let's examine that service layer now.

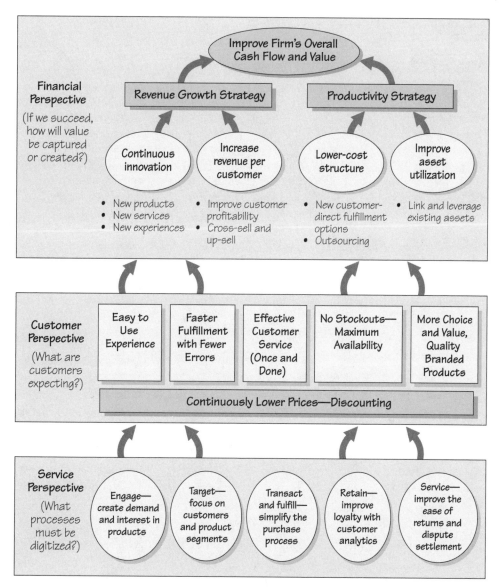

Figure 4.4: The Easy To Do Business With Strategy Map

The Services Layer—Enabling Composite Processes

Once the focal point is clear, companies must begin to define what multi-channel processes (or end-to-end services) need to be improved to achieve the desired results. Services orchestrate a sequence of well-defined business processes across

Table 4.1: Composite Processes in Self-Service

Multi-Channel Processes	Definition
Target-to-Engage	Planning, creating, executing, and measuring marketing activities
Engage-to-Close	Managing, negotiating, and closing sales opportunities
Transact-to-Fulfill	Managing orders, warehouse picking and packing, shipping, invoicing, returns, and financial settlement
Retain-to-Sell	Recording, consolidating, and analyzing customer interactions for cross-sell and up-sell opportunities
Request-to-Resolve	Requesting help with returns, resolving service problems, tracking resolutions and escalations, and enhancing service agreements

multiple applications to achieve a business target. Table 4.1 defines these services in relation to self-service. They tend to be different combinations of basic processes—engage, target, transact, retain, and service.

Customers' demands for better service across channels have been getting louder during the last decade. They would like to avoid engage-to-close experiences like the one we're about to describe. A cable TV operator wanted to lure customers from its satellite dish competitors. It launched a local advertising campaign that promised a $500 credit to customers who traded satellite TV dishes for cable subscriptions. The cable TV operator routed the overloaded call lines to an outsourced call center in the Philippines. Frustrated customers talked to agents who had no knowledge of the local ad. Meanwhile, the Web site listed in the ad crashed every time customers tried to access it. This scenario, hardly uncommon, illustrates the lack of coordination between marketing campaigns, call centers, and the Web channel.

Amazon.com offers a better example of how to create multi-channel services. Consider the target-to-engage service. Taking advantage of its 30 million-plus customer database, it can target and engage customers on behalf of its retail partners, especially for special promotions. If Circuit City wants to clear its inventory of 1,000 Sony big-screen TVs, it can use Amazon.com's mailing list to create a promotion with a clearance price. Within a few hours of the online promotion, all the TVs will likely be sold through the Amazon.com Web site. The cost of this campaign is rather small when compared to a traditional campaign.

End-to-end service efficiency of this magnitude is a major accomplishment, and it's hard for most retailers without a significant IT budget to compete against.

As long as Amazon.com continues to be ETDBW and drives the costs of various services down, other retailers are better off outsourcing their Web channel to Amazon.com than doing it in-house. We anticipate that within five years Amazon.com will become the dominant service platform for the retail industry.

Figure 4.5 shows the structure of a typical multi-channel service platform. It has four key parts: 1) the portal or interaction layer, 2) the composite process layer, 3) the business process management layer, and 4) the enterprise application layer. The multi-channel service platform helps unify a myriad of disparate

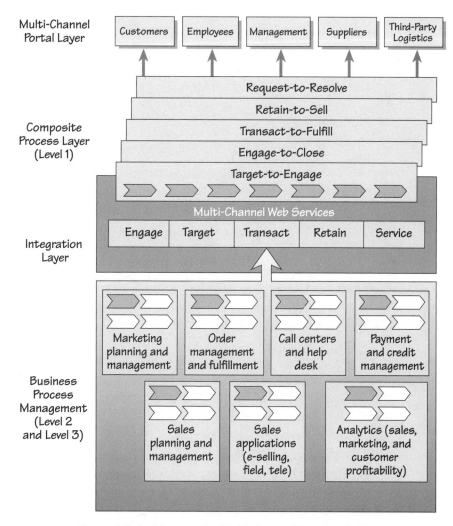

Figure 4.5: Architecture for Multi-Channel Service Platform

business processes and functional applications across the enterprise in a number of ways to address particular business challenges.

As a result, the shift from a function-centric CRM model (marketing, sales, and service) to a process-based CRM model (target-to-engage, transact-to-fulfill) is a scene that is being played out in almost every organization. This may sound relatively simple, but it is an enormous undertaking. The new CRM model requires breakthrough ways of thinking about end-to-end processes. This shift can also explain why many CRM projects that didn't pay enough attention to the design of composite processes are failing or delivering less value than expected.

> The bottom line: Multi-channel service designers are desperately needed. Why? When new channels, in conjunction with old ones, offer a variety of options and possibilities, service designers must filter them, molding them into what customers actually want. The best multi-channel services take into account the engineering of features and functions, as well as the marketing goals of customer satisfaction and brand identity.

The Business Process Management Layer—Translating Services into Processes

Services are built from composite processes. These composite processes are composed of processes that, in turn, are made up of subprocesses and tasks. For instance, a composite process, transact-to-fulfill, is made up of several processes, such as searching, ordering, and tracking. Each of these processes, like ordering, is made up of subprocesses such as order entry and credit card payment. The subprocesses, like order entry, are made up of multiple tasks, such as fill shipping information into a Web page, fill credit card information, and so on.

Most organizations already have thousands of processes segmented by channel. For instance, in the call center, most companies have in place elaborate processes that link a series of discrete subprocesses to describe what happens when a customer calls to place an order. It doesn't make sense to reinvent these processes. The design challenge is how to compose new services from the customers' perspective by utilizing and integrating what already exists.

As part of its transact-to-fulfill service for other retailers, Amazon.com has implemented a robust distributed order processing service. Let's see how this one process triggers related subprocesses. A typical consumer orders products through his channel of choice (either Amazon.com's own Web site or the retail partner's Web site). Orders are handled by the Amazon.com's sales order processing system. Each order can be filled by deliveries from any of the five Amazon.com-owned warehouses, drop-shipped from a vendor's warehouses (like Ingram books), shipped from a partner's warehouse (like Office Depot), or processed and held for in-store pickup (like Circuit City).

Order data is then distributed to the appropriate partner. The goods are managed and delivered to the customer directly from the third-party CRM system. After the goods are delivered to the customer, the delivery status is reported to Amazon.com's sales system. All relevant information regarding the order/ delivery status is stored centrally in the customer order. Invoicing for services between Amazon.com and the vendor/partner is tied to order delivery status. This model is only one example of the many possibilities. Any number of suppliers and transport companies may be involved. Suppliers may be part of a consolidated company or may also be external organizations.

Since 1995, Amazon.com has spent several billion dollars integrating all these processes and subprocesses. Its efforts were aimed at building a robust, internal process integration layer that could support the company, as well as its thousands of vendors and millions of customers. This integration layer is what separates Amazon.com from the rest. Competitors, no matter how hard they try, have failed in their attempts to replicate it.

The design of processes, subprocesses, and task automation is complicated even in a single channel environment. Now overlay the multi-channel requirements and "brick-and-click" possibilities, and it is not difficult to see why companies are struggling to get it right. In our opinion, the design, management, and integration of business processes are increasingly what separates the good companies from the rest of the pack.

Integrating Enterprise Applications—Linking Processes via Integration Layers

Visualizing and designing customer-centric processes are necessary and usually achievable. Layering these processes systematically on multiple business units, applications, and databases is where most CRM projects fail. The complexity is often overwhelming. Consider the case of Delta Air Lines, a major, worldwide airline. In the late 1990s, Delta found that in order to meet customer service objectives, it had to integrate processes across 13 business units. These business units were in turn accessing information stored on 30 separate customer databases and 40 flight databases that used 70 applications.[9]

In the past, when unexpected events, such as weather disruptions or flight delays, occurred, it was difficult to synchronize all the applications and databases.

Delta had no way to share data between the systems without human intervention, as the airline depended on manual reentry of data—a time-consuming effort that left customers and employees unaware of the causes of delays and their remedies. Delta needed to integrate its databases and applications so that information about various events would flow across all systems. The company envisioned a solution that would transform information silos into an interconnected system to be called "Delta Nervous System." A key part of this effort was the introduction of a process integration layer that orchestrated and distributed data to all applications that needed it.

Some variation of Delta's integration problem confronts every company, but the complexity and scope will differ. Customer-centric processes require multi-million dollar investments in process integration technology that bring together customer information scattered across internal applications (CRM, ERP, financials, and legacy systems) and outsourced functions (telemarketing, manufacturing, and logistics). It is easy to spot companies that don't have this process integration layer. The outcome: fragmented applications that create disjointed service, lost opportunities, and a limited view of the customer.

The concept of customer-centric process integration technology has matured considerably in the last decade. Figure 4.6 illustrates the evolution in the structure of CRM applications and the nature of integration performed in these projects. The figure shows the homegrown structure of CRM systems in the 1980s. These homegrown applications were often written internally at great cost, and application integration within these projects was usually not standard.

In the 1990s, companies began to reject building homegrown applications in favor of buying bundled applications or packaged software. Examples of these suites include Vantive (now PeopleSoft), Siebel, and SAP. Embedded in them were various best-practice processes and subprocesses. These packages saved companies money since they didn't have to hire an army of consultants to do subprocess design and reengineering. This "buy versus build" approach made it easier for companies to deploy functionality quickly, especially if they didn't customize the applications too much.

CRM suites popularized the embedding of processes within applications. Consider the generic customer service process flow that is incorporated into the Interaction Center module of the mySAP CRM suite. A customer contacts a company via the telephone, fax, e-mail, or Web chat. The Interaction Center finds the customer's data, which includes a complete history of his past interactions. The customer explains his problem to the customer service rep, who uses the Inter-

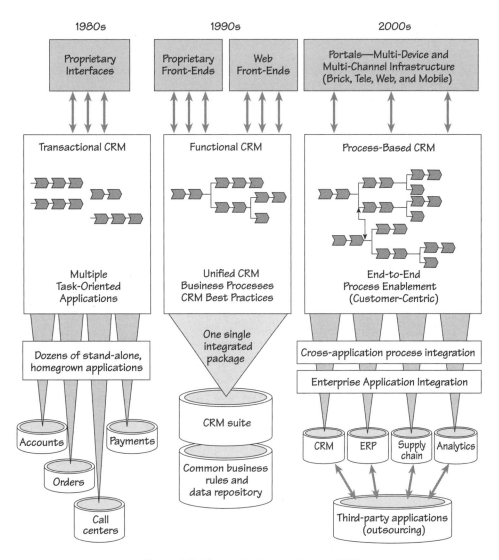

Figure 4.6: Moving to Process-Based CRM

active Intelligent Agent to search the company's knowledge base for applicable solutions. These solutions are then e-mailed to the customer.[10]

As companies gain experience from implementing various CRM packages, they are realizing that the competitive advantage is no longer derived from customizing small fragments of processes but from integrating the entire end-to-end process. For companies to deliver high-quality service, the applications that handle various business processes must work together. Operations such as sales, marketing, inventory, fulfillment, and finance can no longer operate as islands; they must connect seamlessly, without manual intervention, in real time, and be able to handle huge volumes of data. As a result, the scope of CRM is broadening to include inventory management, fulfillment, and service. This new process-based CRM is often called extended order management.

Companies tackling multi-channel problems have welcomed the expanded scope of CRM in integrating multiple legacy and packaged applications. Business processes can now be executed across multiple applications, departments, organizations, and enterprises. However, companies may be reluctant to adopt process-based CRM because they fear the costs associated with such a move. Some firms estimate that 30–40 percent of the cost of new applications is spent linking disparate business processes and applications rather than delivering new business functions.

Managers must understand process integration issues before they invest millions of dollars. Many find themselves frustrated when they discover that the multi-million dollar investment they made in Enterprise Application Integration (EAI) software is not delivering the ROI the salesperson promised.

Multi-Channel CRM Service Platforms—The Vendor's Perspective

Companies want CRM applications that integrate software, such as manufacturing, supply chain management, and logistics systems. Let's look at what various vendors are offering to solve the current integration problems. Peruse the following headlines:

- Siebel Systems announced that Universal Application Network (UAN) is the solution for reducing the cost and complexity of enterprise integration, enabling organizations to develop and deploy effectively cross-application business processes.

- SAP AG announced that xApps represents a new breed of applications called cross-applications. xApps builds on existing applications within and across enterprise boundaries, extending value by delivering cross-functional business processes.

These announcements are remarkably similar. They are both advertising the same thing—the ability to create customer-facing service platforms for companies. Since we covered SAP's xApps in Chapter 3, we will look at what Siebel and its partners, IBM, Accenture, TIBCO, WebMethods, and SeeBeyond, are trying to do.

What exactly is UAN? UAN is an approach for designing and developing cross-application business processes. The UAN solution comprises three basic components: 1) a library of prebuilt business processes, common object models, and transformation maps; 2) a design tool for modeling and configuring; and 3) an integration server that coordinates interapplication communication. Siebel's new version includes an embedded set of UAN-based application services interfaces that expose Siebel's proprietary application processes as Web Services.

How is this relevant to our discussion? UAN is a toolkit of processes for building a multi-channel service platform around Siebel's CRM suite. Its intent is to make it easier for companies to connect Siebel's CRM suite to homegrown systems and packaged applications developed by other vendors. Most vendors are concentrating on application and integration technology. Trends like Web Services, XML, business process management, and enterprise application integration are often thrown around for effect. While these tech trends are useful and necessary, they are often disconnected from the Easy To Do Business With focal point. This is the message we want to be certain we are conveying: Linking the business value to the underlying applications takes time and a unique skill set.

If you take a step back and look at the big picture, you will see a distinct pattern: Many vendors are vying to provide tools to build service platforms. Figure 4.7 illustrates the five core areas in emerging multi-channel CRM service platforms. Most vendors are developing and selling their solutions based on these five themes.

JC Penney—Product Returns in a Multi-Channel Setting

One area of multi-channel CRM that has become a huge issue is returns management. To attract and satisfy customers, retailers in the last few years have instituted extremely liberal return policies. Part of this strategy involves taking back products in a simple and convenient manner. With the emergence of multi-channel shopping, the problem many retailers face is how to align their various sales channels with their returns process.

Returns are becoming a sizable headache. Many retailers face a high percentage of product returns (returns are approximately 6 percent across all retailers). Product returns represent a mundane function that traditional brick-and-mortar retailers have been refining for years. In a multi-channel setting, it is not simple anymore; returns are one of the biggest impediments to online purchases. For

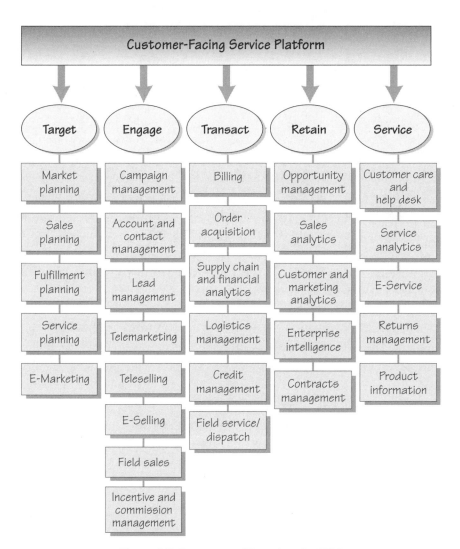

Figure 4.7: Features and Functions in CRM

multi-channel retailers like JC Penney and Sears, there are five distinct end-to-end processes that have to be mapped out: 1) buy online, return by shipping it back; 2) buy online, return offline in the store; 3) buy via catalog, return by shipping it back; 4) buy via catalog, return in the store; and 5) buy in the store, return in the store.

What kind of returns management service platform can support all five variants? In each of these options, the returns process is defined as the management, tracking, and disposition of returned products from the consumer to the return center for reprocessing, disposal, or destruction. The goal is to maximize the value of the returned product and minimize handling costs. The process requires reversing the direction of the fulfillment chain, which has implications for physical and information components of the business process. Let's look at a company that is regarded as a master of multi-channel product returns—JC Penney.

Incorporated in 1924, JC Penney is a holding company that operates through its two wholly owned subsidiaries, JC Penney Corp, the 100-year-old department store chain, and Eckerd Corp, the drugstore chain. JC Penney manages department stores in all 50 states, as well as Puerto Rico and Mexico. The major portion of business consists of providing merchandise and services to consumers through department stores, catalogs, and its Web site. The company markets family apparel, jewelry, shoes, accessories, and home furnishings to households with incomes of $30,000–$80,000. After being in business for 79 years, JC Penney is considered a best practice in the multi-channel returns process.

Multi-Channel Forward Fulfillment Process

To comprehend how products are returned or travel backward, we should first examine how they travel forward. Customers can buy products through three channels: 1) department stores, 2) catalogs, or 3) the Web site.

> **Department Stores.** JC Penney currently maintains 1,075 traditional brick-and-mortar stores that carry a wide variety of merchandise available for purchase.

> **Catalog Sales.** Shoppers can select products from the 1,400-page catalog and place their order using an 800 number. At the time of ordering, the customer is provided with two choices of delivery: 1) the order can be shipped via either UPS or regular mail; or 2) it can be shipped to a catalog desk located in a nearby department store for customer pickup.

> **Web Sales.** When a customer orders online, the order is automatically routed to an order processing system. A confirmation e-mail is sent to the customer within thirty minutes of submitting the order. The fulfillment and shipment process is similar to that of a catalog sale. Once the order is shipped, an invoice e-mail is sent. The item is then charged to a credit card.

After the order is placed, processing begins immediately, and the order is forwarded to one of the fulfillment centers where it is shipped according to the customer's delivery choice. Most catalog orders are ready for pickup in three to five working days. JC Penney contacts the customer when his order arrives at the local store for pickup. The merchandise is held at the store for ten days. In the case of a no-show, the item(s) is returned to the warehouse, and the customer's account is credited for the merchandise plus applicable sales tax. If he opts for home delivery, the order usually arrives in three to five business days.

The Product Returns Process

From a customer relationship perspective, the goal is to make the return process as simple as possible. Retailers like JC Penney want to improve customer service on the return side because they believe this will enhance customer loyalty. Let's look at how the process actually works by first seeing how customers return items to JC Penney.

A product purchased from any channel can be returned in one of three ways:

1. The customer can physically return an item to any store. This is the quickest and easiest way to receive an immediate refund or credit.

2. The customer can return merchandise by mail. A mail return requires the customer to complete a "Returns or Exchange" form and send it back along with the item.

3. The customer can call customer service and schedule a home pickup for the return. It can take as many as seven days before UPS arrives to pick up the merchandise.

Figure 4.8 illustrates the different modes of return. The two issues facing retailers in managing returns are 1) improving the customer's experience and 2) tightening the merchant's operating efficiencies. Merchant operating efficiencies include tracking and monitoring product returns as they affect the credit process, financials, and cash flow forecasts. Most customer service policies specify that the customer should be reimbursed instantly, but for the retailer, returning goods to suppliers and securing a credit note can take weeks.

Behind the Scenes—Inside the Department Store

The first step of JC Penney's return process is filtering, or permitting only "qualified" items to enter the returns process. In the second step, the customer with a qualified return is refunded. The item then joins a collection of returned items. The pool of return items is sorted into categories or "buckets." Items in the same bucket travel along the same path, which is determined by the mode of disposal.

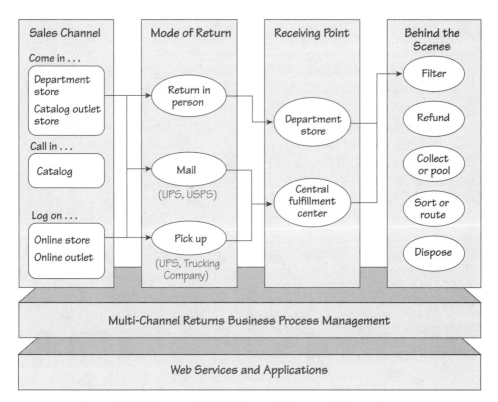

Figure 4.8: JC Penney's Multi-Channel Sales and Returns Process

Depending on the condition of the item, contractual obligations with the vendor or supplier of the item, and the demand for the product, a retailer may have one or more of the following options available: return to stock, return to vendor, sell as new, sell via outlet or discount, sell to secondary (gray) market or auction, donate to charity, repair/remanufacture/refurbish, or send to materials recycling/landfill.

In the case of JC Penney, not all disposition decisions are made at the store level. Store managers are rewarded for disposition of the item first through the retail store. If the item is not sold in the store, then it is sent back to the central fulfillment center (CFC). The CFC sorts, processes, and ships the items to their next destination. Consolidating returns at the CFC offers many benefits such as labor savings, decreased transportation costs, and space utilization.

Managing Returns Is the Next Big Efficiency Frontier

Companies have spent years fine-tuning selling to the customer but have neglected the reverse loop. In some retail sectors, up to 20 percent of goods is returned to the store; this figure rises to almost 30 percent for online operators and specialist fashion retailers.

Returns are becoming a "profit-killer" for retailers as more and more manufacturers (especially overseas) are offering off-invoice discounting in exchange for no returned products (zero-returns policy). In a low-margin business, the financial impact of badly managed returns can sink a company.

At the same time, returns are getting more complicated. Legislation in the European Union, particularly in Germany, is emphasizing recycling more, causing the costs associated with returns to climb. There is an obvious need for end-to-end service platforms that lower the cost of returns.

New players, such as GENCO with its R-Log (retail reverse logistics) service platform, are stepping forward to fill the gap. R-Log captures inbound stock, determines asset disposition, tracks inventory location and movement, monitors cut-off volumes, and triggers product return. We expect to see more traditional IT vendors move into this area by integrating the returns management process more tightly into their CRM applications.

Seven Points to Ponder

> Discovery consists in seeing what everyone else has seen
> and thinking what no one else has thought.
> —*Albert Szent-Gyorgi*

The multi-channel blueprint addresses the strategic issues and operational challenges inherent in delivering new services to existing customers (in contrast to creating services for a new customer base). Developing new multi-channel services requires both an internal (inside-out) perspective on existing capabilities and an external (outside-in) perspective on what customers want and need.

Executing a multi-channel strategy is difficult. Asking the right questions is critical.

1. *Are your channels aligned?* Now, more than ever, organizations recognize the opportunity to affect business outcomes positively by leveraging channels. Your ability to achieve organizational objectives depends

on how well you align your channels with customer objectives and leverage your technology.

2. *Do you understand multi-channel service design?* Operationally speaking, designing and engineering business processes that support multi-channel service for customers are a relatively new science. Most schools of thought center on process design and optimization for only one channel.

3. *Do you realize that the CRM problem is changing?* As technology allows organizations to create more customization options for customers, a brand-new set of problems arises. Blending channels to meet the diverse needs of "segments of one" is extraordinarily difficult. This complexity escalates when firms have legacy infrastructure.

4. *Do you know how to take into account the customer viewpoint?* A multi-channel blueprint requires a significant amount of self-service consumer behavior analysis. Without considerable forethought, it is easy to bypass simple and technologically easy-to-implement approaches for expensive and complex applications.

5. *Are you effective?* Performance management initiatives track and measure individual channels but fail to make the vital link between multi-channel service and business performance. A holistic blueprint perspective allows managers to isolate channel underperformers.

6. *Is your transitional plan working?* Developing a vision of the ideal multi-channel model state is easy. The difficult part is designing and executing the transition from its current state to the new multi-channel blueprint.

7. *Are you paying attention to returns?* Multi-channel returns management is a serious issue. Returns can be a particularly difficult and costly puzzle for merchants. A reduction in both the number of returns and the cost of those returns is an unavoidable business priority for retailers.

Multi-channel service platforms will be a priority for organizations. Anecdotal data indicate that organizations consider it vital to manage customer relationships more effectively and that they are willing to spend money on these projects. As such, the broader CRM market, of which service platforms are a subset, should grow more rapidly than other areas of applications software. Read on; you're not done. Service platforms are incredibly useful in a number of areas, and we highlight spend management next.

CHAPTER FIVE

Spend Management Blueprint: Enabling Supplier Management Services

What to Expect

"Procurement as a set of services" is moving from the realm of possibility to gritty execution. In the search for profitability, many CFOs are asking their purchasing departments not just to streamline purchasing processes, but to control the overall spending across all categories. Most purchasing departments have responded by making discrete cost reductions, for example, in travel and office supplies. These areas are the first step. In the nonstop battle to deliver lower costs, innovative services formed around spend management are the new battleground.

In this chapter, we explain the business problems and long-term trends shaping spend management. To provide the reader with the necessary background, we also briefly illustrate the evolution of the technology behind spend management. We then delve into the design of spend management blueprints (focal points + service platforms). The chapter ends with a discussion of service parts procurement—a topic that is beginning to take center stage in the battle to control costs.

Introduction

Supply management, spend management, spend optimization, supplier relationship management, e-procurement, strategic sourcing, reverse auctions, catalog management, consortia, exchanges, and private hubs—what do all these buzzwords have in common?

All are part of the Low Cost focal point. This strategy hinges on reducing the money spent on purchased goods and services. Every business buys direct materials (raw materials, service parts), indirect materials (travel, office supplies, computers), and professional services (temporary staffing, consulting). For most businesses, purchased goods and services account for a significant percentage of expenses. For instance, ExxonMobil employs 4,000 purchasing professionals that manage more than $30 billion in spending. Even a slight reduction in these expenses could improve the bottom line and dramatically increase profits.[1]

Purchasing, strategic sourcing, procurement, and just plain buying are the many names of a core activity with one objective—controlling costs. Anyone with bottom-line responsibility knows that managing the source-to-pay process is necessary to keep costs under control. Source-to-pay is a business process that deals with sourcing, contract management, procurement, invoicing, reconciliation, and control and compliance. It brings together Web-based analysis (finding savings opportunities), sourcing (getting the savings), and procurement (keeping them).

To set the stage, let's look at some common procurement problems. A wood-products manufacturer sold cabinets under multiple brand names in thousands of retail outlets, home centers, and specialty retailers. The company spent more than 50 percent of product cost on raw materials. The business challenge was to reduce the cost of sourcing. The symptoms the company was interested in tackling included

- Inability to measure supplier performance (delivery, quality, and service),
- Inability to view data that spanned multiple manufacturing plants, and
- Inability to share business information within the sourcing department or with suppliers.

Now consider this strategic problem: A large manufacturer buys more than 1,500 products and services from 2,000 suppliers and spends more than $10 billion across four business units. The company has been experiencing flat top-line growth and increasing margin pressure. The CFO realizes that if the company does not cut its costs, it may lose 15 percent of its market share in the next three years to cheaper competitors. The CFO presents the chief procurement officer with the following mandates:

- Reduce total spending by 7 percent,
- Decrease the number of suppliers by 30 percent, and
- Improve invoicing and payables accuracy to 90 percent.

Finally, let's consider the emerging after-sales service parts procurement problem. Your car breaks down for the fourth time in a year. You get it towed to a dealer. The dealer diagnoses the problem as a broken alternator and informs you that it will take him seven days to get the part from the manufacturer. You fume and wonder why procuring a standard part takes so long. At that point, you make an executive decision never to buy that brand of car again. A clear case of a not-so-happy customer!

Management in a variety of industries (appliances, medical equipment, telecommunications, utilities, automotive, and defense) is analyzing after-sales service parts sourcing and procurement for cost savings. These industries typically have to maintain an inventory of parts (e.g., for replacement, warranty, or recall) for both routine maintenance and unexpected repairs. The total cost of storing, insuring, and moving spare parts to meet certain service level agreements (SLAs) can be very high. Also, inaccurate planning for expensive, slow-moving parts leads to expensive "buy" decisions. As a result, managers are interested in optimizing service parts inventory levels and managing the end-to-end procurement process. (We describe the after-sales service parts problem later in this chapter.)

To solve these different procurement problems, businesses are beginning to focus on "spend management"—aligning processes, resources, and technology to control billions in spending. Consequently, more attention is being paid to implementing service platforms that enable the shift from inside-out procurement process automation to an outside-in spend services digitization perspective.

The goal of spend management services is to deliver cross-enterprise value. This requires a robust service platform that can support best practice spend management strategies and allow companies constantly to measure and improve their results so they can find the savings, get the savings, and keep the savings.

Evolution of Procurement

Since the beginning of civilization, one business formula has not changed: Profit = Revenues – Costs. When revenues plateau or begin to decline, the spotlight is shifted to the big "C"—Costs.

The notion of spend or cost management is as ancient as business itself. You could say that Christopher Columbus went in search of India to find alternative, cheaper, and more plentiful sources of supplies. His procurement objective was to find a new route to the fabled gold, herbs, and spices of the East by sailing westward over what was presumed to be open sea.

A little more than 500 years later, Internet entrepreneurs are trying to pull a "Columbus" by creating new digital pathways for e-procurement. However, the journey toward e-procurement has not been smooth sailing. It has been buffeted by economic fluctuations that resulted in rapid expansion and contraction, a classic boom-bust cycle.

The Boom-Bust Cycle of E-Procurement

Do you remember when business-to-business (B2B) and e-procurement were the rage? The peak of the boom was in 2000 when procurement seemed to be the first area where the Internet and Web technology could bring tangible improvements across the supply chain. Reverse auctions, public e-marketplaces, private trading exchanges, and e-procurement promised to reduce prices while increasing process efficiency.

B2B was hyped as one of the most solid bets on the Internet. The prevailing logic was that big companies could capitalize on the Internet when they made purchases. The Internet could also help them track inventory and create new ways to streamline business operations.

Unfortunately, B2B went through a predictable innovation cycle. The first phase of the cycle was a frenzy to be associated with the concept. Then came the "heavy lifting" part, where making the concept work took time and proved more difficult than anyone imagined. Financial markets got bored, venture capitalists lost interest, and many promising start-ups died for lack of funding. Big companies that embraced the concept started distancing themselves from it.

The third phase began when the glitz evaporated. This was the behind-the-scenes execution phase in which the benefits from the B2B technology started to kick in—just not as quickly as anyone had thought. This was the period when users slowly developed the technical infrastructure, service offerings, and expertise required to realize the full potential of B2B. Investors and customers circled back to the technology, but with a decidedly more cautious outlook.

We are at the beginning of phase three today. The long-term promise of better procurement and supplier management is still there, but the tools and methods have evolved considerably.

E-Procurement—From a Technology Focus to a Process Focus

During the boom-bust cycle, procurement digitization—the automation of the cycle of requisition to order, fulfillment, and payment—noticeably matured both in terms of business value and technology infrastructure. Figure 5.1 illustrates the

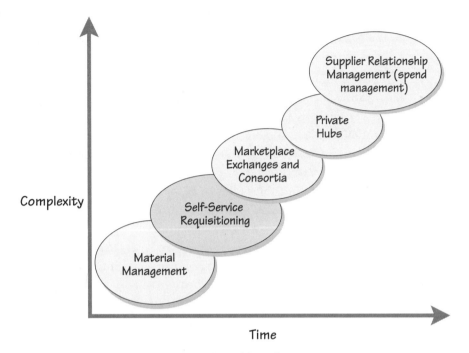

Figure 5.1: Evolution of Spend Management

changes from material management to spend management that took place in a relatively short period.

Before the Internet, most purchasing departments focused on direct materials, which include expenditures on components, subassemblies, and raw materials. These expenditures are the largest segment of corporate spending, representing more than 50 percent of total costs. The application that streamlined this was materials management.

However, material management applications had limited scope. They did not include nonmanufacturing procurement for expenses such as travel and operating supplies, which were largely paper based. As a result, it is quite common to find three problems: 1) insufficient information to make good decisions, 2) scant control over the end-to-end procurement transactions, and 3) inadequate ability to create an integrated set of sourcing/procurement processes.

Solving these problems was the quest of many early B2B ventures that supported the requisitioning or buying process. They developed software platforms for internal catalog management, self-service ordering, and approval cycles. (Ariba is one vendor that got started in this period.) The market demand for digitizing the requisitioning process was quite strong. To resolve the issue of making decisions with incomplete information, companies decided to empower employees with self-service requisitioning.

Digitizing the buying process within the enterprises' four walls was not enough to multiply productivity. Companies realized that the end-to-end process (from requisition to approval to purchase order to supplier to receiving) needed digitization. It didn't take long before the platforms that made self-service possible were expanded to enable end-to-end transaction management via various B2B portals.

During this period, three types of B2B portals emerged: 1) public, independent e-marketplaces run by a neutral company, 2) consortia run by groups of large corporations, and 3) exchanges that primarily allowed buyers and sellers to find each other. Thus, the processes linking end users to approvers and organizations to suppliers were extended using connectivity within organizations or connectivity between organizations.

Public and consortia marketplaces were aiming to digitize four different categories of spend:

1. **Indirect Spending**—Spending on materials that will be consumed but do not become part of a product or service that is sold to customers. Examples include office supplies, telecommunications equipment, food services, and travel expenditures.

2. **MRO Spending**—Spending on maintenance, repair, and operations (MRO) supplies (e.g., tools, parts, and lubricants used to maintain factory equipment). This category also includes after-sales service parts.

3. **Services Spending**—Spending on professional services, for example, temporary staffing, consultants, and contract workers. For many businesses, this is the largest category of spending after direct materials.

4. **Direct Spending**—Spending on goods and services that will become part of a product sold to customers. Examples include raw materials and components.

At the peak, there were 1,500 plus marketplaces. Less than 200 survived. One reason for the attrition was that each was solving one piece of the overall business problem: spend management. They did, however, help educate mainstream companies and create awareness about online procurement in a very short period (1998–2001).

As large companies gained experience digitizing the procurement process, they realized that solving it piecemeal or outsourcing it to a third-party marketplace was not going to create value. Many observed that supporting their internal business processes, connecting with multiple suppliers, and dealing with exceptions required much more control over the technology infrastructure than was provided by a marketplace model. These business needs resulted in another structural shift from neutral public marketplaces to private hubs.

In parallel, the macroeconomic environment swing from revenue growth to draconian cost control has influenced organizations to broaden their focus from transactions into services (which some refer to as supplier management and others as spend management). Advanced firms are digitizing not just the end-to-end transaction but the entire lifecycle—sourcing, procurement, supplier enablement, payment, reconciliation, and spend analysis.

What these companies have discovered is that spend management does not center on technology, but on enabling fiscal discipline. Its goal is to strip down existing procurement processes and to provide companies with a single platform to control their spending.

> The bottom line: Procurement innovations—e-marketplaces, reverse auctions, sourcing tools, and content management applications—are allowing companies to interact with suppliers in ways that were impossible a few years ago. The structural changes in procurement processes have revealed to companies a new way to achieve savings and create new buying mechanisms. Unfortunately, these changes have also created process design and efficiency challenges for suppliers who are struggling to comply with mandatory price reductions.

Long-Term Trends Shaping Spend Management

The cost reduction requirements that made B2B attractive in early 2000 are still intact. In this section, we will look at the long-term trends driving the transition from e-procurement to spend management. They are 1) continuous cost reduction, 2) procurement transparency, 3) global sourcing, 4) flexible integration, 5) process automation, and 6) spend analysis.

Continuous Cost Reduction—Nonstop CFO Focus

If your competitors' costs were lower than yours, could they lower prices, erode your market share, stay profitable, and drive you out of business? This is precisely what Wal-Mart, Dell, Intel, and GE do to their competitors. Companies will be unceremoniously left behind if they don't manage their company's costs efficiently.

In order for profits to increase, revenues must go up, or expenses must keep going down. Revenue growth is difficult for mature industries. As a result, CFOs, especially those whose companies have recently done several mergers and acquisitions, are struggling to manage costs and its alter ego, spending.

Let's say after a merger, a hypothetical large chemical company has 35,000 active suppliers, 2,000 of which account for 80 percent of the total spend. The CFO's goal is to analyze the total supply base by examining what is being purchased from each supplier and eliminating overlap. She intends to consolidate purchasing to drive meaningful, incremental volume toward 50 preferred suppliers who, in turn, provide better prices. This step is known as supplier rationalization.

However, multiple systems supporting many decentralized procurement processes make supplier rationalization a difficult task. They tend to sabotage every effort to consolidate and analyze spending. The challenge is to identify the areas most in need of attention, develop a plan to reduce costs, and then systematically manage all key purchasing interactions across the enterprise to deliver the planned spend reductions.

No spend management platform exists for CFOs. Several have summed up this omission saying, "The sales team has a CRM system, manufacturing has an SCM solution, and finance has ERP systems, but what one, centralized purchasing platform does the firm have?" This is exactly what a new class of service platforms called enterprise spend management (ESM) seeks to provide.

> The bottom line: ESM allows companies to consolidate their analysis, sourcing, contracting, procurement, and reconciliation processes into a single, cohesive platform. It seeks to provide the enterprisewide visibility and control that CFOs need to manage and leverage their spending efficiently.

Procurement Transparency

Procurement has traditionally been a paper-intensive process. Peering into the "black box" (or purchasing department) to perform basic tasks like checking an order's status is usually extremely time-consuming. Opening this black box and understanding what is going on inside is a big step forward in creating transparency.

In procurement, the concept of transparency manifests itself in four ways:

1. **Price** — Are we getting the price negotiated in the contract?

2. **Availability**—Who has the product we need immediately and in what quantity?

3. **Supplier**—Who else makes this product?

4. **Commodity**—Is a substitute, alternative product available?

Transparency in all four of these dimensions can substantially improve the efficiency of the end-to-end process, especially in a fragmented industry.

Consider the case of the food service industry. A manufacturer generally gives different product codes and descriptions to various distributors for the same product. With 2,000 food and consumer product manufacturers selling through 20,000 distributors to 750,000 operators of restaurants, hotels, golf courses, and cafeterias, there is very little transparency.

Without transparency, operators have difficulty tracking rebates, credit memos, payables, and discounts for a specific product, given all the different product codes floating around. The industry is too fragmented for manufacturers to deliver directly to operators. As a result, marketplaces (e.g., FoodService.com or Instill.com) sensing opportunity, stepped in to let buyers or operators order from one portal but fulfill through multiple distributors. These portals allow buyers to get a consolidated view of their procurement, pricing, and consumption, resulting in better process visibility and transparency.

> The bottom line: The lack of transparency in the procurement process can cost companies millions in unnecessary expenses due to longer cycle times, information management overhead, communications cycles, and delayed response times.

Global Sourcing as a "Need-to-Have" Capability

A British insurance company engages an Indian firm to write 10 million lines of code. An Australian airline carrier wants a vendor who can repair small-plane engines. These are examples of global sourcing, a trend aimed at tapping the worldwide marketplace to 1) find additional suppliers, 2) access leading-edge technology, 3) reduce total costs, and 4) meet localization requirements.

Why is global sourcing a priority? Suppose a business has revenues of $1 billion and annual profits of 10 percent, or $100 million. The company's cost of goods sold equals 70 percent of revenues, or $700 million. Cutting production costs by 5 percent, approximately $35 million, would boost its profits by $35 million. Why? Because every dollar saved in procurement contributes directly to the overall profits. Economics is probably the most significant driver of global sourcing.

One prevalent method of global sourcing is reverse auctions. These are growing in popularity and are being widely adopted for raw materials (for example, 5,000 pounds of plastic resin), commodities (for example, 10,000 pounds of cement), and even temporary staffing (for example, 15 programmers for an ERP project).

How do reverse auctions work? Typically, they involve a single buyer soliciting bids from qualified suppliers who bid down to their lowest price. Let's say you are a large company and you are buying 1,000 PCs with 17-inch flat panel monitors and two-year onsite service. You invite Dell, HP, IBM, Gateway, and Sony to participate in a reverse auction. You set the opening price at $800 per PC. The first supplier offers to sell at $750 per PC. The second offers to sell at $700. (Downward price movement defines a reverse auction.) Let's say the auction was held between 3 p.m. and 4 p.m. At precisely 3:59 p.m., Dell Computer offers to sell each PC for $400. The other companies look at this price and decide they cannot beat it and make a profit. Since whoever has offered the cheapest price at 4:00 p.m. will be first in line to get the contract, Dell is declared the winner.

There are three types of reverse auction service platforms:

1. Web-Based Full-Service Providers (for example, FreeMarkets)—any company can go to them, and they take care of the end-to-end procurement process.

2. Web-Based B2B Exchanges (for example, Transora in the retail industry)—companies can go to the industry-specific exchange, and it takes care of the process for the client.

3. Enterprise Software Providers (for example, Ariba)—companies buy the software and can run the entire auction themselves.

The Internet is making global sourcing almost effortless and has produced amazing results. A field study of large companies (companies with annual revenues in excess of $2 billion) shows that effectively executed sourcing initiatives yield an average of 7.2 percent in total direct procurement savings and 5.4 percent in total indirect procurement savings. Together, the collective savings opportunity exceeds $350 billion for the largest corporations.[2]

> The bottom line: Before the Web was used for sourcing goods and services, buyers often had to rely on a small set of suppliers. As a result, buyers might have paid higher prices or obtained lower quality than they would in a more efficient market with better information and alternative sources of supply. The global sourcing trend coupled with reverse auction platforms is attacking this problem with a vengeance.

Faster, Smoother, and More Flexible Integration Is Necessary

Are you integrated with your top five suppliers? How about your top 100? Procurement interactions between businesses are complex, as well as labor and information intensive. Getting the right information to the right constituency at the right time is a challenge in a single large organization, let alone multiple complex enterprises.

Purchase orders can be sent out via mail, fax, e-mail, electronic data interchange (EDI), or extensible markup language (XML). For many companies, only a handful of suppliers represent enough business to warrant the large investment required for EDI. Most global organizations have invested years and millions of dollars in EDI solutions just to connect their top ten or 20 suppliers. These suppliers (usually of direct materials) were selected based on the 80/20 rule, that is, 80 percent of business is done with 20 percent of suppliers. The assumption is that because most corporate spend is channeled through these few suppliers, they are the ones that matter.

In some industries, shaken up by the volatile economy and a heavy dose of mergers and acquisitions, the 80/20 rule may not be true anymore. For these industries, all suppliers are important. Automating the sourcing processes across the entire supply base, not just the top twenty percent, is one of the fastest, easiest ways to pull excess costs out of the procurement puzzle.

Intel is one company that has made significant progress in business-to-supplier integration. The company expects to process $5 billion, or 10 percent, of its purchases using RosettaNet—an XML-based integration standard.[3] RosettaNet lets trading partners automate application-to-application interactions responsible for order management, shipping, receiving logistics, invoicing, and payments. Intel says its long-term goal is to squeeze as much as $500 million in annual costs out of its procurement operations. Much of these savings will come from ceasing to use EDI to communicate with suppliers and customers. EDI tends to be rigid, which is a label firms cannot have in a fast-moving industry.

Effective XML-based integration between suppliers and companies is bound to drive costs down in the long term. Companies want to tap into XML-based integration to make B2B interactions—all collaborations, not just buying and selling—more efficient. Channeling intercompany processes and information through a common service platform can create unprecedented levels of efficiency and process transparency.

> The bottom line: XML-based integration is replacing EDI as the fastest, easiest way to wring excess costs from procurement. Business-to-supplier integration removes both the delay and paper from the process.

Self-Service Desktop Procurement—Better Process Automation

Are your employees allowed to procure online, or are you clinging to tradition and forcing them to fill out multiple forms to get office supplies? Thankfully, an irreversible trend in purchasing is occurring: Digital information is replacing paperwork.

Paper-based or semiautomated processes are costly and time-consuming. Often they include the rekeying of information, lengthy approval cycles, and overly involved financial and administrative personnel. The cost per transaction ranges from $75–$300. Frequently, it exceeds the cost of the items purchased. In addition, these painfully slow processes commonly result in fulfillment delays to end users, leading to productivity losses.

Although self-service procurement appears straightforward, it is tricky to implement. This is partly because there are multiple parties involved in the end-to-end processes. For instance, obtaining office supplies in a large firm involves the employee, the supervisor, the purchasing department, the supplier, and the receiving division. Designing a process that seamlessly connects the different parties in a cohesive workflow requires paying attention not just to automation, but something called workflow monitoring and coordination.

Organizations incur greater costs when they cannot monitor and coordinate procurement. Many lack the systems that enable them to monitor purchases and compile data necessary to see who is buying what. In addition, these businesses suffer from a problem known as "maverick buying," which occurs when personnel do not follow internal guidelines as to which suppliers to use for purchases. When preferred suppliers are not used, organizations pay a premium. Maverick buying accounts for one-third of operating resource expenditures, costing companies a 15–27 percent premium on those purchases.

Paper-based procurement processes also increase costs for suppliers. When buyers are unable to control purchasing and channel orders, preferred suppliers don't get the necessary volume and therefore lose revenues. Suppliers also suffer from inefficient, error prone order fulfillment and customer service processes. Many dedicate significant resources to entering information manually from faxed or phoned-in purchase orders and processing paper invoices. They also spend large amounts on customer acquisition and sales costs, including the production and distribution of paper catalogs. Without automated and integrated solutions, both buyers and suppliers incur extraneous costs in conducting business.

> The bottom line: Enormous inefficiencies exist because businesses tackle complex procurement processes manually. The long-term trend is to digitize workflows and streamline integration so that information can be passed smoothly and costs can be reduced.

Spend Analysis—Monitoring and Controlling Contracts

Who are your top suppliers? How much are you spending in each category? What is the correlation between contract and invoice prices? If you consolidated the spend with one supplier, would there be substantial savings? These are some of the what-if questions being raised by more sophisticated companies. Spend analytics that show how much is being spent when, with whom, and on what are sorely needed. Spend analysis is also attacking other common business problems such as

- Lack of shared contract information among widely distributed business units,

- Limited details about suppliers and spending patterns (that is, what is being spent with whom), and

- No enterprisewide visibility because of multiple nonintegrated systems and disconnected processes (this happens when catalogs, contracts, and orders are not standardized across the enterprise).

Spend analysis is used to monitor supplier performance continuously. This monitoring is accomplished by collecting transaction data from back-end systems to derive key performance indicators (KPIs) for service level, quantity, and price reliability. KPIs provide useful feedback and can be used to compare the performance of suppliers for the same product or product category. They can also assist companies in determining whether to terminate or improve a supplier relationship.

Spend analysis is an important data management issue. The volume and fragmented nature of procurement data—transactions, commodities, and contracts—require significant time investments for collecting, standardizing, and categorizing. Historical spend data comes from various sources and disparate systems: accounts payable, general ledger, suppliers, and purchasing card files. Collecting the data can be a nightmare. Once consolidated, there is still the challenge of resolving data structure issues and classifying it into standard categories for analysis.

More complex spend analysis of direct materials looks at sales forecast and production capacity, as well as spend history. Corporate business objectives (design changes, capacity changes, volume goals, and new product development) also are taken into consideration.

> The bottom line: Spend analysis has to be aligned with business priorities. The spend management service platform needs to give different groups within the organization access to consolidated data that they can slice and dice by product, price, price trends, and delivery cost to gain useful insights.

Creating Spend Management Blueprints

Many companies have tried to digitize their procurement processes. Most have had disappointing or, in some cases, disastrous results. The obstacles they met have been time, cost, and impatience. Of these, impatience has been the biggest stumbling block in executing large-scale change projects. Procurement digitization modifies existing practices and requires a methodical (slow) pace of implementation.

We have noticed that organizations often rush to implement e-procurement with tactical three- to six-month projects. A typical project works like this: A team of five to ten personnel is assembled. Given the tight deadline, they quickly identify and narrow down the scope of the procurement processes to be digitized. Then the work begins on modeling the processes and defining workflows. The team next defines functional and technical requirements and moves swiftly through hardware and software installation, customization of the Web front end, encoding the catalog interface to integrate with suppliers, and end-user training. With much fanfare, version 1.0 is released.

After a few months, the CFO asks for a report on what savings are resulting from the implementation. A consultant is hired to provide a neutral, third-party assessment. She writes a report that says few employees are using the procurement system and the implementation is flawed because it addressed a limited part of the business problem. She recommends another six-month study to figure out how to get ROI from the initial investment.

By this time, senior management is frustrated. They have lost the appetite to invest more money to fix the existing version or create new change management programs to enable adoption. They realize that they have three possible routes: 1) scrap the project and write off the investment, 2) put it in maintenance mode and allocate minimal resources to it, or 3) initiate a long-term view by assessing how to fit the existing project into a spend management blueprint.

Most companies select option one. A tenacious few make the third decision. They realize that it is early in the procurement digitization cycle and that it makes sense to learn from the implementation by looking at what went right and what went wrong. These companies are advocating staying the course. They realize that the basic applications of e-procurement are only the opening move in a much longer chess game.

If we were to offer only one insight to organizations embarking on a spending management initiative, it is this: You must have a comprehensive spend management blueprint. Figure 5.2 illustrates the various layers of such a blueprint. Let's look more closely at each one of these layers.

Spend Management Focal Point

What is your long-term corporate focal point? If it is being a low-cost producer, how do your various spend management initiatives align with this strategy?

Consider the following: The focal point at Boeing, an aerospace and defense giant, is to provide world-class products at an affordable price and in the least amount of time. The U.S. Department of Defense, Boeing's biggest customer, is exerting tremendous pressure on the company to be innovative and yet control the costs of the final products. Because of this pressure, centralized spend management is a core part of Boeing's operating strategy. It has to manage production costs and its surrogate, spending. Boeing's goal is to use the Web to lower procurement costs continuously while maintaining efficiency through collaboration, visibility, and better integration.

Making sure the spend management objectives (efficiency, requisition control, and better supplier relations) line up with the overall business objectives is difficult. Some companies are clear in terms of what they want to accomplish; the majority are not. If you are not certain of what the overall spend management strategy is, it's a good idea to figure it out. The logic behind this is

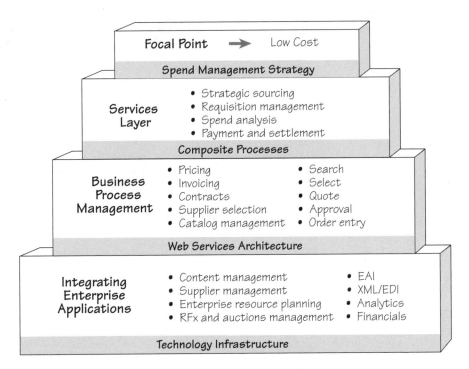

Figure 5.2: Spend Management Blueprint

self-explanatory: If you don't know precisely where you are going, you cannot get there quickly.

Ask yourself these questions: *What specific business value are you trying to create? Reductions in which spending categories would make the most difference to your company's ability to thrive?* Clarifying a spend management focal point is slow, painstaking work. It requires patience and does not come easily to companies without long-term focus or to those that are under tremendous financial pressure to complete short-term projects with immediate ROI. Of course, no organization is without limitations—time, skilled people, budget—so each must make decisions about how to spend scarce attention and resources best.

The Services Layer—Enabling Composite Processes

CFOs are asking their chief procurement officers the ultimate question: Is it possible to take a holistic view of spend management and provide internal clients with a range of high-quality business services?

How can you begin? A first step is focusing on translating the focal point—Low Cost—into a set of end-to-end services. Ask what new business services need

Table 5.1: Composite Processes in Spend Management

Composite Processes	Definition
Sourcing	Managing RFx (request for quote, RFQ; request for information, RFI; and request for proposal, RFP), auctions, and negotiating contracts
Contracting	Managing pricing, catalogs, and contracts; order routing; invoice reconciliation; and supplier integration
Procurement	Controlling the execution against contracts and the requisition to fulfillment process
Payment	Handling invoices, discounts, rebates, disputes, and return processes
Analysis	Evaluating spending, contract compliance, supplier performance, and quality against preset performance indicators and benchmarks

to be in place to meet the spend management objectives, not what disparate applications need to be integrated.

What services do all organizations need for managing spend? All companies need sourcing, contracting, procurement, payment, and analysis (see Table 5.1 for more detail). Each of these services represents a composite process or a collection of processes. For instance, sourcing is a very intricate collection of processes comprised of 1) preparing and distributing detailed requests for quotes (RFQs), 2) identifying high-quality, global suppliers, 3) educating and preparing suppliers to bid online, 4) conducting offline negotiations, 5) supervising a real-time, interactive online auction, and 6) negotiating the contract.

Procurement is another composite process; it spans requisition to invoicing. Let's look at the end-to-end procurement process from the viewpoint of an employee and the applications that actually support the process. The following steps are a far cry from what most people imagine as a two- or three-part process at most:

1. **Requisition**—an employee searches a catalog and creates a shopping basket (Ariba Buyer);

2. **Requisition Approval**—an employee request is routed by e-mail to his manager for approval (Microsoft Outlook);

3. **Purchase Order**—after approval, a purchase order (PO) is created and transmitted electronically to the supplier (SAP ERP);

4. **Supplier Sales Order**—the PO is converted into a sales order in the supplier's ERP system (Peoplesoft ERP);

5. **Acknowledgment**—after supplier validation, a PO acknowledgment is sent back to the buyer using EDI (Vitria EDI Server);

6. **Warehousing**—the supplier's ERP system sends a fulfillment order to the supplier's distribution center (Manhattan Associates Warehouse Management System);

7. **Shipping**—a warehouse worker picks, packs, and ships the product to the buyer (FedEx Ship Manager);

8. **Transportation**—FedEx Ground transports the product to the receiving dock of the buyer (FedEx Cosmos Tracking System);

9. **Receiving**—a worker receives the shipment, signs for it, and records it in the ERP system (SAP ERP); and finally

10. **Invoicing**—the supplier electronically sends an invoice to the buyer, invoking the payment process (SAP Financials).

The actual process is more complicated than what we presented. We glossed over some of the details to give you a snapshot. The interesting point is that each of these ten steps in the requisition-to-invoicing service interacts with a different underlying enterprise application. Designing a new requisition-to-invoicing service platform that integrates the various discrete processes just mentioned is the problem giving CIOs grey hairs. The messy reality is that services like requisition-to-invoicing depend on the integration of vast amounts of data, much of which resides in legacy and custom applications. Connecting these different applications in the context of an end-to-end process is the essence of the spend management service platform.

Some large corporations are beginning to design spend management service platforms that serve as the hub for all spending processes and associated data. Figure 5.3 gives you a schematic of its structure: 1) the portal or interaction layer, 2) the composite process layer, 3) the integration layer, and 4) the enterprise application layer.

The spend management platform helps combine and coordinate the process modules in a number of ways to address particular business challenges. Unlike

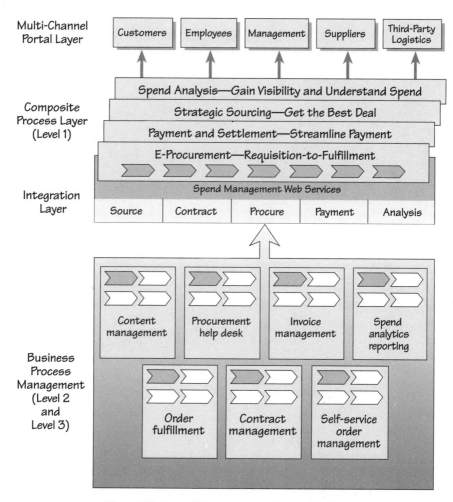

Figure 5.3: Spend Management Service Platform

most enterprise systems that automate important internal operations, the platform will automate both internal processes—such as smoothing out the paperbound process of procurement approvals and invoice matching—and reach beyond into supplier networks to create more high-value partnerships.

Finally, the spend management platform's objective is to provide complete integration within and between businesses by enabling processes to work together via the Internet. Total information sharing among processes means consistent data throughout organizations.

The Business Process Management Layer—Translating Services into Processes

Services, the subject of the previous subsection, are composed of various subprocesses—tasks and data resources. For instance, requisition-to-invoicing (Level 1) is composed of ten major subprocesses (Level 2). Each of these can be deconstructed into tasks (Level 3).

Most of the early digitization work examined automating individual subprocesses (Level 2). We have barely scratched that surface. There is a tremendous amount of subprocess design work left to be done in moving from paper-based purchasing to brick and click, let alone the next generation of brick, click, and mobile processes.[4]

Business analysts typically face a host of design challenges. The first is: What are the detailed Level 2 and Level 3 processes—subprocesses, tasks, workflows, and resources—that need to be digitized to support the Level 1 services?

Take the self-service requisitioning process (Level 2), which is typical of the online purchase of office supplies. The basic tasks that make up this type of requisitioning include logging in to the portal, searching a content catalog, selecting products from the catalog, creating a shopping basket, checking out, getting manager approval for the purchase, and forwarding the request to the purchasing department.

Or take the request for quote (RFQ) process (Level 2), which is characteristic when purchasing organizations search for new supply sources. The steps of the RFQ process are requesting a quotation, selecting the supplier subset, receiving bids from the suppliers, evaluating the bids, choosing a bid, informing the supplier of your decision, and, the final step, converting the bid to either an order or a contract, or conducting a reverse auction.

Companies have collectively spent billions of dollars digitizing these Level 2 and Level 3 tasks and delivering them via B2B portals. Most companies failed in their e-procurement initiatives because they were expecting that all the processes were going be 100 percent digitized. They got discouraged when they realized that only a fraction of the entire process was digital and that a significant part remained paper based. Business analysts must think very carefully about how to create information flows that are part digital and part paper.

Which brings us to the second process design challenge that business analysts face—no process is 100 percent digitized. So, how do we create hybrid procurement processes that are part online and part offline (or paper-and-click)? For example, you can order online, but the fulfillment is invariably offline. How should the online process fragment be connected effortlessly with the offline process fragment so that there is no need to enter data twice?

Consider the problem with payables in the United States, where most of the B2B invoicing, payment, and settlement is done offline. Despite tremendous advances in technology, the payment model, centered on paper checks, has not changed much. Thus, the digitized source-to-order online processes have to be interfaced with paper-based offline invoice and payment processes. These hybrid process designs are often the source of many bottlenecks. Maneuvering around this inefficiency is an interesting design challenge.

The hardest part remains: How should the subprocesses (Level 2 and Level 3) be embedded in a service platform? How should existing applications like ERP, marketplaces, and private hubs that have already digitized some of the Level 2 and Level 3 subprocesses be leveraged? The tremendous investment in enterprise applications has to be leveraged. It would be naïve even to think that companies are going to replace them anytime soon. That is exactly the reason a new services platform that sits on top of existing procurement applications is emerging.

Integrating Enterprise Applications—Mapping Processes into Applications

Most CIOs have had this question posed to them: Is it possible to create one unified spend management platform that covers the different types of spend and spans multiple business units and suppliers?

Enterprise applications have already begun implementing bits and pieces of procurement processes. For instance, most ERP platforms have a catalog of direct materials. To make it useful on the Internet, the process fragments housed in various back-office applications would have to be integrated into a bigger services picture.

Only a few years ago, integration meant little more than forging point-to-point software links between three or four basic business systems. Those days are gone. Integrating and linking with the various process fragments embedded in multiple internal ERP and enterprise applications and external supplier systems are going to keep consultants and programmers busy for the next several years.

Supplier integration remains one of the biggest unresolved issues in spend management. In many cases, the top 20 suppliers are easy to get on-board with the digitization effort. For a large corporation, it is the other thousand or so that pose the problem. These suppliers may be small, and they resist investing in technology in which they see limited value. If suppliers are not integrated into the service platform, it is hard to see how costs can be reduced over time. Understanding how to overcome the resistance of suppliers and get them to commit is more art than science. Companies that succeed at this will definitely be at a competitive advantage.

Mapping spend management process design into enterprise applications is nowhere near being done. From a business value perspective, we are quite far from where we need to be. E-procurement today revolves around fragmented Web portals, each implementing a unique set of processes. In order for organizations truly to embrace spend management, the process fragments behind the Web portals must integrate and connect with other process fragments, as well as with existing systems and applications.

As Figure 5.4 illustrates, with complexity mounting, companies are shifting their attention from individual ERP or e-procurement applications to the issue of integrating all the enterprise applications using a Services Oriented Architecture (SOA). Initially, e-procurement applications were considered the center of the spend management universe because of both the business functionality they offered and the built-in integration they promised. However, even if a firm successfully installed every module an e-procurement vendor sold, it would have covered only a small percentage of the business functionality needed to support services like requisition-to-fulfill. Thus, other bought-and-built applications will continue to be a fact of life. But eliminating the reliance on a single vendor strategy mean that firms need another approach—a service platform that encapsulates both business process management and enterprise application integration.

Spend Management Platforms—The Vendor's Perspective

In the previous section, we presented a top-down business approach to spend management by addressing three questions:

1. How do you take a high-level spend management strategy and translate it into end-to-end composite processes (for example, an order-to-cash process)?

2. In moving from service design to execution, what subprocesses do the overall end-to-end services translate into?

3. How do you go about combining existing, heterogeneous enterprise applications to support new cross-functional, end-to-end composite processes?

To meet the rigors of spend management, organizations now seek a more powerful, comprehensive, and process-driven approach to corporate procurement. A cadre of vendors realized that customer requirements are changing.

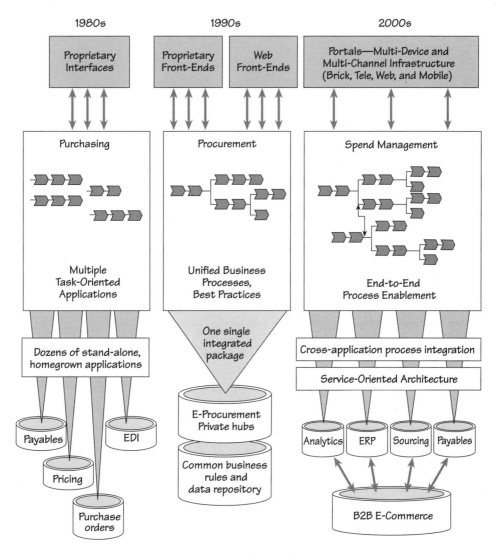

Figure 5.4: Service Integration as the Emerging Focus

Ariba, FreeMarkets, SAP, Oracle, PeopleSoft, and others are hurrying to offer these new spend management platforms.

Integrating various process fragments into meaningful services delivered via portals is precisely what these vendors are tackling. What are the core elements of the service platforms that they are selling? Figure 5.5 provides a bird's-eye view of the composite application building blocks of the spend management platform.

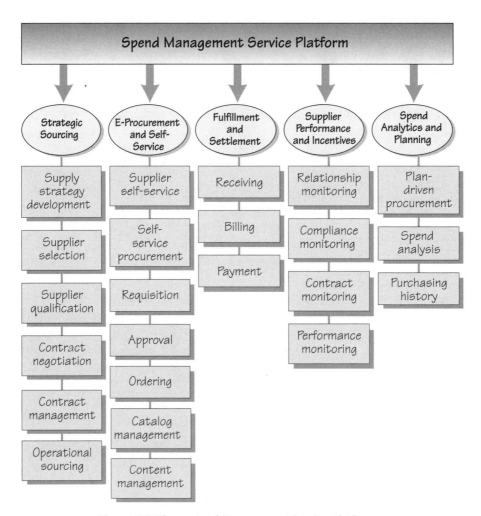

Figure 5.5: Elements of Procurement Service Platforms

Each of these building blocks can be combined in a number of ways to address particular challenges.

When you develop your spend management blueprint, you need to assess each of the modules closely so that you can evaluate whether the solution can lead your company toward its desired end result. All the modules have some capabilities in common: the capacity to harness information continuously from multiple underlying systems and the data model to assess it in the right context.

Fortunately, the techniques have caught up with the times, and new service platforms that might help take some of the cost, guesswork, and complexity out of this undertaking are emerging. Properly implemented, they can help companies save time and money and liberate them from tasks that don't add value.

Service Parts Procurement—An Emerging Service Platform

In a musty basement, a service technician attempts to repair a washer/dryer from the 1980s. It seems like a scene from the 1950s, but, in fact, it's still a large part of the twenty-first-century business of after-sales service.

After-sales service has been regarded as a secondary necessity, but hardly glamorous. This perception is changing. As executives turn from growth to cost control, they recognize that properly executed strategies for service management lead to value creation. Happy customers tend to be good customers.

Efficiently managing service assets, including parts, people, facilities, and equipment, has a direct impact on the bottom line. Take the manufacturing industry. Profit margins on most equipment sales aren't what they used to be. Service is the new competitive battleground, offering a new source of recurring, eye-catching revenues. Manufacturers in computers, consumer electronics, appliances, and even the auto industry generate profits by selling high-margin, multiyear service or warranty contracts on low-margin equipment.

The telecom industry takes service management very seriously. Competition and cost pressure have been intense as the industry rapidly evolves due to deregulation, ongoing consolidation, and technology convergence. As a result, telecom companies like Nokia, Nortel, and Lucent are being forced to do better after-sales service management. Lucent has concentrated on managing the outbound flow of service parts from its own facilities, contract manufacturers, and distributors to service parts depots for its $5 billion worldwide services division. Its challenge was to choreograph the movement of thousands of parts (sourced from multiple locations) that make up a given installation order with the arrival of service technician teams. The goal was to keep all the supply partners in sync to avoid costly inventory buildup and underutilized service technicians.

Third-party after-sales service providers are another case in point. In every industry, there are companies that provide equipment service under contract for manufacturers. For instance, Sears, Roebuck & Co. provides repair services to various appliance makers—Whirlpool, GE, Maytag, and Kenmore—through more than 80 product repair centers. The retailer's HomeCentral subsidiary is the world's largest appliance repair operation, with more than 13,000 technicians who make 11 million in-home repairs annually. These mobile technicians need Web-based solutions that let them interact closely with headquarters to order parts, as well as plan and deliver service. For third-party service operations like Sears that operate 24/7/365 on a global scale, efficiency and tight coordination are key ingredients of success.[5]

The aftermarket is an area where there is a lot of spend; thus, it's not surprising that spend management is focusing on aftermarket service parts sourcing and procurement. Before we look at the processes, let's examine the business drivers affecting service management.

Why Focus on Service Parts Management?

Several factors contribute to the intricate nature of field service management today: shorter product lifecycles, tighter service contract obligations, constrained resources, an increased cost of downtime, and high customer visibility.

Shorter Lifecycles and Obsolescence. Competition is increasing the rate of new product introduction and the proliferation of product configurations. As product lifecycles shrink, more older products need to be serviced, thereby increasing the amount of service knowledge and parts requirements. Furthermore, increasingly complex technology requires more specialized knowledge and experienced personnel to diagnose problems.

Service Contract Obligations. Often equipment uptime is vital to an organization's operations. Hence, it is more common for customers to demand stringent service level agreements (SLAs) before buying equipment. These agreements have explicit limits on response time to repair failures. The service organization must have the spare parts, technicians, and travel proximity needed to meet these agreements. Many SLAs include financial penalties for not meeting the performance specified.

Constrained Resources and Budgets. In today's economy, service organizations must supervise a variety of resources and budgets. Like all budgets, the service one is tight and has to be allocated to various resources (parts, people, facilities, and equipment) in a manner that optimizes service levels.

High Customer Visibility. Levels of service that were acceptable in the past are not any longer. Customers do not tolerate installation or repair backlogs of weeks. Even in areas like appliance repair, telephone installation, or regular maintenance, competition is making it more important to service the customer quickly and get the job done right the first time. If not, the customer will switch to another provider.

Defining the Business Problem

Equipment uptime is a key factor in determining customer satisfaction. Service parts availability and the ability to fix broken equipment rapidly can hit the bottom line. This is why companies are asking sourcing and procurement related questions like

- How can we get the right part to the right place at the right time? How can we create a service parts distribution network that reduces costs but still performs well?

- What kind of customer service targets should we expect if we increase our service parts inventory investment or improve procurement for a specific set of critical parts?

- What parts and what quantity should be carried in the field repair vehicles (warehouses on wheels) to increase the chances of solving the service problem on the first visit?

A significant part of after-sales service management is sourcing and procurement. By now, you are probably wondering why the techniques used for manufacturing procurement can't be used for service parts. There are a number of differences between manufacturing parts procurement and service parts procurement, the primary one being planning and forecasting. In a manufacturing environment, inventory planning, which drives procurement, is based on sales forecasts and orders. This is often called a plan-to-produce process.

Service parts, on the other hand, are stocked for unpredictable equipment failures. Orders you can plan for, but failures you cannot. You just have to react. So, a streamlined problem-to-resolution process is critical. Techniques that work for a plan-to-produce process don't necessarily work well for a problem-to-resolution process.

Another main difference: There is both good and bad inventory. As parts are replaced in the field, many are returned to be refurbished. That means not only can the same part move in and out of inventory several times, but a reverse logistics process must also be established so parts can be received from the field in a timely manner.

Yet another issue is parts inventory storage. While the location of manufacturing inventory is directed by the location of the manufacturing facility, service inventory has to be as widely dispersed as the customer base. Parts are kept in service vehicles, in depots, and at customer locations. Quantities are kept small and demand varies considerably. Depending on the industry, some of these parts can cost upwards of several hundred thousand dollars and may be used only once over several years.

Procurement as a Key Part of Service Management

There are three parts to the service parts management equation:

1   **Planning**—looks at what parts should be stocked in what quantity and where.

2.   **Sourcing**—addresses how a part that is not in stock can be procured and delivered (via FedEx or DHL) to the point of need. If the part is in stock, then sourcing is mainly a matter of replenishing the inventory.

3.   **Tracking**—deals with centralized inventory management (service warehouses and depots) and decentralized inventory management (customer location and service trucks) functionality to track usage and movement of spare and refurbished parts.

Fast and efficient sourcing is becoming important as companies are reducing inventory levels to cut the amount of capital tied up in assets. Another reason is to avoid "just-in-case" inventory. A computer company discovered its field engineers would order several parts if they weren't sure exactly what they needed, and frequently didn't return the excess parts to inventory. In cases where the wrong parts get shipped, it can take ten to 20 days to get a part returned from the field, which means additional inventory on hand to make up the difference.

Putting a mobile computer in the hands of field technicians can help by allowing them to log their own transactions and place parts orders, often in real time. If they have part-related questions on-site, they can browse catalogs via a search engine that can sift through an inventory of millions of parts with descriptions and images, and product, brand, or code numbers. Contrast this with the old process where many parts catalogs were heavy, bound volumes.

The mobile device is acting as the portal to the service management process. All the information service technicians need to estimate repair costs, order parts, fix appliances, bill customers, and process payments is available on the laptop connected to back-office applications via wireless networks. Typically, radio antennas hidden on the service van's roof connect it with a mobile data network. Also, when the service technician is making the repair, the laptop communicates with the van over a shorter-range wireless local area network (Wi-Fi).

Linking the mobile service technician to the back office allows the company to look into inventory buffers. This helps reduce common problems affecting spend management: hidden inventory from technicians stockpiling parts, duplicate inventory due to lack of visibility, and obsolete inventory that weakens the balance sheet. Organizations need better processes to monitor and track field procurement transactions and enforce control processes.

Service management is gaining the attention of service-oriented corporations around the world. Several vendors, such as Servigistics, Xelus, and SAP are now creating spend management platforms under the label of enterprise service management (ESM) for this market.

Seven Points to Ponder

> The mind once expanded to the dimensions of
> larger ideas never returns to its original size.
> —*Oliver Wendell Holmes*

Procurement, also known as business-to-business (B2B) commerce, has always been one of the fundamental activities of any business. In recent times, the technological foundation that supports procurement practices has changed drastically. Organizations are beginning to see procurement as a service, not an activity that solely consists of purchasing—ordering goods and services. This requires taking a holistic view to see where end-to-end services can be further digitized and how concrete cost savings can be delivered.

Spend management service platforms make this easier. The future looks bright and full of innovation for procurement. We leave you to mull over the following:

1. Procurement has undergone a digital makeover. While businesses have always had to purchase materials, they have not always possessed concrete methods to reduce their purchasing expenses. One viable method called spend management systematically aligns the processes, resources, and technology to control spending.

2. Harnessing spending is more than controlling costs—it's freeing up capital that can be returned to the core business to power new initiatives, invigorate existing lines of business, and increase profitability.

3. The biggest benefit from automating procurement processes is reducing hand-offs that result in costly errors.

4. In order to reduce errors, the procurement solution must include a user-friendly, secure system that links end users, approvers, and administrative personnel via an integrated service platform that connects buying organizations with suppliers.

5. The service platform has to sit on top of the organization's existing application investments by working with and connecting to multiple financial, human resource, and enterprise resource planning systems.

6. The system should provide data reporting and tools that enable analysis of end-user spending patterns and provide insight into savings opportunities.

7. Finally, instead of regarding spend management as a discrete set of applications, CFOs are beginning to view spend management as a portfolio of cross-enterprise processes that transcend specific, strategic business unit boundaries.

Organizations may not be able to control the greater economic environment in which they operate, but they certainly can control the money they spend. Managing what you spend regardless of the business climate is always a good idea. Spend management will be an area of focus for many years to come.

CHAPTER SIX

Supply Chain Blueprint: Creating an Adaptive Enterprise

What to Expect

Fluid and fast paced, that's the accurate description of today's supply chain. The volatile economy has compelled organizations to put their supply chains under the microscope to control costs further and to improve responsiveness to market demands. As a result, organizations are hastening to tweak their business processes to introduce innovation, flexibility, and advanced supply chain capabilities into the very fabric of their business models.

Supply chain management is the quintessential horizontal process, easily cutting across the boundaries of purchasing, manufacturing, transportation, inventory management, warehousing, and distribution. Streamlining this process continues to be one of the top areas where significant investments are being made. Many of these investments reflect the widespread belief that the next wave of productivity will come from optimizing the set of cross-company business processes that link enterprises to their customers and suppliers.

In this chapter, we explain the business problems and long-term trends shaping supply chain blueprints. To provide the reader with the necessary background, we also briefly illustrate the evolution of the technology behind supply chain management. We then delve into the design of supply chain blueprints (focal points + service platforms). The chapter ends with a best-practice case study—Eastman Chemical and their fourth-party logistics provider Cendian.

Introduction

Value chain management, e-fulfillment, adaptive networks, supply chain performance, event management, supply chain analytics, fulfillment optimization, distribution management, logistics and transportation management, 3PLs, and 4PLs—what do all these buzzwords have in common?

Each is part of the focal point of fast order fulfillment and service. Taking a sales order from a customer and delivering the finished product to that customer is the essence of business. Doing this faster, with fewer errors, and at a lower cost is the ongoing business challenge. The long-term trend is apparent: Disjointed supply chains are slowly being transformed into real-time integrated models that help companies manage demand variability and complexity and align their upstream strategies with distribution processes.

Why is this critical? In every industry, sales margins are shrinking due to competition. At the same time, manufacturing and order fulfillment are getting more complex. Competition is constantly forcing companies to streamline manufacturing and distribution efficiency while improving their flexibility and responsiveness to fluctuating market conditions.

Balancing production efficiency and business flexibility is difficult, especially when a company's supply chain spans multiple continents, tying suppliers in one part of the world with a plant in another to serve customers in a third location. In response, many organizations are reengineering and digitizing their supply chains to reduce manufacturing cycle times, switching from mass production to order-driven manufacturing, increasing their use of outsourcing, and sharing more information with suppliers and customers.

The retail industry is quite advanced in the race to digitize supply chains. Consider the case of Home Depot (HD), the home improvement retailer. HD is the second-largest retailer in the United States with over 1,300 stores. A typical HD store stocks approximately 40,000–50,000 items, including variations in color and size. Behind the scenes, HD buys its merchandise from more than 500 manufacturers in approximately 40 countries. More than 80 percent of that merchandise is shipped directly from the vendors to the individual stores. HD has seven import distribution centers and 29 lumber distribution facilities located in the United States and Canada. It also operates three transit facilities where merchandise is received from manufacturers and immediately cross-docked onto trucks for delivery to stores. HD's aggressive strategy of growth by acquisition and divestiture further complicates its supply chain operations. For instance, in

2001, HD sold its five stores in Chile to a former joint venture partner, Falabella. In 2002, it sold its four stores in Argentina. On the acquisition side, HD acquired TotalHOME and Del Norte in Mexico.

For HD, the tricky part in competing globally is delivering the right products to the right markets at the right time. With globalization, sourcing managers expand their search for the best value and are rewarded with attractive supply sources in nontraditional locations; the supply chain challenge is efficiently moving the product from remote locations to the point of consumption.

A huge opportunity to improve supply chain performance exists. Consider this: The high-tech supply chain—considered to be one of the most efficient in the world—still can do better. This supply chain (from component manufacturers to final assembly to retailers) holds, on average, 100 days of inventory—a $100 billion buffer to avoid stockouts. Despite this, 10 percent of the time a retail store will not have the product the shopper wants. It takes an average of 40–50 days to send a demand signal to a manufacturer or a supply signal to a retailer. Obviously there's considerable room for improvement.[1]

Digitizing the supply chain is a business priority that even economists are noticing. In his testimony to U.S. Congress, Federal Reserve Chairman Alan Greenspan said, "New technologies for supply chain management and flexible manufacturing can perceive imbalances in inventories at a very early stage—virtually in real time—and can cut production promptly in response to the developing signs of unintended inventory building."[2]

The stakes are high. While the majority of firms are still trying to understand how to digitize simple supply chain processes (order entry, EDI integration), a small set of first movers such as Eastman Chemical and Intel are racing to digitize and integrate multiple composite processes (demand-to-fulfillment, build-to-order) to deliver even higher levels of performance. The other firms, whether they are ready or not, have to react to the challenge posed by the leaders in their respective industries.

Evolution of Supply Chain Management

In the mid-1980s, a company often referred to as a supply chain innovator was Benetton. Started by Luciano Benetton and his sister Giuliana, Benetton became Europe's largest clothing producer. Its success stemmed from its ability to transform the clothing business into a well-lubricated supply chain. The three elements of Benetton's strategy were 1) computer-aided design in styling and

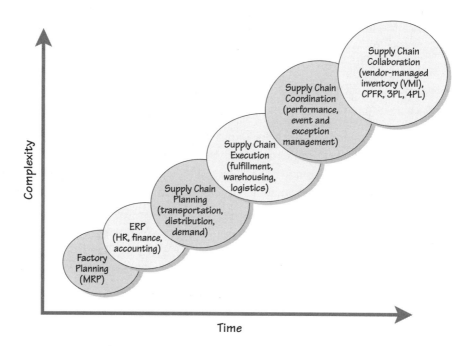

Figure 6.1: Evolution of Supply Chain Management

pattern cutting, 2) a sophisticated international information system that linked its 4,000 stores, and 3) its automated warehouse.

Supply chain management (SCM) has evolved steadily since the pioneering efforts of Benetton. As Figure 6.1 illustrates, SCM now encompasses the planning and scheduling of manufacturing and related logistics, from raw materials procurement through work-in-process to finished goods distribution (which includes direct-to-customer delivery). SCM's composite business processes cover buying, making, moving, storing, and selling the product.

SCM has matured from its initial roots in factory planning, which used a technique called manufacturing resource planning (MRP). MRP systems calculate production schedules by working backwards from an order due date, utilizing fixed production and supplier lead times. Early MRP products were proprietary systems and often required extensive customization to support diverse manufacturing processes. MRP's methodology and architecture did not permit companies to accommodate rapidly changing business conditions and customer requirements.

Technological changes—client/server architectures and relational databases—prompted the evolution from first-generation MRP systems to second-generation MRP systems. While offering significant performance improvements and increased flexibility, these systems still had similar underlying data structures, methodologies, and application logic and, therefore, many of the same limitations as their MRP forebears. Much of MRP's design was also applied to distribution resource planning (DRP) systems, which focused on the transportation and distribution of finished goods.

In the early 1990s, several software vendors (for example, SAP and Baan) developed enterprise resource planning (ERP) systems, which combined MRP and DRP solutions with other enterprise management applications such as financial, accounting, and human resources. Although ERP systems provide substantial benefits by integrating a broad array of business functions, the supply chain decision support capabilities of ERP systems are still plagued by the limiting planning and scheduling methodologies utilized in their MRP and DRP modules.

In the mid-1990s, software vendors, such as i2 Technologies and Manugistics, approached supply chain management from a new direction and addressed many of the limitations inherent in traditional ERP systems. This approach enabled businesses to plan and schedule the principal elements of the supply chain by simultaneously considering internal constraints—manufacturing facility capacities and human resource availability—and external constraints—supplier lead times and customer requirements. The initial focus was on production planning functions such as raw materials procurement, capacity planning, and shop floor scheduling. The later emphasis was on distribution and transportation logistics planning.

It dawned on companies that they could be great at planning but not very effective at execution. In the mid-1990s, parallel to the growth in supply chain planning, a new breed of software vendors (Manhattan Associates and EXE Technologies) began specializing in supply chain execution, particularly warehouse management systems (WMS). They sought to manage complicated fulfillment and distribution challenges better by providing the ability to control all activities within a warehouse. Industries such as retail, automotive, consumer packaged goods, electronics, grocery, wholesale distribution industries, and third-party logistics (3PL) were initial targets for execution solutions.

With planning and execution capabilities in place, the more advanced companies are moving to solve the problem of coordinating the multi-party supply chain. This has resulted in several new areas under the umbrella of supply chain event management (SCEM). SCEM bridges the current chasm between supply chain planning and execution by gathering the real-time visibility of expected and unexpected events taking place in the supply chain and adjusting accordingly. For instance, there is a container shortage in Los Angeles. Detecting this event, the SCEM application adjusts the transportation schedules. This is an adaptive supply chain.

Today, planning, execution, and coordination form the foundation of the larger SCM platform. The goal is to improve the end-to-end business processes. The market agrees, as is evident in the shifting focus toward collaborative process design.

Take the collaborative planning, forecasting, and replenishment (CPFR) initiative that the retail industry is driving. CPFR is a concept that allows collaborative processes linking manufacturers, retailers, and carriers across the supply chain, using a set of process and technology models for dynamic information sharing. CPFR lets the suppliers manage the inventory on the store shelf; for example, Frito-Lay manages the potato chip shelves in a Kroger supermarket.

This is markedly different from the traditional approach to replenishment where if a stockout occurred, the buyer (Kroger) would place an order with the supplier (Frito-Lay). In this scenario, the supplier received no advance warning of demand fluctuations from the buyers; thus, they had limited flexibility to adjust their production plan. The buyer would also carry safety stock of the same items to safeguard against the possibility of no available supplies. The results of this conventional approach were higher levels of inventory in the chain and lower levels of customer service and responsiveness.

Through CPFR, the seller (Frito-Lay) can provide value-added services by performing replenishment planning tasks for buyers. By increasing visibility into actual consumer demands, inventory consumption, and sellers' stock levels, CPFR allows sellers to make better decisions on how to deploy goods across various buyers, which leads to better customer service levels, reduced inventory levels, fewer stockout situations, and lower sales cost. Automated processes allow both parties to benefit from reduced cycle time and lower overhead.

Where are we today? The supply chain software market is consolidating around service platforms capable of integrating multi-application, multi-firm business processes. Companies are differentiating themselves with process innovation and management, not software capabilities. Let's study a few trends that are shaping market dynamics.

Trends in Supply Chain Management

In this section, we will look at the trends collectively, necessitating the transition from traditional demand planning to more comprehensive supply chain service platforms.

Low-Cost Manufacturing—Outsourcing

Companies making anything from cars to tools to food products are asking themselves: Do we need to make this ourselves? Why not outsource?

First spawned by apparel makers that needed to keep costs low and later honed by computer manufacturers that wanted to cut the time it took to bring products to market, outsourcing is going mainstream. The benefits of outsourcing are 1) lowered costs, 2) conserved capital, 3) accelerated time to market and time to volume, and 4) more flexibility.

In the electronics industry, original equipment manufacturers (OEMs) are outsourcing more of their production functions to electronic manufacturing services (EMS) companies. The OEM, or integrator, is typically responsible for only the design and end assembly of the asset. EMS providers such as Flextronics, Celestica, and Solectron are responsible for reducing costs by relocating plants to lower-cost locales, such as China; using industrial park manufacturing where everything is centrally collocated; and emphasizing full-cycle services (design engineering, services, and repairs).

In the personal computer and peripheral sector, outsourcing is widely practiced. It is often said that every supply chain in the PC business goes through Taiwan, where orders for all the big IT brands have been quietly getting filled. With competitive prices and high quality, Taiwan has become the world's largest producer of notebook computers, motherboards, scanners, modems, mice, monitors, and keyboards. Everyone from Nokia, IBM, Hewlett Packard (HP), Dell, and Apple to major Japanese manufacturers rely on the value that Taiwan's EMSs are offering.

Automakers, too, are building less of their products. In Brazil, Volkswagen invited suppliers to collocate their operations within its bus-and-truck plant south of Rio de Janeiro. Inside Volkswagen's walls, suppliers finish parts and assemble modules on production lines. DaimlerChrysler and Ford Motor have adopted similar models in the search for new, low-cost manufacturing options.

Outsourcing is changing the structure of the manufacturing supply chain. The manufacturing chain has evolved from a vertically integrated supply chain to a multi-tier, multi-company environment in which each tier is heavily dependent on the plans of the earlier tiers. Outsourcing is a big cause of this change.

> The bottom line: Outsourced manufacturing demands superb coordination running on real-time information. Outsourcing without electronic linkages is no longer an option. Poor communication and coordination inevitably will result in supply chain glitches.

Matching Supply and Demand in a Volatile Environment

Internet order submission is a high-priority opportunity for many companies. Ideally, they would like to use the Web to improve shared supply chain processes, reinforce distributor relations, eliminate manual processing, and support a growth strategy. Many companies are also hurrying to implement aggressive plans to automate customer order entry and offer self-service order management to align supply with demand better.

Two major supply-demand match problems face most companies:

1. Lost sales due to mismatched demand and supply. For instance, you are making white shirts when the market wants blue shirts. The resulting situation: a blue shirt stockout.

2. Retained inventory due to supply chain uncertainty and process inefficiencies. You are holding 10,000 components at $100 each, when the market suddenly switches to new technology with a price point of $50 each.

Product stockouts in the retail industry occur at an average rate of 8.2 percent and represent 6.5 percent of all retail sales.[3] Nearly half of the stockouts lead to forfeited sales. Other intended purchases at the time of the customer visit may also disappear. All this translates into the loss of significant margin, not to mention a possible increase in marketing expenses for winning back disenchanted customers.

The ready answer for stockouts has been to increase inventories. If inventory is in the pipeline, including the stores, then consumers never have to deal with products being out of stock. Unfortunately, inventory is cost-prohibitive in terms of capital consumption and expense. The total inventory across retail is worth nearly $1 trillion, whereas sales are $3 trillion.[4]

Uncertain demand causes high inventory levels. The more unpredictable demand is, the more inventory is required to manage the risk. In addition, the further away from the consumer an inventory buffer is in the value chain process, the more demand variability that inventory buffer will have to address. This phenomenon is known as the bullwhip effect; it is created by the lack of coordination of downstream demand information with supply processes back through the supply chain.

> The bottom line: In reality, inventory hides inefficiencies in processes and generates unnecessary storage and increased handling of products. Within stores, too much inventory of the wrong products affects sales productivity and new assortment opportunities. Inventory-congested supply chains can even slow the time to market for new products.

Collaboration—Maximizing Utilization of Assets

Leading organizations are employing collaborative approaches to reduce their costs. Sometimes this means sharing assets (manufacturing plants, warehouse and transportation capacity, and equipment) with other companies.

Logistics management is a popular collaborative approach. Companies' supply chains usually comprise geographically dispersed facilities where products are acquired, transformed, stored, or sold. Logistics connects these facilities and ensures that products flow smoothly. Typically logistics accounts for 10–14 percent of a product's cost, so reducing this cost is a strategic priority. Logistics, historically managed internally, is now being farmed out to third-party logistics providers, or 3PLs, to cut costs and increase flexibility.

Companies select 3PLs because they have improved negotiating leverage, better tracking and tracing skills, capital for investment in logistics assets and state-of-the-art technologies, expert staff, and well-designed and executed processes. However, although outsourcing to 3PLs often provides solid, one-time cost reductions, it does not deliver the ongoing savings that businesses desire.

Today, 3PLs supply transaction execution services formerly offered by inhouse shipping and transportation departments. The trend is for 3PL providers to become more involved in planning, optimization, and process management. Large companies with multiple business units accordingly have multiple 3PL providers. The multiple 3PLs of one company can be managed by yet another party—a lead logistics manager, or 4PL. These 4PLs represent the next significant evolution in supply chain collaboration.

Why 4PLs? Consider the problems that 4PLs like Nistevo are solving. Transportation is a vast industry riddled by inefficiencies, including an estimated

$30 billion wasted each year by empty trucks. General Mills, a large producer of packaged consumer foods, has a problem that vexes most companies that ship goods: trucks that are empty on the return trip. Drivers carrying loads of Betty Crocker cake mixes, Cheerios, or Yoplait yogurt were hauling an empty trailer on one leg of the trip as often as 15 percent of the time.

In an attempt to save money by better utilizing empty trucks, General Mills collaborated with other manufacturers, such as paper products maker Fort James, to use a 4PL to find empty trucks. Say General Mills has a truckload of Wheaties to send to Atlanta, Georgia, but no load to fill the truck as it returns to its Minneapolis, Minnesota plant. The 4PL software scans the other companies' shipping schedules and finds that Fort James has a load of Brawny paper towels that needs to go from Atlanta to St. Paul. The software alerts both companies, as well as the carrier. General Mills and Fort James pay less per mile, and the carrier does not have to find a backhaul. Everybody wins. The result: transportation costs are reduced by up to 10–15 percent.[5]

A 3PL allows companies to take assets off the books and obtain a better return, but 4PLs coordinate the entire supply chain and provide additional savings. A 4PL is a supply chain integrator that assembles and manages the resources, capabilities, and technology to deliver a comprehensive supply chain solution. Taking a best-of-breed approach, 4PLs leverage the capabilities of 3PLs, technology service providers, and business process managers to provide greater cross-functional integration and broader operational flexibility.

> The bottom line: Companies are realizing that sharing transportation capacity saves serious money. This simple solution is only just emerging due to 4PLs. What does this trend mean for supply chain applications? Demand for new platforms that allow real-time information sharing to match requirements with effectively positioned assets and excess capacity is growing.

New Forms of Differentiation—Reverse Logistics

You buy a pair of jeans online. They are delivered to your doorstep after a week, but by then you don't want them anymore. You walk into the store and return them. The money is credited to your account, and you go on your way.

Do you ever wonder what happens to products after they are returned? Today, given the ease of online purchasing and flexible return policies, people are more inclined to exchange impulse purchases. Product returns, remanufacturing, and recyclables are becoming critical to the overall business model of many companies. In fact, the value of products returned by U.S. consumers to the nation's retailers each year exceeds $100 billion.[6]

Product returns are merchandise that is sent back due to consumer returns, damage, seasonal inventory, restock, salvage, recalls, and excess inventory. Product return is more consequential in some industries. For instance, book publishers have their books returned by distributors or retailers 20–30 percent of the time. Direct or catalog retailers face even higher rates. It is not unusual for a direct retailer to have return rates of more than 35 percent.

The process of moving returned goods from their current destination to their originating company for the purpose of capturing value, or proper disposal, is known as reverse logistics. For many industries, managing the reverse flow is critically important. Within specific industries, where the product is high-value, margins are low, or where the return rate is greatest, reverse logistics activities can make or break a company.

Consider the auto parts industry, where the remanufacturing and refurbishing activities around certain returned parts are substantial. The remanufactured auto parts market is enormous. It is estimated that 90–95 percent of all starters and alternators sold for replacement are remanufactured. There are nearly 12,000 automobile dismantlers and remanufacturers operating in the United States alone.[7]

> The bottom line: With today's competitive pressures, efficient reverse logistics are important to a firm's overall profitability. Most return processes are paper-intensive and span boundaries between firms or business units of the same company. Digitizing the returns process end-to-end is becoming a priority.

Adaptive Supply Chains—Monitor, Alert, and Act

Two problems confront all supply chain organizations: a lack of visibility into how supply chain operations are actually being executed, and an inability to identify and respond to operational issues that cause plan deviations before they hit the bottom line.

Forward-thinking companies are resorting to closely monitoring the performance of their supply chains, detecting problems (such as orders that are at risk of shipping late or inventory that is about to run out), alerting all relevant participants in the supply chain community, and collaboratively resolving the issues before they result in excess cost or lost revenues.

Consider Seagate Technology, a manufacturer of disc drives. To maintain certain service level agreements (SLAs) with customers, Seagate must balance on-time delivery expectations with optimum inventory levels. Complicating this alignment is Seagate's own distributed application architecture, in which each region maintains its own order management and inventory systems.

To get visibility into each region, Seagate invested in a supply chain event management (SCEM) application from Vigilance. This SCEM application detects orders at risk of not shipping on time by applying the following business rules: orders that cannot be shipped by the customer request date, orders on hold for more than a certain amount of days, and orders that are missing data in order to ship correctly.

If the SCEM application detects these events, it immediately notifies the responsible manager via e-mail for corrective actions. This alert links them to a common, Web-based exception desk for further action. Here managers assess, assign, track, and collaborate to resolve the event quickly. If the event goes unresolved, the SCEM application automatically escalates until the event is resolved. The monitor, alert, and act capabilities of SCEM applications have made it one of the fastest growing segments in supply chain digitization.

Clearly, companies need real-time visibility, as well as the ability to readjust rapidly. They want to 1) monitor performance across the supply chain through preset business rules, 2) be alerted of operational issues in real time, and 3) act on critical operational problems through Web-based collaboration and closed-loop control.

> The bottom line: Companies need to shorten their response time to business events that affect performance. The speed at which companies can deal with exceptions—a sudden stockout of a critical part or weather conditions that delay a shipment to a key customer—will determine who wins the race.

Supply Chain Blueprint

Observing these trends, companies cannot help but ask themselves new and difficult questions: How can we create an adaptive and flexible supply chain model that changes with the business? How can we form a process layer that can deliver high levels of service at reduced costs? How can we lower the risk associated with process change by utilizing integration?

Moving from an integrated supply chain vision to a blueprint that delivers results is a multi-year journey. Look at Nike, a leading apparel and footwear maker. In fall 1999, Nike was ready to spend $400 million to streamline its supply chain and further automate the way it produces, ships, and sells shoes. It seemed like a no-brainer.

Instead of taking a month to plan and start producing a new line of sneakers, a new supply chain system "promised" to narrow that window to a week. By better matching supply with demand, the company thought it could avoid being stuck with warehouses full of shoes that were going out of style, while boosting sales of the trendier pairs that everyone wanted.

Translating the vision to reality hasn't worked out exactly according to plan. In early 2001, Nike announced that it expected its earnings to fall by one-third, to about $0.35 per share, dramatically lower than the earlier projections of $0.53 per share. The culprit? The new supply chain software, which executives blamed for causing factories to crank out too many unpopular models. To offset shipping delays for hot-selling shoes, Nike shipped them by plane at $4–$8 a pair, compared with about $0.75 by boat. In the meantime, unhappy retailers like Foot Locker had to discount heavily to sell the less-popular styles.[8]

During a conference call with analysts, Nike CEO Philip Knight said, "This is not a particularly fun hour for me. I guess my immediate reaction is, 'This is what we get for $400 million?'"[9] Knight went on to say that it could take up to nine months to overcome the supply glitch. Other footwear firms took advantage of Nike's problems and began to steal market share. Its predicament is an expensive example of an increasingly common problem when complex technology is adopted too quickly and too widely.

Where Are We Today?

Despite the constant reminder to think of supply chains as a process enabler and integrator, the dominant thinking in SCM wrongly centers on discrete applications—planning, execution, and coordination. Due to the fragmented nature of technology execution, the supply chain is not a smooth chain, but more like a bunch of links that might or might not connect. Participants in the supply chain process are frequently separated from each other and, more important, from the consumer, with less-than-optimal results to show for it.

As you might expect, fragmented execution is not delivering the expected results. Some companies have achieved significant results while others have not, primarily because of poor information, disconnected systems, and the miserable lack of collaboration. Poorly integrated supply chains are a big problem and are on the radar screen of almost every company.

Data integration, while useful, is insufficient. Process integration, its finicky relative, needs to be addressed for major improvement. For instance, delivering "Every Day Low Price" is extremely difficult if some participants in the chain are not efficient. It's comparable to team sports: Unless everyone on the team is synchronized, it's difficult to perform well. So, the emerging challenge for executives is: How does your company get every trading partner in harmony? What is the process for making this happen?

The answer to these questions lies in the creation of a supply chain blueprint. As we have explained, every blueprint can be segmented into four layers: the strategy, services, process, and applications layers (see Figure 6.2).

1. The strategy layer defines the supply chain focal point and provides the framework for defining the operating targets.

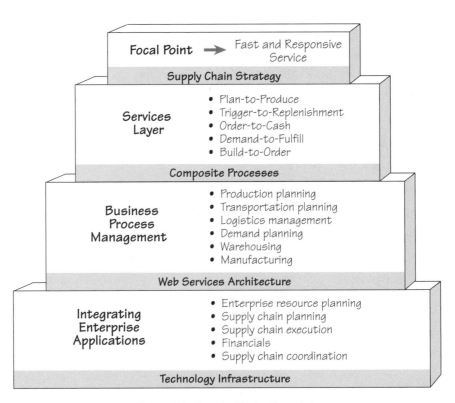

Figure 6.2: Supply Chain Blueprint

2. The business services layer provides the execution framework. Think of this as a composite process layer that supports the operating model. It determines which processes are going be digitized to deliver against the operating targets.

3. The business process management layer identifies the individual processes that combine to form the composite processes in the previous step and then digitizes those processes in a controlled application to support the service strategy.

4. The applications layer is the foundation and infrastructure behind various processes, or the technology plumbing and wiring that links the systems, databases, and applications.

Let's look at each one of these layers in more detail.

Supply Chain Focal Point—Fast Service

Every SCM blueprint must begin with a laser-sharp focus on the business rationale and the drivers of value. This helps everyone understand the "why" of the undertaking. It also provides guiding principles for management. Furthermore, it greatly helps to prioritize activities, particularly when management and partners temporarily lose sight of the forest for the trees, which sometimes happens in multi-year projects.

The U.S. Department of Defense (DoD) is attempting one of the largest supply chain digitization efforts. Defense logistics is very large, costly, and inefficient: more than $80 billion in yearly operating expenses, almost one million government personnel involved, over 1,000 different information systems, and almost $60 billion in inventory.

In addition, the DoD's focal point has shifted. The DoD developed and perfected the "mass" logistics model of the twentieth century to deter and defeat cold war forces engaged across well-defined battle lines. This model, conceived during a period of relatively slow and expensive transportation and paper-based information, features several echelons of inventory and maintenance to enable timely response to the warfighter needs of forward deployed forces.

The priorities have changed. The threats of the twenty-first century are creating a vastly different battleground than previously encountered; highly mobile, dispersed forces will engage throughout an area of operation. To support needs for rapid mobilization and sustainment, the DoD is transforming its mass logistics system to a highly agile system that delivers logistics "on demand." A key element of this transformation is replacing the multi-echelon infrastructure with rapid, accurate logistics and information.

Given the size of the problem, a series of projects is being launched to change the supply chain. One is happening within the U.S. Marine Corps, which is in the midst of digitizing its supply chain to move from a "mass fighter" model to a more agile model where military missions, objectives, and frequencies change. The customer of the supply chain is the warfighter and, ultimately, the joint commanders, who want capability—not complex, unwieldy supply lines. The goal is a revision of how marines get food, ammunition, and support matériel like mail.[10]

To understand the focal point better, we recommend using a technique called strategy maps. The supply chain strategy map, shown in Figure 6.3, defines how

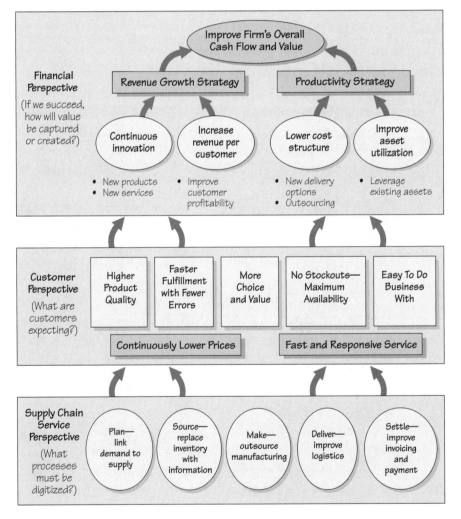

Figure 6.3: Supply Chain Strategy Map

supply chain objectives and processes link to enable overall corporate performance. The other component of this undertaking is getting the timeline right, both in the near term for tactical reasons and in the long term so that commitment can be maintained when the going invariably gets tough.

> The bottom line: When developing a supply chain focal point, it is important to state the revenues, costs, investments, and profits expected from supply chain digitization. Fuzzy supply chain objectives—increased sales, organizational streamlining and alignment, administrative and operational efficiency, improved cash flow, and improved return-on-assets performance—must be carefully defined and linked to overall corporate performance.

The Supply Chain Services Layer—Enabling Composite Processes

What services are needed to support a focal point? Once business targets are set, the task of defining what services or composite processes need to be improved to achieve those targets begins.

We list the composite processes involved in supply chain digitization in Table 6.1. These services are combinations of plan, source, make, deliver, and settle—the core activities of supply chains. The services perspective helps to eliminate functional stovepipes and replace them with processes that focus on creating value for customers. The integration is then extended to suppliers and customers to create a fully integrated supply chain.

Who is the best at supply chain service design? The retail industry. Its early efforts were practiced under the umbrella of vendor-managed inventory (VMI). More recently, collaborative planning, forecasting, and replenishment (CPFR) is gaining momentum as the next version of VMI. CPFR takes a holistic approach to supply chain management among a network of trading partners. Similar trends to integrate the order-to-cash process (planning, execution, and critical monitoring of the value chain) tightly are under way in other industries.

Inventory is a major cost factor; everyone wants to fulfill customer demand quickly while minimizing inventory. Consider the case of NEC Solutions, a subsidiary of Japan-based NEC Corp. To ward off competition from Dell Computer and attain a better supply-demand match, NEC Solutions is working feverishly to increase visibility and streamline the flow of information among sales, parts procurement offices, overseas production facilities, and distribution systems.

Table 6.1: Composite Processes in Supply Chains

Composite Processes	Definition
Plan-to-Produce	Involves planning, sourcing, producing, warehousing, and coordination
Trigger-to-Replenishment	Involves low-stock level trigger, replenishment order to warehouse, picking, 3PL delivery logistics, and financial settlement
Order-to-Cash	Involves managing orders, picking, shipping, invoicing, returns, and financial settlement
Demand-to-Fulfill	Involves creating a sales forecast, sending forecast to contract manufacturer, sourcing, producing, 3PL warehousing, and coordination
Build-to-Order (Order of one)	Involves product configuration, checking availability, collecting payment, engaging suppliers for product, merging products, direct delivery product to customer, and returns

NEC has developed a supply chain service platform using technology from i2 Technologies. This service platform enables the digitization of several composite processes. One of NEC's objectives is to forecast sales accurately while ensuring that demand changes are immediately incorporated into production planning. For instance, if the demand for a certain configuration goes up, then production is able to adjust quickly to the demand spike. Because of better integration, NEC claims that the lead time between preparation of production plans based on sales figures and actual production and shipping has been shortened from ten to four days.[11]

The retail and high-tech industries are well aware that they are competing in a low-margin market with price deflation (the value of the PC drops 5–7 percent every month).[12] As a result, the supply chain becomes the differentiator. The market leaders in these industries are racing to create proprietary supply chain blueprints (focal points + service platforms).

Figure 6.4 illustrates the structure of a supply chain service platform. The platform is made up of what are considered strategic processes at the corporate level (need-to-have processes for supporting the operating plan). The figure also

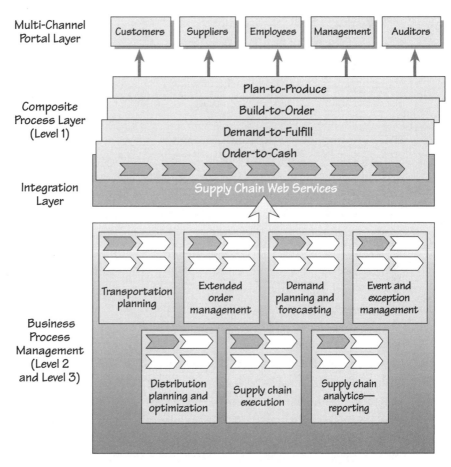

Figure 6.4: Architecture for a Supply Chain Service Platform

illustrates how the strategic processes are based on a set of smaller functional processes (typically called the business process management layer).

> The bottom line: The retail and high-tech supply chains have highlighted the need to view value creation as a set of services with inputs from suppliers and outputs to customers. This is the essence of the service layer—how to create and capture value from disjointed processes. These services have to work within the existing enterprise systems to create a "single version of the truth," leveraging rather than recreating functionality.

The Business Process Management Layer— Translating Services into Processes

What is the current state of process management in supply chains? After a lot of work, we are finally at a point where many companies have at least digitized basic processes. Taking an order on a Web site is no longer worthy of a press release. It has become an integral part of the supply chain toolkit. This is a very important step as it allows the composition of complex services from more simple process fragments. (This is similar conceptually to being able to build cars from modular assemblies.)

How does this work? Let's say the corporate objective is to create a set of services that enables faster fulfillment of customer demand. This can be subdivided into three Level 2 processes: streamline customer requests and orders, plan and manage material flow, and coordinate delivery. These Level 2 processes further consist of Level 3 processes. Some of the core Level 3 processes include managing orders, forecasting demand, and directing the transport network. This exercise sounds deceptively simple.

To understand this process decomposition better, consider build-to-order (BTO) service in the PC business. The BTO service (Level 1) is an end-to-end collection of processes commonly used to make products according to the unique specifications of the customer. The first step of the BTO service is a customer order (Level 2) that triggers the manufacturing planning process (Level 2). Manufacturing planning for PCs is made on the level of specific assemblies and components. In fact, highly accurate demand planning on the assembly level (Level 3) is very important to reduce the delivery time. It is possible in this (Level 3) process to plan for all the components for individual customer requirements. There is a constant link between the sales order and the production order. This leads to tracking the progress of the customer order.

The task of process decomposition and aggregation is a complex undertaking. People tend to trivialize the need for process management. This is where initiatives often run into problems. Actually, process management is becoming a field unto itself under the umbrella of supply chain process management (SCPM). SCPM builds off much of the work done around process design and improvement in Six Sigma and quality management. SCPM has five well-defined steps although implementation varies by organization. They are

1. **Process Clarity**—defining service activities as a series of related core processes and critical subprocesses;

2. **Process Mapping**—diagramming all current flows of information, as well as value and service expectations;

3. **Data Collection**—tracking and analyzing the performance of a subprocess with strong reliance on measurement and hard data;

4. **Process Analysis**—redesigning a process to improve performance; and

5. **Continual Improvement**—utilizing a methodology to document, standardize, and improve processes.

Organizations tend to do these steps with different levels of sophistication. It might be time to ask: How sophisticated is my process management capability? At which of the following stages are you?

- **Stage 1** could be characterized as ad hoc and even chaotic. Few supply chain processes are defined, and success depends on individual effort.

- **Stage 2** is when the basic processes are well-defined. The necessary supply chain process discipline is in place to repeat earlier successes on projects with similar applications.

- **Stage 3** is when many basic tasks are already digitized in the form of supply chain applications, and effort is being expended to make them reusable. The integration process is documented and standardized for the organization.

- **Stage 4** occurs when new supply chains can be constructed quickly. If there is an acquisition, you don't have problems integrating their process into yours. You are able to create new business value by designing innovative supply chains.

The bottom line: Everyone talks about the importance of supply chain processes, but few, other than manufacturers, have a good idea of all the different processes that constitute a complex supply chain. As a result, many critical supply chain digitization decisions are based on hunches and few facts. This invariably causes problems during implementation.

Integrating Enterprise Applications— Mapping Processes into Applications

Supply chain executives are asking CIOs: Is it possible to create one unified supply chain platform that covers the different types of applications and spans multiple business units and suppliers?

Conceptually, integrated supply chains may not seem like a big deal, but implementing one is anything but easy. Why is integration within a company time-consuming and costly? Largely because current versions of enterprise applications, like Web-based order entry and self-service order management, access one business application at a time, making it difficult to link the activities relating to a specific supply chain process that sits on all the applications. This is a widespread business problem.

Stovepiped applications that support isolated process capabilities are contrary to a company's need to link business processes. The disconnected applications interrupt the flow of information and force hand-offs among different systems, technologies, and data models. As a result, creating a business process that can support the information flow from order to payment is very challenging.

Most of the discussion about integrated supply chains in the late 1990s might have been a little premature since the foundation applications (planning, scheduling, and execution) were not developed enough. Imagine trying to build a tall building on a shaky foundation. The engineers were telling you that it couldn't be done, but management was insisting that it must. No wonder the first-generation supply chain projects did not work as planned.

Both the integration problems and application maturity issues are being resolved. Planning and forecasting have greatly improved over the last decade. The tools used to analyze data and generate forecasts also have gotten better as computing power became cheaper, as have data integration and quality. At the same time, the business world better comprehends the importance of supply chain integration. All of these factors will tremendously boost the popularity of supply chain service platforms and integration projects worldwide.

SCM Service Platforms—The Vendor's Perspective

The transition from function-centric, supply chain management models (planning, execution) to process-centric (order-to-cash) is clearly happening. Companies are demanding that SCM applications become more than stand-alone planning, execution, and coordination tools and offer better end-to-end integration internally and externally to other software, such as CRM.

A cadre of vendors realizes that customer requirements in SCM are leaning toward service platforms. The marketplace is pleading with them to stop selling products and start selling solutions, but many vendors are not ready. As a result, it looks as though the gap is growing between what customers want and what vendors are selling (see Figure 6.5).

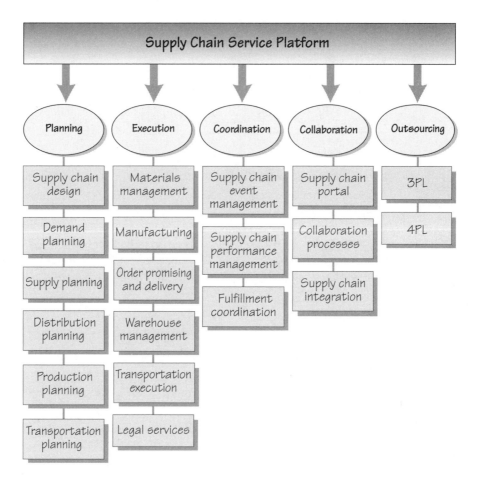

Figure 6.5: Features and Functions in SCM

A cursory examination shows that most SCM vendors—i2 Technologies, Manugistics, SAP, PeopleSoft, Oracle, and J.D. Edwards—are offering the following functionality:

- **Demand Management**—allows companies to work with their key customers to monitor and manage demand, replacing inventory with information.

- **Supply Management**—enables a company to work with suppliers to plan production, purchasing, and transportation across the value chain by taking into account capacity and material constraints of the company and its suppliers.

- **Collaboration and Inventory Visibility**— lets companies more accurately gauge inventory for better planning. It also aligns an organization's planning and execution processes with its trading partners.

- **Transportation, Distribution, and Logistics**—provides a complete solution for planning, execution, and monitoring. It allows companies to analyze what-if scenarios, monitor the status of shipments, and decide and replan as changes occur.

- **Factory Planning and Scheduling**—analyzes cost, profit, and service trade-offs for production and generates an optimized plan for plant, department, or production facility.

To integrate the various functional pieces, companies often have to turn to another set of vendors—WebMethods, Seebeyond, Tibco, Vitria, or Mercator—who are offering various enterprise application integration (EAI) toolsets. At the same time, there is yet another group of vendors—Vigilance, Evantra—offering supply chain event management (SCEM) toolsets. Overall, the situation in SCM is chaotic and confusing for managers. Taking advantage of this chaos are some enterprising Old Economy companies, such as Eastman Chemical, that are filling the gap with industry-specific service platforms.

Eastman is enjoying success because many SCM, EAI, and SCEM vendors are losing sight of the customer's perspective. You can have the most leading-edge technology available, but if it's not easy for organizations to integrate and create economic value, chances are they won't stay with you for long.

Eastman Chemical—Creating a Logistics Service Platform

In the last few years, Eastman Chemical has built an excellent reputation as an industry forerunner in digitization, using it to differentiate itself in a maturing industry and generate incremental revenues. Technology has been a critical component for Eastman. As Roger Mowen, senior vice president of developing businesses and corporate strategy, stated, "You can hardly think about incremental process improvement without some form of technology being integrated into that strategy."[13]

Based in Tennessee, the global chemical company manufactures a broad portfolio of chemicals and generated sales of $5.3 billion in 2002. The company was founded in 1920 to produce chemicals for Eastman Kodak Company's photographic business. It became an independent entity in 1994 when Kodak spun off its chemicals business.

Eastman operates 41 manufacturing sites in 17 countries and supplies major chemicals, fibers, and plastics products to customers throughout the world. The company's products and operations are managed in five operating units divided into two divisions—Eastman and Voridian.

Growing Focus on Supply Chain Efficiency in the Chemical Industry

Some chemical industry background might help you understand where Eastman is heading. The chemical industry is in the midst of a pronounced slump. Several trends have led to this state, including flat growth and deflationary prices, greater buyer knowledge and access to information, an increasing number of suppliers due to lowered trade barriers, and a traditional operating culture at odds with the new economy.

Investors are pressuring companies to minimize fixed capital investments, improve production capacities, and lower costs. Not surprisingly, chemical manufacturers are turning to efficiently managed supply chains to pull them out of the slump. Specifically, they aim to develop effective logistics solutions that deliver value and lower costs. The $1.5 trillion industry has 8,000–10,000 chemical shippers, who combined spend nearly $160 billion annually on logistics, and has one of the highest average supply chain costs, close to 12 percent of revenues.[14]

The Eastman Division saw an opportunity to leverage its solid expertise in chemical logistics by providing a fully outsourced logistics service that optimizes the logistics network within the supply chain. A Web-based logistics service platform was seen as the key to realizing the opportunity.

As Terry Begley, vice president of global customer supply chain at Eastman Chemical, stated, "When we talk about the scope of the supply chain at Eastman, we emphasize that it is the flow of information, as well as materials, from the supplier of the raw materials to the delivery of finished goods to the customer, and even understanding the demand of the product by the end consumer."[15]

Supply Chain Technology—A Competitive Weapon for Eastman

Despite being the seventh-largest chemical manufacturer in the nation, Eastman has become a reputable industry leader in building and profiting from IT. An early believer in SAP, Eastman implemented R/2 in 1989 (and later R/3) in more than 90 percent of its divisions. Let's look at examples of how Eastman is using technology in the areas of customer and technical service, supply chain visibility, and new service innovation.

Customer Service. Eastman is an industry leader and was one of the first to implement and use e-business technology to market products to customers. All of Eastman Division's global customers have the choice of obtaining products and services through Eastman.com or through any of the global customer service centers. Customers who choose to use the Web site can conduct a wide range of business transactions, such as ordering online, accessing account and order status, and obtaining product and technical data. Eastman generates more than 10 percent of its annual revenues from Eastman.com.

Technical Service. For over 30 years, Eastman chemists and engineers have built programs to answer routine customer questions. Now these programs have been Web-enabled as "Technical Wizards" and placed on the company's Web site. Among other tasks, Technical Wizards can calculate the amount of an Eastman antioxidant needed in a food product or obtain engineering properties and regulatory status for 83 solvents.

Does this sound technical and complex? That's the idea. With 15 wizards currently up and running, Eastman is providing expertise to worldwide customers. The Wizards reduce technical support service costs, while improving customer collaboration. The Wizards help differentiate Eastman from its competitors.

Supply Chain Visibility. Another vital innovation at Eastman was improving its connectivity to its customers and suppliers. The company was early to recognize that in an economy where it is difficult to gain and maintain customers, better connections and the resulting improved service are central to building customer loyalty. By using XML technology from WebMethods to connect to suppliers and customers, Eastman created visibility in the supply chain, giving itself a view of its trading partners' inventories. The enhanced visibility enables more accurate planning decisions. The company buys more than 15 percent of its raw materials over the Web or through direct XML-based connections with key suppliers.

New Service Innovation. Eastman is expanding beyond the core business of chemicals and plastics manufacturing to develop less capital-intensive service businesses that allow it to take advantage of its long-term customer relationships, operational skills, and technological capabilities. The organization has more than 80 years of experience managing a complex, global supply chain. It procures $2.5 billion of raw materials, energy, and services and manages 8,800 product/package combinations and 200,000 shipments per year. Eastman also provides customer service and order management for more than 10,000 customers.

Eastman leveraged its enviable expertise in chemical transportation and logistics to create a new business. In 2000, it launched Cendian Corporation, a lead logistics provider for small and midsize chemical companies. Cendian supports Eastman's worldwide logistics requirements and supplies outsourced logistics services to more than 50 other chemical manufacturers globally.

Cendian—A 4PL Service Platform for the Chemical Industry

Cendian manages a range of logistics services for its clients, shipping chemicals in and out of more than 80 countries via truck, rail, sea, and air.

Cendian offers a state-of-the-art service platform to interface with customers, which minimizes capital investments for its clients, including Eastman. This innovative technology, in combination with a service provider network, enables Cendian to deliver increased supply chain efficiencies and improved economies to its clients. Its service provider network spans more than 300 preferred logistics service providers operating worldwide.

The company's service platform consists of the following elements:

- **Transportation Planning and Execution.** Seamless worldwide delivery of domestic and international chemical shipments utilizing robust transportation planning software, targeting the optimal route and mode alternatives, and selecting the best equipment and service providers.

- **Client Services.** Assigns clients dedicated service representatives who are trained logistics professionals and are responsible for proactive logistics management. They utilize real-time data to track shipments, anticipate exceptions, and ensure that there are no interruptions in transit.

- **Commercial Settlement.** Proactively alleviates administrative challenges and labor investments by managing all aspects of freight payments, freight audits, and claims processing on behalf of its clients.

- **Performance Management.** Ensures consistent, high-quality execution by continually evaluating service providers based on safety compliance, on-time performance, availability, and reliability.

Cendian stands apart in a crowded market of fragmented logistics providers with its global network, its ability to offer full outsourcing services with chemical industry knowledge, and its capacity to offer end-to-end logistics execution. Cendian offers value to small and midsize businesses (SMBs) in three major areas:

1. **Volume Leveraging from Multi-Shipper Network.** SMB firms provide limited volume that results in higher contract rates with chemical shippers and carriers. Cendian's service platform can combine volume from many chemical shippers to work toward more efficient, lower-cost solutions. With more than $1 billion of chemical logistics services under contract, Cendian leverages its purchasing power to help cut costs.

2. **Network Optimization to Improve Asset Utilization.** Chemical shippers are limited by their own network in optimizing shipments. That is, shippers send trucks with full loads of freight forward, but they return empty on their way back. Cendian's platform can look across multiple shipper networks to optimize a bigger collective network.

3. **Technology Integration and Business Process Improvement.** The logistics information across the entire chain, from shipper to carrier to customer, is not well integrated. Cendian has information from all parties for decision support, the benefits of which include better execution and greater information visibility. Through better measurement and performance tracking, Cendian's platform improves on-time delivery results. By providing information about shipments on demand, the platform further allows adjustments to be anticipated and communicated before shipments are late.

Cendian represents a 4PL focused on logistics management. It is built on top of a multi-modal, global transportation network of more than 300 preferred logistics service providers. Before becoming a member of Cendian's network, the company evaluates and certifies each service provider based on safety, security, and chemical compliance standards. Using an infrastructure comprising connectivity software, rigorous logistics planning tools, and sophisticated Web-based technology, Cendian's logistics planners select the most efficient modes and carriers, consolidate orders, and generate essential shipment documentation.

Eastman saw a compelling chance to build on its selected capabilities and leverage "intellectual assets" into a new service business with Cendian. Years of head-to-head competition with the world's largest chemical companies have led the company to develop world-class capabilities and unique IT assets. The key to sustained, profitable growth is translating this knowledge into products and services that the market needs. This will allow the company to build less capital-intensive, higher-margin, service-oriented businesses. As Susan Armstrong, a supply chain associate at Eastman Chemical, stated, "Value capture is what we're really all about right now because we've made such a huge investment in technology. The challenge is to get the benefit out of it."[16]

Seven Points to Ponder

> Do not go where the path may lead,
> go instead where there is no path and leave a trail.
> —*Ralph Waldo Emerson*

The concept of integrated supply chains has been around for a while, but the technologies that will make them a reality are just starting to mature. Stories of SCM implementations gone horribly awry are plentiful and well publicized. Rather than just technology failures, most of the SCM disappointments involve deficiencies in strategy, execution, or business processes. There is much to learn from these early cases. The problems seem to fall into three categories: 1) fragmentation, 2) buy-in, and 3) focus.

Fragmentation of efforts is a huge problem. Every firm begins an SCM effort with a pilot initiative that upgrades some key process, perhaps planning or delivery. It soon becomes apparent that improving processes here and there, while useful, does not have the overall enterprise impact sought.

Buy-in is problematic, too. The people at the forefront of supply chain efforts, from call center reps to delivery drivers, need to buy in to the program. These people are central to success. Invariably, companies thrust supply chain efforts on employees without thought as to how they influence their individual jobs, needs, or preferences. Not surprisingly, these projects invariably backfire.

Lack of focus usually derails supply chain projects also. How can the supply chain initiative support the broad corporate strategy (financial and customer value)? What value are you trying to create? Simple but deadly questions. If you cannot answer these questions in thirty seconds or less, then your company does not have a clear focus.

Integrating processes across functions and enterprises to deliver value has long been the vision of SCM. Keep the following points in mind when you undertake any supply chain digitization effort:

1. The focal point has to be the basis for supply chain process design. Creating a blueprint around a focal point such as Fast Service necessitates an integrated blueprint that ties the enterprise strategies and processes to those of its trading partners.

2. SCM blueprints require a robust infrastructure—an application infrastructure and a set of technologies that enable shared business processes.

3. A change management methodology—a program that facilitates the business process changes within each participating enterprise—is necessary for the success of an SCM project. This aspect of SCM is often overlooked, causing poor ROI.

4. With the business environment constantly in motion, supply chain blueprints supporting virtual or extended enterprise models (retail, high-tech, and automotive) are becoming more complex and dynamic.

5. Application integration is going be a challenging problem in supply chains for years to come. There is no simple way to deal with integration issues. The best way is to assume that things will change and to choose the integration option that provides the most flexibility.

6. Satisfying the customer means digitizing supply chains. The goal is to link planning and execution across multiple enterprises, thereby enabling optimized, closed-loop decisions that drive the synchronization of supply and demand for each participant on the network.

7. Never lose sight of the fact that SCM is a business problem. Doing it right unlocks value—fewer stockouts, reduced total costs, lower markdowns, and less inventory in the chain. Not doing it right will destroy value.

In this chapter, we detailed the emerging role of service platforms in architecting supply chain blueprints. Supply chain digitization is the next frontier for companies. It will complement, but not replace, the internal productivity efforts already undertaken by companies. SCM represents an ongoing opportunity of value creation for firms, shareholders, and customers.

CHAPTER SEVEN

Employee-Centric Blueprint: Enabling Human Capital Management

What to Expect

Every business is a "people business." Besides the customers, the other important people in any business are the employees. Despite the slogans, employee-facing processes often take days or weeks to complete. Employee information is scattered, human resource (HR) application integration is weak, and there are multiple points of failure. Many structural and process problems need to be overcome.

Our objective for this chapter is to give you better insight into emerging employee-facing blueprints. We illustrate the business problems and long-term trends that are driving HR blueprint investments. We also illustrate the steady evolution of employee-facing processes from transaction HR to human capital management. We trace the technological evolution from human resource management systems (HRMSs) to HR marketplaces. Then we go into the details of blueprint (focal point + service platform) design. We conclude with a best-practice case study of General Motors.

Introduction

In response to globalization, technology, and economic pressure, companies are organizing internally in new ways. Organizations feel relentless pressure to improve employee productivity. Becoming an employee-oriented enterprise and making it easier for the workforce—full-time, part-time, temporary, or contract—to do their job are essential.

Technology and human resources are now inseparable. Take the case of Wal-Mart, which has implemented the world's largest employee-centric portal as a key part of its overall efforts to keep costs down. Handling routine personnel matters for 1,400,000 employees used to cost the retailer a fortune. Today, the employee portal handles tasks such as online benefits enrollment, 401(k) allocation changes, and modifications to personal data. Without the employee portal, this work would take place over the phone or face-to-face with an HR representative and would be loaded with paperwork.

Pipeline, Wal-Mart's self-service portal, eliminated the need for most of these front-line clerks. The point-and-click portal delivers a wealth of information including company news, benefits information, insurance sign-up, the internal telephone directory, and company policies.

Pipeline is a vital conduit for management to reach associates no matter where they are based. Wal-Mart relies heavily on its associates. Some stores have as many as 500 associates. The savings from eliminating the paper used to communicate with associates is staggering. Another company, Ford Motor, estimates that it lopped off more than $1 million in annual expenses just by distributing health-care brochures online.[1]

Wal-Mart is also using Pipeline to reduce back-office operating costs. Before Pipeline, basic and complex questions regarding pay, benefits, and other issues would have been directed to the company's HR help desk. Now many are redirected to the self-service portal and significant staff reduction is possible. The cost of a customer representative staffing an internal HR help desk is conservatively estimated at $1.50–$2.00 per call. In comparison, the cost of obtaining information or enabling a transaction via the portal is less than $0.05. Multiply this difference by the number of transactions, and it's easy to see how the savings can be significant.

Most companies install employee-centric portals for one compelling reason: People are expensive, accounting for nearly two-thirds of some corporate budgets.[2] Thus, improving employee productivity makes good business sense. At most companies, changing an address or transferring an employee is a multi-step process that includes downloading a form, filling it out manually, placing it in an envelope, and mailing it to HR. An HR employee then opens the envelope and types the information into the human resource management system (HRMS) application. It usually takes two employees well over an hour to make an address change. Clearly, the process can be streamlined.

It's hardly surprising that a top priority for management is to reduce overall operating costs while increasing workforce productivity. Management often turns to the HR staff for help. HR managers are quite familiar with the resulting conundrum: They must help reduce not only workforce costs, but their own overhead costs as well. They're also asked to maintain or even enhance services while cultivating a more productive and motivated workforce.

Balancing these conflicting objectives—achieving cost savings in the near term while enhancing productivity in the long term—is the challenge facing almost all areas of HR. The complexity and costs of HR are rising while the cost of delivering self-service information is dropping. As a result, we are beginning to see high-cost activity being replaced by lower-cost technology (see Figure 7.1).

The solution for balancing the conflicting objectives of the short and long term is to digitize HR processes. Embedding best practices for repeated employee interactions into new service platforms is becoming part-and-parcel of modern business. Employee-centric technology initiatives in many large organizations account for as much as one-third of HR departments' operating budgets. The money is being poured into different types of HR process digitization initiatives; spending it wisely is an ongoing challenge.

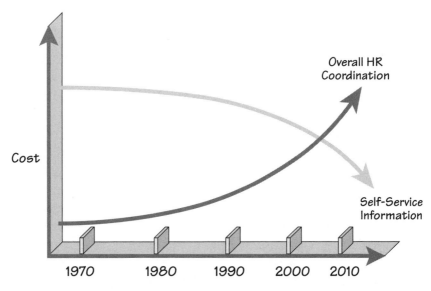

Figure 7.1: Replacing HR Coordination with Self-Service Information

Evolution of HR Digitization—Processes versus Platforms

It is critical to understand the different ways that organizations can achieve productivity gains and cost savings with HR digitization. Two distinct dimensions of digitization-related activities are taking place simultaneously. These are

1. The process perspective centers on the broader theme of business value creation and services. This is usually the agenda of HR professionals and executive management.

2. The technology perspective concentrates on a narrower theme of HR portals, applications, and integration. This is the domain of vendors and IT departments.

Companies may have active projects from both perspectives concurrently. While the two types of projects are related, they tend to use different terminology to describe the same goals. It is important to understand both perspectives in order to organize some of the prevailing chaos.

Process Perspective—Types of HR Process Digitization

HR professionals who approach digitization from the process angle try to find where their respective companies can recover time lost on mundane activities and where consolidated and redesigned processes can better serve employee needs.

They shoot for integrated cross-enterprise processes that deliver a superior employee experience, align workers with corporate objectives, enhance employee productivity, and, of course, lower costs. They can't meet those goals without a systematic roadmap that guides them through three stages: transactional HR, strategic HR, and human capital management (see Figure 7.2).

1. **Transactional HR** is the stage when HR personnel aim to improve certain core administrative tasks and transactions. The goal is to reduce costs by automating nuts-and-bolts tasks such as payroll services or employee record management. Until a few decades ago, HR departments kept employee records on index cards, and everything was handled on paper. Thankfully, those days are ending with HRMSs. Today, these systems are finally streamlining administrative transactions and eliminating variation, resulting in substantial time, staff, and budget savings. However, putting records online was only the first step.

2. **Strategic HR** entails moving from transaction automation to higher-value processes, for example, providing enhanced services to the workforce. Strate-

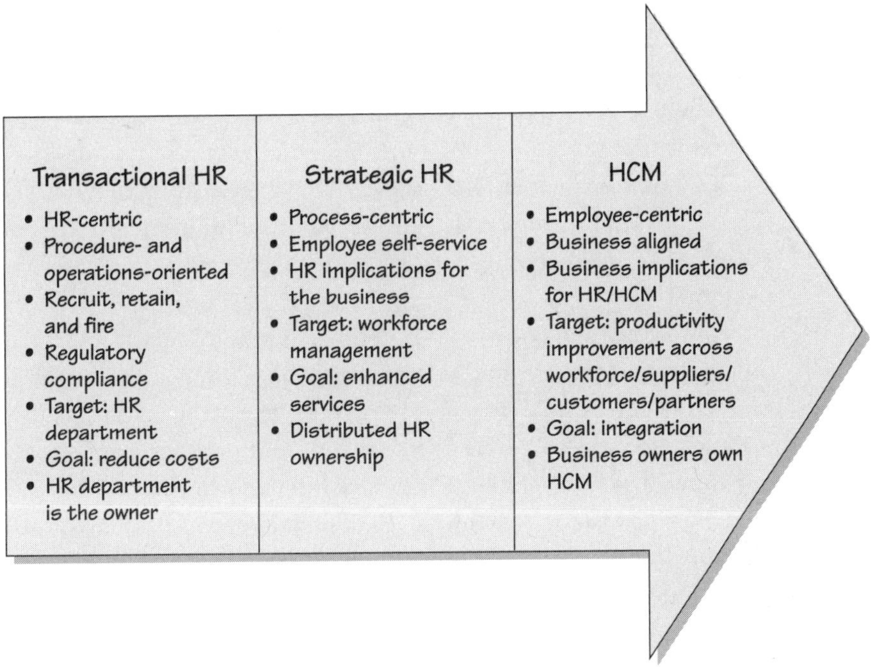

Transactional HR	Strategic HR	HCM
• HR-centric • Procedure- and operations-oriented • Recruit, retain, and fire • Regulatory compliance • Target: HR department • Goal: reduce costs • HR department is the owner	• Process-centric • Employee self-service • HR implications for the business • Target: workforce management • Goal: enhanced services • Distributed HR ownership	• Employee-centric • Business aligned • Business implications for HR/HCM • Target: productivity improvement across workforce/suppliers/customers/partners • Goal: integration • Business owners own HCM

Figure 7.2: Evolution of the HR Process Problem

gic HR processes, such as knowledge management, aim to solve chronic problems that cross multiple functions of an organization. Employee self-service, which has evolved from online transactions to more complex process management, is capable of this. For instance, from a single portal, new employees can enroll and manage various health-care and benefit programs. Self-service also is an option for managers. They can easily initiate job requisitions for open positions, plan staff salaries for the coming year, conduct performance appraisals, and create development plans all through a portal.

3. **Human Capital Management (HCM)** is the stage when employee, managerial, and HR processes are optimized simultaneously. The scale and scope of an HCM initiative is much bigger than a strategic HR project. At this phase, companies aim to manage and mobilize multi-divisional workforces better; improve employee operational processes; and align the workforce with operating goals, driving better operational performance. HCM requires new employee-centric business process solutions that integrate multiple isolated applications. Companies often try to implement HCM strategies without

having a robust transactional HR system or any strategic HR processes in place. This is usually a recipe for disaster.

Where are the top 5,000 organizations today with respect to these three phases? The advanced organizations (10 percent) are beginning to implement HCM service capabilities. The majority (50 percent) are laying the groundwork for strategic HR capabilities. The rest are either building Web-based transactional HR processes or migrating their existing proprietary systems to a Web-based platform.

Advancing from one phase to another is a major undertaking. It requires significant people, process, and systems changes. For instance, moving from a transactional HR model to a strategic HR model requires the unique ability to look at processes from the employee's perspective. What information does an employee in a warehouse or on the shop floor need to perform better? What information does the supervisor need to improve her productivity? These questions are vastly different from those in the transaction HR environment—What does the HR manager need to do her job?

The administration-centric, transaction-based process model devoted to efficiency has run its course. Productivity will stall if companies neglect to look at processes from employees' perspectives. The reality is that employee-driven business processes—from benefits management to time management—depend on the integration of vast amounts of data, most of which resides in legacy and custom applications.

Technology Perspective—Evolution of Employee Service Platforms

What does the future hold for HR technology as it moves far beyond automating paper-based legacy systems to incorporating applications that measurably improve the speed and quality of all aspects of workforce management?

Over the past decade, the applications supporting HR have steadily evolved. As Figure 7.3 shows, digitization of employee-centric processes is taking place in a series of steps, from core HRMS transaction automation systems to more advanced HR marketplaces, such as those seen in the areas of benefits management and business process outsourcing (BPO).

Despite the evolution of HR applications, the business fundamentals driving them have not changed much over the years. The two basic long-term goals of HR applications remain intact:

1. Control HR administration costs, while boosting employee productivity, and

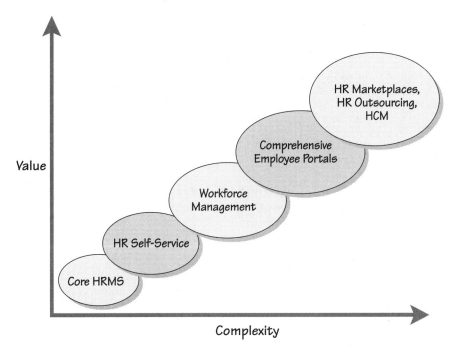

Figure 7.3: Evolution of Employee Service Platforms

2. Direct the HR personnel and other managers to value-creating functions by reducing the amount of mundane or unproductive administration.

What has steadily changed is the scope of HR applications. From simple task automation in the early 1990s to massive suites with incredible functionality in the early 2000s, the evolution in application features and functionality has been stupendous. PeopleSoft literally has a module for everything an HR manager could potentially want. The challenge today is not features or functionality, but value capture and extraction—understanding what needs to be done and integrating the various modules to solve an employee problem.

The urgency for HR process reform is growing. More employees use the Web in their daily life, and they are raising the expectations bar. Employees are asking questions such as, If I can manage my personal finances online with Fidelity Investments or pay my taxes online, why can't I do the same with time tracking and other data entry applications on the corporate intranet? Why do we need endless amounts of paper for everything?

As technologically savvy employees become more familiar with self-service applications, they begin to ask for more features so they can address more needs.

This closed-loop (technology changes processes, processes change technology) phenomenon, along with market trends, has caused HR applications to evolve in many different directions.

Employee portals are proof of this closed loop. They are mushrooming to provide alternative methods for managing and communicating human resources, benefits, and payroll information. Portal functionality ranges from 24x7 self-service to e-learning. The common theme is supplying employees with access to company information, policies, and online learning, enabling them to manage their workday, as well as allowing businesses to monitor individual performance.

Accenture, a global management and technology consulting firm with more than 70,000 people in 46 countries, illustrates the productivity improvements that are possible with portals. The company has eliminated paper and digitized almost all employee-centric processes. Take, for instance, manager self-service processes. Instead of filling out endless forms and forwarding them to HR for approval and processing, managers can initiate and complete administrative workflows on their own. Digitization has led to controlled costs and increased annual revenues of more than $13 billion.

Despite its potential, HR process digitization in most organizations is constrained by the vagaries of application integration. Employee-centric process digitization is often hindered by a lack of integrated data, usually housed in disconnected systems such as payroll, recruiting, and time management. Vendors promising a "complete suite" of integrated prepackaged applications are racing to solve this complex issue. The ability to capture the full range of data found in legacy and custom applications is required for executing next-generation employee-centric platforms.

Long-Term Trends Shaping Employee-Centric Investments

Employers, regardless of geography or industry, are encountering unprecedented challenges managing their workforce. Changing technology, critical skill shortages, and an aging population in many developed countries have increased competition for talented employees. At the same time, employees' expectations relating to compensation, benefits, and other HR services are rising. Employers must respond effectively to these challenges to remain competitive.

We identified six trends that will contribute to the growth of employee service platforms. They are 1) HR outsourcing, 2) more frequent mergers and acquisitions, 3) changing workforce demographics, 4) a more complex regulatory environment, 5) synchronized employee and corporate objectives, and 6) better benefits management. Let's look at each in further detail.

Cost Reduction Trend—HR Process Outsourcing

What do Bank of America, British Telecom, International Paper, Prudential Financial, and Unisys have in common? They are all practicing some form of HR outsourcing, which is where manufacturing was 20 years ago and information technology was ten years ago. In the perpetual quest to be efficient and economical, companies are transferring traditional HR duties to outside companies. Payroll, recruiting, pension management, health-care benefits administration, and workers' compensation are among the first tasks that employers outsource.

Getting back to basics, improving your business focus, freeing up time and resources—these are often the reasons driving HR outsourcing. The root cause is that companies are organizing in new and fluid ways to be competitive. They are relying more on autonomous, short-term, project-based teams composed in part of temporary or contract workers. Everybody is looking to tighten his belt in any way he can. People are asking questions such as: How do we cost-effectively find, recruit, and retain the right people? How do we ensure that we keep pace with innovation and have the knowledge that is required to compete?

As the structure of the organization changes, new questions need answers. How many tasks should be outsourced? This simple question dictates what kind of employee-centric platform has to be deployed.

It's important to understand the difference between simply outsourcing one or more services, such as payroll or recruitment, and completely outsourcing via a professional employer organization (PEO) or coemployment solution. A PEO offers an end-to-end suite of HR solutions designed to share the responsibilities associated with being an employer. As coemployer, a PEO assumes many of the legal burdens such as health benefits, workers' compensation, unemployment insurance, payroll, and tax compliance. The PEO industry began to emerge a decade ago; today, there are more than 2,000 PEOs. AdminStaff, ADP, Randstad, Adecco, Manpower, and Ceridian all compete in this sector.

PEO outsourcing is an outlet for companies that want to focus on their competencies and offload specific tasks, but it isn't always smooth. Take our company, a research and advisory firm. We outsourced payroll to a well-known PEO, and each month new problems arose. From paying employees twice to inaccurate checks, outsourcing became less of a productivity multiplier and more of a productivity destroyer. We finally fired the company but still had problems. We received a state government letter more than a year later stating we had outstanding issues with prior year payroll taxes. The PEO was supposed to have taken care of this task. The takeaway: Although outsourcing sounds like a way to save costs and reduce time spent on tedious tasks, you must be prepared for unforeseen problems.

On the other side of the outsourcing spectrum is simple task outsourcing. Recruiting portals such as Monster, CareerBuilder, and HotJobs exemplify task outsourcing. They allow HR to farm out some of the tedious, time-consuming tasks of resume management. Before these portals flourished, companies used professional recruiters, who were efficient but costly. They often charged 25 percent of the new employee's salary; thus, if you were hiring a consultant for $40,000 a year, it would cost you $10,000 to bring that candidate on board. Utilizing a service such as Monster.com, where you can submit a new job posting for about $300, is notably more economical and quicker. For small companies or HR groups trying to save money, these new digitization services are becoming an accepted way of doing business. The downside: HR has to spend much time sifting through resumes. Time versus cost is the trade-off.

> The bottom line: As companies focus on their core competencies, they are scouting outsourcing options for one service like payroll or for an end-to-end suite of HR solutions provided by the fast-growing PEO industry. Regardless of your needs, we emphasize that HR outsourcing is a trend that bears monitoring.

Organizational Structure Trend—Mergers, Acquisitions, and Divestitures

Fueled by global overcapacity, competitive pressure, and new technologies, in the last decade mergers, acquisitions, and divestitures (MADs) have wrought a new corporate landscape. MADs are becoming increasingly complex and prompting the need to combine corporate cultures and human resources programs quickly and effectively. More recently, with the financial markets rewarding focused execution over vision, divestitures are more prominent.

Linking balance sheets is the easy part of merging. The hard part is integrating employees and the work they do. Often when business combinations fail, it is due to inadequate integration of human capital. As a result, one of the critical needs of a MAD environment is capable and continual communication with the entire workforce.

Organizations in MAD environments using traditional communication methods—newsletters, broadcast e-mail, and voice mail—generally find that they are unable to relay strategy shifts, changing priorities, and other news to employees fast enough. For large, geographically dispersed workforces, this problem is particularly acute—newsletters remain in inboxes, e-mails are filed away, and voicemails are deleted. The result of these deletions and dismissals has a serious bottom-line impact: employees that execute according to outdated priorities and operating plans.

In the midst of organizational overhauls, employees still want answers to their questions and the empowerment to use that information. They don't relish spending precious hours trying to figure out where information is stored. They want transparency in a MAD world.

> The bottom line: Companies must develop employee service platforms to assist with premerger planning, postmerger integration, and other changes incurred by MADs. Communication is critical to success, especially in the MAD environment.

Demographics Trend—Changing Workforce Needs

The faces making up today's typical workforce are changing. Demographic trends, along with more mobile and diverse workers, are prompting companies to redesign and customize employee communication, career development, compensation, and benefit plans so that they can attract and retain employees.

Understanding the individual employee and his unique perspective is an important goal. One-size-fits-all HR strategies are not ideal when you have four distinct generations working together in the same office. These four generations are

1. Retirees—Aged 65 and older, they value benefits and loyalty.

2. Baby Boomers—Aged 46 to 64, they value individuality and benefits.

3. Generation X—Aged 21 to 45, they value career growth, learning, and compensation.

4. Generation Y (also called Generation Next)—Aged 16 to 21, they value teamwork, good times, and community.

Companies' staffs are in constant flux due to new talent requirements, the business climate, and an unprecedented aging of the workforce. As a result, the capabilities of the workforce need to be ever reconfigured and aligned with the business priorities. Once you understand more fully what each demographic is interested in, you'll have a much better sense of how technology can help.

> The bottom line: Dialogue between employers and employees is necessary for understanding what different generations and demographics seek in the workplace. Generic HR strategies will not attract or retain employees who are more mobile than ever and do not hesitate to switch jobs.

Regulatory Trend—Complex and Changing Regulatory Environment

Corporate HR operations are subject to a number of laws and regulations that apply to payroll practices, benefits administration, employment practices, and data privacy. For instance, global firms that have employees around the world must deliver HR services in compliance with the legal and regulatory requirements of multiple jurisdictions.

Employee benefit programs in most countries are subject to complex government regulations. Keeping up with government compliance across the whole spectrum of employment laws can be a huge headache. In the United States, some areas of compliance include discrimination, workplace safety, civil rights, and taxes. Two well-known regulations are COBRA (the Consolidated Omnibus Budget Reconciliation Act of 1985 that requires most employers with group health plans to offer employees the opportunity to extend their health-care coverage temporarily under their employer's plan) and HIPAA (the Health Insurance Portability and Accountability Act of 1996 that protects health insurance coverage for workers and their families when they change or lose their jobs).

Regulations are modified frequently as governments respond to social policy issues. In response, HR must implement changes in plan designs. Employers throughout the world are increasingly seeking human capital consultants and PEOs to assist them with plan design, compliance, and regulatory advice. Keeping abreast of new compliance laws and actually altering plans accordingly is one thing. Implementing and communicating these changes to affected employees is another. This is why digitizing regulatory change management processes makes sense.

The bottom line: The need to adapt to regulatory changes presents internal challenges since traditional HR systems can't readily incorporate data from outside sources. As a result, most HR departments rely on mountains of Excel spreadsheets to track their most critical information. This results in further fragmentation and an inability to present a comprehensive view.

Employee Alignment Trend—Sync Employees with Corporate Objectives

Firms recognize that the effective management of employees contributes to shareholder value. However, a chasm usually lies between where the organization wants to go and where employees are going. There is a growing disconnect between employee behavior and business objectives. While employees may be meeting performance standards, shareholder value is reduced if employee behaviors are not tied to the organization's strategic goals.

However, employees face two challenges in focusing their daily efforts on truly value-added activities. First, they are typically burdened with administrative tasks such as completing paper forms for time reporting, leave requests, and scheduling that distract them from more productive activities. Second, corporate objectives are often not communicated to employees; thus, they are uncertain if they are concentrating on the daily tasks that are important to achieving corporate objectives.

To attack the problem head-on, organizations must align employees with corporate objectives in two ways: first, by devising HR solutions that reduce the burden of administrative responsibilities, which interfere with value-added tasks, and second, by providing performance management and incentive management modules that ensure every employee clearly understands how her day-to-day objectives contribute to corporate strategy, personal incentives, and career development.

The bottom line: Communicating corporate goals to all employees is critical to ensure they concentrate on tasks that move the company closer to success. Failure to align individual goals to company goals leads to time wasted on unnecessary tasks. Productivity will go down as costs go up.

Benefits Management Trend—Provide Flexibility

Benefits are of two kinds: retirement and health-care. Assets in employer-sponsored health and retirement plans are increasing rapidly. The need to manage these plans effectively—in terms of structuring benefits, managing liabilities, and maximizing the plans' value in attracting and retaining employees—has never been greater.

The collective size of benefit programs nationwide is staggering. In 1998, U.S. employers contributed more than $120 billion to pension and profit-sharing plans, and the assets of U.S. retirement plans exceeded $8 trillion. In the United States, the combined effect of limited retirement savings, concerns regarding the continuing viability of government-sponsored retirement and health-care programs, and rising health-care costs underscore the importance of benefits programs to both employers and employees.

One benefit most U.S. workers are familiar with is the 401(k) plan. This is an employer-sponsored savings plan for employees that allows them to save for retirement through payroll deductions. Since its introduction in 1981, the 401(k) has wielded a powerful financial influence on more than 50 million American workers. Providing employees the tools to manage, administer, or change their 401(k) is a necessity in many companies.

Sometimes benefits are offered through a flexible program usually called a "cafeteria plan." Employees enrolled in this plan can use pretax dollars to choose from a long list of additional benefits offered, which might include unreimbursed medical expenses or dependent care. The tax savings to both business and employee can be enormous, but their value diminishes when paper-based processes are utilized.

As outsourcing trends increase in benefits management, so does the demand for integration and flexibility. The boundary between enterprises and their benefit business partners is becoming blurry. Entangled relationships in which a change triggers a reaction across multiple tiers of HR suppliers make it imperative for organizations to work even more closely together and to integrate their heterogeneous system applications.

> The bottom line: The growing demand for employee service platforms stems directly from the size, complexity, and rapid changes associated with benefit programs. Providing self-service for employees to manage their own benefits equates to huge cost savings for the company.

People, Process, and Technology—Creating New HR Services Blueprints

These emerging trends have influenced all companies, small and large, and are dredging up difficult questions that in the past—an era of permanent employment—were never an issue. Managers are furrowing their brows with questions such as, How can we create an HR operating model that changes with the business? How can we create an HR process layer that enables the delivery of high-quality services at reduced costs? How can we lower the risk associated with HR process changes by better utilizing application integration?

More important, what is the HR focal point, and how do we execute against it? Figure 7.4 illustrates the employee-centric blueprint built around the Productivity Multiplier focal point.

What does a productivity multiplier look like in the real world? Consider the following scenario: When Lynn Smith first logs onto her PC, a personalized HR screen, call it myHR, appears. From this screen, Lynn is able to access a variety of HR-related information 24/7 from the office or home. She has secure access to

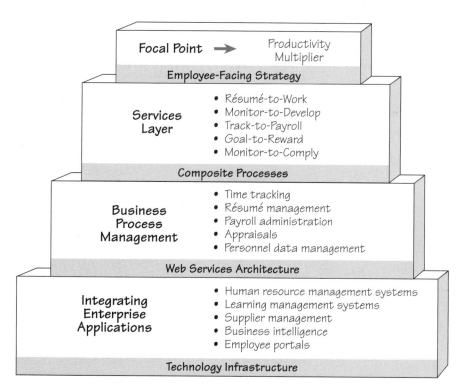

Figure 7.4: Employee-Facing Blueprint

her personnel information, such as pay, benefits, and individual performance evaluations. In addition, Lynn is able to complete many HR tasks online, such as changing insurance beneficiaries, without filling out any paperwork or involving HR. If Lynn needs assistance, she can access an HR representative by e-mail, online chat, phone, or fax. She is also able to use myHR to access more general HR information and resources, such as internal job postings, training, and relocation policies. myHR can also link to other non-HR functions and databases within the company, such as e-mail and role-based applications. Finally, myHR can give Lynn access to personal information, such as her "to do" lists, contact information, and calendar.

From the perspective of Lynn's employer, myHR aids in the development, application, and dissemination of HR best practices, thereby reducing costs and improving productivity. myHR also makes the process of HR administration substantially more efficient by removing the need for intermediaries in many mundane HR functions. In addition, employers have greater assurance that the data collected through myHR will be reliable and consistent because it is entered and reviewed by employees. myHR is also a vehicle through which employers can disseminate company information, such as announcements targeting a particular segment of employees.

To create this self-service scenario, an organization needs a blueprint. Every employee blueprint is conceptually segmented into four layers:

1. The focal point layer defines the real business impact—productivity improvements, employee satisfaction, or cost savings—that needs to be accomplished.

2. The services layer defines the critical composite processes that support the focal point. Employees, managers, and administrators prefer to deal with holistic end-to-end processes, not piecemeal fragments.

3. The process layer is where the core business processes are defined and then digitized using various applications to implement new employee experiences and support the services strategy.

4. The integrated enterprise applications layer is the foundation and infrastructure of a business, or the technology plumbing and wiring that link systems, databases, and applications together.

A key objective of an employee blueprint is to align HR strategy, process, and applications. The point of an employee-centric blueprint is to improve your business processes from the employees' perspective. Applications and technology are only a means to achieving that end. With this in mind, let's look at each one of these layers in more detail. (Remember as you read further that a digitization blueprint = focal point + service platform. A service platform = services + processes + applications.)

Defining the HR Focal Point

The HR focal point allows management to define the business goals for human resources, such as productivity improvements, employee satisfaction, or cost savings. The HR strategy map translates these business goals into an operating plan. Figure 7.5 illustrates a generic HR strategy map that outlines the cumulative expectations of all perspectives—financial, employee, and services.

Where do you begin? Before you start your employee-centric initiative, you must define the specific financial benefits you expect it to deliver. This may sound obvious, but many projects fail because this "obvious" step is ignored. The financial perspective defines the business case or ROI of the entire blueprint. The first step is to analyze the employee base in terms of revenue or productivity contribution. Continuous improvement and increased revenue-per-employee models provide a robust understanding of how employees contribute to growth.

Consider the case of Royal Ahold, a Dutch conglomerate. Ahold, with supermarket operations in the United States, Europe, Latin America, and Asia, is a food provider with annualized sales approaching $66.6 billion. The company operates more than 9,000 supermarkets, hypermarkets, and specialty stores, and serves more than 30 million customers weekly. It wants to retain more employees and improve HR business processes by automating corporate and store HR transactions through Web technology. Ahold's long-term HR priorities are clear:

- Decrease the amount of time that HR departments and store management spend answering informational queries and processing business transactions.

- Rid HR functions of paper, while improving one-on-one communication with associates. Employees generally want more insight into the inner workings of their employers, as well as an understanding of how they personally fit into the overall company goals.

- Maximize employee satisfaction and morale. In the grocery and retail industry especially, employees' actions directly affect customer satisfaction. So, morale is a key performance indicator.

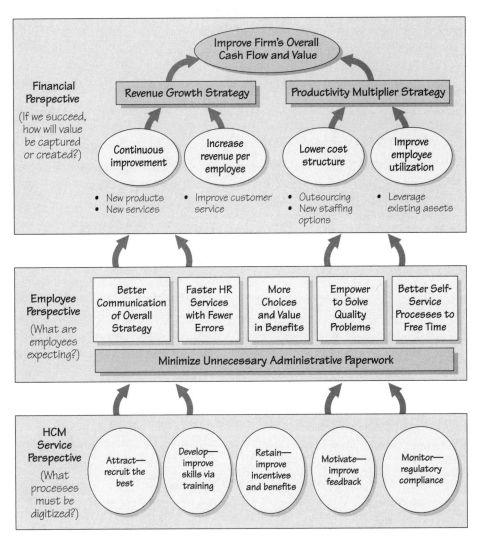

Figure 7.5: Employee-Facing Strategy Map

Ahold embarked on its manager and associate self-service (MASS) portal project with Workspace, an HR portal vendor, to deploy a wide range of self-service functions. A Web-based benefits portal that oversees and communicates complex benefits and policy information is a key part of the solution. This portal will include instructions and decision support content, as well as approval workflow.[3]

The targeted outcome at Ahold is a self-service portal that grants employees access to personally relevant information about benefits, policies, and procedures, and performs day-to-day HR functions via the Web whether the employee is at work or at home. The logic behind this: Employees have jobs to do and want processes simplified so they can complete their work.

Managers at Ahold now realize that defining HR objectives and constructing a strategy that will allow it to achieve and communicate its focal point is an essential first step in constructing its blueprint. The next step is to identify the key processes of the services layer that will support the new strategy.

The HR Services Layer—Enabling Composite Processes

Productivity comes from employees, not procedures. The idea that HR services need to be employee-centric is not a radical one; however, it is not reflected in corporate HR processes. Most are designed to consider what the business wants, not what the employee wants. Thus, workforce processes everywhere are in the early phases of being redesigned outside-in with the employee and manager in mind.

What new services lead to empowered employees and more productivity? Services are organized around the five primary management processes of attract, develop, retain, motivate, and monitor. By describing services with these process building blocks, very simple or very complex services can be developed using a common set of definitions. Examples of these HCM services or composite processes are shown in Table 7.1.

Why are companies moving toward services? The primary reason is to hold competitors at bay. As companies pursue differentiation through better customer service, lower operating costs, and superior products, they constantly have to deconstruct and reconstruct the right mixture of employee-centric services that will get them to their goal.

Table 7.1: Composite Processes in HCM

Composite Processes	Definition
Résumé-to-Work	Encompasses recruiting, hiring, and workforce enablement
Monitor-to-Develop	Covers training, evaluating, and assessing employees
Track-to-Payroll	Includes tracking projects, schedules, time, and payroll
Goal-to-Reward	Involves aligning goals, managing compensation, incentives, and benefits
Monitor-to-Comply	Includes labor relations and vendor sourcing

In designing each new HCM service, organizations have to define what business problem they're trying to solve: finding, hiring, and compensating employees; improving employee effectiveness; retaining employees; managing administrative tasks; or complying with the law. Most of these problems are cross-enterprise, often requiring real-time integration across multiple applications. Organizations must carefully map how their existing services address these business problems and whether employee-centric portal applications can help them reach desired improvements. This is where most efforts fail.

Figure 7.6 illustrates the behind-the-scenes structure of emerging cross-application employee service platforms. The figure also shows that the once-

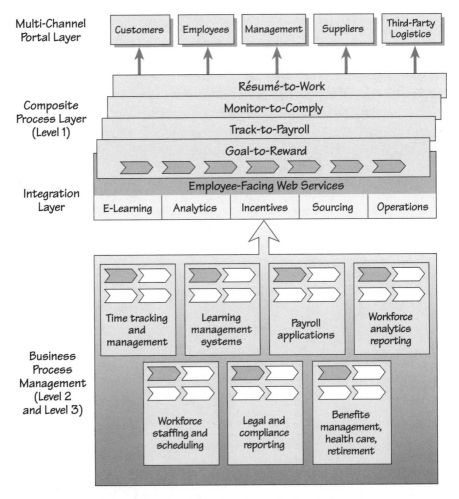

Figure 7.6: Architecture for an Employee-Facing Service Platform

independent disciplines of portals (with their user focus) and human resources management systems (with their transaction and administrative applications) are now converging around employee service platforms. The portals really become windows into the aggregation and delivery of services.

The employee service platform acts as an integration layer that connects, integrates, and orchestrates the various business process fragments into a cohesive service. Aggregating discrete business processes into seamless services is the challenge that companies are wrestling with.

> The bottom line: Many large and midsize companies are in the process of migrating from strategic HR capabilities to human capital management (HCM) services. We expect this journey will take many years to complete. The state of the art in HCM services is implementing end-to-end HR processes across heterogeneous applications. As a result, understanding how to design integrated business processes to solve workforce issues and streamline day-to-day operations is becoming a "must-have" skill.

The Business Process Management Layer— Translating HR Services into Processes

The rationale for employee-centric services is obvious: Make your employees more successful, and they will ultimately make you more successful.

Services are created from a core set of complex, multi-application, multi-function building blocks. Services describe the business activities associated with all phases of satisfying an employee's need. Table 7.2 outlines some of the emerging cross-enterprise process categories (Level 1) and related detailed processes (Level 2) necessary to support better employee experiences.

Many companies already have various Level 2 processes that are in different stages of digitization. For instance, HRMS applications like PeopleSoft, Lawson, or SAP have digitized many different process fragments over the years. Thus, organizations are not starting from scratch; significant investments have already been made. This is a key point as it helps shape the nature of the employee service platform.

Interestingly, these cross-enterprise processes (Level 2) are part brick and part online. The design of hybrid employee processes is undoubtedly one of the bigger challenges. Many projects have failed because managers ignore the fact that being 100 percent digital is not going to happen (at least not in the near

Table 7.2: Detailed HCM Services Categories

Human Capital Management Services (Level 1)	Specific Processes (Level 2)
Workforce Planning Services (Résumé-to-Work)	• Recruiting, hiring, and temporary staffing • Contractor administration • Relocation management
Performance Management— Alignment, Organization, and People Development Services (Monitor-to-Develop)	• Alignment with organizational objectives • Training and skill enhancement • Employee development and assessment • Employee communications
Employee Self-Services and Data Management (Track-to-Payroll)	• Time tracking and payroll • Employee data and records management • Tracking projects and schedules • Employee and manager self-service (e-HR)
Benefits Management— Total Compensation Services (Goal-to-Reward)	• Incentive plan • Accounting services (travel and expense reimbursement) • Benefits (health-care and retirement)
Workforce Management Services (Monitor-to-Comply)	• HR service centers and contact centers • Labor and employee relations • Third-party vendor sourcing and management • Policy and legal compliance

future). Most processes will have offline and online components. Hybrids of the two are known as "brick-and-click" (or "click-and-mortar") processes.

Organizations are figuring out how to combine to their advantage their brick-and-mortar operations with their online presence. Employees appreciate having consistent information when they make decisions. Whether an employee seeks information through a face-to-face encounter with HR personnel, a touch-tone telephone menu, a Web page, a telephone representative, or a kiosk, the information and the experience provided should be the same regardless of which channel it came from. Our research tells us it is not easy to implement a multi-channel process.

Enterprise Applications—Mapping HR Processes into Applications

According to the new model of service integration, employees of the twenty-first century will deal directly with processes via multi-channel portals rather than with the monolithic HR applications of the 1990s. Integrating disparate enterprise applications under a multi-channel process banner is daunting but necessary for productivity and efficiency.

Even after several decades, translating business processes into applications remains a big problem. Figure 7.7 shows the evolution of this translation process in three phases. In the first phase, discrete tasks—payroll, time tracking, benefits, and résumé manager—were coded directly into the homegrown applications.

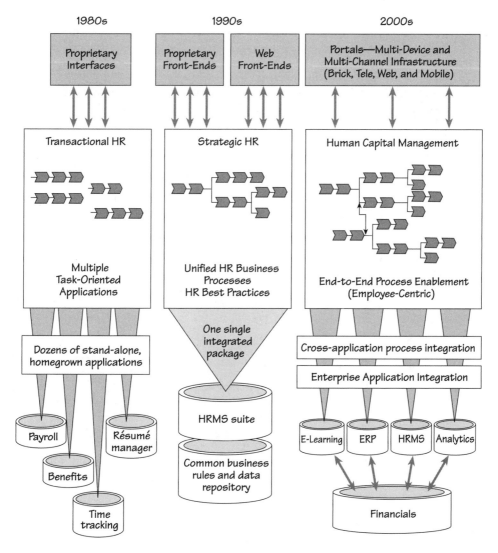

Figure 7.7: Service Integration as the Emerging Focus

In the second phase, these discrete tasks were brought together under the banner of integrated software packages, like HRMS. The widespread theory of the 1990s was that most HR processes should be managed by a single, centralized application (à la HRMS). The complexity of these packages has grown tremendously over the years.

In the third phase, multiple large-scale enterprise level processes under the banner of HCM have to be mapped to a multi-application back office. The emerging employee service platform links the front-end processes and back-end applications.

The theory of the 1990s (integration under one application suite) is being tossed aside for a new theory of the 2000s (integration supporting the need for speed and flexibility in the face of a volatile economy). How can you be flexible, leverage existing investments, and enable employee-centric processes? By creating an integration platform that fuses together an array of components.

Employee service integration differs subtly but importantly from the efforts of the past in that the employee, not the organization, has to be the primary focal point for what is being integrated.

Employee Service Platforms—The Vendor's Perspective

Organizations are working overtime to figure out how to create integrated processes that increase employee satisfaction. The long-term challenges are plain: How should the end-to-end processes that are delivered through a self-service portal be built? How should the fragmented processes be combined to create value for employees?

Vendors realize that customer requirements in employee self-service are shifting, leading to a new era of business value delivered through next-generation applications. As a result, various vendors—Workspace, Peoplesoft, SAP, J.D. Edwards, Oracle, Siebel, and others—are dashing to deliver the new generation of employee-centric platforms.

What are the core elements of these service platforms? Figure 7.8 delineates the application building blocks of the employee service platform. Companies can integrate the functionality from modules in a number of ways to design different services. These building blocks include:

- **Workforce Analytics and Planning**—Analyze workforce trends, leverage key performance indicators, and align your staff with new organizational objectives.

Figure 7.8: Elements of Employee Service Platforms

- **Workforce Operations**—Manage HR business processes from recruitment to retirement with Web applications.

- **Performance and Incentive Management**—Align your workforce with corporate objectives through carefully designed and well-executed incentive plans.

- **Workforce Sourcing**—Administer and optimize the efficiency of the workforce, empower employees, and recruit and retain key talent.

- **E-Learning**—Deliver the right learning to the right employees at the right time.

Each one of these larger building blocks is composed of a set of smaller functional modules. In general, each functional module encapsulates a well-defined process. For instance, an e-learning building block would be composed of processes to manage corporate learning using a variety of delivery methods, including Web-based, instructor-led, and virtual classroom training. Employees could browse the course catalog, enroll in classes, receive training, view a training library, and take skills tests.

Recommended courses could be taken online and, upon completion, employee skill profiles would be updated to reflect this newly acquired knowledge. In addition, managers would have access to their direct reports' test results.

When you create your HR blueprint, evaluate how much progress you've made for each of the building blocks mentioned in Figure 7.8, then evaluate where your company is in comparison to where it wants to go.

General Motors Case Study—Ease of Self-Service

General Motors (GM) is a diversified automotive business with interests in communications services, locomotives, finance, and insurance. The size of GM is staggering. The company has revenues of approximately $180 billion from more than 200 countries. Its manufacturing operations in over 50 countries produce 15 percent of the world's cars and trucks. GM has about 2,800 joint venture and alliance relationships and a gigantic global workforce of approximately 315,000 hourly and salaried employees. The business pays more than 465,000 pensions and touches 1.2 million lives with benefits in the United States alone.[4]

Business Challenges Facing GM Human Resources

Traditional HR departments within large, multi-national corporations like GM tend to be inundated with the logistics of managing processes across many departments spanning multiple countries. In addition to the logistical complexities presented by an employee base of this magnitude, the HR function is complicated by factors such as varying legal regulations from country to country, a multitude of employee benefit plans, and, of course, mergers, acquisitions, and divestitures.

In addition, GM, like other multi-nationals, has multiple HR groups—one at the corporate level and additional human resources departments for each separate business unit within the corporation. These HR groups typically do not have a central repository of information and lack a coordinated communications infrastructure.

As a result, the HR processes of large, multi-national corporations generally are redundant and inefficient. In addition, the sheer number of third-party vendors used by an HR department to handle discrete functions makes managing the process challenging. By necessity, these departments predominantly have focused on administrative functions and typically have neither the time nor the resources to devote to strategic planning. At the same time, many are facing a dramatic reduction in resources, and cost-cutting efforts primarily have focused on reducing staff, rather than reengineering service delivery.

Focal Point—Increasing Employee Productivity

The pervasive use of the Internet makes the integrated service delivery model for HR finally feasible. In 2000, GM recognized the need to bring self-service capabilities to its huge employee base. Back then, Rick Wagoner, CEO of GM, said, "This is all about speed, flexibility, and offering our employees options that will assist them in juggling the demands of work and home in the Internet age." Providing services to GM's employees and retirees in a fast, convenient, and easy-to-use way became a strategic objective for GM.

GM's objectives for the employee portal included:

- Raising the productivity of all GM employees while increasing service and quality.

- Improving transaction accuracy, thus saving the company money (less rework).

- Reducing costs at the multiple call centers through self-service.

- Giving all employees (salaried, hourly, retirees) more control by providing a portal for employee and retiree relationship management.

The company's goal was to reach the maximum number of employees and connect them to the business, whether they were at home, at work, or on the road. By using the Internet to move HR delivery to a largely self-service model for both current workers and retirees, GM was seeking to achieve cost reductions of approximately 25–30 percent.

However, this is easier said than done. To date, many Fortune 500 companies have not captured the immense power of the Internet because no consistent mechanism exists to centralize or organize the large amount of information generated by HR processes. The Internet's use in HR departments has been sporadic and largely limited to e-mail communications or simple transactions. Moving beyond this was the basis for "mySocrates."

The Employee-Centric Solution—mySocrates

GM's first-generation portal worked well but reached a limited number of employees because of computer access limits. The portal's architecture was also limited in terms of scalability and flexibility. In addition, the portal offered only company content and minimal personnel information. The company reviewed feedback from employees after its debut and began development of a more scalable and robust portal.

In the second generation, GM used Workscape and Sun Microsystems to develop the next version of the employee portal, known as "mySocrates." The mySocrates portal was developed using Workscape's Employee.com product. For deployment, GM used the Sun ONE portal server. Scalability, reliability, and availability were critical as the portal supports more than 32,000 concurrent users and receives more than 3,000,000 hits per hour.[5]

Some issues that were overcome along the way included

- Fractured intranet strategy, that is, hundreds of Web sites,

- Integration with multiple ERP systems and legacy systems,

- Leveraged niche HR applications that provided a broad variety of employee content,

- Improved end-user services (secure, convenient) via a single user sign-on and authentication process, and

- Universal connectivity or Internet access for employees without PCs.

With mySocrates, employees have access to millions of pages of information and can tap hundreds of previously stand-alone, internal Web sites. GM employees have the option to use mySocrates or contact a GM human resources representative. It's unlikely, however, that GM will continue offering both options forever. In as little as five years, GM may make the Internet portal the only way for employees to complete many HR-related tasks. This could be a problem for employees who aren't comfortable using the Internet.

The GM portal streamlines employee communications, indexes relevant content from hundreds of sources, consolidates hundreds of existing internal Web sites into a single point of access, and brings collaboration and productivity tools to one place on the desktop (see Figure 7.9).[6] It also expands the employee experience by allowing employees to customize the portal for fast and easy access to the resources they need, from business applications to personal information, such as 401(k) status and benefits.

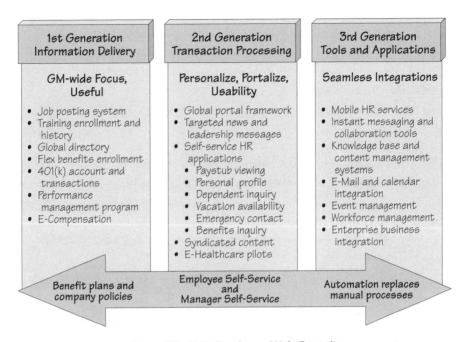

Figure 7.9: GM's Employee Web Capacity

GM and Labor Productivity

All these innovations at GM add up to labor productivity, which is rising in both blue-collar and white-collar jobs. In the last three decades, labor productivity improvements came very slowly and sporadically despite advances in technology. However, all this changed in the 1990s when we witnessed impressive gains: nearly a percentage point rise in annual U.S. labor productivity growth compared with sluggish increases in the preceding years. One percent per year may not seem awe-inspiring, but, when compounded over many years, it results in a significant increase. Can this improvement in labor productivity be a direct result of investments in employee-centric service platforms?

Taken together, the sustained increases in employee productivity of the late twentieth century due to technology is noteworthy. We believe considerable gains from the IT revolution have yet to ripple through the economy, and history is on our side. The benefit of the nineteenth century invention of the internal combustion engine was not manifest until after the 1920s; the effects of the technical breakthroughs in electronics, chemicals, and pharmaceuticals during the 1930s were not fully felt until after the 1950s. Similarly, in the 2000s, the productivity impact of the Internet, corporate intranets, and other enterprise applications is just being recognized.

Seven Points to Ponder

> Minds are like parachutes; they work best when open.
> —*Lord Thomas Dewar*

Much has been written lately on the importance of the customer, the cost of obtaining new customers, and the value of the customer throughout his lifecycle. Companies are now realizing the same is true for employees. There is a high cost of recruiting, motivating, retaining, and training new and existing employees. The benefits employees bring to the company as they gain expertise over time are indispensable.

Employees have now been given center stage. The reason: Satisfied, focused, and well-trained employees deliver excellent service. Companies are relying on employee service platforms to give workers easy, widespread access to information assets that can promptly answer myriad queries. The goal is to guide the right employees to the right contact channels at the right times.

Companies have found they can save a lot of money by providing employees with the resources to help themselves. For businesses striving to gain competitive advantage, it is no longer a question of whether to adopt employee self-service, but when. Ponder our seven points, and see if you are doing all that you can do to make your workforce productive.

1. Companies are finally focusing attention on an asset that has long been taken for granted—the employee. *How well do you know your employees, HR needs and what they want in terms of self-service?*

2. People are pricey. They constitute a significant part of most corporate budgets; therefore, making the most of the staff you have by improving employee productivity makes excellent business sense.

3. Productivity dwindles when employees are forced to spend time on paper-based processes. HR professionals try to recover this lost time and streamline processes to serve employee needs better. Productivity will stall if companies neglect to look at processes from the employees' perspective.

4. Advanced companies are organizing a wide range of separate systems (document management systems, ERP applications, department intranets, data warehouses) to deliver online personalized information, communications, and transactions to employees, managers, and even contractors.

5. You can lead a horse to water, but you can't make it drink. The same challenge exists for organizations developing employee-centric service platforms. Putting HR processes on the Web is easy; getting employees and managers to use them is not.

6. Success is not simply a matter of automating static HR transactions. Employee-centric service platform deployments must be based on corporate strategies that identify realistic business needs and payback models.

7. When implemented properly, employee self-service HR platforms offer one of the highest return-on-investment rates of any technology area. Companies stand to reduce operating overhead, improve employee productivity, and, in some cases, increase customer satisfaction.

The next decade will be explosive in terms of changes on the employee side. In industry after industry, companies are overhauling day-to-day employee-centric HR processes to make them faster, more flexible, and more user-friendly. Perhaps you are ahead of the curve.

CHAPTER EIGHT

Product Innovation Blueprint: Enabling Product Lifecycle Management

What to Expect

New products are the lifeblood of every company; without them, growth and profitability cease to exist. Yet the area of product lifecycle management (PLM) is not as well understood as it deserves to be. PLM has suffered the additional problem of being overrun by swarms of acronyms, which include CAD, CAM, CAE, PDM, NPD, and CPC. What does each mean? How do they all fit together in the context of PLM? These are the questions this chapter will answer.

PLM is a collection of cross-application business processes. Executing the PLM vision requires a blueprint that reduces the cost and complexity of cross-enterprise integration. In this chapter, we illustrate the business problems and long-term trends that are driving PLM investments. We also illustrate the steady evolution of PLM from its early roots in CAD. We explore how the concept of service platforms is quietly inspiring the new wave of PLM solutions. We conclude with two best-practice case studies: Nike and New York Times Digital.

Introduction

New product development (NPD), new product introduction (NPI), collaborative product development (CPD), collaborative product commerce (CPC), product data management (PDM), computer-aided design (CAD), computer-aided manufacturing (CAM), and computer-aided engineering (CAE)—what do these buzzwords have in common?

Each one of them directly relates to the Product Innovation digitization focal point. Product innovation is a top priority for industries such as consumer products, pharmaceuticals, automotive, high-tech, and even media companies. They view it as a way to reach new audiences, expand market share, enhance customer loyalty, and increase profitability. The intent of innovation is to develop new or improved products that help businesses stay in front of the competition.

For survival, firms must continually generate new product ideas with distinct customer value because the competition follows very quickly with cheaper look-alikes. Customer and competitive pressures are causing interesting structural changes in product innovation. In years past, engineers were the drivers of product innovation; they managed the sedate pace at which products were designed and manufactured. Today, customers are in charge, and engineers are scrambling to meet their demands for more options, styles, and features. Even marketing is feeling the heat, as they have to complete faster customer needs assessments and product launches.

Products bind companies to their customers. Consider the consumer electronics segment of home-related technology—digital cameras, game systems, digital TVs, DVD recorders, flat-panel displays, and car navigation units—where intense competition constantly drags prices down. This creates three interesting strategy problems:

1. How can companies constantly improve product designs to reduce manufacturing costs, thereby allowing firms to decrease consumer prices?

2. How can companies produce new designs that are aligned with what the market wants and is willing to pay for?

3. How can companies market new products to consumers in order to gain market share?

We think that the answers to these questions facing the consumer electronics industry lie in the developments taking place around product lifecycle management. With the cycle time for innovation-to-market shrinking, companies that don't invest in digitizing the product development processes will have a hard time competing with the likes of Sony, Samsung, and Nokia, which are creating new products at a torrid pace.

Parallel to the faster pace of innovation, the scope of product innovation is broadening from a single firm to a multi-firm collaborative model. Consider the aerospace and defense industry. In October 2001, Lockheed Martin, the defense contractor, won a $200 billion contract to build the Joint Strike Fighter (JSF), a new family of stealth fighter planes for the U.S. Defense Department. Living up to the terms of this mega-contract will require some intricate teamwork on Lockheed's part. More than 80 suppliers will be working at 187 locations to design and build components for the JSF. It is up to the technology group at Lockheed's aeronautics division to link them all together. The U.S. Air Force, Navy, and Marines, as well as Britain's Defense Ministry, are responsible for giving their input, tracking progress, and making changes.

The magnitude of this collaboration is staggering. People sitting at more than 40,000 computers will work together to get the first JSF in the air in four years—the same amount of time it took to get the simpler F-16 fighter from contract to delivery in the 1970s. Lockheed and its partners will be using a system of 90 Web software tools to share designs, track the exchange of documents, and manage deliverables. A project this huge requires a sophisticated service platform to keep all related activities moving in sync.

Procter & Gamble (P&G), a consumer packaged goods giant that markets 300 brands to five billion consumers in 140 countries, is also searching for ways to streamline and automate the processes that support research and development (R&D). P&G invests nearly $2 billion a year to develop and improve its products. To increase R&D productivity, the company sought a way to manage the creation, review, approval, distribution, and storage in a single database of all technical specifications for its 300 brands, such as Clairol or Old Spice.

For P&G, the core R&D process begins when technical specifications for a product or a material in a product are created. These specs may apply to packaging, test methods, processing methods, supplier approvals, and other operating procedures. The spec is then routed for peer review, revised based on comments, and formally approved. Coordinating the work processes around specification management requires significant effort and time. To streamline specification management, P&G invested in a service platform that combined collaborative work processes and a document management system for managing all technical specifications.[1] The business value: Specifications are reused, rework is eliminated, and costs and time to market are reduced. The business value is even more considerable when the service platform extends outward to P&G's suppliers.

Clearly, firms are interested in improving R&D. Why? Because product innovation can be very risky. If not done properly, the losses can be significant. It is estimated that RCA lost $580 million on its SelectaVision videodisc player; Texas Instruments lost over $660 million on its home computer business. Other historical costly product failures include the Newton handheld (Apple Computer), Polar-vision instant movies (Polaroid), OS/2 (IBM), Zap Mail (Federal Express), Edsel (Ford), New Coke (Coca-Cola), and Arch Deluxe sandwiches (McDonald's).[2]

Because so many new products fail, firms are anxious to learn how to improve their odds of success. At its core, product innovation is a set of complex, collaborative processes—design-to-order, need-to-concept, concept-to-prototype, and manufacture-to-launch—that span multiple organizations and functions. These product innovation processes are application independent and need to be deployed across a diverse set of applications, as well as multiple divisions and business units. All of these processes can be grouped under the umbrella of PLM. To understand the new developments in PLM better, it is important to know its recent history.

The Evolution of PLM

With more companies than ever looking to create and launch new products quickly, no class of enterprise software is growing faster than PLM. This entire segment has its roots in technical drawing. Product drawings and specifications kick off every new product development effort. Twenty-five years ago, nearly every drawing produced in the world was done with pencil or ink on paper. Minor changes meant erasing and redrawing, while major changes often meant recreating the drawing from scratch, resulting in expensive delays.

PLM was born in 1982 when CAD (computer-aided design) was introduced and changed the way design was done. A CAD program enables users to draw polygons, ellipses, multiple parallel lines, and different parallel curves easily, enhancing the designer's productivity and speed. In short, CAD led companies to produce better designs that are almost impossible to produce manually and eliminated unworkable designs during the conceptual design phase.

Today, CAD is an integral part in the design-through-manufacturing life-cycle across industries including aerospace, auto, heavy equipment, consumer durables, and healthcare. CAD is much more than drawing lines by electronic means. One reason to use CAD is competition. Companies usually turn to CAD to produce better designs more quickly and inexpensively than their competitors.

The next challenge was to link CAD to CAM (computer-aided manufacture) wherever possible. A typical design involves drawing a part in a CAD program right up to the completion of the design phase and then making layers of the geometry required for the CAM processing software. The description of the part created in a CAD program is translated into an appropriate format, such as DXF or IGES, and then loaded into the CAM program, which is then used to create tool paths needed to manufacture this description. Some examples of CAD/CAM programs are PRO/Engineer, CATIA, Unigraphics, Ideas, Autocad, Solidworks, and Solidedge.

In the next phase, CAD/CAM, or CAE (computer-aided engineering), evolved to automate and optimize more process management. The reason for this evolution is not difficult to trace. When tools for authoring 3-D design data (specifically, value-priced parametric solids modelers) became respectable in the mid-1990s, the industry's focus shifted from data authoring to data management of the product development process

Product data management (PDM) emerged next. PDM was devoted to solving the problems of CAD file management—managing documents, drawings, and other product design files. These systems are generally used for archiving files, accessing data, and controlling revision levels as engineers proceed through the design cycle.

As the industry evolved, the scope expanded beyond engineering departments. By the early and mid-1990s, companies dictated development of more sophisticated applications to address issues such as change control and configuration management. Hosts of related technologies, such as visualization, began to appear and were quickly used to enhance the capabilities and value of PDM implementations. By the end of the 1990s, the industry gained additional experience with these systems, and best-practice methods were developed. These practices were combined with available technologies to provide solutions focused on specific industry problems.

In recent years, the role of PDM has expanded outside the enterprise. Referred to as cPDM (collaborative Product Data Management), it includes the use of other technologies, such as Web interfaces, portals, 3-D visualization, and XML-based data exchange capabilities, which facilitate tremendous levels of collaboration beyond engineering, both inside and outside of companies.[3] These collaborative tools provide an effective approach to defining and managing work processes, coordinating activities, and enabling better communication between workers, departments, and enterprises.

What PDM is to product, PLM is to process management. PLM adds the methodology of cradle-to-grave lifecycle management to the picture. PLM is not just automation of the process—it's building the entire product lifecycle on a service platform, the benefits of which are endless, for example, reuse of information, reduced time to market, and a unified set of processes. Examples of PLM vendors include Parametric, MatrixOne, EDS, and IBM. Figure 8.1 summarizes the steady evolution of the computer-aided platform market.

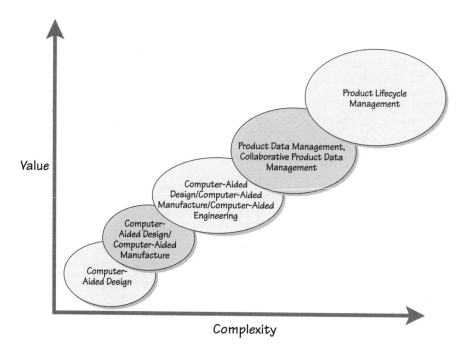

Figure 8.1: Evolution of Product Innovation Platforms

> The bottom line: CAD systems are useful in design and analysis. Product data management systems are good at managing all the bits and pieces of data and geometric definitions that go into the design. PLM provides the process support to make and service the product. To be a successful in novator, a company must have a common service platform to share in formation across the entire enterprise and throughout the complete product lifecycle.

Long-Term Trends Shaping PLM

A focus on developing new products has always characterized the most successful manufacturing firms. The product innovation process comprises four phases:

1. The **inception** phase covers predevelopment activities.

2. The **creation** phase includes the development stages of generating a product concept and seeing it through until it is a working prototype.

3. The **realization** phase deals with prototype to volume manufacturing.

4. The **launch** phase is concerned with customer adoption.

Each phase has its own characteristics, requirements, and management peculiar to it. During the inception phase, market research and R&D specialists generally play major roles. Designers usually lead the central creation phase, while people in production, engineering, and manufacturing dominate the realization phase. Marketing supervises the launch phase.

All four need to work closely together as the cycle time from concept to launch is compressed. Several trends are further influencing these phases to function as one well-oiled machine.

Accelerated New Product Design

We turn to General Motors (GM) to begin the discussion of our first trend. Under pressure to deliver double-digit earnings growth, GM is concentrating on faster product innovation. The process starts in the design studio; GM uses CAD and CAE tools to represent each part of a vehicle's physical properties—dimension, weight, and so forth. A complete vehicle can be designed and engineered on the computer, saving the company valuable time. The design process finalizes the form and function of the product before engineering begins.

In parallel to product innovation, GM is accelerating new product launches. For instance, in 2002, GM introduced the Vectra, a mid-size car, as well as an enhanced version of the Saab 9-3 sport sedan. In 2003, it has introduced the upscale Signum sport wagon and the Meriva, GM's entry into the subcompact minivan market. The company is leaning hard on its engineers to bring new products to market quickly. GM, for instance, has accelerated development of its new Astra compact, a key car in its European lineup, by 12 months, for an early 2005 launch.[4]

The problems of faster product development are not unique to the automotive sector. The pharmaceutical sector faces similar business challenges as drug makers seek to cut years and millions of dollars from the development cycle—drug discovery, clinical trials, U.S. Food and Drug Administration (FDA) approval, controlled manufacturing, and distribution—of new medicines.

Take, for instance, the clinical trial process of testing and reporting on the safety and effectiveness of new drugs. Getting a new drug to market can cost as much as $500 million and take up to 15 years.[5] Nearly half of that time is spent on clinical trials. Data from more than 95% of the thousands of clinical trials conducted annually is captured using a pen-and-paper approach, which often results in mistakes. To improve the efficiency of the process, pharmaceutical companies are developing new Web-based solutions to automate the multi-year, multi-billion dollar process that involves data capture, clinical research record keeping, patient tracking and reporting, and electronic report submissions to the FDA.

As companies speed up their design cycles to develop "gotta-have" products, they must be very careful. Since much of a product's cost is determined during the design phase, companies have to put all their ideas on the table, weigh numerous variables, iterate quickly, and make important decisions. Otherwise, they will lose significant money downstream.

> The bottom line: Competitive global markets, rapid technology advances, and increased customer demands continue to squeeze product lifecycles and market windows. To succeed, companies must rapidly introduce, improve, and reduce the cost of their products.

Emphasis on Time to Market and Quality

In the past, there was a trade-off between time to market and quality. Today, however, companies must get both right. Consider the challenges faced by Bose when it developed the Bose Lifestyle 20 music system. The company's engineers were given the assignment of building a unit that contained a multi-disk CD player and an AM/FM tuner; however, they were told to scale it down to the size of a single-disk CD player. Small wasn't enough. The unit also had to look good. And, of course, it had to be launched as soon as possible.

The Bose engineers addressed the design problem by using an integrated CAD/CAM/CAE platform. They first designed each of the components for the stereo and then combined the designs into a master to see how the components would mesh. The platform allowed them to see their hypothetical unit in 3-D, which enabled them to identify problems and fine-tune the specifications.

By using the CAD/CAM/CAE platform to build the music system, all parties involved in the project—electronics designers, manufacturing engineers, and vendors—were able to provide input and ultimately produce a high-quality product. Bose's latest offering continues the company's tradition of stylish, small, well-made music systems.[6]

Shipbuilding has also benefited from the introduction of CAD and PLM. Building anything from a submarine to a cruise liner can cost in excess of $500 million dollars and take between three and five years to complete. CAD and PLM have ushered in a new era of shipbuilding. Gone are the days of manual designs. Meyer Werft, a high-tech shipbuilder known for its challenging and complex designs, has championed shipping digitization. The fruit of its efforts: The time from order to delivery was reduced from 36 months to 18 months, and later to 12 months. Digitization has effectively given the company the power to double its production without increasing its workforce.[7]

Essentially, a high-quality product can reach the market faster if repetitive development tasks are eliminated and rework minimized. This not only helps to decrease time to market, but also provides speed to volume. Increasingly, companies view volume increases as important as time to market. The logic is simple: Production must move fast enough to match demand.

> The bottom line: Time to market and quality are taking equal precedence at companies. CAD and PLM help companies achieve both, while yielding the additional bonus of facilitating communication among the different factions on a team project.

Expanding Health, Safety, and Environmental Regulations

All products, new and old, are subject to a growing number of regulations focusing on environment, health, and safety (EH&S). Keeping up with these rules and laws can be a time-consuming, tedious effort. It involves carefully tracking regulations, shipping requirements, waste-disposal restrictions, product documentation, and other compliance information.

For example, in the highly competitive pharmaceuticals market, it is necessary to perform efficient, global management of data and documents related to consumer safety and the environment. The legacy data processing systems that companies have traditionally used for this purpose are unable to meet growing demands.

Aventis Pharma, a pharmaceutical enterprise in Germany, replaced its labor-intensive and costly legacy system with a PLM service platform from SAP. The goal: better integrated logistics and sales processes, more synergies, and the ability to use and standardize EH&S information worldwide. The platform makes safety data available on company intranets and dispatches safety data sheets from sales and distribution to customers when required—all in accordance with regulatory requirements. This ability to better integrate business processes has helped Aventis reduce its production and monitoring costs.

Regulations not only concern engineering, but also production, sales, distribution, and other areas of the company. Managing EH&S issues is critical. Failure to comply with regulations can lead to stiff fines, penalties, and potential lawsuits.

> The bottom line: The necessity of addressing complex environmental, health, and safety issues is forcing companies to invest in PLM platforms. Handling EH&S issues effectively can pay off in terms of reduced risks to customers, lower costs, and an enhanced brand.

Custom-Configured Products

A growing number of digital consumers want custom-configured products. As a result, manufacturers are under fire to provide any customer with a Web browser the ability to "build" custom products by choosing from a list of available product features and options. The trend is evident in apparel, computers, cars, cosmetics, and footwear.

Custom-configured products let customers do the designing; call it self-service design. Reflect.com, a division of P&G, symbolizes this trend. On its Web site, visitors can customize makeup and other products for their skin and hair. You start by answering questions about skin tone, hair texture, coloring, and favorite fragrances. After you supply the personal data, lab technicians match them with ingredients and mix those with base formulas. Finally, they inject your chosen scent and deliver the personalized products to your doorstep. However, it's not cheap. Customized shampoo at Reflect.com can cost several times more than regular brands.

Companies are approaching this custom-configured world with caution. The reason is simple: While the front-end processes are relatively easy to do on the Web, the back-end processes are much harder to change. Custom products can result in supply chain and even factory redesign. Nike spent six months working with suppliers in Asia to tailor its manufacturing for custom-made sneakers.[8] If not thought through completely, the manufacturing costs can quickly escalate out of control.

> The bottom line: State-of-the-art production is critical in responding to the demand for personalized merchandise. Profits hinge on error-free manufacturing that adjusts quickly to orders.

Engineering Digital Products

Managing the end-to-end product lifecycle of digital products is a brand new problem. In certain industries like photography, video games, media, and education, products are becoming all digital. The products are created, delivered, consumed, and stored online. Examples include digital music, gaming, digital video, advertisements, and e-learning content.

How does this work? Consider the case of CNN. It has created a digital asset-management system called Media Source that can archive the 30,000 hours of video collected each year. The business value: Digital files don't deteriorate like analog video, which has a shelf life of 20 years. Media Source is used for all daily news production. If you are editing a story on India, simply type in the keyword, and the system will search for the latest raw images and finished news pieces that match. Once producers find the clip they want, they type its ID number into a digital order, and an electronic schedule queues up the clips to run on the air.[9]

Digital products have a unique product lifecycle: creation, production, packaging, distribution, promotion/marketing, and usage. Now consider this scenario in the publishing industry: Simon & Schuster is implementing an enterprisewide digital asset management (DAM) solution for its collection of digital content and information. The objective is the creation of a centralized, integrated repository that manages and extends the life of digital assets such as books, cover art, author photos, and marketing materials.[10]

Clearly, managing the content lifecycle is an integral part of Simon & Schuster's business. The service platform works across different levels, providing a common front-end interface that makes for easy electronic storage, retrieval, and distribution of key assets for all employees. In addition to archiving assets upon completion, the design of the DAM solution allows employees to find and use the most recent version of the digital asset.

What is the business value? The service platform is expected to provide faster access to artwork and marketing materials for all departments, increased access to asset usage rights, greater flexibility and creativity in producing customized sales materials, fewer exchanges of files and printouts, and reduced printing, copying and shipping costs.

The bottom line: The lifecycle of entirely digital products must be managed. Digital asset management and enterprise content management are used to describe this emerging service platform for digital products.

Accelerated Online Product Launches

Having a great product is not useful if customers aren't aware of it. Capturing and retaining the interest of customers is quite difficult. Companies are constantly searching for untapped ways to launch new products that both separate their products from the competition and result in consumers adopting it more eagerly.

Yahoo! is becoming a premier destination for new product launches by firms such as Pepsi, Coca-Cola, Universal Studios, and DaimlerChrysler. Through its twenty different Web sites (mail, finance, games, and others), Yahoo! reaches more than 237 million individuals worldwide each month. To segment this audience further, Yahoo! uses a combination of paid keyword searches, online classifieds, and "rich media" ads, which incorporate video, animation, and sound effects.

Yahoo! has become a service platform for online media campaigns. Consider its offering called AdVision, which enhances online branding campaigns by engaging users after they click on a banner, button, or any other ad unit. The viewer's click generates a custom-branded page rich in media that contains streaming audio, video, flash, HTML, graphics, and more. By maintaining the viewer's attention and offering multiple forms of content, AdVision presents marketers a much better platform for branding campaigns than static Web sites.

The ability to reach customers online is not being lost on consumer products and entertainment industry professionals charged with accelerated product launches. An effectively placed advertisement on Yahoo! can generate significant traffic to product sites. Universal Studios, for instance, uses Yahoo! in conjunction with online media placements, to support movie launches such as *The Bourne Identity*.[11] The transition of Yahoo! into a global product launch service platform has been an interesting evolution to observe and track.

> The bottom line: Using the Web to launch products is a new trend. As more and more customers go online, marketing professionals have to learn to utilize the power of the Web as an important product launch vehicle.

People, Processes, and Applications—Creating PLM Blueprints

Improving a process as complex as the product lifecycle can be daunting, but companies must undertake it if they desire new ways of meeting or exceeding rising customer expectations at a manageable cost. Improving the product lifecycle entails identifying which parts of the product lifecycle are not competitive, understanding which customer needs are not being satisfied, establishing improvement goals, and implementing enhancements.

Industry has lacked a standard way to manage and model PLM processes. Because of this, manufacturers and service providers were unable to use a common blueprint in the effort to improve their R&D performance. Moreover, the absence of a common means to describe PLM services renders software selection difficult and usually expensive. Instead of finding the right tools for improving specific competitive gaps, businesses made huge investments in software that failed to address their particular problem. All too often, available software products forced companies (often unwittingly) to revamp their PLM processes to suit some default criterion.

Unfortunately, many organizations don't have integrated PLM processes, and manufacturing, engineering, and product design do not communicate well. In addition, there is the other problem of the product lifecycle: the whole dynamic nature of product creation, production, logistics, and intellectual assets, which includes the people in finance, human resources, and so on. The need for a holistic blueprint that coordinates the various layers is sorely needed. Figure 8.2 illustrates this blueprint.

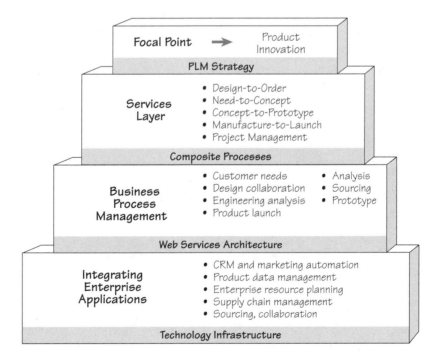

Figure 8.2: PLM Blueprint

PLM Focal Point—Accelerated Product Innovation

In the high-tech industry, some products have a short, six-month lifetime and a production cycle time of three months. Eliminating weeks from production time directly contributes to the bottom line.

The overriding first principle of digitization is that bottom-line improvements must govern everything firms do. To support this objective, two PLM operating goals stand out: 1) growth from new products, and 2) profitability from product improvement. Every product innovation strategy has to meet these objectives.

Celestica, a contract manufacturer in the computer and communications industry, knows this well. The company started small with two design and manufacturing facilities and grew rapidly to thirty-one in a few years' time. This tremendous growth, via acquisitions, created an environment of incompatible design systems. In a low-margin, highly competitive environment, fragmented PLM tools were beginning to affect revenues.

Celestica's management realized that they had to switch to a single platform that unified the company. Its customers wanted to deal with one common platform, not a bunch of different applications. Also, the inconsistency among design facilities meant that if one factory was idle while the other was running over capacity, designs could not be easily moved. To address these structural problems, Celestica invested in a PLM platform from MatrixOne.[12]

In Figure 8.3, we map the problem Celestica and many others face, and show how the financial objectives relate to the product/customer perspective. The strategy map illustrates how to link the product/customer perspective to the core PLM services perspective, which is organized around the five primary management processes of concept, design, engineering, manufacture, and launch. The entire product lifecycle can be described using these process building blocks.

The strategy map describes the business activities associated with all phases of satisfying a customer's demand. Everyone understands that products are critical for a company's growth and profitability; coming up with the ones that customers need and are willing to pay for is where a coherent strategy map can help.

The PLM Services Layer—Enabling Composite Processes

Five basic composite processes (or end-to-end services) provide the building blocks for the services layer. The services are

1. **Design-to-Order.** Empowers customers to self-innovate by enabling them to configure products to their specific requirements and evaluate whether the configuration can be built.

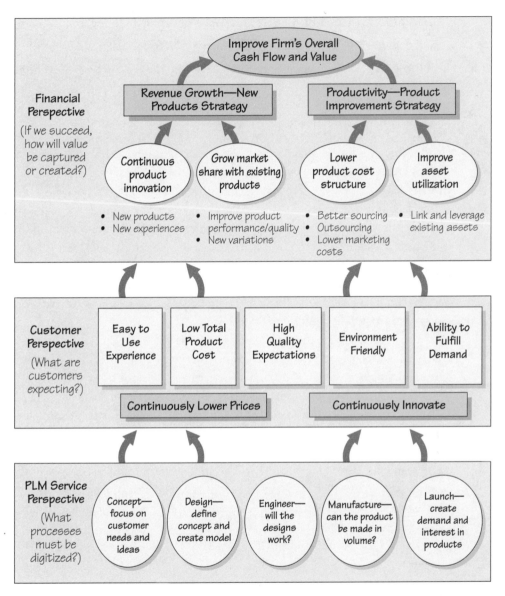

Figure 8.3: PLM Strategy Map

2. **Need-to-Concept.** Includes customer requirements, idea generation, product concept, business viability, and feasibility analysis.

3. **Concept-to-Prototype.** Covers conceptual design, product definition, actual design, design reviews, engineering analysis, and prototyping.

4. **Manufacture-to-Launch.** Encompasses engineering, sourcing, volume manufacture, change management, and product launch.

5. **Project/Program Management.** Manages innovation projects including phase (stage) gates, project planning, visibility into global projects, tasks, and deliverable status.

To explain the concept-to-prototype service better, let's look at an example. In the Shinjuku district of Tokyo, one company produces virtually 100 percent of the handset molds used in the highly competitive mobile phone market. Customers, such as Kyocera and Sony, can have their finished products delivered just three days after placing an order with the company.[13] The company does this by creating the mold designs in CAD. A designer cannot know just by looking at the CAD image whether a design will work; therefore, the output is fed into a laser-shaping machine for creating the mold. This way the design can be adjusted with micron-level precision. Laser-shaping machines cost tens of millions of dollars, but the results are well worth the investment. In today's rapid-fire world, concept-to-prototype speed is often a decisive factor in a company's competitiveness.

The process flow of the concept-to-prototype service begins when an external or internal customer asks for a new product to be developed. This customer provides the responsible product managers with thousands of unstructured or partly structured documents relating to the concept. The design team's initial task is to analyze and prioritize this huge amount of information. After creating features and customer requirement structures, and obtaining verification from the customer, the prototype process is initiated via effective cooperation between the design and engineering departments. The strength of the concept-to-prototype service is based on all ideas, documents, structure information, process information, and early layout information being centrally collected and managed on one platform.

Figure 8.4 illustrates the structure of the PLM platform that supports the different services.

The Business Process Management Layer— Translating PLM Services into Processes

Services are built on a set of business processes. The need-to-concept service, which is gaining importance as new product development becomes driven more by customer needs, is composed of four processes: 1) understanding the customer requirements, 2) generating ideas, 3) developing a product concept, and 4) screening the proposed concepts.

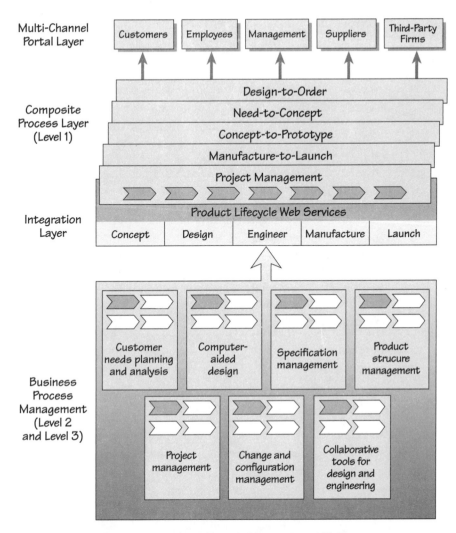

Figure 8.4: Product Lifecycle Management Platform

Each of these four processes can be further divided into subprocesses. For instance, understanding customer requirements has various subprocesses for gathering stated and unstated customer needs and prioritizing customer and market needs.

Let's look at a popular technique for understanding customer requirements that we call "Voice of the Customer." The VOCAL technique has five major sub-processes:[14]

1. **Verify**—Capture the customer's voice by conducting one-on-one in-depth interviews with customers to explore their experiences, attitudes, beliefs, and feelings.

2. **Organize**—Extract the customer's voice by analyzing data from the interviews to identify the themes and opinions that represent the wants and needs of the customer. Through a detailed analysis, a comprehensive set of unique customer needs is created.

3. **Conduct**—Validate the customer's needs by conducting more detailed interviews to confirm that the themes identified are correct.

4. **Analyze**—Utilize statistical analysis to identify the needs that best represent what customers want and to show which needs are key drivers of their satisfaction and preference.

5. **Leverage**—Analyze the data further to pinpoint and prioritize opportunities, leading to superior new product and service designs.

As you can see, the subprocesses themselves can spawn other tasks at crucial points; thus, managing the entire end-to-end service is a complicated endeavor.

Integrating Enterprise Applications— Mapping Processes into Applications

From a technical perspective, PLM is a process management system that bridges the gap between design, engineering, manufacturing, customer service, procurement, and the back-office financial and human resource systems. Processes have to be mapped to technical capabilities. Some of these capabilities are product and process configuration integration, change control, process creation, workflow, access management, simulation and visualization, as well as storage, security, and other data administration capabilities.

Figure 8.5 highlights the different applications that processes have connected in the evolution of PLM. In the current stage, the functionality of PLM is delivered via portals. Based on their role (design, engineer, and supplier), users get Web-based access to the internal and external content, applications, and services they need to do their jobs.

The value of a portal-based model is that all users share common data to create what is often called a "single version of the truth." In other words, at the heart of any PLM platform is a data model that manages product, process, plant, and data entities and their interrelationships.

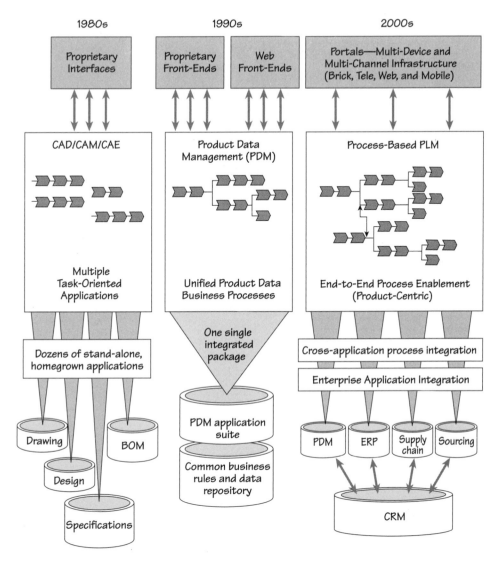

Figure 8.5: Moving to Process-Based PLM

How does all this work? Let's say you are designing a new vacuum cleaner using a PLM platform. You first define the functional structures that represent the basic components of the product. Then you add more detail, completing the product documentation by including design drawings, specifications, and part numbers. As you define the product structure and its variants, you can begin to model manufacturing processes and factory layouts. This means you are simultaneously constructing the details of your product, manufacturing processes, and factory production. For each of these three functions, PLM lets you define the basic structures first and refine them later.

For example, you can model your vacuum cleaner as a logical construct. All you need to know is that this vacuum cleaner will have a dust tray, wheels, motor, and handles. Moving downstream, engineers don't need to know that piece-parts A, B, and C, and piece-parts X, Y, and Z have to go together in a particular set sequence. All they need to know is that there will be a motor and a wheel assembly to be integrated. The same holds true for production engineers who don't have to memorize the material numbers.

Suppose the vacuum cleaner prototype has been released to manufacturing. Entering a model number into the PLM system will drive all the manufacturing processes, resources, and plants associated with making that product. Entering a facility number, even a production line ID, will lead to what products are being produced there. Likewise, entering a resource descriptor will show what product and processes are being produced.

Both design and manufacturing engineers can check what processes and tools are assigned to what parts and assemblies, thereby quickly identifying what could be affected and who can resolve any associated issues in the case of the classic—and typical—late design change. Our vacuum cleaner example is a simple scenario that demonstrates the power of a PLM platform.

PLM Service Platforms—The Vendor's Perspective

When Albert Einstein was teaching at Princeton, he gave a final exam to a class of graduate students. After reading over the exam, one of the students raised his hand and, looking rather confused, said, "Professor Einstein, these are the same questions you gave us last year." Einstein smiled and said, "Yes, but the answers are different."

What Einstein meant was that intellectual discovery is not a static exercise. It requires a constant infusion of imagination—the ability to see something new in the familiar—to recognize that different answers sometimes provide better solutions to the same old questions. That's how progress is made. In business, as in Einstein's exam, the basic questions about product innovation are the same— What do customers want? What features will they pay for? — but the answers are fluid. This is the dilemma of the PLM vendors: The high-level needs are the same (create great products), but the details of how to achieve this goal are changing.

Clearly, businesses want PLM service platforms at their disposal. However, most vendors are still offering only segments of functionality (see Figure 8.6).

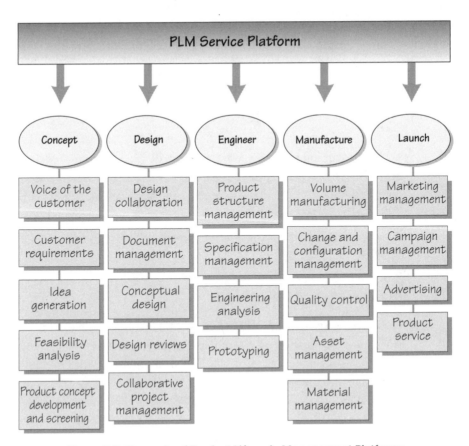

Figure 8.6: Elements of Product Lifecycle Management Platforms

The cost of integrating the various PLM pieces is rapidly becoming a significant barrier to the deployment of new business applications.

Some of the more advanced PLM vendors like Parametric, MatrixOne, Agile, EDS, Dassault Systems, and IBM aim to reduce measurably the cost and complexity of application integration, enabling organizations to develop and deploy cross-application business processes effectively. The next-generation PLM service platforms include three primary components:

1. **Best-Practice Business Process Library**—A library of prepackaged industry-specific PLM business processes based on best practices that are prebuilt. These business processes can be executed across multiple applications, departments, organizations, and enterprises.

2. **Business Process Design Tool**—A selection of PLM business process design tools for modeling and configuring existing business processes and creating new ones.

3. **Integration Server**—An integration server to execute business processes and coordinate interapplication communication based on XML and Web Services industry standards.

It is becoming clear that vendors must develop flexible PLM service platforms that allow organizations to select best-in-class applications and ensure that they are not locked into vendor-specific proprietary architectures. The goal is a vendor-independent service platform that enables organizations to respond to new product opportunities, optimize organizational performance, and realize business value from existing systems.

Nike Footwear—A PLM Case Study

One of the most innovative PLM firms is Nike, the apparel and footwear company. The company that later became Nike started in 1964 when Phil Knight, an accountant and ex-collegiate runner, talked his University of Oregon coach Bill Bowerman into joining him in creating a new shoe company called Blue Ribbon Sports (BRS). The initial investment in BRS was $1,000.

The inspiration for the idea was a trip that Knight took to Japan where he found a company, Onitsuka, which made good track shoes. In the first year, BRS sold 1,300 pairs of Onitsuka Tigers and pulled in $8,000 in revenues. They sold directly to runners who were hungry for better shoes. Knight sold pairs out of his car at track meets and running events.[15]

In the early days, Bowerman was designing the shoes and sending them to Onitsuka for manufacturing. However, by 1971, the relationship with Onitsuka had soured. Knight decided BRS needed its own brand and a distinguishing mark to put on the shoes. The name Nike, the Greek goddess of victory, was chosen and the famous swoosh logo was created. BRS severed ties with Onitsuka and found other suppliers. In 1972, with 45 employees, the company had sales of $1.96 million. To fuel growth, Knight secured financing from a large Japanese trading company, Nissho Iwai.

You probably know the rest of the story. Nike exploded to become a very large and complex organization. Today, Nike is a $10 billion global brand with operations in 140 countries. Footwear constitutes the majority of Nike's business, comprising 60 percent of annual sales; the rest is in apparel and equipment. Its mission: "Bring inspiration and innovation to every athlete in the world," with the footnote "If you have a body, you are an athlete."[16]

Evolution of Athletic Footwear Design

In 1974, Nike introduced the best-selling Waffle Trainer. The shoe was based on a design Bowerman crafted using a rubber compound and a waffle iron; it offered superior cushioning and was lightweight. Bowerman understood his customer, the athlete, well. He always asked, Is this necessary? Does this create value for the runner?

Bowerman, of course, didn't use computers. In the early days, the design technology of shoe soles was based on clay, wax, or foam. This method originated in the second half of the nineteenth century when individual cobblers working either alone or with one or two apprentices produced practically all shoes. The advent of the sewing machine enlarged craftsmen's shops and converted them to factories. Eventually, the footwear trade relocated from the small backyard workbench of the local cobbler to the design studios of companies staffed by designers, sculptors, and engineers.

As sophistication grew with more ergonomic design, new technology began taking hold. Today, foot scanners produce a digital representation of feet and have made plaster casts obsolete. By using digital modeling tools, designers can create complex midsoles and outsole designs, which previously could only be made by hand. These digital forms are used in downstream processes such as rapid prototyping, grading, tooling design, and machining. The advantages are a reduction in product development time, improvement in design quality, and decreased manufacturing costs.

Digital technology helps Nike to see the entire shoe as a holistic system; the key is not any one piece but the integration of multiple pieces—the upper, the lacing system, the midsole, and the outsole.

The Mold Process—Computer-Aided Engineering

Prototyping is a crucial step in the product development process at Nike. With shortening lead times, the company created a software program that works with CAM software to speed up the fabrication of prototype molds.

Prototypes are nearly the only opportunity to test a product rigorously before production begins in hundreds of combinations of sizes, colors, and graphics. To meet the need for quickly built, tight-tolerance tooling for its prototypes,

Nike invested in high-speed, precision mold-cutting machine tools for its mold and tooling center (MTC). It also invested heavily in manufacturing software.

To make and test design prototypes, Nike uses multiple types of molds—rubber molds for outer shoe soles; foam molds for inner soles, midsoles, and uppers; injection molds for inserts between the outer and inner soles; and blow molds for its distinctive encapsulated air soles (or "airbags," as Nike labels them) found on the outsoles of many of its shoes.[17]

The MTC can design, generate mold tool paths, and machine a set of three or four prototype molds for the various components of a new shoe design in five days. Nike could potentially go from concept-to-prototype in less than a week.

The Next Generation of Design—Design for the Environment

Nike is taking footwear PLM to a completely different level. The company is pursuing the concept of environmentally sustainable product design (SPD). The increasing volume of environmental legislation, primarily coming out of Europe, is driving Nike to explore new materials. In looking at alternative, future materials and their required R&D, Nike faces capital expenditures in equipment and chemistry to the tune of several million dollars.

Creating sustainable products requires more than just new molds; it necessitates designing, engineering, and building new manufacturing equipment and processes. It is a major R&D process. However, before all the decisions are made regarding a major capital investment, the trade-offs and implications—such as use of leather, tanning agents, and energy—must be understood. Product lifecycle assessments are helping Nike understand the potential impact of its decisions.[18]

Nike faces stiff challenges in integrating SPD into the standard product development and design process. Until now, conceiving and creating products at Nike has been a smooth process. The challenge will be to take environmental issues and translate them so that product teams understand how they implicate the design of their product.

The New York Times—Creating Digital Products

What do you think of when *The New York Times* is mentioned? Perhaps a famous newspaper? Certainly not product innovation. What could be innovative about a newspaper organization?

New York Times Digital (NYTD), the Internet division of The New York Times Co., operates NYTimes.com and Boston.com and survives by being innovative and agile.[19] Since its launch in 1996, it has extended the brand using several new digital products:

Breaking News. Established in 1999, a "Continuous News Desk" team updates stories from writers and rewrites wire stories for NYTimes.com and its news service.

Multimedia. Uses Flash animation, audio, video, and interactive graphics to enhance news stories.

E-Mail. On both the news side and the business side, e-mail is used to extend its reach and generate revenues.

Targeting. Every user must supply demographic information and an e-mail address to access content. The company uses this information for personalization and targeting.

Brick-and-Click Content. Generate cross-media packages for existing subscribers.

What is the strategy? NYTD intends to reach beyond being an online newspaper and establish itself as a dominant player in digital content. It also wants to create an unshakeable infrastructure that will allow it to develop digital products easily, build different revenue streams, and compliment the distribution and reputation of *The New York Times.*

What will it take? Achieving brand differentiation, developing revenues, and maximizing the existing platform are three goals of the NYTD team. Tactically, the efforts are channeled into three areas: content development, technology infrastructure, and advertising development. The efforts translate into revenues in three ways: 1) display advertising, 2) classified advertising, and 3) premium content and licensing.

Product innovation is ingrained in every step. Consider, for example, display advertising, which constitutes the majority of the revenues. NYTD has capitalized on a rapidly changing advertising market. It has been able to innovate beyond banner ads to big ads, pop unders (unsolicited ads that launch underneath an open browser window), Surround Sessions, and video ads.

Let's look at Surround Sessions, which exemplify advertising product innovation.

Next Generation of Online Advertising—Impressions via Sessions

The online advertising sector has been reeling, failing to make an impact with small-sized banners and short exposures. In 2001, NYTD, feeling the pinch, responded with an innovative ad product type called Surround Sessions. This product allows a single advertiser to control every major ad position and maintain total share of voice across multiple pages of the Web site. A Surround Session exposes a user to the messaging of an exclusive advertiser for an extended period in an effort to improve advertising efficiency. Users see ads from only one advertiser for the duration of their visit to the Web site.

Surround Sessions could prove advantageous to advertisers because they receive exclusive sponsorship in major ad positions during a user's visit. Agencies can create sequential advertisements that tell a story or make the sale over the course of several pages—circumventing the cramped creative confines of a single banner. Ideally, this could produce better online ads.

Although a Surround Session continues until the user leaves the site, NYTimes.com packages and sells sessions using a minimum of five pages of ads. That means if a user abandons the site after viewing only three pages, the advertiser pays nothing for that session. Likewise, should a user view ten pages on the site, the session's five additional pages of ads are delivered at no cost.

Targeting is also possible and is based on how a user enters the site. Surfers that start with the NYTimes.com's business section are categorized as business users and would receive ads from a related advertiser.

Going Beyond Surround Sessions—Site Sessions

Building on the success of Surround Sessions, NYTD has launched a Site Sessions advertising format. Site Sessions allow a single advertiser to be featured in exclusive placements across its major ad positions for a specific period, similar to the advertising format used in radio and television.

The thinking here is that the ability to purchase specific, desirable times during the workday allows advertisers to reach their target audiences online at the particular times of day when they may be making purchasing decisions. The Internet dominates daytime media use in the same way that television dominates evenings. Daytime is prime time on the Internet.

Due to the positive results from its Surround Sessions campaign, American Airlines decided to be the first advertiser to adopt Site Sessions. NYTimes.com combined the specific period of time concept with targeting made possible by the registration system for NYTimes.com. As a result, the site's users in different time zones across the United States viewed the American Airlines ads between 9 A.M. and 10 A.M. Monday through Wednesday.[20]

New Products from Old Material—Archive Packaging

While virtually all of NYTD remains free and ad-supported, the company is exploring selling some of its own antiques. For instance, "Glory Days: Baseball in New York 1947–1957" is a package of archival Times sports articles, as well as multimedia quizzes and audio interviews focusing on the heyday of the Yankees. For $9.95, users can access this premium mini-site for one year. This is a niche product, intended for Yankees fans.

Archive packaging makes business sense. Breaking even is easy to do with archival repackaging because any publication's old content is already paid for. Subsequent uses are pure profit. Aside from drilling archives for the best articles and photos, digitizing some old sports content, and getting the in-house development team to wrap it in a presentable template, very little up-front investment needs to be made.

Archive packaging is a major trend online. NYTD, along with all online content providers, faces the eternal question of new media business models: What will users pay for? The company is pursuing multiple strategies: developing homegrown products, offering partner products for sale, and experimenting with subscriptions for games. In the media industry, the design and introduction of new premium products is in its infancy.

Digital Product Lifecycle Management—The New Frontier

Digital products, such as music, movies and games, are the next frontier of product innovation. However, going from a physical to a digital model for media companies is not going to be easy. Take the case of AOL TimeWarner. The megamerger was all about creating a behemoth that delivers multi-channel media services to the customer. While the merger was sound in theory, executing it via channel integration and synergy among various business units has proven to be extraordinarily difficult. Many companies are facing similar problems, as the media business model transition gets under way.

Forward-thinking media companies today are growing their businesses with new and innovative products that clearly establish brand value and differentiation. These organizations recognize that they are known for their products, not their back-office systems. As a result, the product development process is central to their business strategy and long-term success.

Seven Points to Ponder

> The backbone of surprise is fusing speed with secrecy.
> *Carl von Clausewitz (1780–1831)*

Product innovation is indispensable in translating market demands into improvements to existing product lines. It's also critical in the creation of new product classes that allow companies to dominate emerging markets. In addition, the speed of the product development process, by defining specifications, parameters, and characteristics that differentiate the product, has become the key to success in today's competitive markets.

The importance of PLM cannot be emphasized enough. The entire product lifecycle—from concept to engineering to launch—is rapidly being digitized. Customers, competition, and the market are pressuring companies to digitize these processes and release products in record time. Companies that don't invest in product lifecycle digitization are going to be left behind. To remain competitive, a company must gauge its success based on seven measures:

1. Time to prototype: How fast can you test the feasibility of the idea?

2. Time to volume: How quickly can you produce at a volume that attracts enough revenues to cover cost?

3. Time to market: How fast can you get the product to market?

4. Time to adoption: How can you coordinate a successful launch campaign to drive customer adoption?

5. Time to profit: How can you generate revenues that exceed production and marketing costs?

6. Time to modify: How quickly can you make changes to accommodate customer requests, and how much do these changes cost?

7. Time to retirement: How long before the product can be retired?

Manufacturing quality—a longtime competitive differentiator—is approaching parity across the board; therefore, meeting customers' specific demands for innovative products is emerging as the next critical opportunity for competitive advantage. Companies that learn how to manage their product lifecycle adeptly will eventually become the new success stories in the global marketplace.

PART III

Creating a Services Blueprint

CHAPTER NINE

Vision to Execution: The Blueprint Methodology

What to Expect

Services digitization has moved from the realm of vision and possibilities to the realm of action and results. Organizations are tired of PowerPoint presentations that promise "significant revenue improvements" and "sizable costs savings." Clearly, the era of "the next big thing," "the new new thing," and disruptive innovation is over. We expect that the next decade will be the era of operational details and painstaking execution.

So, how do you go from theorizing about digitizing your business to actually making it happen? How do you align the critical parts of business—strategy, processes, and technology—to create value? In this chapter, we explain the different facets of execution with respect to digitization and how to formulate a blueprint to implement enterprisewide digitization. The chapter ends with the important issue of governance—whose job it is to create and manage that blueprint.

Welcome to the Company, Mr. VP

To paraphrase Sir Winston Churchill loosely, technology-induced change is a riddle wrapped in a mystery inside an enigma. Although some consultants and vendors may wish the enigma to remain so, change is in the air with respect to how technology is leveraged. As managers gain more experience with large-scale technological change, they are beginning to look for ways to loosen the shackles of application and infrastructure vendors and to scrutinize their technology investments to determine what return on investment (ROI) has resulted (if any) and how to improve it.

Let's consider the case of Mega-Corp, a fictional conglomerate, to illustrate the challenging issues in managing digitization. Mega-Corp, like many of its peers, is struggling to create business value after a period of unfocused technology investments. It has tried everything: setting up sleek Web sites, creating a separate business unit for e-business, and investing millions in enterprise applications. Yet the business is underperforming, and customers are unhappy. To fix these problems, the company decides to create a new management position titled "Vice President of Services Digitization." This person will be put in charge of digitizing the company's critical processes from the customer's perspective and will work closely with the CFO and CIO.

After an intense series of interviews, you get the job. On your first day, you walk through the front doors, raring to go. Excitement soon melts into apprehension as you recognize the sheer size of the initiative you have chosen to spearhead. There are fifteen business units, each one of which has leadership that traditionally did its own thing. The business units are fiercely independent and resent being told by headquarters which projects to undertake and how to allocate their technology dollars.

Facing resistance rather than open arms, what do you do? Where and how do you get started? Should you run for the door, never to be heard from again? Our emphatic answer is no. Resistance to change is fairly common. Although digitization is a difficult undertaking, if you persistently follow a solid roadmap, you will be successful.

Believe it or not, your job is easy compared to that of some of the project managers staffed on mega-engineering undertakings. Let's go back to 1931, the height of the Depression, when thousands of U.S. workers came to the Black Canyon on the Arizona-Nevada border to tame the Colorado River. They began construction on what would be the largest dam of its time: the Hoover Dam. Before the dam could be built, workers had to divert the powerful river from the construction site by blasting tunnels as big as four-lane highways right through the canyon walls. For the next five years, the Colorado River gushed through these diversionary tunnels while 8,000 workers toiled in the harsh, dry canyon bottom. Amazingly, they completed the dam in less than five years, ahead of schedule and under budget.[1]

Still not impressed? Then consider this: In 1998, Japanese engineers stretched the limits of design with the completion of the Akashi Kaikyo Bridge, the longest suspension bridge in the world. The bridge stretches 12,828 feet across the Akashi Strait to link the city of Kobe with Awaji Island. The design constraints were challenging. First, the Akashi Strait is a busy shipping port; therefore, engineers had to design a bridge that would not block shipping traffic. Second, they had to compensate for the weather. The Akashi Strait experiences some of the worst weather on the planet. Gale winds whip through the strait. Rain pours down at a rate of 57 inches per year. Hurricanes, tsunamis, and earthquakes rattle and thrash the region almost annually. Sounds like it was a pretty complicated project.[2]

Overcoming odds and achieving incredible feats are part of the human psyche. Digitization, too, is just another challenge that can be overcome. Like all major engineering projects, it requires careful planning, project management, and execution.

The first step of the digitization journey is planning. Planning invariably starts with asking the question: Is there a concrete need for digitization? In other words, a critical first step is to assess and understand how people throughout the organization regard digitization. Do they see digitization simply as new technology or as a significant business issue?

Why is understanding and managing perception important? Well, if the employees, customers, suppliers, and management affected by digitization don't embrace the need for change, then your company's digitization initiatives will fail. Digitization must be based on a desire for change. Change for change's sake or simply copying a competitor's initiative will not work. In other words, the destination has to be clearly defined.

While you educate the various constituents that change is necessary, you need to begin organizing a team that can plan, coordinate, and manage digitization across the enterprise; in other words, execute systematically. Let's look at why execution is an ongoing problem.

Your Challenge Is Not Strategy, but Execution

In 1999, *Fortune* featured a story based on research by Ram Charan and Geoffrey Colvin that looked at why executives fail. Their conclusion was simple: CEOs falter when they fail to execute their strategies. The authors argued that strategies need not be brilliantly formulated for companies to achieve success. They do, however, have to be executed well. The message: Execution is much more important than strategy formulation.[3]

Successful execution of digitization initiatives is a rising problem. Why? While some firms have clearly benefited from new technologies, others have found the payoff slow or nonexistent. For instance, the Gartner Group found that 55 percent of all installations of customer relationship applications did not produce any results. In 2000 the Standish Group found that of 280,000 IT projects tracked, only 78,000 were classified as successful.[4] That is only about a 28 percent success rate.

Why such poor results? Generally, the cause is poor execution planning and little understanding of constantly changing user requirements. Too many organizations simply try to fly by the seat of their pants and pay no attention to formal planning. Execution is always difficult because it often involves upsetting the status quo. Efforts to bring about change usually woefully underestimate the difficulty of this task; thus, they fail due to the lack of leadership and patience.

We have seen many situations where managers are quick to make decisions based on incomplete information or faulty assumptions. Few bother to test the assumptions (does the customer really want X, Y, or Z?), which translates to problems downstream that require asking questions afterwards. The result: Companies develop applications and services without truly understanding the intricacies of the processes, the needs of their customers, or the complexity of the change required. The good news is that these problems are solvable with prudent execution management.

It is often said that digitization execution involves juggling three balls—time, cost, and quality. Most corporations have several hundred projects happening in parallel to implement digitization in several divisions, across a division, or throughout the whole organization. Managing multi-project digitization is more like a troupe of circus performers standing in a circle, each juggling three balls and swapping balls from time to time. The complexity is astounding.

To overcome execution complexity, digitization is usually broken down into multiple projects. It is not surprising that digitization of complex processes like order-to-fulfillment is proving to be quite tricky. The result: large productivity differences within firms, even when divisions employ similar information technologies and produce similar services. Performance differences between the best and the worst users of technology within a single company can be on the order of 5:1. Intrafirm variations of this magnitude are significant, both financially and competitively.

In parallel, the broader business climate is somewhat volatile. The business case for funding ongoing execution is not the same. Gone, probably forever, are the go-go 1990s, when companies used Y2K, breakneck growth, and dot-com competition to justify their multi-million dollar technology investments. In the economic downturn of 2001–2003, corporate technology projects have been scaled back or cancelled altogether. One thing is certain: CFOs and corporate boards want to get more out of every technology dollar. Answers need to be found fast. As profits decline, accountants run out of tricks, mergers and acquisitions no longer cloak inefficiencies, and the overwhelming pressure to grow organically, streamline, and digitize processes builds.

> The bottom line: Organizations need to follow a systematic execution or roadmap leading them to a digitization strategy that delivers long-lasting process improvements with bottom-line results. To meet this need, we present a blueprint management framework for establishing a coherent enterprise digitization map and launching tactical initiatives.

Do You Have a Unified Blueprint to Manage Enterprisewide Execution?

Imagine taking a caravan of thousands of employees on a journey with no map, no schedule, no one in charge, no logistical support, no way to keep everyone informed, no scouting reports to assess and update progress, and no navigational instruments. Sheer madness, yet that's how most companies handle the journey to digitization.

A blueprint maps a course for creating value. The objective is to help companies avoid the dead ends they encounter when they don't plan where they are headed. There are three levels to blueprint planning:

- **Macro-Level (Focal Point Planning).** At this level, your main charge is to understand why digitization is needed. Assess where you are today and where you need to be. You should be able to understand, monitor, and adjust your digitization goals. This includes defining the focal point, mobilizing assets, governance, and planning a set of initiatives. Examples of widely used business methodologies for macro-level planning include SWOT Analysis or Balanced Scorecard, which we will discuss shortly.

- **Meso-Level (Services and Related Processes).** This level deals with improved translation of individual digitization focal points into initiatives, which have to be clarified further into a set of services. Services, as we have articulated throughout this book, link vision and results. The more detailed steps of this level are understand, model, and redesign the cross-enterprise business process for a click-and-brick world. Examples of widely used process methodologies for meso-level planning include Six Sigma, Lean Enterprise, and KAIZEN (a method of gradual improvement or doing "little things" better).

- **Micro-Level (Technology Management).** Last, we have the micro-level, where the processes are mapped into application and infrastructure. Integration, technology implementation, change management, and versioning to attain operating objectives happen here. Technology management, the umbrella term for all these activities, is the challenge of managing individual initiatives, and doing it quickly to beat the competition. Examples of widely used IT methodologies for micro-level planning include IT portfolio models, federated architecture, and other software engineering methods.

Figure 9.1 shows how the three levels of the blueprint framework interrelate. Currently, different methods are being used to plan and measure activities at each level.

- Top management talks the macro language of Competitive Strategy, SWOT Analysis, and Balanced Scorecards.

- The different operational lines of business speak the process languages of Lean Enterprise or Six Sigma.

- IT departments converse in the micro language of enterprise application portfolio models, software maturity models, and software engineering methods (like the iterative development methods).

So, yes, everyone is busy planning, but no one is linking the activities. This often leads to an alignment problem. This point cannot be overstated. Most companies have alignment issues between the strategy, operations, and IT because they all rely on different management methodologies. There is no common language that incorporates all three. As a result, it is important to understand the relationship between these various methods and place them in the context of a blueprint that integrates these multiple perspectives.

Making all these methods talk to each other is going to be a significant part of your job, Mr. VP. Your corporation does not need another new management method; it needs a better way of linking the existing ones to create value.

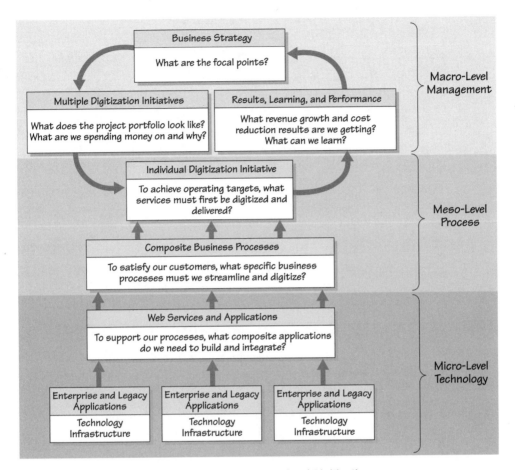

Figure 9.1: The Three Levels of Digitization

The bottom line: A blueprint is a unified way of translating the operational strategy of the firm (derived from the focal point) into specific service digitization initiatives. These service initiatives are further mapped into technology initiatives. The goal is not to replace existing methods like Six Sigma, Balanced Scorecard, and IT Portfolio models, but to link them in a meaningful way to create coordinated value.

Macro-Level—Creating an Operating Strategy Using a Balanced Scorecard

As speed and execution take precedence over size and vision, companies are modifying their corporate strategies accordingly. Corporate strategy has three parts: strategy formulation (Porter's 5 Forces Model), core competency analysis (SWOT Analysis), and strategy execution (Balanced Scorecard).

Table 9.1 illustrates how the three parts of corporate strategy fit together. Strategy formulation is an assessment of whether an organization is doing the right things and how it can be more effective in what it does. The essence of core competency analysis is assessing whether an organization can use its internal strengths to take advantage of external opportunities. Strategy execution helps convert strategy into specific operational objectives (focal points). Digitization, at the highest level, is driven by these operational objectives.

Table 9.1: Three Facets of Strategy

	Competitive Strategy Formulation— Michael Porter's 5 Forces Model	Core Competency Analysis—Strengths, Weaknesses, Opportunities, Threats (SWOT)	Strategy Execution— Balanced Scorecard
Goal	Competitive strategy formulation	Stimulate dialogue and organizational learning	Strategy measurement and control
Time Focus	Present and future— Long-range planning	Present and future	Past and present
Targets	Set by competitive environment	Periodically reevaluated based on business	Fixed boundaries set by operating plan
Value	Analysis of industry segmentation, value chains, and competitive advantage	Self-awareness— What are our core competencies?	Frequent data-driven adjustment
Methodology	None—Intuitive	None—Descriptive	Strategy maps
Business Objective	Anticipating and changing	Anticipating and changing	No execution surprises

In general, the goal of strategy execution is to measure and control

- Performance, or running the business to get products and services out to customers and get paid, and

- Innovation, or changing the business to ensure that it is competitive.

The challenge is to do both simultaneously. The Balanced Scorecard is one popular method for managing both objectives. Scorecards include strategic objectives and performance measures in areas such as financial, customer, internal processes, and innovation. The strategic objectives and performance measures within the Balanced Scorecard framework are derived from the vision and strategy of the organization. Companies using the Balanced Scorecard as a core strategy management system include Exxon Mobil, the U.S. Army, AT&T Canada, JP Morgan, Hilton Hotels, Sears, UPS, Wells Fargo, and Wendy's International.[5]

The Balanced Scorecard provides a relatively simple but comprehensive operating framework that management can use to link the strategic activities to the ultimate goal of financial value creation.

At the top of the framework is financial performance, for example, a return on assets, which is driven by a unique customer value proposition. This is in turn delivered by the right set of business processes (the value chain). At the base of the hierarchy is innovation and growth, which provide the capabilities and infrastructure for continually evolving value propositions and processes. The cause-and-effect linkages within the Balanced Scorecard hierarchy can be powerful tools for strategy evaluation.

Although the resulting operational improvements have often been good, many companies have been frustrated by their inability to translate the high-level landscape map that the Balanced Scorecard provides into specific details that drive sustainable results like reduced inventory, improved order fill rates, and more satisfied customers. To fill this gap, companies are using Six Sigma, a more detailed process improvement technique.

Meso-Level—Creating a Process Strategy with Six Sigma

Strategy has to be converted into operational processes. In the last three decades, the continuous yearning for productivity, lower costs, quality, and speed has spawned a remarkable number of operations tools and measurement techniques: Total Quality Management, Lean Enterprise, benchmarking, outsourcing, Six Sigma, process improvement, reengineering, and change management. Bit by bit, they are taking the place of classical long-range planning methods like forecasting, positioning, and competitive advantage.[6]

Six Sigma is the latest in a long line of operational process improvement methods. It was initially pioneered at Motorola and popularized by General Electric and Allied Signal (now Honeywell). Today, thousands of organizations, including discrete manufacturing (Caterpillar and 3M), process manufacturing (Dow Chemical), and service firms (Bank of America, Home Depot, Telstra, and Starwood Hotels), have adopted the data-driven technique to fine-tune existing products and processes.

Why has Six Sigma become a boardroom issue? As the environment moves from managing profits through acquisitions or aggressive accounting, back-to-basics process improvement looks safe and irresistible.

Six Sigma is an amalgam of old methods. Remember Total Quality Management (TQM)? Many consider Six Sigma to be a new and improved version of TQM and ISO 9000. There are more similarities than differences between them. Six Sigma does not come with any new analytical tools that TQM wasn't already using in the 1980s. However, it does have some standard methodology and organizational guidelines that are unique. Philosophically, Six Sigma revolves more on improving profitability with measurable targets, whereas TQM focuses on improving quality with fuzzy targets. The fundamentals have not changed.

The foundation of Six Sigma is simple. Companies are filled with ad hoc processes, and few employees truly understand why the processes do the things they do. In order to streamline these ad hoc processes, it is necessary to look at them through a microscope called DMAIC:

- **D**efine the customer-critical parameters,

- **M**easure how the process performs,

- **A**nalyze the causes of the problems,

- **I**mprove the process to reduce defects and variation, and

- **C**ontrol the process to ensure continued, improved performance.

Every process under scrutiny goes through the DMAIC approach to develop a best-in-class output. In fact, once brick-and-click processes are defined, streamlined, and improved, they become good candidates for digitization. We strongly believe the Six Sigma perspective is the absolute right step before digitization and leads to the best results. We are not unique in this approach. Charles Schwab, Cisco, Siemens, and others are advocating the same.

Table 9.2: Basic Terms in Six Sigma

Terms	Definition
Critical to Quality (CTQ)	The features and functionality customers are looking for in a process or service
Defect	Failing to meet customer expectations or service level agreements
Process Capability	The scope and designed performance outcome of the end-to-end process
Variation	The difference between best-case and worst-case performance
Stable Operations	Controlling variation to deliver consistent performance
Design for Six Sigma	Engineering a process that incorporates all the basic concepts of Six Sigma

The value proposition of Six Sigma is the creation of a consistent vocabulary, a team-based approach to problem solving, and a highly quantitative approach to measuring results (see Table 9.2). In Chapter 10, we will describe Six Sigma in greater detail and illustrate the mechanics of the method.

Micro-Level—Creating a Technology Strategy

Process design has to be translated into an architecture. The architecture of digitization—which includes hardware, software, other IT resources, and the rules and procedures used to coordinate them—largely determines the productivity of the people and assets in the organization, the quality of products and services, and the responsiveness of the organization to customer needs. A sturdy foundation must be established or your efforts will collapse at the first sign of adversity.

Consider the application and infrastructure problem of The Walt Disney Company. Disney is a diversified worldwide entertainment company, operating in four segments: media networks, parks and resorts, studio entertainment, and consumer products. Across these segments, two-dozen business unit CIOs are planning and executing more than 1,000 projects that support more than 4,000 systems and are sourced from about 1,300 technology vendors.[7]

These projects tend to span a range of processes such as auctions, customer relationship management, or collaborative manufacturing. Often, different

Disney single business units (SBUs) were doing similar projects, but working independently with very little knowledge sharing. The challenge for Disney is smart alignment—how to streamline, integrate, and leverage technology investments faster throughout the entire company. Wasting millions of dollars reinventing the same effort is inefficient, poor management.

Nestlé SA, the world's largest food and beverage company, is also not immune to this problem. It has developed a global business excellence initiative (GLOBE), which is a long-range project to harmonize and simplify its business process architecture (meso-level) worldwide and achieve greater efficiencies in the company's critical information systems for financial reporting, purchase orders, inventory management, distribution, and sales volume monitoring.

GLOBE's objectives are 1) to create shared business services to leverage the global footprint of Nestlé; 2) to integrate Nestlé internally across different business units to be more competitive; and 3) to harness the power of e-business applications, with a focus on customers, channels, and consumers, to create new value.[8]

Three key micro-level IT elements support Nestlé's operating objectives: process enablement, which includes SAP ERP and internal productivity projects; application integration, which includes Enterprise Application Integration (EAI) platforms and middleware tools; and infrastructure standardization and consolidation, which includes hardware, software, and networking tools.

Both the application and overall technology infrastructures typical of organizations like Nestlé or Disney are presented in Figure 9.2. Aligning business services, application resources, IT resources, and network resources to create value and manage risk is a constant managerial headache.

IT architecture planning is very difficult because most of the complex planning is done using ad hoc methods at different levels, such as applications, databases, and infrastructures. Unlike other business disciplines, the hybrid nature of IT really does not have a robust scientific base to support decision making. This results in inconsistency and a lot of costly trial and error.

Consider the application layer where the build-versus-buy decision often dictates which planning method—Financial Portfolio Theory or Software Engineering—is chosen. For instance, if your corporation does not build applications but tends to buy best-of-breed applications from various vendors, then the application portfolio model might be useful. This model is derived from the Investment Portfolio theory and makes the basic point that applications are like stocks in a portfolio. Managing risk is the overall objective.

If your organization does not believe in buying applications but rather in building them from scratch, then various software engineering method-

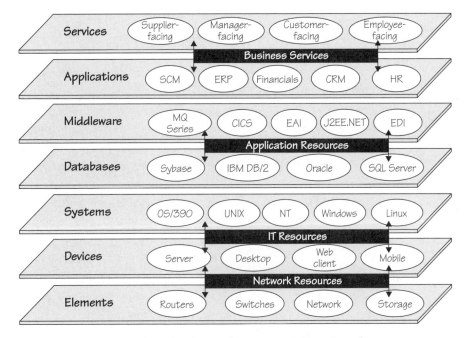

Figure 9.2: Technology Infrastructure Is Very Complex

ologies are more suitable. These techniques range from waterfall models and rapid prototyping models to object-oriented models. The oldest is the waterfall model in which the previous phase in a sequence has to be finished before the next phase begins. The phases are analysis, design, coding, testing, deployment, and maintenance.

In Chapter 11, we will describe some of the other micro-level planning models in greater detail. Bringing these layers together under the context of various digitization focal points is one of the hardest tasks facing senior management.

How Are You Going to Coordinate the Macro-, Meso-, and Micro-Levels?

Many organizations can point to one or two successful projects, but few achieve superior performance on a consistent basis. Even fewer show steady improvement in their digitization efforts over time. Yet getting better and better at digitization management is the key to competitive advantage.

Effective digitization requires a coordinated approach, not the current piecemeal approach evident in most organizations. In the latter, costly resources are expended on IT projects with limited understanding of how they all fit together and add value. We see this problem again and again.

Let's turn to a large insurance firm to make our point. Of 28 lines of business found in the corporation, ten of these are each implementing a stand-alone CRM application to get closer to their customer. Each business unit has invested in the application licenses, process consulting, and integration consulting without coordinating with the other business units. This typifies the logic that every business unit espouses: We need to move fast; the other units are slower than we; they are going to hold us back; when we finish, we will show them how it should be done.

This kind of thinking leads to many duplicated efforts (which increase overall costs), wasted resources, and confused customers. Instead of living up to the Easy To Do Business With focal point, the resulting mishmash of implementations forces customers to wade through hundreds of Web sites and dozens of call centers to find and obtain service. Woe to the customer attempting to obtain a price quote on five products. This entails visiting multiple Web sites and filling out many forms, each of which requires nearly identical data.

Clearly, the lack of an integrated customer-centric architecture creates underlying redundant activities and processes, resulting in unnecessary burdens and costs. This problem is especially acute in organizations that are structured around product lines.

Let's look at a large bank that organized itself around product lines, that is, credit cards, mortgages, investment banking, and relationship banking (checking and savings accounts) are all separate divisions. After several failed Web projects, the bank's management realized that creating cross-cutters—services that cut across divisions—to solve the customer needs was difficult but desperately needed in the Internet world. They also came to realize that customers could not care less how the bank was internally organized. Customers want to be able to do business with the bank across channels. The management was faced with either providing new integrated services or losing customers to a company that would.

Organizations have to create a management infrastructure conducive to successful change. This infrastructure needs to do the following:

- **Manage coordinated change.** Organizational change is more effective when changes can be planned and implemented in a holistic and integrated fashion without jeopardizing current business activities.

- **Align strategy, processes, and tactics.** Processes act as glue, linking strategy and tactics and avoiding the alignment problems of most organizations.

- **Support process management** by providing a process framework, analytical tools, and reporting, so that senior management can direct, monitor, and evaluate the change process.

- **Administer resources** by providing prioritization, scheduling, changing scope, exception, risk modeling techniques, and more efficient uses of scarce resources.

- **Integrate** multiple, simultaneous, interacting digitization projects with their corresponding applications, infrastructure, and finite resources.

Clearly, managing digitization is incredibly challenging. Blueprint management attempts to address the lack of proven techniques to tackle large programs of digitization and change.

Coordination: You Need to Create a Blueprint Management Office

We want to reiterate that digitization is a multi-year endeavor. One critical, ongoing job of the CIO's office is providing program management services (PMS) to help coordinate and execute digitization in a changing, multi-project environment. Blueprint is the term we use for the generic field of PMS as it relates to process digitization.

A blueprint for digitization focuses on the key operational imperatives of alignment, integration, capability, and measurement.

- **Alignment**—define strategic business initiatives and align the complex, multi-project efforts with shifting business goals.

- **Integration**—synchronize budget processes and organizational structures with the overall portfolio of projects.

- **Capability and Efficiency**—manage organizational capabilities, resources, and supporting infrastructure to control the quality and risk of projects.

- **Measurement and Learning**—measure success and implement a formal learning process so that the same mistake is not made twice.

Like many managerial practices, digitization is as much an art as a science. After many years of experimenting with different strategies for digitization, we have learned that getting the strategic alignment right is the key to everything that follows. As Roger Mowen, senior vice president of developing businesses and corporate strategy at Eastman Chemical, stated, "It's about those companies that

Table 9.3: Tough Questions for the BMO

Project-Related Questions	People-Related Questions
Who needs to be involved?	**Who** will be affected by process digitization?
What is the potential benefit of various initiatives?	**What** will be the impact on the workforce and customers?
When will each project begin and end?	**When** will the change be felt?
Where will digitization be of value?	**Where** will the benefits come from?
Why should the existing way of doing things change?	**Why** will people embrace the change if it results in the loss of jobs?
How big should the change be?	**How** will the workforce issues be dealt with?

over 10–15 years have transformed themselves through a set of actions. It's not a silver bullet though; it has got that incremental and continuity of purpose over a long time to improve the business model and focal point."[9]

Many companies make the mistake of pursuing digitization with spirit and initial funding but with no structure to make changes a permanent part of their business. As a result, the digitization changes take place on the fringe and very little of it is infused into the core operations. We see this frequently where projects are abandoned halfway because no one owns the task of diffusing the change throughout the organization. As a result, the return on investment is low or even negative. It happens with all new technology but can be addressed with better management practices and patience.

The blueprint management office (BMO) can provide that structure by asking questions related to projects on one hand and adoption on the other (see Table 9.3). The BMO defines the scale and scope of digitization initiatives and allows organizations to ground their transformation efforts better. It also creates the necessary boundaries to discourage misdirected energies and resources.

Structure of the Blueprint Management Office

The BMO is a shared, centralized division dedicated to ongoing process digitization. Ideally, the BMO consists of specialized, experienced staff with functional

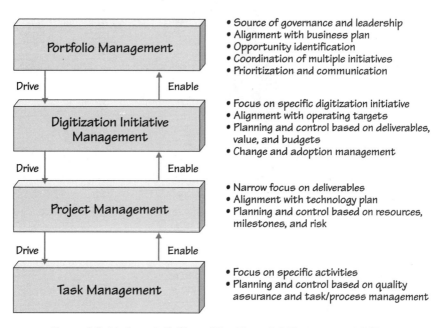

Figure 9.3: Various Activities of the Blueprint Management Office

expertise in business, technology, engineering, management, and processes. Structurally, the BMO must be responsible for the following activities as they relate to digitization (see Figure 9.3):

- **Governance**—developing a continuous process of project evaluation, selection, and management, which is enabled by the right balance of corporate control, budgets, and latitude for decision making.

- **Identifying Opportunities**—creating the right projects in the right order by leveraging investments and avoiding unnecessary duplication of infrastructure and major components.

- **Single-Source Accountability**—ensuring a single point of contact to executive leadership. This helps to relay more effectively project status, issue escalation, project sponsorship, approval, project prioritization, and resource allocation.

- **Monitoring and Reporting**—providing greater visibility of enterprise-level project performance by measuring and reporting key performance metrics. It should also give real-time status snapshots of the portfolio of projects within the program.

To execute these steps, the BMO demands a formal structure that shields it from the political and budgetary tug of war. Often, initiatives are shut down after a first milestone failure; a proven management structure will safeguard against this corporate reflex. The good news is that the BMO can be built quickly, efficiently, and relatively inexpensively.

What Power Does the BMO Have?

When they are first instituted, most blueprint management offices are given a lot of responsibility but very little power. This leads to frustrated folks in the BMO as they encounter problems that they are powerless to fix.

Understanding the three BMO approaches should help you to control the situation better.

- Directive Control is when the BMO mandates enterprise behavior by setting policies, rules, and resources.

- Limited Control is when the BMO directs enterprise behavior, but not all stakeholders are under direct control.

- No Control is when the BMO is limited only to influencing the behavior of key stakeholders.

Directive control is used when key enterprise stakeholders (for example, line of business managers and strategic business unit directors) are under a single management structure. This provides direct control over organizational and technology architecture. The structure used is a classic hierarchy with a top-down definition of roles, responsibilities, policies, procedures, and incentives.

Limited control is employed when the key enterprise stakeholders are outside the hierarchical influence. The structure is a shared resource model that reuses complex domain knowledge, existing infrastructure, and enterprise relationships. The BMO gains efficiency (enabled through reuse of knowledge) but loses performance (in actually making things happen). For instance, the BMO group has control of the technology architecture but no control over organizational dynamics. They can influence the infrastructure decision but have no say about the applications that run on them. In this case, the issues that hold back change are more organizational than technical.

No control is when the BMO can influence standards or broker relationships but does not have responsibility (or power) to implement anything—organizational or technical. This is more or less an observer type of status that is very typical of corporate strategies. At one large bank, the BMO group was asked to study problems and recommend solutions to senior management. Management listened to the recommendations but did nothing to change the status quo. They were too busy fighting other fires. Sadly, the no control approach is quite common when there is no senior management commitment to digitization.

Logically, directive control is the most likely of the three to yield results, but it requires very strong leadership capable of making tough decisions. In this scenario, change often necessitates creating an integrated perspective from multiple stakeholders' feedback and a commitment to making things happen.

Mr. VP, what type of control approach are you going to adopt? Which one allows you to make the most impact on the organization? Is senior management going to let you go that route? Is senior leadership refocusing performance metrics away from local fiefdoms?

Staff the BMO with Service Thinkers

Typically BMOs are staffed with project managers or process flow analysts. They are not enough. You need to find people who understand what services thinking is all about. Let's crystallize the difference:

- **Process-Centric**—inside-out design of workflows driven by what managers think the customer wants.

- **Service-Centric**—outside-in design of workflows driven by a superior understanding of what the customer wants.

Clearly, we are in between eras. Everywhere, strategists, senior, and mid-level managers are caught between process-centric models (current state) and service-centric models (future state). The old techniques of the manufacturing economy (process-centric) that are widely practiced and taught have to be complemented with the more sophisticated process techniques of the information economy (service-centric). Otherwise, the return on investment from the billions of dollars spent on digitization projects every year will continue to be measly.

Since design from the customer's perspective is a critical aspect of digitization, you need to surround yourself with people who understand what customer-centric means. Users are the heart of every focal point: They define what is important in a new design. They expect performance, reliability, competitive prices, on-time delivery, service, correct transaction processing, and much more. In every attribute that influences customer perception, just being good is not enough. Delighting customers is a necessity, and this translates into three core design elements: What is the multi-channel customer experience? How do we

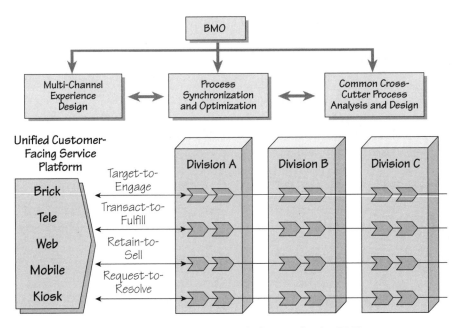

Figure 9.4: Service Design Challenges for the BMO

synchronize and optimize channels to deliver the experience? How do we create the necessary behind-the-scenes cross-cutting processes? The BMO team has to be responsible for these three core elements, otherwise they will never be successful (see Figure 9.4).

Service-centric designs are both new and complicated. They require substantial enterprise-level changes that have to be carefully orchestrated. One thing is certain: There is a need for managing and coordinating enterprise-level change. Management of digitization—at the macro-level (organization), meso-level (cross-enterprise processes), and micro-level (individual technology projects)—is very primitive. Why? While technology has evolved at a rapid pace, management practices for the creation, migration, and integration of hundreds of applications and legacy systems have not. Let's look at an example of a supply chain digitization project managed by a BMO.

Example of a BMO Project—Supply Chain Digitization

The BMO's purpose is to manage multiple types of digitization initiatives—single view of customer, integrated view of supply chain—that may be going on in parallel. For instance, to implement a real-time, adaptive supply chain, one company began by establishing an executive team facilitated by the BMO subgroup called the supply chain council (SCC). The charter of this group was to organize and manage the entire supply-demand network.

First, the SCC created a model of the business that identified key processes, constituencies, and business capabilities. This step involved gathering information, setting the performance baseline, and conducting a competitor analysis. The next step was taking inventory and mapping the current state of the supply chain application portfolio.

After defining the present state, the target state for the supply chain application portfolio had to be defined. Selecting the right projects to work on is critical. This involved asking questions such as whether all the projects underway were practical to pursue, whether some should be dropped, whether they made business sense, if the projects had an owner, if they fulfilled some part of the business strategy, and if there was a comfortable mix between "frontier" and "maintenance/utility" projects.

The final step was building a management control mechanism that included a performance measurement framework for what the ideal system should be able to achieve. After this, the SCC created the necessary policies to empower frontline employees to prevent problems and manage day-to-day operations. Finally, the SCC learned from the implementation and began to adjust the performance metrics and policies.

The supply chain blueprint formulation approach allowed the company to assess the fit of its proposed projects with its current architecture; it also provided early warning of the risk involved when the fit was not good. Without this warning, it is quite feasible that millions of dollars would have been spent before the alignment problem was identified, let alone diagnosed.

> The bottom line: We're entering a new phase of digitizing cross-enterprise processes from a customer- or service-oriented perspective. The challenge is not so much the vision, but getting there. Firms need to plan, prioritize, coordinate, and monitor many overlapping and competing digitization projects better with limited funding and resources.

Seven Points to Ponder

> Obstacles are those frightful things you see
> when you take your eyes off your goal.
> —*Henry Ford*

Digitization can be thought of as transformation on a large scale. Firms that believe major changes are occurring in their business are the most likely to undertake digitization. Firms are motivated to transform most often either because they conclude that very different operational challenges are arising that will greatly reduce the effectiveness of existing ways of doing work, or because they see an opportunity to develop new forms of operations that will yield great advantage in the future.

The move to digitization requires a coordinated approach where a combination of technology, governance, and internal process change combine to bring about a dramatic leap in effectiveness. The sooner you accept that digitization is not about technology, the sooner you can begin drawing up a holistic blueprint for digitization, without which your efforts will not achieve the intended objectives. Of course, this is common sense, but you would be surprised at how many people try to implement complex strategies without a well thought-out plan.

For process digitization to work, we have found that the following organizational elements are crucial:

1. Digitization requires a multi-faceted approach. It covers the macro- (strategy), meso- (operational processes), and micro-levels (IT applications and infrastructure). Having a clear conceptual understanding of how all three levels fit together is probably the number one reason why certain companies are more successful than others.

2. Digitization, like other change programs, requires a committed, actively participating executive leadership team. Management makes the difference. The magnitude of impact management has on digitization, in our experience, is not 10–15 percent, but more like 50–75 percent.

3. Digitization requires full-time, trained managers advocating enterprise-level change. The blueprint management office is not a luxury but a necessity. Unless there is someone responsible and empowered for making digitization happen, it is not going to happen.

4. Intense focus on business process thinking and centering efforts on the customer are required for digitization. The whole organization must relentlessly pursue customer value. The job of IT and operations is not to keep servers and processes running but to satisfy customer needs.

5. Project selection is often where the good companies separate themselves from others. Projects must be picked according to their ability to yield real ROI, such as reduced costs and increased revenues.

6. There must be unwavering alignment between existing initiatives, strategies, and metrics. The importance of adopting a holistic perspective cannot be understated. Different decisions at different levels in the organization should interrelate and reinforce one another.

7. Continual learning and improving are absolutely critical. Digitization is a dynamic rather than a static process. As a result, group learning is as important as individual learning.

Implementing digitization will not be the easiest task you've faced. We warn you that it will be even harder if you have fuzzy goals, too many objectives, an excessively broad scope, ill-defined or immeasurable metrics, no clear tie to financials, and disconnection from the strategy or operating plan. Good luck!

CHAPTER TEN

The Analysis and Design of New Services: Meso-Level Blueprint

What to Expect

Each digitization effort begins with the challenge of translating the vision for the project into tangible services. What does the user want? How do you architect the end-to-end workflow to deliver value? So, at its core, digitization is a problem-solving activity. Every initiative has a horizontal process or a multi-channel workflow design problem that is holding up performance. If your organization has decided to digitize its composite processes, the logical next step is to ask what, when, how, and why.

In this chapter, we present a detailed methodology based on Six Sigma that addresses the issue of how to analyze and improve existing processes and then subsequently design new end-to-end services while keeping the customer in mind. We also present the emerging topic of new job design as technology changes conventional jobs.

Moving from Strategy to Process Design

As the old saying goes, the devil is in the details. While there is a plethora of literature on process improvement, there is very little practical knowledge and insight into the detailed design of new customer-centric composite processes (for example, order-to-cash or multi-channel processes). This is often the area where enterprise projects break down.

For projects to be successful, deep dives into As-Is and To-Be processes are a necessity. It is common to see consultants and management waving their hands and talking high-level stuff. Few want to get their hands dirty and dig deep into the tangled inner workings of the organization. Sophisticated service platforms cannot be engineered without significant investments of time and resources in process modeling, design, and analysis.

Successful digitization efforts are possible only by carefully engineering processes in the context of the overall change effort. In Chapter 1, we talked about the three basic types of change: process improvement, strategic improvement, and business transformation. To illustrate the difference between them, consider this simple analogy: Process improvement is painting your house; strategic improvement is remodeling the kitchen; and business transformation is tearing down the house and rebuilding on the same lot.

The impact, effort, and scope of each are different depending on the industry. No two industries are precisely the same, but it's remarkable how many industries are affected by the same trends. This holds true even for education and government—the last bastions of brick and mortar. Let's look at some services design challenges in e-government where some significant projects are under way.

Evolving to Brick and Click—New Multi-Channel Government Services

Government organizations worldwide face dramatic changes, fueled by a marked increase in constituents' demand for integrated and transparent electronic services. Nearly every type of government—local, state, and federal—is involved in a widespread modernization and reform effort frequently called e-government. The goals are clear: Improve and automate processes, reduce costs through self-service, and streamline citizens' access to tax, licenses, and revenue information.

What is driving these changes? Vocal citizens, who are demanding better value for the taxes they are paying. They want accessible, convenient, and consistent online services. They are tired of taking time from their busy schedule and standing in line at a government office filling out paperwork. It seems like a story straight from the pages of science fiction: two parallel worlds—one, a highly digitized, multi-channel private sector versus the other, a highly paper-oriented, uni-channel government sector. The challenge is to upgrade government processes, applications, and infrastructure for new multi-channel services.

Existing government services have to change and provide a better user experience while being resource efficient. This is not going to be easy. Consider the recently established Department of Homeland Security (DHS), one of the most extensive reorganizations of the U.S. government since the 1940s. DHS is undertaking one of the most ambitious and expensive service platform initiatives in history. The agency's charter is to integrate numerous federal agencies, local governments, education, and private sector corporations to fight terrorism.

DHS's biggest challenge is the design, implementation, and optimization of new cross-agency processes that integrate various field, back-office, third-party applications, and other information silos. However, the processes that support the broader objective should drive technology investments, not the other way around. Since this is such a new initiative, the conundrum is that the customer of these new processes is currently unclear. So, the approach that DHS has to take is an iterative one—design, build, understand, and revise.

E-government efforts like DHS represent some of the most complex and radical efforts to move from a uni-channel (brick only) service model to a multi-channel (brick, tele, Web, and e-mail) service model. They also involve significant parallel changes in process design from an agency-centric model to a people-centric one capable of serving a broad constituency—private citizens, businesses, and employees.

Now that we have established the need for multi-channel services, let's examine the ever-present challenge of cross-enterprise services such as order-to-cash.

Evolving to Cross-Enterprise—New Order-to-Cash Services

The new services design problem is also evident in cross-enterprise scenarios. Take, for instance, the order-to-cash process. Most manufacturing companies think of this process in terms of receiving an order and seeing it all the way through to getting the cash. It's a long process that begins with lead generation, marketing campaigns, and order entry; this is the realm of customer relationship management (CRM). When a customer's electronic order arrives, manufacturing is scheduled, and parts availability is verified; this is the realm of enterprise resource planning (ERP). The order is then guided by applications such as distribution planning and order fulfillment; this is the realm of supply chain management (SCM). Finally, the order is sent to warehousing, shipping, and billing; this is the realm of financial applications and accounts receivable. Soon, you're all the way back to customer service and CRM.

This end-to-end process typifies the way companies operate, but not the way they use enterprise applications. Organizations have automated little fragments of the entire order-to-cash process using applications like CRM, ERP, and SCM. Part of the problem is that companies have defined the problems incorrectly. For instance, they thought that B2B Web sites solved the supply chain process problem. As companies look for more leverage and value from technology investments, they are focusing less on narrow process fragments and more on entire services. These services are built on cross-enterprise service platforms that address a range of interdependent integration and digitization issues.

What is the new services design challenge? Translating the high-level vision of macro-level focal points and strategy into everyday cross-enterprise services. What makes this even harder is that evolving technology capabilities coupled with morphing customer priorities make services design a nonstop issue.

The continuous service evolution concept should not be a big surprise for managers, but it usually is. For instance, many companies think that their work is done after they invest large amounts of time and money automating their internal business processes by purchasing and installing complex ERP, CRM, and SCM systems. Little did they realize that they were making only the first investment. The next big investment decision facing them is to integrate all these prior investments to support more sophisticated composite processes.

The evolution of business processes in organizations is conceptually similar to the evolution of species. In the long run, only the fittest or those most suited to the current environment survive.

The Growing Importance of Service Analysis and Design

Companies and government organizations need to ask, Do we have a detailed understanding of what the end-to-end process looks like? Are our end-to-end processes effective? Is the customer happy with our current way of doing business? Can it be improved? If so, what process improvement method should we use? It is imperative that every services analysis and design effort should be concerned about being effective and efficient. Effective means doing the right things; efficient means doing them fast, cheap, and well.

Converting digitization objectives into systematic results requires a complex combination of process improvement, new service design, and systematic change management. Change management issues need to be thought of earlier in the design cycle, not after the cycle is completed. This simple fact was often ignored by many organizations that attempted first-generation e-business. All were in a hurry to implement quickly. A lot spent millions on technology but later were shocked and disappointed to find that few customers or employees were really using the applications. Overcoming this adoption resistance is an obstacle facing many organizations. Our research shows that digitization strategies consistently underestimate the difficulty of getting people to change.

The bottom line: Digitization initiatives seldom fail because of technology. They sputter and die without process definition and change management to sustain them at multiple organizational levels. A methodology for undertaking this arduous journey of change is acutely needed.

Picking a Meso-Level Change Management Methodology

Before designing services, it is important to pick a process improvement methodology. This is not as easy as it looks. There are many of them—Six Sigma, Voice of the Customer, Lean Enterprise, Theory of Constraints, Total Quality Management, Process Reengineering, Toyota Production System (TPS), and Activity Based Management.

What is common to all these methods? They represent a variety of methodologies and improvement tools used to pursue quality at the factory shop floor, end-to-end manufacturing operations, and service operations. They also form the meso-level process foundation for digitization. The common belief in all these quality improvement methods is that organizations should aim for zero defects in all aspects of their operations. This is achieved by relentlessly improving business processes.

Every meso-level method aims to improve both the business performance and the customer experience. More often than not, it challenges the status quo. As a result, simply automating the existing As-Is processes is not an option. Every digitization initiative should have Six Sigma or an equivalent process improvement method as its first step. Unfortunately, few do. In their hurry to implement enterprise applications, companies often gloss over or sacrifice the time-consuming but pertinent details.

A well-known cliché in the software industry is garbage in, garbage out (GIGO). If the existing processes are not redesigned and improved, the digitized processes are not going to be efficient or effective. A significant number of digitization projects don't formally follow an improvement method. Why isn't every digitization initiative preceded by a process improvement effort? Because managers like to believe in the vendor's sales pitch: "Trust us. Our software, developed by brilliant programmers, will address all your process problems." Until it is too late, many do not realize that they should have changed their processes before they bought the software. This scenario is so common that you wonder if people ever learn from their mistakes.

Technology is an enhancer, plain and simple. It is not a substitute for process thinking or understanding where inefficiencies (or waste) are or how to eliminate them. It is a well-known fact that much performance improvement can be obtained by simply tweaking existing processes to eliminate waste. What technology does is further turbocharge the overall improvement. In other words, if you don't know how to drive, buying a Ferrari is not going to solve the problem. The Ferrari is an enhancer of the overall driving experience; it cannot address your lack of driving capability in the first place. Similarly, if you don't have the right processes in place, it does not matter what applications you buy.

Picking a Performance Improvement Method

Now that we have clearly stated the need for a process understanding and improvement method, the question facing you is: How do you choose the right methodology? Which one is best suited for services digitization since each methodology sets out to accomplish different strategic and operational objectives?

Table 10.1 shows some of the characteristics of common change methodologies—Total Quality Management, Process Reengineering, Lean Enterprise, and

Table 10.1: Comparing the Popular Methods

	Total Quality Management	Process Reengineering	Lean Enterprise	Six Sigma
Goals	Meet customer expectations	Breakthrough solutions	Eliminate waste to create value	Reduce variation in all enterprise operations
Focus	Product quality	Business processes	All enterprise processes and people	All sources of product/service variation (bottom-line bias)
Scope	Business unit	Business unit	Enterprise value stream	Enterprise
Change Process	Incremental	Radical change	Evolutionary systemic change	Process-specific; continuous
Methodology	Statistical quality control	Ad hoc process mapping	Value stream mapping	DMAIC methodology
Business Objective	Improve efficiency and shareholder value	Increase enterprise performance and customer value	Deliver value to all stakeholders	Minimize waste and increase customer satisfaction

Six Sigma—that are being used in corporations to address the issue of general process improvement. While they differ on certain dimensions, the underlying methods are similar in their approach, as they all sprang from the same root: the statisticians Walter Shewart and Edward Deming.[1]

Let's look at Six Sigma, a method that is getting the most traction in the marketplace. We will highlight the basic concepts behind Six Sigma, the momentum behind it, and how it being used.

Six Sigma—Dominant Performance Improvement Method

The most popular improvement method in recent years is Six Sigma. In every generation there is one method that becomes the dominant standard. Right now, it looks like Six Sigma is the one for process analysis and design. It is by far the method that has the most organizations as its devotees. As they say in the stock market, don't fight the market. If the market adopts Six Sigma as the standard, it makes sense to look at digitization through the Six Sigma lens.

Motorola engineers developed the Six Sigma concept at the end of the 1980s.[2] In 1988, Motorola won the Malcolm Baldridge Award for quality. Immediately, the media began reporting success stories emanating from Motorola that sparked the interest of other companies. One popular and frequently cited success story was pager redesign. The new pagers that Motorola was making were costly— about $1,500—and took a long time to manufacture. In an 18-month period, Motorola's engineers, using Six Sigma, redesigned processes to create a pager that sold for a few hundred dollars and took only 72 minutes to produce.

Six Sigma was credited with bringing a process focus to Motorola and making it a market leader in the early 1990s.[3] Six Sigma practically became a household word in the mid-1990s as Allied Signal and General Electric (GE) started to report sizeable operating performance improvements that they too attributed to the quality improvement method.

Other companies took note, and since then, there has been an explosion of Six Sigma adoption. The logic behind its popularity is not hard to grasp. Six Sigma is aimed at defect reduction. A defect is an outcome that is not intended. For example, a sales order that is not filled correctly is a defect. Parts that are not inspected are defects. Late delivery is a defect. There is nothing redeeming about defects, which cause customer dissatisfaction and, in turn, company problems. In the case of a car or appliance company, defects result in excessive warranty costs. So, when defects are eliminated, customers are happier, and the savings and the efficiency go right through to the bottom line.

Six Sigma's core message is simple: You can't create value for the company without first creating value for the customer. In recent years, there has been a movement toward defect and variability reduction in services. Many hospitals adopted Six Sigma to reduce prescription errors. One used it to map the process of prescriptions as they originated with a doctor's scribble, were filled by the pharmacy, and then administered by nurses. Most mistakes came from errors in reading the doctors' handwriting. The hospital reacted to this discovery by implementing a program requiring doctors to type the prescriptions into a computer, slashing errors.[4] Companies have discovered that the discipline of data analysis, an integral part of Six Sigma, is especially useful in reducing variation.

These companies and others are wisely laying the foundation for digitization by putting the Six Sigma methodology to improve processes in place first.

Six Sigma's Momentum

Six Sigma is a serious undertaking. Like every methodology, it takes patience, money, discipline, and experience. There are no shortcuts. However, some of the published results (which we describe) have been astounding and probably well worth the expenditures.[5]

- GE is estimated to have spent more than $600 million on thousands of Six Sigma projects and estimates that its ROI from the investment totaled more than $8 billion since 1999 alone.

- Dow Chemical credits Six Sigma with its savings of more than $750 million since 1999.

- Bank of America predicted that Six Sigma would save it $1 billion in 2002 alone through error reduction, process streamlining, and enabling cross-platform selling.

Some companies are using Six Sigma to reposition themselves aggressively. Consider GE's efforts in the words of Jeff Immelt, chairman and CEO, "We've lowered material costs through digitization, online auctions, things like that. We've reduced our reinvestment ratio from 1.4 to 0.9. We've created capacity through Six Sigma. A lot of our digitization resources and investments are in place. And we've generated 3–4 percent total cost productivity during this time period. . . . And we've increased digitization in Six Sigma, so at a time when we're taking total costs down and total employment down, we're making the strong redeployment call so that we can get the most out of this market."[6]

Doug Oberhelman, group president of Caterpillar had this to say about Six Sigma: "There are literally thousands of other cost containment projects going on at Caterpillar, and Six Sigma is at the core of most of them. . . . We didn't realize at the time what Six Sigma could do. We certainly do now. We really started Six Sigma in early 2001. This is the end of our second full year. I know we haven't published numbers on the benefits of Six Sigma. I can tell you I don't know where we would be without it today. It is becoming engrained in the way we think and do, and I think the Caterpillar culture is particularly conducive to something like this."[7] (Caterpillar's objective is to cut costs by $1 billion in three years.)

Six Sigma is also being employed on the multi-channel customer-facing side to create a better customer experience. Thomas Patrick, CFO of Merrill Lynch, described how Six Sigma has benefited the company's Private Client business, which provides wealth management services for individual investors: "We continue to leverage our multi-channel service strategy to increase our share of clients' business and continue to invest in growing the retirement services business. . . . Private Client has also made a number of client service enhancements as it continues to improve the client experience and reduce costs. For example, through Six Sigma initiatives, Private Client has been successful in reengineering the monthly client account statement and mailing processes. These changes have led to an increase in client satisfaction by increasing ease of use and speed of delivery."[8]

With these types of results, it's not surprising that Six Sigma went from the shop floor to the boardroom rather quickly. However, few firms are seeing the linkage between Six Sigma and digitization. They are thinking of Six Sigma only as a process improvement method. They are not seeing that Six Sigma lays a very powerful foundation for services digitization. Forward-thinking companies like GE saw this connection in the late 1990s. Other firms with large Six Sigma investments need to start thinking about how to leverage the Six Sigma investments into a services digitization advantage.

Six Sigma = Culture Change

We talked a lot about the importance of change management earlier in this chapter. Digitization can learn a lot from the efforts of Six Sigma, which wrestled with many of the same issues, such as how to bring about enterprise-level changes to drive quality. Many companies and individual business units see Six Sigma as more than a quality or process improvement technique; they are using it as a rallying cry to change the organization.

According to Dan Burnham, chairman and CEO of Raytheon Corporation, a U.S. defense contractor: "If you see Six Sigma as a culture changer—something that will profoundly affect the organization—then, by definition, it takes the passion and obsession of the CEO to make it happen. We saw Six Sigma—in particular, Raytheon Six Sigma—as a way to profoundly change our culture."[9]

Part of the culture change is getting employees to talk the same process language. Grass roots adoption is critical. History has shown that Six Sigma has failed when executives forced it on unwilling employees. Experienced CEOs will tell you that you can't change a large company all at once; you have to go process-by-process and unit-by-unit and get buy-in from the entire organization.

Why is buy-in important? Joseph Juran, one of the pioneers of the quality movement said, "I know of no company that took less than six years to achieve a position of quality leadership within their industry. Usually it took closer to ten years."[10] It took Japanese companies more than 30 years to shed their reputation of poor product quality. This implies that, in many cases, the digitization initiatives will outlive the executive team that introduces it. Hence the danger when it is seen as being imposed by a strong-willed individual.

Like Six Sigma, successful digitization initiatives have to create a grass-roots culture change at the employee level.

Criticism of Six Sigma

Since we presented the positive side of Six Sigma, it makes sense to balance it by presenting the opposing side. Every methodology has its followers and its opponents, and Six Sigma is no different. Opponents claim that it is nothing new, only old tried and tested methods being reformulated. There are plenty of people who assail it as a "marketing ploy" by consultants looking for quick money. Some of this is true as Six Sigma, like all buzzwords, blurs in meaning and stands for multiple things: a vision, a philosophy, a symbol of change, a metric, and a methodology.

The cult-like following of Six Sigma is creating a backlash. Opponents of Six Sigma feel that quality needs to be built into product. The argument is that the whole organizational culture needs to put quality into planning and drive quality throughout the entire organization (not just inspect poor designs). Companies that follow this model are Honda, Toyota, and Mercedes Benz. The Japanese and Germans are fanatical about quality. Over the years, they have built their own production quality systems, such as Toyota Production System, that have many of the same attributes as Six Sigma.

Despite the criticism, we think Six Sigma is a better framework and approach to defect reduction and process improvement than many other alternatives. The challenge is applying it to problems for which it is suitable.

Steps for Service Digitization

By this point, you are probably thinking: Six Sigma and digitization, I still don't see the connection. Well, let's try to reestablish the connection. An efficient end-to-end multi-channel service does not just happen; it must be designed with the customer in mind and implemented across multiple applications. In other words, the existing way of doing business literally has to be disassembled into its fundamentals and reassembled to meet new objectives.

Disassembling and reassembling processes are the theme of this chapter. To undertake this effort, you have to understand the process inefficiencies that cause time, resources, and money to be wasted. Eliminating waste and creating new value implies a willingness to redesign the current way of doing things.

To bring about effective change, you must first understand your unique situation. The rest of this section helps you to assess your current situation so that you may create and implement an optimum change strategy for your company. We use an iterative yet simple model to guide you in this process. The Six Sigma DMAIC process—define, measure, analyze, improve, and control—should help you to channel these change management efforts.

If you already have defined a digitization focal point, then it is time to make your process conform to Six Sigma standards. Let's analyze each of these steps, which are illustrated in Figure 10.1.

Define

Always start with the users. Figure out what they want and how to satisfy them better. Take a "50,000-foot view" to identify the key output variables (the buzzword for this is critical-to-quality), and list what is important to customers. Do you feel your customers' pain? This also involves collecting, defining, and communicating all the background information on the product, process, and customer or end user.

The vast majority of an organization's knowledge is tacit, that is, it is based on experience and has been neither articulated nor explicitly represented. The challenge is to make the tacit knowledge explicit. The detailed steps for making this happen include:

1. **Define the Focal Point**—What is your business? This is a simple but provocative question. Define the digitization focal points by conducting the following analysis: What are the five critical-to-quality issues the customer cares about? What is the value of the identified focal point for the company and the customer? What are the resulting outcomes expected for the business? What

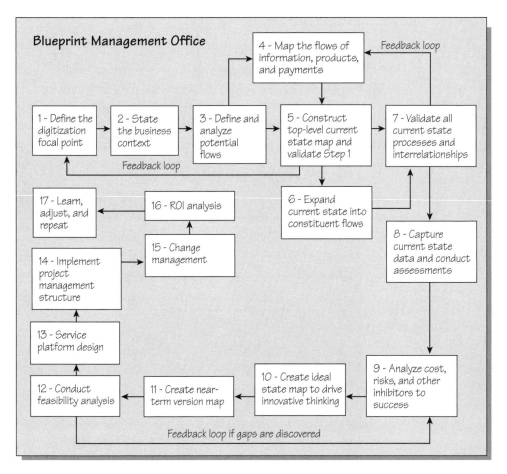

Figure 10.1: Steps for Service Digitization

are the major processes or organizational flows that support this focal point? Who are the key value stakeholders? Getting close to the right goals is far more important than achieving the wrong goals more efficiently.

2. **State the Business Context**—Define the scope of the business context. Perform analysis of any external influences (societal, environmental, technological, and political), and any destabilizing forces that may be internal or external (policies, laws, demographics, and trends). Change involves numerous people with many creative ideas. Delineate your boundaries clearly (who the customers are, who the suppliers are, what the inputs are, what the expected outcomes are). The output of this step is a business case—what

do we want to accomplish? For instance, in a project involving digitizing accounts receivable, the objective is to reduce end-to-end ship-to invoice process cycle time from an average of 12 days to an average of 3 days.

3. **Be the Customer**—Take a moment and look at your organization from the customers' perspective. What do they see? Digitization requires you to look at the processes from the customers' perspective, not yours. In other words, study processes from the outside-in. By understanding the transaction life-cycle with the customers' needs in mind, you can discover what they are seeing and feeling.

   Voice of the Customer (VOC), an interview and analysis technique, is a useful method for gathering firsthand information about what the customer is looking for. With this knowledge, you can identify areas where you can add value or improve from their perspective. Consider this scenario at a telecom company: Customers are extremely unhappy about billing errors. The company frequently sent out invoices that contained errors about rates per minutes. The company would charge customers $0.10 per minute when they should be billed $0.05 per minute. One of the VOC findings was that the problem was especially bad for customers who had multiple products (land-line, cell phone, and DSL Internet service). This problem was causing multi-product customers to switch carriers. The loss of this high-dollar value segment of customers was resulting in significant bottom-line impact.

4. **Map the Service**—What composite processes are needed to serve a customer? Assess and map the end-to-end high-level flows of products/programs/services, information, and payments as appropriate. Without a high level of understanding of how you or your customers complete an activity, you'll never know how to change it for the better.

Figure 10.2 illustrates the gap between expectation and reality. Why does the gap exist? After several years of evolution, process flows tend to get complicated. Companies buy other companies; they sell off some companies. They grow from 100 to 10,000 employees. Workflows become convoluted. The challenge is to think of new ways to simplify those flows.

Measure

After you finish defining the high-level processes, you must begin studying the details. Developing the detailed process decomposition is the foundation of digitization. It keeps efforts grounded in "reality." The detailed steps include:

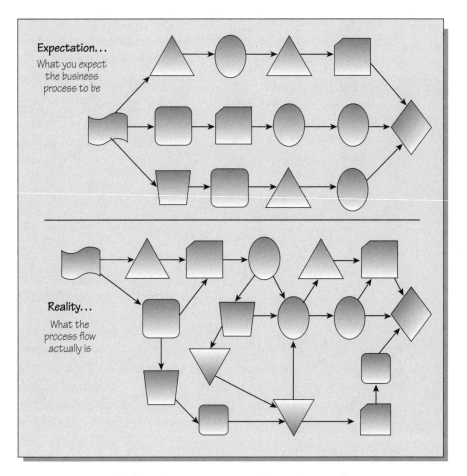

Figure 10.2: Process Expectation versus Reality

1. **Draw an As-Is Map**—Start with current state (the level one processes from Step 4) and validate boundaries, values, outcomes, and mission. Adjust the initial assumptions as necessary to reflect reality. The output summarizes current reality in a visual map that allows the whole organization to see the opportunity. Understanding assumptions behind a process is an extremely important step. Certain processes are the way they are for a reason. Not understanding these reasons will create problems downstream.

2. **Drill Down**—Take each portion of the current state and drill down one layer to the next level of constituent processes, flows, or components (see Figure 10.3). Drilling down one layer of processes makes the interaction of the vari-

ous flows more apparent and allows more data to be gathered and analyzed. Drilling down is a tedious and time-consuming process and often a step where companies begin to lose interest. Extracting details of the different ways Level 2, 3, and 4 processes are being done in the real world takes quite a bit of detective work.

3. **Conduct a Process Walk-Through**—What is causing the process breakdown or inefficiency problems? What causes variations? Variation is what you encounter when you walk up to the counter and get great service once and lousy service the next time. Variability is the enemy of consistency and customer satisfaction. Overlay the soft stuff (workforce issues) with the hard stuff (technical components) of the flow not already captured and mapped.

4. **Perform Linkage Analysis**—Capture relevant data that is measured in terms defined by the company and understood consistently. That is, capture the metrics or information available and perform an analysis/linkage. Conduct assessments to capture other metrics and create a comprehensive view.

Talk to the people who actually perform the work that you are studying as they are the most knowledgeable about how to improve the workflow and eliminate variation. Then start measuring and refining. Remember to benchmark current customer satisfaction constantly because that is your ultimate measure of success.

Figure 10.3 presents a widely used method of process decomposition. The ability to take high-level services and systematically decompose them into processes, subprocesses, and eventually into tasks is well understood in engineering and operations but not in other areas of business, say marketing or HR. This is a problem since marketing tends to lead many customer-facing services initiatives and HR many employee-facing services initiatives.

Analyze

The next action is to develop a practical To-Be map for what you would like to achieve in the near future. To reach this point, you have to change your processes to maximize customer satisfaction and identify performance gaps and improvement objectives. This often involves slicing and dicing the As-Is data to understand the existing process conditions and problems that create customer dissatisfaction.

The detailed steps include:

1. **Conduct a Process Analysis**—Analyze and capture bottlenecks, flow, value inhibitors (whether social or technical), costs, risks to flow, and risks to

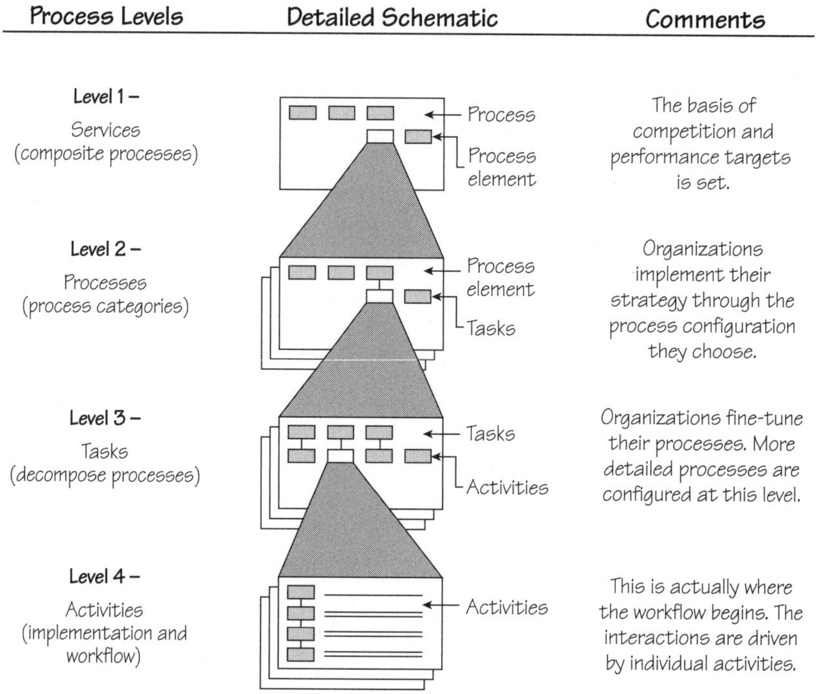

Process Levels	Detailed Schematic	Comments
Level 1 – Services (composite processes)	Process / Process element	The basis of competition and performance targets is set.
Level 2 – Processes (process categories)	Process element / Tasks	Organizations implement their strategy through the process configuration they choose.
Level 3 – Tasks (decompose processes)	Tasks / Activities	Organizations fine-tune their processes. More detailed processes are configured at this level.
Level 4 – Activities (implementation and workflow)	Activities	This is actually where the workflow begins. The interactions are driven by individual activities.

Figure 10.3: Established Methodology for Drilling Down the Process Levels

success criteria. Group these findings into priorities and analyze them to understand how they affect service, wait time, resources, and money. Prioritize the list of changes into short-term and long-term and assess the impact of each proposed process change.[11]

2. **Create an Ideal State**—The ideal state should include process, technical, and social elements. Perfection is impossible, but reaching for it stimulates breakthrough thinking and analysis that will create a more robust future state.

3. **Develop a Version Map**—Take your ideal state and work backwards. Create a To-Be version map achievable in a relatively short-term window (six to nine months) based on that ideal state. Versioning is a commonly used method of moving toward an ideal state. See Table 10.2 for an example of an As-Is process and the first version of a To-Be process.

4. **Conduct a Feasibility Analysis**—Assess and analyze the gaps in the ability to achieve the next version. Create a balanced set of measures/metrics for success and confirm behaviors generated conform to the future state directives.

Table 10.2: As-Is Processes versus To-Be Processes in Procurement

Paper-Based Purchase Order Processing (Steps in As-Is process)	Digitized Purchase Order Processing (Steps in To-Be process)
1. Receive a purchase requisition 2. Obtain drawings and material specifications 3. Copy drawings 4. Copy material specifications 5. Write letter/request for quotes 6. Collate letter/request for quotes/drawings/material specifications 7. Post to several potential suppliers 8. Receive queries from suppliers 9. Refer to engineering department 10. Reply to query 11. Receive written quotations 12. Analyze quotations 13. Select supplier 14. Place purchase order	1. Receive a purchase requisition via a portal 2. Post drawing/material specs/other details on secure Web site 3. E-mail inquiry and temporary passwords to potential suppliers 4. Hold competitive bidding event (reverse auction) 5. Select supplier 6. Place electronic purchase order

Simply tweaking the old work processes may not be enough to implement these changes. You may have to invent new ones.

Improve and Implement via Service Platforms

Customer-centric design is consistently giving customers what they want, when they want it. Once the root causes of problems are determined, the goal is to implement solutions that minimize, reduce, or eliminate them altogether. The detailed steps include:

1. **Design the Service Platform**—Establish and implement actions/programs/events to drive the creation of value and elimination of inefficiency to achieve the future state. This is where the new service is translated in detailed subprocesses that are part of the service platform (see Figure 10.4).

2. **Develop Project Management Structure**—Create necessary project management infrastructure (including organizational structure) to ensure leadership, integration, course corrections, validation, and accountability for

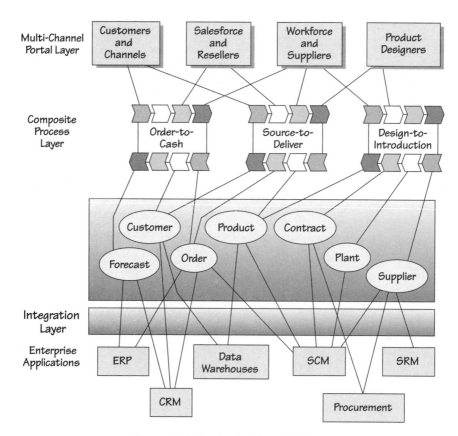

Figure 10.4: Service Platform Design

changes. Analyze risks, change management issues, and other inhibitors of successful implementation.

Control and Learn

Evaluation is the final goal of the DMAIC program. In this step, the firm analyzes before and after data, monitors the overall project, and documents the overall user acceptance. The detailed steps include:

1. **Manage Change**—Establish a change management program to drive adoption. Simply implementing the applications and taking a "build it and they will come" approach usually fails. People tend to resist imposed change; thus, overcoming it requires a deliberate strategy. Create a marketing and commu-

nication plan to ensure stakeholder enrollment, ownership, and accountability for all actions and ongoing analysis.

2. **Analyze the ROI**—What value did you actually get from the effort? Quantifying the return on investment is a great way of forcing everyone involved to understand that there is a financial goal that anchors process digitization. Based on the ROI, decide on a renewal period to revisit and adjust the future state (a continuous versioning view) on the path to the ideal state. To make this happen, you need to collect detailed data on end-to-end process performance (for example, time from order taking to order fulfillment).[12]

3. **Learn**—Repeat the entire process for the next version, but reflect first. Usually, managers have little or no time for reflection. This important step helps articulate various dysfunctional underlying dynamics that are causing problems.

Implementing anything new is always tricky and often has unintended consequences. In 1998, for example, Marks & Spencer, the U.K. retailer, decided to cut procurement costs by sourcing products from the cheapest possible supplier. It shifted much of its buying to overseas vendors with low-cost labor. However, the company failed to design the necessary business processes and managerial controls needed to handle a global logistics operation. Overseas sourcing that appeared profitable on a narrow local cost basis generated extremely high shipping and handling costs. The company's profit margins were cut in half between 1998 and 1999, and by 2000, its shares had lost nearly half their value. According to an industry executive, "Their biggest problem is that they've lost control of their supply chain."[13]

The moral of the story is that things happen after implementation. It is rare that everything goes smoothly. You need to have the necessary project management structure and skills to be able to react and fix the problems quickly before they become full-fledged catastrophes.

Workforce Changes—New Job Design

A critical task for the blueprint management office is redefining jobs. Superior performance is ultimately based on the people in the organization. The processes, applications, and procedures play an essential role, but the value truly stems from the employees—their skill, ability to solve problems, and motivation.

As service platforms transform jobs, it becomes necessary to redeploy the workforce to tackle different activities. Downsizing the organization is not the sole answer. Glance at the following announcements:

- Humana, a health-care insurer, plans to cut about 2,300 jobs (or 17 percent of its workforce) and consolidate seven customer service centers into four. The job losses were partially driven by large investments made into automating claims processing.

- Aetna, the second-largest U.S. health insurer, cut more than 8,000 jobs as its technology investments help to lower operating costs and generate the same amount of revenue with fewer employees.

Evidence of white-collar job loss due to digitization and outsourcing is beginning to accumulate, especially in the service sector. Replacing white-collar labor with technology is an irreversible mega-trend. However, successful replacement requires careful attention to a little-known science called job design. Job design is the creation, assessment, and definition of a job that includes making sure both employees and technology are being used optimally.

People resist using technology when it gets personal. The problem is not new. People have been rising up against new technology since the Industrial Revolution when followers of Ned Ludd smashed mechanical looms in the British Midlands between 1811 and 1816 to protest the seismic changes wrought on weavers and their communities. Despite the early resistance, the Industrial Revolution changed jobs forever. Since the early 1800s, the structure of business and labor has always been intimately linked to the new technologies. For instance, British workers steadily moved away from scattered shops or homes to organized factories. Steam, waterpower, and costly machinery enabled a concentration of labor in factories close to the power source and transportation hubs. Concentration of labor allowed efficiency and specialization, which in turn increased productivity.

The historical pattern of technology changing jobs is repeating. In the 2000s, the structure of white-collar labor is changing with catalysts like the Internet, wireless, and cheap computing. The constraints of distance, language, and culture are being breached with technology and globalization. Processes that were entirely paper-based are getting streamlined, digitized, and self-serviced. As a result, excessive layers of bureaucracy are getting slashed everywhere.

Resistance is natural when the status quo is threatened. It is difficult to let go of old ways and move quickly to new ones. This is true for literally every human being. Creating incentives for embracing new methods is part of designing jobs well.

We present the following example to bolster our argument. A large computer manufacturer traditionally sold computers, servers, and software to the customer through its direct salesforce and reseller channels. To increase efficiency, the company decided to create a new self-service channel. The expectation was that customers would serve themselves for standard products and would contact the salesforce for more complex, high-end products.

The company spent several million dollars building the new self-service portal. The portal was technically perfect, but fatally flawed in its process design. Self-service customers could get quotes for products online but had to go offline and fax the order to the call center (due to the legal department's insistence on a paper signature). The process, instead of going from a paper-based model to a digitized self-service order model as planned, became paper to online to paper. Not what the company had envisioned and definitely not what the customer wanted!

The role of the salesperson in the new process also became extremely fuzzy. When should he contact the customer? What should he do when the customer contacted him about orders placed online? How should he cross-sell and up-sell if customer contact is moved online? A whole set of important questions emerged. In the meantime, the salesforce was distracted by all these issues and unable to close critical deals. As a result, the company could not meet the revenue targets.

Whose responsibility is it to design the new click-and-brick jobs? It's certainly beyond the purview of traditional human resources. It requires a detailed understanding of how service platforms are affecting people and their job functions.

Most organizations do not choose to redesign jobs; they choose to let employees go. This is one potential way to solve the problem, but not an ideal one since downsizing works only when the job is eliminated. It rarely works when the job has to be reconfigured. Redesigning jobs is perhaps an unforeseen but necessary task in the journey toward digitization.

The bottom line: The most sophisticated service platform will not work if people are not interested in using it. People innately resist technology when it directly affects their jobs. Redesigning jobs is a crucial element of digitization that is currently being overlooked.

Seven Points to Ponder

> A journey of a thousand miles must begin with a single step.
> —*Lao Tzu*

An organization is only as good as its processes. When designing new services, the following issues must be considered:

1. Services are provocative. They help companies move beyond the question of what processes should be automated to address the challenging question of what value is intended from digitization.

2. Organization outputs are produced through processes. The objective is to leverage existing investments in enterprise applications and create value, based on the customer needs.

3. A process improvement methodology is critical. We favor Six Sigma, which is a disciplined, uniform approach to problem solving and process optimization that expresses customer requirements and expectations in quantitative terms.

4. Utilize a methodology to analyze and eliminate defects in processes. The Six Sigma approach outlines specific methods to recreate the process so the defects and variations can be minimized. At its core, Six Sigma is process reconfiguration based on data, understanding of statistical tools, and customer focus.

5. Operationally speaking, creating new services requires both an internal perspective on existing capabilities and an external perspective on customers' interaction with the service. Organizations do not always recognize circumstances in which introducing a new service will necessitate developing additional operating capabilities.

6. Two important questions should drive the introduction of a new service: 1) What customer needs are met by the new service? and 2) What process capabilities does the service require? Once a firm understands the process capabilities needed to support a new service, it can determine whether existing capabilities can be leveraged or new ones must be developed.

7. Organizations rarely recognize that additional job skills are required when digitization initiatives are implemented. Those that do often underestimate the difficulty of developing those skills.

This chapter emphasizes two important and often overlooked aspects of digitizing services. By no means the only two relevant considerations, they nevertheless play a prominent role in the offering of new services. By focusing on existing processes and new customer needs and examining how these dimensions are linked to one another through services, we gain insights into when and how to offer new services.

CHAPTER ELEVEN

Making Digitization Happen: Micro-Level Technology Blueprint

What to Expect

The micro-level IT architecture (the infrastructure and applications) of a typical organization is designed to support inside-out processes. As the game changes to an outside-in service-centric model, the underlying IT architecture has to change rather drastically, and it has to be in place before services can be designed, implemented, and delivered.

The Internet and emerging distributed computing models are replacing traditional, carefully crafted, centralized IT architectures. In this chapter, we delve into the micro-level technology blueprint (IT architecture) using several business examples. Our goal is to show the range of decisions a typical CIO will have to deal with.

Introduction

We are at the cusp of a massive infrastructure upgrade cycle to support service-centric (cross-enterprise and multi-channel) models.

Consider the following: A financial services firm in the Netherlands embarked on a program to redesign its IT architecture so it could bring new banking products to the market more quickly; increase its ability to give each customer personalized service; reach more customers through new channels; and, at the same time, cut IT costs. The firm began this effort after a major reorganization. Its strategy changed from being a bank structured along product lines to becoming an integrated financial services provider arranged according to customer segments.

Not surprisingly, after this reorganization the IT architecture could no longer meet the business requirements of the different divisions. It was too slow for the brokerage unit, too fragmented for the retail banking unit, and much too inflexible for the quickly changing investment banking environment. The IT architecture was a mess—the customer database alone had more than 2,000 proprietary interfaces. This level of custom code made simple changes time-consuming and expensive.

To get an idea of the size of the effort involved in an infrastructure upgrade project, consider the case of Nextel Communications. Due to its tremendous customer growth, Nextel needed to upgrade its business system infrastructure, especially billing applications, to support its business needs. It also wanted to put a platform in place to service over 10 million subscribers and accommodate future growth. In 2000, Nextel began a multi-year project called Business System Overhaul. The overhaul spanned three countries, six time zones, and eleven vendors. Over two million hours of software customization was necessary. It is estimated that over 800 business processes were redesigned and 25,000 users had to be trained.[1] This helps to show the massive effort involved in upgrading infrastructure.

IT management everywhere is haunted by questions. With extremely limited funding, how do we go about rearchitecting the IT application and infrastructure portfolio to achieve business goals? Are these goals clear enough to suggest whether the rearchitecture outcome should be a centralized or decentralized model? Should it be process-driven or application-driven? These are fascinating questions. They might put some business people to sleep, but for a majority of IT professionals this scenario is a recurring nightmare. The challenge is constantly balance to long-term flexibility with short-term demands.

Short-Term IT Decisions versus Long-Term IT Decisions

Most managers who are not in IT do not understand their organization's micro-level technology blueprint. Given the recent Six Sigma trend, they may comprehend their products and processes; they may even recognize their customers and quality impediments. However, they usually don't have a sufficiently detailed grasp of how their technology blueprint enables their business to get products made or services delivered. This lack of understanding creates a problem, as important IT decisions tend to be short-term rather than long-term oriented.

Long-term IT planning is absolutely necessary. The pace and nature of change in the business environment does not permit a step-by-step IT planning approach to developing the digitization blueprint; however, the piecemeal approaches that are often attempted are as dangerous as none at all. Such efforts absorb vast resources—financial, workforce, and even users—and lull the organization into thinking that it is addressing the architectural problem.

Companies are measured on their long-term performance. Whether the focal point is zero defects or increased productivity, the underlying issue is the long-term performance of the IT architecture. To provide the necessary performance, the micro-level blueprint approach—creation, management, and evolution—must adopt a strategy that recognizes and responds to the full range of current technology needs and requirements. Consequently, the technology blueprint effort proceeds on multiple fronts simultaneously.

Given all the positives of long-term IT planning, why isn't it more prevalent? One answer is rather obvious: The average tenure of a CIO is estimated to be around 18–24 months. Most CIOs are not in their positions long enough to make a significant impact. Without leadership stability, the trend tilts toward more short-term oriented decision making.[2]

Princeton University—Digitizing Education

To understand the tension better between short-term versus long-term decisions, consider the challenge facing educational institutions as they struggle to satisfy the digital student. The digital student is unlike any previous generation of students. They are more inquisitive, technologically savvy (most of them use Morpheus or Kazaa), and demanding (why is it taking so long?).[3] They do not take kindly to the phrase "can't be done."

The new digital student is putting a lot of pressure on processes and systems at various K–12 schools, colleges, and universities. Let's look at Princeton University as it races to meet the digital needs of students, alumni, faculty, and employees.

Located in central, suburban New Jersey, renowned Princeton University enrolls approximately 4,600 undergraduate students and 1,750 graduate students. Founded in 1746, this elite, Ivy League institution is the fourth-oldest university in the United States. Princeton, like other modern universities, increasingly communicates with its students, faculty, staff, and alumni through the Web. The university observed this phenomenon early and seized the opportunity to develop a comprehensive strategy to improve and expand its use of the Web.

Three major technology initiatives are taking shape at Princeton to deliver university services via the Web:

1. Improving and expanding the way Princeton's community uses the Web,

2. Web-enabling the client/server-based administrative systems, and

3. Integrating multiple stand-alone portals and aggregating typical administrative applications into a service platform.

These three goals constitute Princeton's Web strategy. As it strives to provide Web access to all university services, it is being forced to rethink everything from brand identity and teaching models to systems architecture and portal strategy.

The Web—A Core Part of the Digital Education Experience

With the campus community, especially the students, becoming avid users of the Web, a strategy is being developed to integrate it tightly into the daily activities of the university. Other drivers for the infrastructure revamp include rapidly changing technology, increased competition for limited resources, and an infrastructure that has grown piecemeal.

The resounding popularity of the Web has created an interesting set of issues. It is estimated that the initial university Web infrastructure took two people one week to implement in 1993.[4] Today, maintaining the Web infrastructure requires numerous people and many man-hours. High-impact Web projects are stymied due to a lack of coordination, standards, and time.

To address these issues and move to a service model, Princeton proactively created a Web strategy task force. The goals of this task force were to propose a strategy for improved and expanded use of the Web, as well as to set policies, guidelines, and an appropriate administrative structure for carrying out the strategy. The policy questions the task force aimed to define and address included:

• How can the Web support Princeton's teaching and research efforts?

• How can the Web support administrative activities and conduct university business?

• How should the Web be used for internal communication?

• How should the Web be used for external communication (for example, alumni, parents, potential applicants for admission and employment, media, and the public)?

- What transactions and forms of e-commerce can be conducted over the Web, eliminating people and paper?

The answers to these questions form the basis of a new phase of infrastructure development at Princeton. This will pave the way for the move from the current three-tier architecture to an n-tier portal architecture.

Serving the Digital Student—Portals and Service Platforms

In Princeton's current environment, resources are scattered, and students need to visit multiple Web sites to locate the information they seek. The university is creating a series of portals to deliver integrated access to these different constituents. Campus portals are applications that provide a single, consistent, and personalized gateway to on- and off-campus information and applications. Where the campus Web site may be a collection of thousands of pages or department Web sites, a portal is a collection of many applications and services.

Why portals? It is estimated that more than 42 Web sites exist with a "princeton.edu" destination address. This creates inefficiency and adds to frustration. Take grades, for instance. Since key information is not in one destination site, students would phone or visit faculty, administration, and staff members with inquiries. Also, with multiple independent destination sites, there is an overlap of features, an absence of a standard security architecture, unnecessary data replication, poor coordination, and suboptimal use of costly programmer resources.

To remedy the existing fragmented user experience, Princeton is considering moving toward one central service platform that would address the current architecture fragmentation problem. The service platform also presents a consistent and secure way to provide access to all key information, including course materials, student records, and financial information. This is similar to personalization projects at other institutions. Figure 11.1 shows the evolution from a custom portal method to a service platform model that can support multiple portals.

Utilizing a new service platform model, Princeton is looking to create new services aimed at the digital student. Princeton has set out to improve use of the Web, Web-enable the administration systems, and integrate stand-alone portals. Although these tasks are daunting, the long-term satisfaction from students, faculty, alumni, and staff will make this challenge worth the effort. Princeton will likely succeed in revamping its IT architecture. When it does, the university's success should be attributed to its ability to insist on a long-term focus.

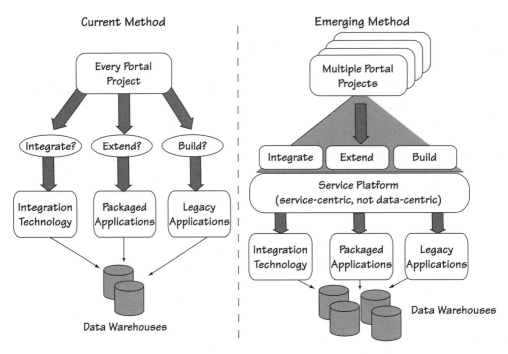

Figure 11.1: Moving Princeton to a Service Platform

Micro-Level Blueprint Planning Models

Organizations make micro-level technology decisions in three ways: 1) planning-oriented, 2) entrepreneurial-oriented, and 3) bureaucratic-oriented.

Planning-oriented decision making is based on long-range holistic considerations. With this style, plans are modified when organizational and environmental conditions change. Entrepreneurial-oriented decision making is based on opportunities that may be within the long-range plan. For instance, when the Internet took off in 1997, most organizations had to resort to entrepreneurial decision making to keep up with the competition. Bureaucratic-oriented decision making is when the firm has rigid procedures and committees that scrutinize *everything*. All innovation pretty much comes to a grinding halt. *Which style is your firm using?*

In the creative phase of digitization, entrepreneurial decision making was the dominant method for architecting a micro-level blueprint. In the quest for speed and to keep up with the dot-coms, long-term implications were often not fully considered. As the market consolidates and organizations become more profit-centric rather than growth-centric, the planning-oriented model is beginning to reassert itself.

In the planning-oriented style, there are five primary IT architecture decisions that have to be made. These are

1. The Project Specific Decision—one project at a time

2. The Data Architecture Decision—enterprise versus business unit versus project

3. The Application Architecture Decision—build, buy, or lease

4. The Portal Architecture Decision—application server versus workflow

5. The Infrastructure Decision—federated, centralized, or decentralized

Figure 11.2 illustrates the decisions every CIO has to make. Each choice results in a vastly different micro-level blueprint. Let's examine the issues involved in each of these decisions. We will only scratch the surface as each of these choices has evolved into a discipline by itself.

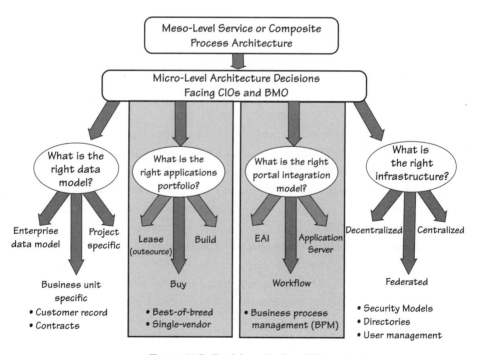

Figure 11.2: Decisions Facing CIOs

One Project at a Time

The primary reason to select this approach is unstable funding. Often, creating grand plans isn't the hard part; finding the money for execution is. Accordingly, the project-by-project mind-set permeates.

Deciding to digitize in this way is very common for small- and midsize businesses. Sometimes, even in big corporations, large-scale digitization projects are treated the same as any other initiative. Each effort is undertaken, one project at a time, in isolation from other projects, with little forethought given to achieving economies of scale, scope, or shared resources.

Without a shared strategic vision in place, each initiative wanders off in its own self-defined direction. In this scenario, directors and managers in business units will focus narrowly on immediate tactical needs; there is little involvement in or awareness of overarching strategic concerns. The results of the single project focus are

- Resource competition resulting in internal bickering and political posturing,

- A failure to embrace any commonality of purpose and technology across the organization,

- Incompatible system designs and no standardization among initiatives, leading to inconsistent customer experiences, and

- Business processes with essentially the same specifications but subtle differences that do not allow them to be interchanged.

A technology blueprint based on discrete initiatives can easily become chaotic when it is developed and managed one project at a time. Off-the-record, many executives will admit to you that their companies are not getting results because the political will or resources are simply not there to drive unification. Without such political courage, the institutional obstacles to well thought-out, comprehensive blueprints stubbornly remain. Like the good politicians they are, top management rhetorically supports common initiatives every chance it gets, but then does next to nothing to make them happen.

Departmental resistance is often the reason individual projects take precedence. Departmental incentives are often driven by parochialism, group loyalty, and a culture based on the concepts of "profit center" and individual P&Ls. As a result, the business lines are loath to implement common projects. This attitude is harmful when you are creating solutions for a common customer. In this fragmented environment, "customer focus" and "one face to the customer" will be impossible to execute—no matter how much effort is expended.

What Is Our Data Model?

A data model is useful for specifying an organization's business information requirements. Data models answer questions such as, What should the customer database look like? What information should be stored in this database? How should an order be represented in the database? What attributes of the order should be captured and stored?

After years of being out of fashion, top-down "data" models are back in vogue as complexity of business processes increases. The rapid rise of the Internet with its many disparate initiatives resurrected an old method first seen in the late 1970s and early 1980s. It makes sense to learn from what took place in the past so that the same mistakes are not repeated again.

Two decades ago, many large companies engaged in "map-the-ocean" projects to create large-scale enterprise data models. The objective was to bring order to the chaos of fragmented databases that the boom in data processing applications was creating. Since the late 1970s, the enterprise data model (EDM) has been the cornerstone architecture for IT development, especially with the staggering growth of relational databases like Oracle.

In the late 1980s, computer-aided software engineering (CASE) evolved under the umbrella of information engineering (IE). Typically, in a CASE environment, the planning tool set would be used to produce a high-level model of the corporate enterprise and its data. This model would depict the structure of the organization and its goals and priorities, as well as represent its business information, business activities, and interactions. The model also meant to identify how data is maintained, accessed, and used.

The goal was noble—create an enterprisewide data model to provide a single, consistent, logical view of business usage of data. Once created, all new applications and databases would conform to and be consistent with the enterprise data model. The outcome was massive data models created by both reverse engineering of existing information systems and forward engineering from stated business requirements along with the information needs of business leaders and analysts.

Unfortunately, most of the EDM projects in the 1980s and 1990s failed. Translating complex and conflicting business requirements into a single enterprisewide data blueprint proved to be impractical. Some projects were quick fixes that caught fire and then died out. Many projects missed the mark and became shelfware. In fact, some projects failed so badly that the mere mention of "enterprise architecture" or "enterprise data models" can send seasoned IT professionals scurrying.

Why did EDM projects fail? The pressure to deliver was too much. Most companies couldn't afford to wait while some group painstakingly built an enterprisewide data model. The lofty goal of creating a single data model in isolation from ongoing projects wasn't practical in a dynamic environment. The idea wasn't flawed; the methodology was. Specifically, the projects lacked iteration and learning within the scope of existing projects.

Fixing the Data Model Problems—Iterative Development

In recent years, some enterprise data modeling problems have been fixed by using a "closed-loop" iterative methodology. Being too focused on the tactical and not enough on broader issues is the longstanding criticism of the enterprise data model approach. The closed-loop feedback process attempts to bridge the two.

The closed-loop model also attempts to resolve a prominent cause of EDM's failure: Most of the work was done in a "clean room" with very little customer participation or knowledge of how the processes actually use the data. To prevent this chasm, companies are forcing their analysts to go out and listen to customers.

If you're going to build a robust EDM, it makes sense for the EDM to be created around what the customers actually want and need. Talk to happy customers; talk to unhappy customers. Find out what's going on in their processes and business. Ask what their concerns are. Knowing where they stand and what they would like will help define the boundaries. It will help you adjust the EDM so that, as customers evolve, the blueprint keeps up with the market.

In today's world, data models are built iteratively as a part of projects under the oversight of the enterprise architect. By managing data models from a larger perspective as a shared resource enhanced by each successive project, the enterprise can gradually develop enterprise data models that are relevant and valuable.

What Is Our Enterprise Applications Model?

Users don't interact with data directly. They interact with applications. An application model is the translator between data models on one side and processes on the other.

In the 1990s, the business and process agendas of large corporations were primarily supported by an application model comprised of enterprise applications, especially ERP (enterprise resource planning), like SAP R/3. A large part of this was due to Y2K remediation and, in Europe, the preparation for a single currency, the euro. Technology historians will likely dub the 1990s the "Golden Age of ERP."

In the late 1990s and early 2000s, e-commerce, CRM (customer relationship management), and SCM (supply chain management) replaced ERP. These applications moved to the top of everyone's agenda as organizations, pressured by financial markets and investors, raced to become customer-focused and growth-oriented. As a result, the application portfolio of many companies began to look like a loosely coupled set of packages (see Figure 11.3).[5]

In recent years, the technological landscape of most corporations has gone from mostly custom applications to one dotted with packaged applications with acronyms like BW (business warehouse), ERM (enterprise resource management), WMS (warehouse management system), HRMS (human resource management system), EAI (enterprise application integration), SFA (salesforce automation), BPM (business process management), and PSA (professional services automation). The media and analyst firms feed the buzzword craze by creating new variants.

To deal with all these different, expensive, and "must-have" packaged applications, which often have complex overlapping functionality, companies began to create cross-functional steering committees. The goal of these steering committees is to come up with a strategy to align business, processes, and applications.

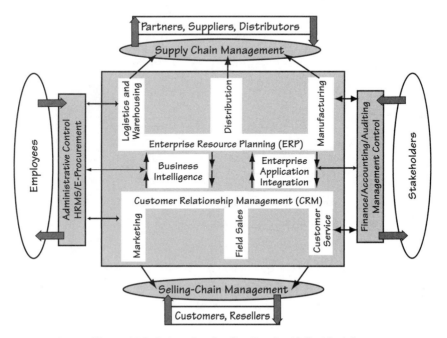

Figure 11.3: Enterprise Application Portfolio Model

The strategy then drives three key activities—selection, evaluation, and execution. In our experience, most steering committees are very active in the selection and evaluation phases. They lose interest in the most critical phase—execution—which creates the actual value.

The decision of build versus buy versus lease is a tough one. Let's look at how the selection and evaluation decisions are made with the widely used portfolio approach.

The Portfolio Method of Application Investment

In most organizations, a centralized, business-driven, top-down investment approach dominates the creation and management of off-the-shelf applications. The main objectives are to minimize risk by looking at technology investments from a financial perspective and to make sure that all the application investments complement the business goals.

The portfolio method originated in the early 1990s, as CFOs and line-of-business managers began to take an active interest in helping fund, create, and manage the application portfolio. The mind-set with which they approached the technology investment and management problem was similar to the structured way they would invest in machines, factories, or warehouses. Investing in these areas is typically done through classic capital budgeting, a staple in introductory finance courses.

Capital budgeting typically involves the following steps:

- Analyzing and ranking all applications based on benefit, cost, and risk criteria;

- Benchmarking, screening, and selecting a portfolio of applications;

- Scoring and prioritizing the existing portfolio;

- Determining whether applications meet stipulated business process requirements; and

- Deciding on the mixture of applications in the overall IT investment portfolio.

Since it is based on financial models, the portfolio method leans heavily toward data and quantitative analysis. As a result, innovative breakthrough projects, which may not have historical data (or media hype) to back them, often have a hard time making it through the process. To get around this hurdle, prototyping innovative application ideas to explore potential and value is a standard practice among IT organizations.

Single Vendor versus Best-of-Breed

The application portfolio can be constructed using three approaches:

1. Single-vendor standardization,

2. Best-of-breed, or

3. Leasing or outsourcing.

Single-Vendor Standardization. Colgate-Palmolive is one of the world's largest consumer products manufacturers. Its products span oral care (toothpaste), personal care (deodorants and shampoos), and household cleaning supplies (soaps and bleach). Colgate-Palmolive has shown a preference for single-vendor standardization using SAP for its applications and IBM for its hardware platform. By globally standardizing SAP as its end-to-end application architecture, the company explicitly trades off the functionality provided by best-of-breed solutions for the reduced integration cost and speed of deployment provided by a standard, packaged solution. Colgate supports the standard architecture by centralizing all development, utilizing a complement of regional shared services centers to handle regulatory and legal customization, and minimizing local IT support staff. This approach allows Colgate to reduce the percentage of IT spending on maintenance and enhancement activities from 90 percent to 50 percent, enjoy economies of speed when rolling out new functionality, and bring new products to market faster, leading to exemplary corporate financial performance.[6]

Best-of-Breed. Best-of-breed (or mix-and-match) integration is when the organization buys multiple packages from different vendors and consolidates them into a seamless whole. As applications become more vertically specialized, companies may not want to buy everything from one vendor. They may want use application integration software to tie together various suites, both inside and outside the organization. That is what EAI, XML, and Web Services are meant to do. They make the Web an integration platform for linking best-of-breed applications. VF Corporation, the world's largest publicly owned apparel company based in Greensboro, North Carolina, is an example of a best-of-breed company. VF designs, manufactures, and markets branded jeanswear, intimate apparel, occupational apparel, knitwear, outdoor apparel and equipment, and children's playwear through its operating subsidiaries. With more than 25 consumer-focused marketing units, 93 manufacturing facilities, more than 70 contractors, and 54 distribution centers around the world, VF operates a complex supply chain. The company uses a best-of-breed strategy with solutions from several vendors, including SAP, i2, Logility, and Gerber.[7]

Leasing or Outsourcing. Leasing is when the company chooses to rent an application. Outsourcing is a form of leasing. We found an example of an outsourcing approach at British Petroleum (BP). Determined to focus its IT resources on projects that enable its core business of oil exploration, BP has taken the dramatic step of completely outsourcing IT infrastructure and several business processes, including accounting, finance, and human resources. In this model, the firm partnered with multiple external vendors and systems integrators to manage its IT infrastructure, utility services (for example, help desk), and solutions delivery. Using innovative contract terms, including gain sharing and mandatory multi-vendor collaboration, BP is able to conserve IT resources for projects that improve the efficiency of its exploration efforts, such as its Highly Immersive Visualization Environments (HIVES), which have increased both decision speed and quality.[8]

Drawbacks of the Portfolio Method

Despite marking a turning point in technology management, the portfolio method of managing applications is top heavy in high-level strategy and poor at dealing with the vagaries of real-world execution.

The method often overestimates the synergy between different applications due to limited feedback from the trenches, where day-to-day execution is done. This problem is similar to one that crops up with mergers and acquisitions, which are often based on optimistic projections that assume few difficulties in integrating companies.

The typical scenarios resulting from the portfolio method are

- The best case: a tightly integrated set of transactional applications that create an effective digitization foundation. Invariably, most of the success is enjoyed at the single business unit level.

- The worst-case: a hodgepodge of packaged applications and legacy applications (or heritage systems) that fail to integrate as anticipated. Much money and manpower have to be dedicated to bring about integration, further eroding the ROI.

Who are the culprits causing the worst-case scenario? In many cases, the executives who made the investment decisions are not even around when the project moves to execution. In fact, there is a group of executives and consultants who simply specialize in enterprise software package selection. The minute the selection is done, they are off to another company. They never stick around for the less glamorous execution phase. Consulting companies and software sales teams love this scenario, as they have very little accountability.

Alas, the application portfolio model's usefulness may have peaked in the early 1990s. The game at the time, of course, was enhanced revenue growth. In the postbubble, sluggish economy, companies are challenged to deliver both cost reduction by increasing efficiencies and improving existing processes and growth by driving integration and innovation across product lines. There is more focus on getting rid of redundancies and cleaning up operations. It's a challenging prospect, but one that has set the perfect stage for portals.

What Is Our Portal Strategy?

Consider the process changes under way in the airline industry, where multiple fragmented applications are being integrated and forced to go real time. The objective is to create a flexible infrastructure that captures and manages the entire lifecycle of events from scheduling, gate assignment, passenger check-in, meal logistics, luggage activity, and runway assignments. All information should always be available in real time to gate and service agents, flight terminals, tower control centers, and customer Web sites. The right information in the right places dramatically reduces flight check-in time, increases on-time departures, and better manages security risks.

The airline business is racing to eliminate costs in a bid to stay competitive. It is not the only industry that faces these pressures. If you haven't already, you will soon. You will probably see the following words driving your digitization plan: integrated, people-driven, nimbleness, agility, adaptive, flexibility, or shared. *Are these words present in your digitization plan?*

If any of these words are present, the odds are high that you are spending or have spent millions of dollars and thousands of man-hours buying, configuring, and deploying portals, which are integrated with various best-of-breed enterprise applications. It is also highly likely that nearly as much money and time were spent developing and maintaining homegrown application integration servers to perform functions unique to your business.

Today, organizations have data everywhere but not a lot of information. For example, you may have multiple policies (homeowner, auto, and term-life) with the same insurance company, but that firm doesn't have the foggiest idea that you're the same person. Sad, but true.

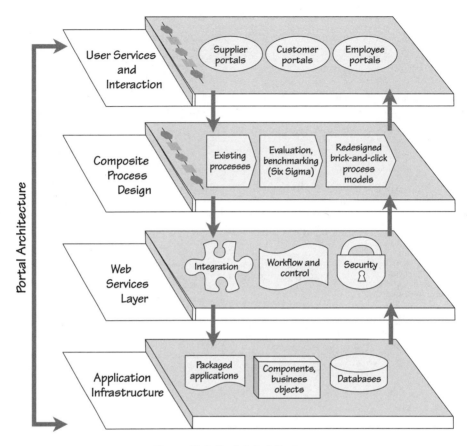

Figure 11.4: Portal Architecture

Thus, most organizations are being forced to find a new way of integrating these diverse and often incompatible applications. The only way to unlock the full value of those investments is to integrate them so they can interact with each other to generate information. If this is your company's objective, then you are a prime candidate for the services blueprint enabled by enterprise portals and Web Services. Figure 11.4 illustrates the elements of a portal architecture.

In the portal architecture, the focus is clearly shifting from discrete clusters of transactional applications like ERP toward cross-functional service integration. It does not take a genius to figure out that the hallmark of any successful, service-oriented company is continuous process innovation with a sharp focus. As the focus shifts, so must the blueprint.

Investing in Portals

Consider the case of FedEx Corporation. Experiencing a slowdown in its express shipping business in the late 1990s, the company decided to improve its service by creating a "one face to the customer" strategy, enabling seamless, role-based, cross-channel customer service. Underpinning this strategy was an "operate independently, compete collectively" philosophy. The outcome was the Arise project, which was a multi-year plan to create a standard customer-facing portal architecture, composed of 30 discrete IT projects. To facilitate the creation of this architecture, FedEx aligned customer-facing functions, including sales, marketing, and IT into a single group to increase the efficiency of application integration efforts. The project is estimated to have cost about $110 million—$50 million for branding and $60 million in technology and organizational changes. FedEx estimates that this portal architecture will yield additional sales equivalent to 50 percent of the company's annual revenue growth.[9]

There are several business trends driving portals:

- Response times are decreasing and business cycles are shrinking. As time becomes a more critical determinant of business success, the pressure builds to be more responsive and to utilize the various assets more effectively.

- The name of the new game is aggressive cost cutting, which dictates a move from a portfolio of discrete applications to more tightly defined solutions that deliver value.

- The Internet and Web technologies are creeping from the fringe of organizations to the core. As the Internet becomes part of mainstream processes, the "classic" foundation has to be overhauled as business process outsourcing becomes a possibility.

Drawing from lessons learned through unsuccessful efforts in the past, a new push is emerging to make the technology blueprint truly process-driven. This is most evident in the work around enterprise portals—customer-facing, employee-facing, and supply chain-facing.

Employee-facing process integration is very active. The enterprise portal idea is simple and compelling: Build a Web- and browser-based system that allows knowledge workers in the enterprise to access all the information they need to do their job, regardless of where that data is stored. By providing access to numerous corporate data sources through a single Web interface, or enterprise portal, employees save time they would otherwise spend requesting reports, contacting colleagues, and waiting for answers from other departments.

The most challenging aspect of any enterprise portal blueprint effort is that current operations must run smoothly while a significant part of the foundation is simultaneously reengineered and improved.

Implementing Portal Blueprints

Eastman Chemical will gladly testify to the value of Web portals. In dogged pursuit of continued corporate growth in a commodity industry, Eastman adopted a three-pronged, long-term strategy: Enable real-time information access, build seamless supplier and customer connectivity, and extract value from mergers and acquisitions. After a decade's worth of business process and IT standardization, the company reduced management layers, increased merger and acquisition integration speed, and lessened its corporate SG&A expense. Eastman estimates that Web portals helped generate millions of dollars in new revenues.[10]

Implementing cross-enterprise portals is an appealing idea; however, it is seldom easy. That's because most enterprise portals on the market are built on a "data center" architecture, which relies on a centralized, enterprisewide planning and implementation program along with centralizing the access to data in one server. This data center approach has two costly liabilities:

- Collecting and restructuring enterprise data to fit the schema of a centralized architecture consumes substantial enterprise resources.

- Up-front planning and development time involves logistical and political roadblocks associated with building a consensus on enterprisewide issues.

As a result, enterprise portal projects built on data center architecture are rarely successful.

Making the underlying structure transparent to users requires all of the major architecture components to be highly integrated. This is slowly happening under the umbrella of enterprise portals and Web Services. At this stage, the business, information, security, applications, and technical infrastructures have yet to be fully optimized.

What Is Our Infrastructure Model?

Centralized, decentralized, or federated are the options from which to choose. How should security, network identify management, e-mail, directory servers, and other shared infrastructure elements be managed? Should every department or autonomous business unit do its own thing (decentralized), should everything be controlled from one location (centralized), or should some standards be set centrally but actions taken locally (federated)?

Technology infrastructures are shaped like political and governance infrastructures. There are three models of power distribution in politics:

- **Unitary:** National government retains all power, with states dependent on its will (similar to centralized command and control infrastructure model).

- **Federal:** States retain powers within a certain sphere and national government has power in a different sphere (similar to federated infrastructure model).

- **Confederal:** States retain sovereign power, national government is dependent on their will (similar to decentralized infrastructure model).

What is the right approach? In an era well known for impractical visions and failed initiatives, the federated approach is proving to be a practical one, especially for cross-enterprise firms and firms with multiple single business units (multi-SBUs). CIOs and CFOs at large corporations are using the economic downturn to rein in the inefficiencies from years of uncoordinated portal buildout. To eliminate redundancy, corporate CIOs are architecting enterprise portals—a single interface and infrastructure for all corporate information.

Yet if a laissez-faire approach to portal deployment is inefficient, so is "over-centralization." Portals with content and workflows dictated by corporate IT risk are being shunned by end users for being too generic and divorced from their real needs. To navigate between these two extremes, CIOs are forging a new federated model in which IT builds a common "shared" infrastructure, collaborates with the line of business on process architecture, productivity tools, and user support, and leaves content and workflow design to end-user discretion.

Business Process Outsourcing Demands a Federated Model

The business drivers calling for the move to the federated model are flexibility and business process outsourcing. Over the last two decades, large and multi-national firms have restructured, resized, reengineered, and divested operations to increase shareholder value. The next chapter of this journey is being written with business process outsourcing (BPO). BPO is a new version of the old saying: Stick to your knitting. That is, concentrate on your core competencies and outsource the rest.

Many of the best-managed and most forward-thinking companies like GE, British Petroleum (BP), and British Airways, are adopting BPO as an operating strategy, allowing them to focus more time and resources on what they do best. The expected benefits of BPO include reduced fixed capital costs, better and faster back-office services, and increased margins from lower operating costs.

BPO is a major disruptive strategy that is causing massive micro-level blueprint changes. Businesses and even governments are rationalizing their resources and focusing on their core businesses, gladly sending noncore functions outside the organization to specialist suppliers, usually with a long-term contract. Examples of these outside suppliers are payroll companies, human resource companies (staffing, insurance plans), logistics, call centers, and back-office information technology specialists.

The trends that are driving BPO include:

- **Globalization.** Markets are global. Talent is cheap and plentiful, especially in Ireland, Russia, China, and India. The tax structure is often more favorable in developing markets.

- **Rising Back-Office Costs.** Noncore business processing is becoming a growing share of total expenditures for companies. Mergers have contributed to redundant and dissimilar back-office processes. By entrusting expensive processes to specialists, companies are attempting to get a handle on their cost structure.

- **Need for Focus.** Being the best at every process from HR to supply chain management is not easy. BPO gives companies access to best practices without the headaches.

- **Standard and Low-Cost Technology.** The Internet, high-bandwidth telecommunications, and Web technology have fundamentally changed the economics of business.

Outsourcing noncore functions tends to cross and even collapse "silos" within organizations. At the same time, the outside specialist suppliers are combining and evolving into a smaller number of large "function organizations"—for example, one or two large payroll companies or a single collections agency.

BPO is also a major contributor to the increasing focus on a multi-SBU shared infrastructure model. These have to

- Decentralize execution so that implementation is faster.

- Decentralize control and leverage investments in applications and infrastructure.

- Align people, information, and business processes across technologies, locations, and departmental boundaries.

Development of the BPO architecture is a new activity. Using the federated blueprint, BPO architectures can be shared by different groups throughout an organization. As a result, opportunities for enhanced interoperability, integration, and cost-effectiveness will be easier to identify and act on. As organizations gear up for another round of technology investments, it makes sense to do it differently this time.

Putting Everything Together

Micro-level blueprint = {data, applications, portal, integration, and infrastructure}. The combination of all these things dictates the overall quality of the technology blueprint.

Each combination has its pros and cons in converting strategy into technology execution. The blueprint depends on the As-Is and To-Be state of the organization. Figure 11.5 illustrates where each approach has been applied during the last decade as we transitioned from e-commerce to e-business to collaborative business.

In the Web-publishing phase of digitization, the method primarily used was one project at a time. To satisfy short-term needs, organizations had multiple Web sites, each developed independently of the other. As we moved to enabling transactions with customers, the method used was a comprehensive data approach. The objective was to make sure that order entry, order fulfillment, and order management were seamless.

The next phase of this evolution was enabling transactions to traverse the entire length of the company, from one end of the value chain to another. To accomplish this, the application approach was the preferred method. The objective was to make sure that the legacy and packaged software organizations had procured over time could work together to support end-to-end integration in a single business unit.

Now it gets interesting. Most of the experience and knowledge that we have built over the years is being challenged as we tear down and rearrange business boundaries. This means that lateral coordination of processes across multiple business units and organizations is the important variable around which the design has to be optimized. The portal model is rapidly becoming the preferred method for cutting horizontally across various silos of digitization.

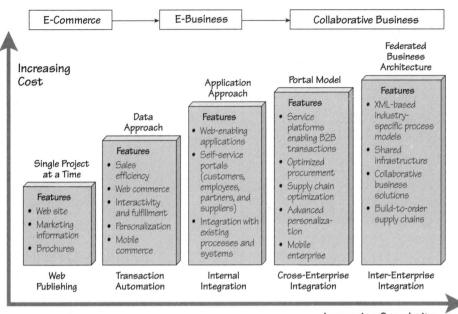

Figure 11.5: Constantly Evolving Technology Infrastructure

Advanced organizations are pushing the performance envelope even further. They are looking to align with the macro economy. That means when customer demand is high, they expand quickly with internal growth, outsourcing, and mergers and acquisitions. When customer demand is low, they contract equally quickly with layoffs, outsourcing, and divestitures. Expanding and contracting with business cycles and economic conditions are the hallmarks of flexible companies. To accomplish this, the federated "business" architecture is becoming the preferred method.

The Need for Federated IT Architecture—The Transformation of Georgia-Pacific

Some organizations are changing too quickly as a result of mergers, acquisitions, and divestitures. This puts incredible strain on the underlying IT architecture. To deal with this strain, there is a growing movement toward federated models where a combination of centralized (shared) and decentralized (dedicated) infrastructure allows more flexibility.

Let's examine Georgia-Pacific Corporation, whose business model epitomizes "rapid change." The transformation of Georgia-Pacific presents a very interesting case study of the challenges faced by CIOs in aligning complex enterprise applications and infrastructure with business strategy. This case study also shows that the best-formulated IT strategies become obsolete as a firm's external and internal environments change. It is essential, therefore, that IT strategists systematically review, evaluate, and control the execution of micro-level strategies.

From a Building Products Company to a Consumer Products Company

Founded in 1927 as a wholesaler of hardwood lumber, Georgia-Pacific (GP) has grown through expansion and acquisitions to become one of the world's leading manufacturers and distributors of household products, tissue, packaging, paper, building products, pulp, and related chemicals. Headquartered in Atlanta, Georgia, with annual sales of more than $25 billion, the company employs approximately 75,000 people at 600 locations in North America and Europe.

A big part of Georgia-Pacific's existing strategy is its bread-and-butter building products division. GP has been among the leading wholesale suppliers of building products to lumber and building materials dealers and large do-it-yourself warehouse retailers like Home Depot.

More than 100 mills churn out plywood, lumber, wallboard, and other building supplies. Georgia-Pacific also has a significant paper manufacturing business. Corrugated boxes and packaging supplies are tumbling off the assembly lines at another 46 plants.

Building products and other commodities have always been the guts of Georgia-Pacific's business, but that's changing. In the late 1990s, GP overhauled its business model. After more than 70 years, the company shed its mature pulp, paper, and building products in favor of consumer household products sold in supermarkets.

From a long-term strategy perspective, GP wanted to get away from the boom or bust business cycles ingrained in its core paper and forest products industry. Pete Correll, chairman and CEO of Georgia-Pacific, expected the building supply business to fall victim to a housing market decline after a period of strong growth.[11]

To diversify its revenue base, Georgia-Pacific acquired Fort James, the maker of Brawny paper towels, Quilted Northern toilet tissue, and disposable tableware like Dixie cups. The $11.3 billion deal made Georgia-Pacific the largest maker of tissue products in the world, knocking Kimberly-Clark out of the top spot. The merger gave GP nearly half of the tissue market in North America and its first foothold in Europe.

To make sure that it could solidly distribute its many products, Georgia-Pacific acquired Unisource Worldwide. Unisource is one of the largest distributors of packaging systems, printing, imaging papers, and maintenance supplies in North America.

The result of these mergers: the vertical integration of the value chain from producing raw material to consumer products to distribution. In IT, a side effect of the acquisitions is the massive integration effort to link the various systems of the acquired companies so that synergies could be obtained.

Spin-offs and Divestitures—Reshaping the Company

Interspersed in the acquisition flurry were several divestures. To reduce company debt and noncore operations, Georgia-Pacific sold all of its timberland holdings to Plum Creek, a real estate investment trust. This divestiture gave Georgia-Pacific the odd status of being a forest products giant that owned no trees. The company also sold half of its white paper business and several pulp mills to Domtar Inc. Nine tissue plants that made commercial products for hotels, hospitals, and other businesses also got the boot to appease antitrust concerns in the Fort James merger.

As you can imagine, GP's revenue mix changed dramatically after its various acquisitions and divestitures (see Table 11.1). The moves eventually gave the company a more predictable revenue stream, cushioning its earnings against the turbulent price swings in pulp, paper, and building products. Income from Brawny, Dixie, and other consumer products helped Georgia-Pacific offset declines in what used to be its core areas.

The volatility is not over for Georgia-Pacific's employees. In 2002, GP agreed to sell a controlling 60 percent interest in its Unisource Worldwide paper distribution subsidiary to Bain Capital, a global private investment firm, for $850 million. Georgia-Pacific's remaining 40 percent interest will be overseen by CP&P

Table 11.1: Revenue Mix at Georgia-Pacific[12]

Before Fort James		After Fort James	
Pulp and Paper	32%	Consumer Products	51%
Building Products	30%	Containerboard and Packaging	26%
Containerboard and Packaging	29%	Building Products	13%
Consumer Products	9%	Pulp and Paper	10%

Inc., the company's subsidiary formed to hold its consumer products, packaging, pulp, and paper businesses.

According to Pete Correll, the decision to sell GP's majority interest in Unisource was based on two strategic factors. First, the value of the original synergies in the combination of Unisource and the uncoated paper manufacturing business was realized in the sale of the majority of those assets to Domtar Inc. Second, due to those divestitures, Unisource had a limited strategic fit with the consumer products and packaging (CP&P) businesses and the building products and distribution businesses.[13]

The Execution Challenge

This GP case study raises many important execution challenges. How could a company that built its empire on pulp and paper go up against consumer heavyweights like Proctor and Gamble and Kimberly Clark? How could a company used to competing against the paper and pulp companies (International Paper, Weyerhaeuser, and Boise Cascade) adjust to the brutally fast pace of the consumer products industry?

Given the short time frame in which the business transformation took place, there was tremendous pressure on the company's operations. When macro-level corporate-level strategies zigzag, the meso-level process and micro-level IT architectures lag behind (see Figure 11.6). In such an environment, employees cannot truly execute. They become frozen because they don't know the context in which to make critical decisions.

The constantly changing strategy of Georgia-Pacific has placed enormous pressure on its micro-level blueprint. This brings to the forefront certain key questions about architecture design:

- How does a company organize its processes, applications, and technology infrastructure so that reorganization—internal changes, mergers, acquisitions, and divestures—is less painful? In other words, what is the blueprint that will help the company evolve? The answer increasingly is converging around a federated approach.

- What is the mechanism for converting ideas into plans that can go into development today and produce results quickly? The answer to this question is a tough one. Speed of execution is often a good thing in the short run but, if not carefully planned, tends to create integration problems over a longer time horizon. Better project selection through more rigorous prioritization and value assessment is an absolute requirement.

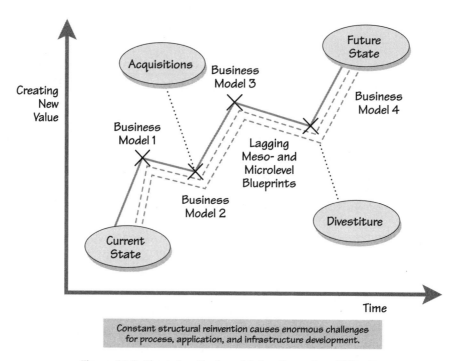

Figure 11.6: Changing Strategy Makes Execution Difficult

After an almost total business transformation, GP management has to settle down and create an architecture that will allow systemic and continuous performance improvement. The case of GP is not unique. During the late 1990s, mergers and acquisitions created companies that are barely integrated. They look fine from the outside but are falling apart inside. Fixing this situation is one of the main reasons why application integration is a top business priority.

Seven Points to Ponder

> A system must have an aim.
> Without an aim, there is no system. . . .
> A system must be managed. . . .
> The secret is cooperation between components
> toward the aim of the organization.
> —*W. Edwards Deming*, The New Economics

The micro-level blueprint is the explicit description of the current and desired relationships among the business model, processes, and information technology.

It describes the target situation that the organization wishes to create and maintain through managing its application and infrastructure portfolio.

With micro-level blueprints, companies are aiming to do the following:

1. Drastically reduce the time horizon for formulating and executing a digitization strategy. For instance, a critical outcome of the micro-level blueprint is to support the concept of service platforms. Through service platforms, organizations are looking to leverage assets: employees, knowledge, products, business relationships, and applications.

2. Evaluate whether an organization is doing the right things and how it can be more effective. Every organization should be wary of becoming a prisoner of its own architecture because even the best ones become obsolete sooner or later. Regular evaluation helps management avoid complacency. Objectives should be carefully developed and coordinated and not merely evolve out of day-to-day operating decisions.

3. Make bigger strategic bets to respond to new business realities. Companies can't afford to spend a whole lot of money in one direction and then find out it was the wrong direction because the technology won't support it. A micro-level blueprint needs to help quickly identify and exploit innovative opportunities within and outside the enterprise.

4. Enhance business performance by unifying formerly isolated business units and improving efficiency. Although it does not guarantee success, the process allows proactive rather than reactive decision making, especially around the theme of integration.

5. Leverage and increase the overall value of enterprise software investments. Most companies are essentially process and information machines that, over the last few years, have been stripped down and substantially rebuilt with new applications and technologies. The engine is warming up. How fast can it go, and what speed do customers desire?

6. Maximize corporatewide return on technology assets. Going forward, the big breakthrough will not be technology; there's more than enough of that out there. The eureka moment will come when we learn how to

manage technology well, harnessing its immense powers to improve and create value continuously. In other words, the focus on e-business is giving way to e-services.

7. Finally, an organization with no coherent micro-level blueprint precipitates its own demise. When an organization does not know where it wants to go, it usually ends up some place it does not want to be. Every organization needs to establish and communicate corporatewide objectives by cutting across vertical hierarchies.

We leave you with a brainteaser: Do services drive IT infrastructure? Or, does IT infrastructure drive services? In an ideal service-centric world, customer needs and priorities drive processes, processes drive applications, and applications drive infrastructure. That is the logical path in a service-centric model. What happens in the real world is somewhat different. Usually the infrastructure is inflexible and the applications are rigid due to the nature of legacy systems. When this is true, the logical path is reversed, infrastructure drives applications, applications restrict processes, and processes curb what customers can do, see, and interact with. *Which scenario describes your organization?*

CHAPTER TWELVE

The Discipline of Execution: A Tale of Two Companies

What to Expect

Throughout this entire book, we have illustrated the movement from e-business applications to services digitization. On the surface, it is hard to refute the idea that companies should strive to implement quality processes and digitization. However, legitimate questions can be raised about their chances of success. For instance, how do you manage and execute initiatives given the constantly changing business direction?

In Chapter 1, we wrote about three types of blueprints: process improvement, strategic improvement, and business transformation. We illustrated examples of process and strategic improvement (GE and Wal-Mart, respectively), but not of business transformation. In this chapter, we present two business transformation case studies—AT&T and IBM—that illustrate how companies have tackled the issue of business transformation in different ways with different results. The point is to show the inherent risk involved in transformation strategies and the type of blueprint and execution needed to manage this risk.

Introduction

Volatile financial markets. Roller coaster demand patterns. Rapidly shifting competitive structures. Emerging technologies. Shifting customer requirements. These are some of the issues that managers lie awake at night pondering, and they all have one thing in common: They impel change. Whatever your company or industry, there is little doubt that your organization is knee-deep in large-scale change or you can see it on the horizon.

Companies constantly have to transform themselves. The challenges and opportunities that confront organizations in the twenty-first century are quite different from those they encountered during the previous century, or even during the 1990s, and greater change is clearly on the horizon. Consequently, merely improving upon today's capabilities will not suffice to meet tomorrow's challenges.

Directional change is the rule rather than the exception in organizational survival and renewal. Companies prepare for directional change with one of two types of macro-level transformation strategies: 1) inward looking (based on an immediate survival need, this entails looking at reorganization and integration as a way of creating value) and 2) outward looking (this strategy examines mergers, acquisitions, or divestitures as ways of creating value).

Which macro-level strategy is your company practicing? Board members and senior management constantly try to align their business models with changing market directions and competitive dynamics. This creates a lot of whiplash in operational strategy and often is the root cause of project failure. Understanding the source of this whiplash is especially important for people on the front lines of digitization projects.

We'll begin with AT&T, whose strategy clearly was to use M&A to transform itself. We will conclude with IBM, whose strategy was to revamp itself with internal reorganization and process digitization. Based on what you have read so far, would you like to venture a guess as to which company's strategy was successful?

The Mergers and Acquisitions Strategy

Industry boundaries are evaporating, and the solid walls that delineated industry expertise are disintegrating. As a result, competitors from previously distinct industries, such as financial services, technology, and healthcare, are scrambling for each other's customers.

Many companies like Vivendi Universal, AT&T, Tyco, and Bank of America established corporate initiatives to acquire assets and roll them up through mergers and acquisitions. Some industries, such as U.S. banking, went into a constant M&A mode. That industry experienced a sustained and unprecedented merger movement from 1980 to 2000. During that period, more than 8,000 bank mergers occurred, involving over $2.5 trillion in acquired assets. The 1990s, especially 1994–98, was a period of numerous large bank mergers; several were among the biggest in U.S. banking history.[1]

The objective of M&A is to be opportunistic either by continuously entering new niches and growing or by divesting marginal operations. A company in the middle of a rapidly consolidating sector faces the following tough challenges:

- Developing a new formula for success after purchasing assets and rolling them up into the existing organization, and

- Integrating acquisitions without compromising customer service quality.

Let's examine the pendulum-like shifts in strategy that occurred at the U.S. business icon, AT&T. Here's a preview of the key takeaway: Executing digitization projects in the midst of mergers and acquisitions is extremely difficult, if not downright impossible.

The Amazing Saga of AT&T

The history of AT&T parallels the history of the telephone in the United States. AT&T's roots stretch back to 1875 when AT&T founder Alexander Graham Bell invented the telephone. During the nineteenth century, AT&T became the parent company of the Bell System, the U.S. telephone monopoly. Bell System provided what was by all accounts the best telephone service in the world. The system broke up into eight companies in 1984 by agreement between AT&T and the U.S. Department of Justice. From 1984 until 1996, it was an integrated telecommunications services and equipment company, succeeding in a newly competitive environment.

Several large-scale strategic shifts took place at AT&T between 1995 and 2002. On September 20, 1995, it announced that it was restructuring into three separate, publicly traded companies: a systems and equipment company (Western Electric, which became Lucent Technologies), a computer company (NCR), and a communications services company (which would remain AT&T.) It was the largest voluntary breakup in the history of American business.

The new AT&T began evolving from a long-distance company to an integrated voice and data communications company. AT&T reentered the local telephone service business, enabled by the Telecommunications Act of 1996. The company successfully launched an Internet service, AT&T WorldNet Service, while selling off operations, such as AT&T Submarine Systems and Skynet Satellite Services, which no longer were a strategic fit.

Diversifying from Long-Distance to Only Soup-to-Nuts Services

C. Michael Armstrong became chairman and CEO in November 1997 and quickly set out to put his stamp on the company. As he wrote in the 1998 annual report: "We're transforming AT&T from a long-distance company to an 'any-distance' company. From a company that handles mostly voice calls to a company that connects you to information in any form that is useful to you—voice, data, and video. From a primarily domestic company to a truly global company."

In 1997, AT&T was strictly a long-distance service, acquiring 79% of its revenues from more than 60 million voice long-distance customers. Despite the size, the long-term trends for long-distance looked bleak. AT&T's long-distance business suffered from increasing competition, weakening market share, and lower profit margins. It also faced great difficulty in entering smaller markets as the local operators had monopolies over the last mile to the home. The only way the organization could get into the customer's home was through an alternate channel: broadband coaxial cable controlled by the cable TV firms.

Armstrong and his team decided to make a series of horizontal and market extension acquisitions to reinvent the core business of AT&T. Over the next three years, the company went on a $105 billion debt-financed acquisition spree to make the "integrated communications" vision real. The major acquisitions included:

- A leading provider of local telephone service to business customers (Teleport Communications Group),

- Two large cable companies, (Tele-Communications, Inc. and MediaOne), the acquisitions of which made AT&T the largest cable company in the United States,

- A top provider of global data networking services (IBM Global Network), and

- A joint venture with British Telecom called Concert that combined the two company's international assets and operations to support the communications needs of multi-national customers.

By mid-2000, AT&T had three rapidly evolving networks (broadband, wireless, and data) and four separate businesses (cable, wireless, business, and consumer).

Blur of Deals—Understanding the Strategic Shifts

According to internal AT&T documents from 1998, all these mergers, acquisitions, and joint ventures were aimed at supporting a series of industry trends.[2] These include:

- **From resale to facilities-based**—To deliver integrated services, AT&T thought that it was necessary to own or control the facilities used to reach end customers. The company decided that they could not depend on just reselling the connections of other companies, especially when those companies were often competitors. The outcome: Buy facilities (what engineers call "controlling the architecture") to ensure quality of service and control of costs.

- **From narrowband to broadband**—The future is a digital, broadband world. Broadband systems transmit data at high speeds to make advanced communications services work. The AT&T long-distance network had been broadband for years, but the final connections to most customers were still pairs of copper wires that carry a narrow stream of information, fine for voice calls but too slow for next-generation services. The outcome: Invest in and buy cable companies.

- **From circuits to packets**—In the old world of voice telephony, every call ties up a circuit or pathway through the network from one phone to the other. In the Internet world, information—whether sound or data—is broken into separate units called "packets" that are reassembled at the receiving end. With packets, many users can share the same pathway at the same time, which is more efficient. More important, advanced packet systems run on the technology standard known as Internet protocol, or IP. The outcome: Invest in companies like @Home or buy companies that can erase the boundaries between TVs, computers, and telephones. Pave the way to new applications such as Internet services delivered over pocketsize wireless phones.

- **From local cellular to digital wireless leader**—The growth of wireless calling is second only to the growth of the Internet as a driving force in communications. AT&T continued to expand its nationwide digital wireless network. With AT&T Digital One Rate service, customers were offered a single rate for wireless calls throughout the United States—no long-distance charges and no "roaming" charges for using the phone outside their primary calling area. The outcome: Invest in upgrading digital cellular network and acquire companies to get scale and subscribers.

- **From a domestic company to a global communications power**—AT&T customers, especially multi-national companies, need end-to-end global services with consistent quality, price, and customer support. To provide that, AT&T has a facilities-based global strategy that gives customers the same technology and support everywhere in the world. The outcome: Complete a global joint venture with British Telecom called Concert and acquire the IBM global network.

AT&T's strategy rapidly evolved from a company that handles mostly long-distance voice calls to a family of four discrete divisions that connects people to information in any form that is useful to them—voice, data, and video—over any of three different networks—wireless, data, and cable.

Breaking Up AT&T, Again

If employees thought that the pace of change in a short time span was amazing, they were ill prepared for the next announcement. In October 2000, after watching the stock price decline from $61 per share to $22 per share, financial markets and large institutional shareholders decided that various divisions of AT&T were more valuable than the sum of their parts.

They forced the divesture of the company. It announced that it would restructure over the next two years into a family of four publicly held companies: AT&T Broadband, AT&T Wireless, AT&T Business, and AT&T Consumer. Also, the company spun off Liberty Media, which it got through its acquisition of Tele-Communications, Inc. (TCI) in March 1999 (see Figure 12.1). The breakup of AT&T illustrates a well-known saying that indigestion is a common postmerger malady.

The logic behind the breakup is that the troubled long-distance business could no longer mask the strengths of other operations and that each business would be more accurately valued based on its own prospects. It remains to be seen whether this theory of "the parts being greater than the integrated whole" actually creates additional value in terms of better service, increased shareholder value, and innovation. That will depend on grueling, inch-by-inch execution.

The case of AT&T illustrates that execution is extraordinarily difficult in the win-now, quarterly results culture, even with the best managers.

Key Lessons Learned from AT&T—Chasing a Moving Target

In a span of ten years, the 123-year-old flagship of the U.S. telecomm industry has gone from being one of the greatest companies in the world to a shadow of itself.

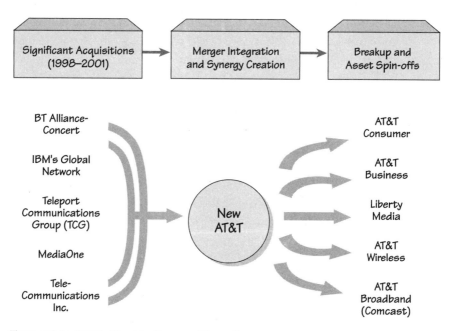

Figure 12.1: AT&T—The Challenge of Execution

With all the mergers, acquisitions, and divestures, it became impossible for even the best managers to execute a chaotic strategic plan. Constant changes make it especially hard for employees in the trenches to follow what's going on in the company.

The lessons learned (the hard way) from the AT&T case study are

- No matter how much employees try, effective execution simply cannot happen when companies try to synchronize corporate strategies with volatile stock prices.

- It is easy to underestimate the costs and logistic nightmares of consolidating the operations of companies with different processes, systems, and cultures.

- Interaction and information exchange throughout an enterprise are more difficult following acquisitions because of the often incompatible business processes and information technology systems of the merged or acquired business.

What is difficult for outsiders to fathom is the impact on employees and project managers who were executing the unification strategy during 1997–2002. They must have worked incredibly hard to merge and assimilate the operations of the acquired companies. All that energy and effort had to be reversed as the company moved from an integrated theme to a portfolio of stand-alone companies. Clearly, one of the toughest challenges for employees is how to execute under uncertainty or subject to zigzag strategy.

IBM's Digitization Journey

In 1993, IBM was in trouble. The company that traced its roots to 1911 as the Computing-Tabulating-Recording Company (CTR) was drowning in red ink. Big Blue posted an $8.1 billion loss, and the stock price collapsed, hitting a 20-year low.

The crisis was triggered primarily by profound changes in the mainframe marketplace and the resulting collapse of profit margins. Unable to translate its sizeable intellectual property into products that were competitive and relevant in the new PC-dominated landscape, IBM saw signs of trauma everywhere.

In the early 1990s, IBM had nearly 400,000 employees in 160 countries. It operated 24 separate business units, which together sold an estimated 5,000 hardware products and 20,000 software products. Efforts to cut costs and stem losses were hampered by the sheer scope and complexity of operations. The fragmentation of IBM's business units had become a major vulnerability, and dismantling the company was increasingly seen as the only way out of the crisis.

Change of Leadership

With a divestiture plan on the table, IBM hired Louis V. Gerstner as CEO in April 1993. Gerstner, who came to IBM from tobacco company RJR Nabisco, was an outsider and knew little about the computer industry. One of Gerstner's first moves was to put a halt to the decentralization occurring at IBM. He reversed the then-current plan to break up the company and committed instead to making all of IBM's parts work together. The logic: Unless everyone was pulling in the right direction and executing the same play, the company was not going to make it.

Gerstner's hunch was that IBM would be better off as a unified company, sharing core assets like research throughout all its product divisions and presenting one sales team to the customer for a suite of products. Through it all, the guiding light came down to two words: customer focus. It proved both galvanizing and clarifying, serving as the principle for reexamination and for resolving many internal debates.[3]

The lynchpin of IBM's strategy was to focus as much as possible on the efficiency and quality of the core business and then start looking to expand. To implement this strategy, IBM structured its transformation journey in a series of phases:

- **Simplification**—Rationalize and simplify products, systems, solutions, and services for all businesses.

- **E-Business**—Reorganize all organizational units, regions, groups, and operating companies around digital processes.

- **Transformation of the Value Chain**—Standardize cross-enterprise processes such as enterprise resource planning, customer relationship management, supply chain management, and product lifecycle management.

- **Extending the Value Chain**—Further extend the value chain outside the four walls of IBM to all partners, customers, and suppliers.

IBM began the journey by simplifying operations, cutting costs, and driving common processes and systems that would be implemented across the entire global organization. These efforts, called One IBM, reflected IBM's goal of going to market as a unified organization and became the guiding force behind its business transformation.

Phase 1—Simplification

IBM was a complex maze when it began the transformation efforts. It went to market as 20 different businesses, each with its own fulfillment, manufacturing, accounting, payroll systems, IT structures, and marketing strategies. None of these processes was interconnected, and unnecessary redundancy was everywhere. Product designs had little commonality of components, foregoing major cost efficiencies. This complexity was difficult to manage and confusing for customers. IBM recognized that they had to do a better job of integrating the global enterprise.

In the early 1990s, the company was ready for simplification. Money was being wasted on duplicate systems and bloated bureaucracy. Recognizing that complexity lay at the root of many of its problems, IBM adopted a strategy of streamlining its core business. This simplification reached across five key areas:

1. **Reengineering Internal Business Processes**—In 1994, cost reductions were realized through consolidation and standardization. In 1996, reengineered processes were globally deployed, resulting in process simplification. Web-enabling of core business processes and systems began in 1998 and continues today. By 1999, customer satisfaction jumped 5.5 percent, time to market was 75 percent faster, and total savings exceeded $9 billion.

2. **Standardized Applications**—IBM's 16,000 business applications were reduced to less than 6,000 by embracing a standardized application architecture built around best-of-breed suites such as SAP's ERP and Siebel's CRM.

3. **IT Infrastructure Consolidation**—Consolidation and standardization of IBM's IT infrastructure were key components of its strategy. In 1993, IBM had 155 data centers, 31 separate private networks, hundreds of different PC configurations, and 128 CIOs. Data centers were reduced to 12, networks were reduced to one, PC configurations to four, and CIOs to one.

4. **Changing Process Accountability**—IBM transformed process management in three ways. First, on a companywide level, it replaced multiple, customized processes with a uniform global process. Second, IT management was pushed to the business-unit level. Third, business strategies were better aligned with management systems, processes, IT, and Web initiatives.

5. **Outsourcing Operations**—IBM Global Services was tasked with application development, integration, infrastructure deployment, and maintenance. This approach has allowed IBM management to focus on strategic issues. It also helped them move from their previous responsibility of managing large technology staffs to concentrate on learning the business, enforcing standards, and reducing redundancies, resulting in both process and cost efficiencies.

IBM's initial transformation success shows that self-contained process silos stifle crucial end-to-end integration across the company. Simply streamlining processes with little thought as to where they fit into the big picture did not address the need for complex cross-business initiatives (CRM, fulfillment, and the integrated supply chain) that promised to leverage the size and scope of IBM fully.

Phase 2—Digitizing IBM Internally

The most important part of IBM's transformation began in 1998 when it committed to becoming an e-business. To do this, IBM had to bring Internet technology into core business processes, fusing business and IT strategy. It had to alter its structure radically and break down internal barriers within the company.

The goal was to rebuild the company on a foundation of simplified and integrated business processes. For this, IBM had to knock down the walls between the operating units to become a single, integrated organization with seamless connections between employees and among the company, suppliers, customers, and business partners. To drive the full benefits of transformation and e-business further, IBM shifted to an end-to-end value chain model in 2001.

IBM's objective in leveraging the Web was to improve productivity and quality and, at the same time, take cost out of everyday processes and procedures. It discovered that tremendous efficiencies can be gained from using the Web to digitize transactions, so IBM embarked on a journey to reengineer common business processes and information systems. Key e-business initiatives were "Shop IBM" Web store, online procurement, online customer support, online business-partner sales and support, and the corporate intranet for training and employee support.

Consider e-procurement, a process in which IBM is considered one of the best in the world. IBM steadily implemented key elements of its e-procurement plan: full coverage of end-to-end processes, transactions, and spending via the Web; 100 percent supplier enablement; and hands-free, paperless procurement. The results were astounding: IBM's purchase order process time was reduced from 30 days (1995) to one day (2001). Contract cycle times diminished from 12 months to 30 days. In the area of paperwork, IBM shrank a typical contract length from 100 pages to six. Lower administrative costs, reduced order cycle times, better business controls, and other e-procurement efficiencies saved the company $377 million in 2000.[4]

Phase 3—Customer-Centric Process Transformation

To continue building on these gains, IBM realized the need to shift its transformation from reengineering and deploying global processes to a more direct link with the company's business models and product offerings. The question was how to organize and configure the processes to fit the way the customer wanted to buy?

Fundamentally, the value chain model takes vertical processes (that's how IBM divisions are organized and operated) and flips them on their side to create cross-enterprise processes. Similar products (hardware, software, and services) are grouped into categories—or value chains—that best represent how value is delivered to customers.

The customer becomes the focus of all processes. The goal is to improve on key performance indicators such as time, cost, quality, and flexibility. To achieve this goal, IBM defined several cross-enterprise value chains based on what customers wanted:

- **High Volume, Easily Configured Products**—personal computer products, low-end servers, and printers

- **Complex Configured Hardware**—mainframes, high-end servers, storage, and printers

- **OEM Hardware Components**—storage and micro-electronics products

- **Software and Operating Systems**—software products such as WebSphere, DB2, Lotus Domino, and Rational

- **Outsourcing and Consulting Services**—all services provided by the IBM Global Services[5]

The objective was to present a single face to the customer by integrating processes from the customer's perspective. To make this happen, processes that interface with customers (CRM, fulfillment) and suppliers (procurement and integrated supply chain) were standardized and integrated across these value chains. Customers expect to interact with the company as a single entity, and the collaboration that takes place between customer- and supplier-facing processes is critical to getting customers the information, resources, and products they want, when they want them.

During the course of this transformation, IBM found that value chain solutions require a keen insight into the company's capabilities and the ability to pull together contributions from all parts of the organization.

Phase 4—Consultative Solution Selling

IBM is on the move again. With several major acquisitions like the $3.5 billion acquisition PricewaterhouseCoopers, IBM is moving into a new phase of its transformation: consultative solution selling. The logic of this becomes clear when you consider the following statement by Gerstner: "Technology changes much too quickly now for any company to build a sustainable competitive advantage on that basis alone. Rather, it is how you help customers use technology." The movement toward providing solutions rather than technology alone is a significant strategic shift in the marketplace.[6]

IBM is taking methodical steps in executing the consultative solution selling strategy. It is focusing on creating solutions for a particular customer segment, namely large customers, which poses a rather interesting dilemma. While most customers want solutions instead of products, they prefer not paying a premium for this extra. Solutions, however, cost significantly more money to customize and create. To get around this problem, IBM decided to limit solution selling initially to large customers who are willing to pay premium prices.

In addition to the value chain solutions, IBM is providing the full solution lifecycle beginning with strategy consulting, management consulting, solution design, hardware, and outsourcing services. To be effective, IBM truly has to understand the customers' needs and strategy. To create ongoing value for the customer, solution selling requires a significant amount of collaboration and a multi-year commitment between IBM and customers. IBM expects to earn a premium because it assumes some of the risk and responsibility for part of its customers' business, spares the customer from the hassle and cost of dealing with multiple vendors, and reduces the effort of having to integrate the components and services themselves.

Even skeptical competitors like Hewlett-Packard, Sun Microsystems, Fujitsu, and Dell are beginning to copy IBM's movement toward solutions. As the business environment becomes more and more digitized, customers will gravitate to vendors that offer an integrated solution that is greater than the sum of components. That is exactly what IBM is betting on in the next phase of its transformation.

Transformation Management—The Blueprint Team

Lack of managerial support and stakeholder resistance are two of the main reasons transformation initiatives fail. To overcome these barriers, IBM has made corresponding changes to its management systems and transformation policies as it evolved. The business transformation office and CIO still drive the overall business transformation strategy, but they have new roles and responsibilities in support of value chains.

Figure 12.2 shows the cross-enterprise processes that cut across IBM. New leadership roles were defined to manage this structure. Roles added to the IBM's blueprint governance model include:

- **Value Chain Owners**—A senior line of business executives is accountable for each of IBM's value chains.

- **Business Transformation Executives**—Each cross-enterprise process has an executive who is responsible for strategy and implementation. He is also accountable for end-to-end business integration, including planning, prioritization, development, deployment, and support.

Figure 12.2: IBM's Governance and Management

- **Customer/Supplier/Employee Collaboration Executives**—These executives are charged with transforming all customer-, supplier-, and employee-facing processes at the corporate level. For instance, the employee-facing executive is responsible for communicating the One IBM strategy to employees worldwide.

- **IBM Business Process Council**—Comprised of managers from cross-enterprise areas, the council sets the enterprise architecture, defines integration, and drives compliance.

- **IBM Enterprise Architecture Board**—Aligned with the business process council, the architecture board formulates the application and data architecture and ensures compliance to standards.[7]

Ultimately, the CIO is responsible for business transformation across all of IBM. The various transformation and e-business investments are rigorously evaluated and channeled through the same model used for managing product development. Executives responsible for these investments build business cases to ensure they are in line with the business needs of the value chains, while generating the highest return to the overall business.

Key Lessons Learned from IBM's Transformation— Hitting a Moving Target

IBM represents a rare success story of large-scale business transformation. As the case study of IBM shows, digitization requires some key ingredients to work:

- A clear and consistent vision (and focal point) that does not frequently change;

- The management talent to pull it off;

- The discipline to implement the vision in a rapidly changing industry; and

- Funding and resources (including the patience to see it through).

In our opinion, the most important ingredient is the consistent focal point that can drive actions. Let's look at the management of digitization, a critical component of execution success.

Services Transformation—Management Is Essential

What do the case studies of AT&T and IBM tell us? Businesses, no matter how successful, must transform themselves. Many firms recognize this and have spent millions clearly defining what transformation is and providing a persuasive case as to why they need to transform.

Unfortunately, many have not yet developed either a transformation strategy or a process to ensure that transformation will come about. That was exactly the gap that this book tried to address: What does a transformation roadmap from e-business to services look like?

The Roadmap for Services Digitization

Digitization is often seen as the art and science of layering the business processes on top of an application or set of heterogeneous enterprise applications to drive new services. But it is more than that. Digitization is really the study of roles, responsibilities, and functions of senior management; the crucial business processes that affect success; and the technology decisions that determine the direction of the organization and its future.

Digitization is moving from an ad hoc practice to a more disciplined subject. Digitization is similar to an engineering discipline such as civil engineering. It takes architectural thinking, discipline, and patience. There are four areas of specialization in the discipline of digitization:

1. **Defining a target strategy.** The competitive landscape is always changing, so strategies must constantly evolve (business and revenue models) to reflect new opportunities and threats from industry and competitive dynamics. While in theory this looks easy, in practice it is not.

2. **Aligning process and technology.** In order to align the two, you must have a clear understanding of multiple business processes, an ability to deconstruct a complex system into its basic factors, and the originality to synthesize and invent. In these functions, there is an increasing trend toward the use of scientific instead of traditional or ad hoc methods.

3. **Designing, implementing, deploying, and maintaining applications, portals, and other solutions that embrace customers, operations, suppliers, and employees.** The goal is to produce the maximum value with the minimum investment and cost while maintaining or enhancing longer-term viability of the enterprise.

4. **Executing and coordinating.** This challenge includes governance, project management, programming, change management, communication, and marketing. Change management, which enables the transition from the old to the new, is by far the hardest and most important step to undertake.

Of these, the least understood area is the fourth: execution and coordination of digitization. One of the insights that experienced managers have told us repeatedly is the need to tackle governance and ongoing management issues upfront. A digitization initiative becomes complex, managed by disparate groups throughout the enterprise. How these different elements are coordinated and kept up-to-date is a key management issue that must be addressed early in the process.

The root causes leading to poor return on technology investments are not technical problems, but management problems in dealing with large-scale change.

Guiding and Coordinating Large-Scale Digitization

The similarities between large-scale enterprise digitization projects and mega-construction projects are uncanny. One of the critical aspects of the mega-projects in civil engineering is the systematic blueprint for the type of construction being undertaken.

Consider the example of the "Big Dig"—the Central Artery/Tunnel Project in Boston, Massachusetts. This project is considered by many to be the "largest, most complex, and technologically challenging highway project in American history."[8] The tunnel project will be eight lanes wide, 3.5 miles long, and completely buried beneath a major highway and dozens of glass and steel skyscrapers in Boston's financial district. What does it take to dig a tunnel like this? A lot of careful planning, hard work, and engineering tricks. Imagine the ways in which a project of this magnitude could go awry if it were not carefully coordinated.

Like engineering projects, the management of large-scale digitization efforts (typically composed of multiple smaller projects) can very challenging. The individual projects may be well conceived and adequately budgeted for, the "to-be" processes carefully engineered, the consultants may be specialists, and programmers may be highly experienced. However, if the efforts of all the participants are not skillfully coordinated and managed, the digitization effort may overrun the budget, fail to meet the schedule, or fall short in technical quality. The larger and more complex the scope, the more critical this overall coordination function becomes.

Throughout this book, we stress this point because enterprise-level digitization is a continuous and open-ended activity. Digitization projects call for a radical change in mind-set and behavior of management and programmers. Digitizing a corporation, government agency, or supply chain—while continuing to conduct business—is a bit tricky. It's sort of like changing all the tires of an eighteen-wheel truck while it's in motion. But even this metaphor doesn't quite capture the magnitude, complexity, and difficulty of transforming a large company in a successful digitization effort.

The Discipline to Implement

Finally, why have some companies succeeded at digitization while others have failed? The stock answer is they tend to have management and employees who don't believe in quick-fix solutions. They have senior management who are willing to stick with a vision for the long term. But there is more to it than that. They are able to execute and deliver short-term financial results while laying the track for the future. We never said this wasn't tricky.

Companies often tend to lose patience when an initiative takes time to produce results. Consequently, they look for quick-fix solutions that don't work or produce sustainable results. As Sun Microsystems CEO Scott McNealy is quoted as saying: "A bad strategy, well executed, will win every time. And a good strategy, poorly executed, will fail every time." The ultimate difference between a company and its competition is, in fact, the ability to execute one project at a time.

A Final Thought—Services Digitization Is Inevitable

> I will not sell the future for a quick profit!
> —*Werner von Siemens (1884)*

Forecasting the distant future is relatively easy: Most processes will be digitized, a majority of customers will utilize self-service, and everyone will do business over mobile handheld devices. The challenge for corporations is readying their foundations for tomorrow by figuring out the new processes that will get them from where they are to where they need to be. Planning and executing the next step in the digitization journey was the focus of this book. Let's review some of the key points that we made along the way.

First, every organization has to become a digital organization in the twenty-first century. They don't have a choice; the competitive pressures are too great. However, as outlined throughout this book, the challenge is to identify what mix of existing and emerging systems and capabilities is required to deal with the new competitive environment, while also exploiting current sources of competitive advantage. Managers face a dilemma. They have to focus on the big picture so that they are looking for the next key transition points. At the same time, the most challenging question confronting managers is not just "How do we innovate?" but also "What processes and services do we digitize?"

Second, in responding to external and internal pressures, companies are asking tough questions without easy answers: How can digitization improve revenue growth and productivity either through better functional alignment, new value propositions, or enhanced operations? How can digitization be incorporated more quickly and cheaply without replacing existing systems? These strategic questions probably top management's agenda whether the business is small or large, is involved in service or manufacturing, or has one office or many offices across the globe.

Third, addressing the digitization strategy problem has proven to be much more complicated than initially thought since deep-rooted structural changes are often required. A skyscraper doesn't start at street level, in fact, the taller the building, the deeper the foundation. This holds true for digitization efforts. Digitizing service processes, streamlining work in the entire system, and automating transactions are deep-rooted foundational business problems. A focal point is critical in steering the organization as it navigates the stormy waters of digitization.

Fourth, how do you execute against the focal point? Companies cannot effectively implement if they are unable to map their focal point seamlessly into processes and applications. One of the key points we emphasized throughout the book was how the design of composite processes is an important emerging issue. Composite processes create value, not enterprise applications. We make this bold statement because most firms have the same processes built on packaged application frameworks, like customer relationship management or enterprise resource planning. In this environment of sameness, how do you differentiate yourself? The obvious answer: by creating more agile process designs that competitors cannot easily copy.

Fifth, how do you digitize composite processes? The leading companies are pushing the envelope in terms of how they are digitizing next-generation processes. These firms are creating cross-enterprise processes (order-to-return) that run on a new multi-channel, cross-application integration layer called service platforms. Progressive managers in this capital-constrained environment are steering discretionary IT spending toward creating services platforms that are customer-, employee-, reseller-, product-, and supplier-facing. They are looking at long-term value in addition to focusing on the fastest payback and highest ROI projects. However, creating multi-channel and cross-enterprise service platforms is hard work, especially in complex, multi-divisional, enterprise environments like General Motors, Citigroup, Ford, and Nestlé.

Sixth, CIOs, IT managers, and architects are facing a big thorny application integration problem as they attempt to digitize cross-enterprise and multi-channel processes and services. They are looking for new tools and techniques. As a result, Services Oriented Architectures and Web Services have become the fastest-growing segment of the IT industry. This is largely because they aim to help organizations capture greater business value from their IT investments. Recent developments are moving the IT industry, and business as a whole, into a services economy. A services economy seeks solutions for its customers. Technology is the engine for creating solutions, not the driver. The solutions are driven by looking at customers' priorities. In this book, we present a blueprint for management that illustrates the underlying concepts of the services economy and explores issues crucial to the impending paradigm shifts in the digital economy.

Seventh, and last, the importance of a blueprint cannot be understated. Translating an organization's focal point into strategic objectives, processes, and applications, which in turn drive operational results, is the critical role of the blueprint. A blueprint provides a framework to coordinate strategy in a consistent and insightful way. Without a blueprint, companies face alignment problems. When the blueprint is not aligned correctly, it shows in the form of customer migration. Customers migrate rapidly from companies with nonperforming blueprints to competitors that are better able to satisfy their priorities.

We think that managing digitization should be a top priority in organizations. Business today offers the spectacle of companies getting their few minutes of fame and quickly fading away. Even seemingly invincible corporate giants have either gone under, gone through "near death experiences," or are going through dramatic cycles of renewal. It's like riding the change rollercoaster as customer priorities, technologies, financial conditions, and competitors evolve constantly. Disciplined leaders and better execution are required to handle this rollercoaster ride. In this high-risk environment, the demand for ideas on how to execute strategy gets louder and louder. Hot new fads are everywhere. The concept of a blueprint can seem like another fad, but look closer, and you will find a significant difference. Blueprint management brings discipline to technology projects and investments. It is not a business fad tied to a single method or strategy, but rather a flexible approach for better performance.

While this book presents a different way of thinking about processes and integration, the heart of its message is excitement about what lies ahead. Remember that what looks like the norm today was likely considered impossible in the past. Until May 6, 1954, when Roger Bannister ran the mile in 3 minutes, 59.4 seconds, the four-minute mile was considered to be beyond human capability. Experts said the heart was liable to burst trying to supply enough oxygenated blood to the legs. Yet after Bannister, an English neurologist, showed the power of scientific training methods and thorough research into the mechanics of running, 300 runners broke the four-minute barrier within two years. Thousands more have since.

For business, a similar thing has happened in recent years. Online transactions that were once considered radical are now mainstream. In every industry, core business processes are being digitized, often in manners that were once considered impossible. In the past, a digitized company was one that allowed the buying and selling of most products online. Now the idea is much larger. Companies are developing blueprints for a digital nervous system that connects anything and everything involved in an organization's business: applications, customers, employees, factories, suppliers, and partners.

Welcome to digitization, a concept that will grab the attention of your enterprise architects and business strategists over the next decade. Due to the dot-com bust, resistance to digitization may be sharp and prolonged, but it is doomed to failure. Digitization is here to stay. As the Borg in Star Trek say: "Resistance [to digitization] is futile. You will be assimilated."

Endnotes

Chapter 1

1. Source: Intel Corporation's 2001 annual report. Also see the company's press release titled "Intel Conducts $5 Billion in RosettaNet e-Business," Business Wire, December 10, 2002.
2. "McDonald's Ends Project," *The New York Times*, January 3, 2003.
3. For more on the high-level general concepts behind business execution, see Larry Bossidy and Ram Charan, *Execution: The Discipline of Getting Things Done* (New York: Crown Publishing Group, 2002).
4. This does not include U.S. Federal Information Technology spending, which will exceed $48 billion in 2002 and $52 billion in 2003.
5. See the Standish Group's *The Chaos Report* (1994 and 1998). Also, visit the firm's Web site for more recent information (www.standishgroup.com).
6. Source: GE's Web site (www.ge.com/en/commitment/quality/).
7. Source: GE's 2001 annual report.
8. Source: The December 17, 2002, investor meeting on GE's 2003 outlook with CEO Jeff Immelt (www.ge.com).
9. During the fiscal year ended January 31, 2002, Wal-Mart had sales of $217.8 billion.
10. Source: Wal-Mart's 2002 annual report.
11. "Associates Viewed 'As Merchants First'," *Chain Drug Review*, July 22, 2002, no. 12, vol. 24; p. 87.
12. Source: same as note 10.
13. Brian Deagon, "Kmart Misses Mark," *Investor's Business Daily*, April 25, 2002. See also Carol Sliwa, "IT Difficulties Help Take Kmart Down," *Computerworld*, January 28, 2002.
14. Based on IDC's September 2002 forecast, annual IT spending worldwide for 2002–2004 will be approximately $1 trillion.
15. Jennifer Baljko Shah, "Agilent's ERP Rollout Hits Expensive Glitches," *Electronic Buyer's News*, August 26, 2002.

Chapter 2

1. Niamh Ring, "After $21M Loss TD Waterhouse to Cut Staff 30%," *The American Banker*, August 23, 2001, p. 2.
2. Jane Black and Olga Kharif "The Battle to Streamline Business Software," BusinessWeek Online, December 4, 2002.

3. Source: Dell's October 2, 2002, analyst meeting.

4. "Processing Claims," *DataQuest,* October 17, 2002.

5. PR Newswire, "Boeing Awards Gold Supplier Certification to Northrop Grumman," September 13, 2002.

6. Federal Reserve Board Chairman Alan Greenspan made these remarks at a hearing of the Joint Economic Committee of the U.S. Congress on November 13, 2002. The chairman was present to give his economic outlook following the first three quarters of 2002.

7. "The Right Prescription," *NASDAQ International Magazine,* September/October 2002.

8. William Borden, "Machines Fill Increasing Number of Prescriptions," Reuters News, January 5, 2003.

9. Source: www.mcdonalds.com.

10. Craig Barrett, CEO of Intel, spoke about the company's real-time business model during a Mastermind interview conducted by analysts at Gartner, Inc., during the Gartner Symposium/ITxpo held in Orlando, Florida, on October 9, 2001.

Chapter 3

1. Source: www.nasdaq.com.

2. Source: Amazon.com's 10-K and 10-Q filings with the Securities and Exchange Commission (www.edgar.sec.gov).

3. Michael E. McGrath tackles this subject in *Product Strategy for High Technology Companies* (New York: McGraw-Hill Trade, 1995).

4. Marc H. Meyer and Alvin P. Lehnerd explore Black & Decker's platform strategy and argue in general for companies to develop product families with common components and technology in *The Power of Product Platforms: Building Value and Cost Leadership* (New York: The Free Press, 1997).

5. Karl Ulrich and Steven Eppinger walk companies through the product development process in *Product Design and Development,* (New York: McGraw-Hill/Irwin, 1995).

6. Peter Marsh, "Platform Development at Whirlpool," *Financial Times,* April 29, 2002.

7. XML began with data description and has evolved to also include communication standards (for example, the SOAP protocol). Early attempts to create online Web Services utilized a variety of proprietary software communication technologies that resulted in custom point-to-point linkages among applications—a laborious and expensive proposition.

8. Different industry groups such as the Chemical Industry Data Exchange (CIDX), Electronics Industry Data Exchange (EIDX), and Voluntary Interindustry Commerce Standards (VICS) are working hard to create domain-specific XML data and business process standards.

9. Source: Case study on British Airways by BEA Systems. For more information on airline management systems, see the British Airways Fact Book, which is included on its investor relations Web site.

10. It is beyond the scope of this book to describe in detail each of these service platforms. There are many other books and Web sites that do an outstanding job of explaining the technology.

11. SAP AG explained its new product xApps in its press release "SAP Launches Cross Applications," June 5, 2002.

12. Visit www.sap.com for more detailed information and white papers about ESA and NetWeaver.

Chapter 4

1. Nadji Tehrani, "19 Years of Call Center/CRM Evolution and the Incredible Growth Continues! What Next?" *Call Center Solutions*, July 1, 2000, p. 4.
2. Jeffrey Cruikshank and David B. Sicilia, "Brain Storms," *Business Month*, July 1988, p. 88.
3. Marvin Reid, "How the Self-Serve Revolution Bred Price Wars and C-stores," *National Petroleum News*, February 1984, p. 92.
4. Bob Tedeschi, "E-Commerce Report; Bolstered by Holiday Shopping, Online Retailers Now Must Try to Flourish Year-Round," *The New York Times*, January 6, 2003.
5. Clifton Leaf, "What Went Right 2002," *Fortune*, December 16, 2002.
6. Steve Ulfelder, "Signed, Sealed, and Delivered," *Computerworld*, September 30, 2002, p. 50.
7. Russ Banham, "CRM Rollouts: Mulligans Required," *CFO.com*, August 1, 2002.
8. The strategy map is based on the Balanced Scorecard work of Robert S. Kaplan and David P. Norton. To read more about strategy maps see Robert S. Kaplan and David P. Norton, *The Strategy-Focused Organization* (Boston: Harvard Business School Press, 2001).
9. Stephanie Overby, "The Incredible Lateness of Delta," *CIO* Magazine, February 15, 2003. See also the case study on Delta Airlines, www.tibco.com.
10. Source: mySAP CRM documentation (www.sap.com).

Chapter 5

1. For a detailed description of procurement-to-pay at ExxonMobil, see A. Baderschneider, vice president, global procurement, ExxonMobil Global Services Company, and his testimony to the House Government Reform Committee, Federal Document Clearing House Congressional Testimony, October 4, 2001.
2. In AMR Research's Executive View series, Tony Friscia writes about "The Good, the Bad, and the Performance-Driven." The report, published on October 1, 2002, centers on performance-driven enterprises.
3. This Intel press release from December 10, 2002, "Intel Conducts $5 Billion in RosettaNet e-Business, Web Services," highlighted that the company had moved forward to its third phase of e-business, business-to-business integration, by using RosettaNet.
4. We delve into this topic in detail in our earlier mobile business book titled *M-Business: The Race to Mobility* (New York: McGraw-Hill, 2002).
5. Barbara Rose, "Sears appliance technicians taking computers to heart," *Chicago Tribune*, April 18, 2002, p. 3.

Chapter 6

1. Source: The 2001 annual report of i2 Technologies.
2. Federal Reserve Chairman Alan Greenspan made this comment while giving the Federal Reserve Board's semiannual monetary policy report to the Congress, before the Committee on Financial Services, U.S. House of Representatives, on February 28, 2001.
3. Source: www.cpfr.org. This Web site concentrates on the collaborative planning, forecasting, and replenishment initiative sponsored by the Voluntary Interindustry Commerce Standards (VICS) association. The initiative hopes to "improve the partnership between Retailers and Vendor Merchants through shared information."
4. Source: Same as note 3.

5. Kim Cross, "Fill It to the Brim," *Business 2.0*, February 2001.

6. James Stock, Thomas Speh, and Herbert Shear, "Many Happy (Product) Returns," *Harvard Business Review*, July 2002, p. 16.

7. The Automotive Parts Rebuilders Association noted this in its 1998 brochure that discussed "Rebuilding/Remanufacturing: Saving the World's Environment."

8. Eric Young and Mark Roberti, "The Swoosh Stumbles," *The Industry Standard*, March 12, 2001.

9. Andy Dworkin, "Nike Cuts Earnings Estimates," *The Oregonian*, February 27, 2001.

10. Ann Roosevelt, "Marines Aim at More Efficient, Effective Logistics," *Defense Week*, September 30, 2002.

11. Ken Belson, "How Dell Is Defying an Industry's Gravity in Japan," *The New York Times*, December 8, 2002.

12. Source: Research conducted at E-Business Strategies, Inc.

13. This information originated from a set of interviews that E-Business Strategies, Inc. conducted with several members of the Eastman Chemical management team—Roger Mowen, senior vice president, developing businesses and corporate strategy; Terry Begley, vice president, global customer supply chain; and Susan Armstrong, supply chain associate. The interviews were conducted on December 7 and 12, 2002.

14. Earnie Deavenport, "Encouraging partnerships: C-commerce and the petrochemical supply chain," *Executive Speeches*, August 2002/September 2002.

15. Source: Same as note 13.

16. Source: Same as note 13.

Chapter 7

1. Carlos Grande, "When the Workforce Becomes the Customer," *Financial Times*, July 16, 2001.

2. According to CIBC's equity research report "Employee Relationship Management" dated February 21, 2001, U.S. companies will spend more than $160 billion annually—nearly $1,500 per employee—to hire, train, manage, and retain their workforces. Of this amount, companies spend about 80 percent on workforce compensation and benefits. The rest is spent on administration.

3. Business Wire, "Workscape to Deploy Strategic Solutions for Ahold USA Aimed at Employee and Manager Productivity Gains," September 23, 2002.

4. Source: The Web site and 2001 annual report of General Motors.

5. PR Newswire, "Workscape, Sun, and General Motors Win DCI's 'Portal Excellence' Award; Design and Deployment of One of the World's Largest Employee Portals Recognized for Solving Strategic Business Problems and ROI Results," May 21, 2002.

6. Source: General Motors' presentation, General Motors' Employee Portal—Liftoff Plus 1 Year: The Sky's the Limit!, given to The International Association for Human Resource Information Management (IHRIM), 2002.

Chapter 8

1. The service platform was built using MatrixOne's eMatrix product collaboration platform.

2. For these and other examples, see Cliff Edwards, "Where Have All the Edsels Gone?" *Greensboro News Record*, May 24, 1999, p. B6.

3. The term "collaborative product commerce" (CPC), proposed by Gartner Group, is often used as a synonym for PLM.

4. David Welch, "Has GM Pulled Opel Out of Its Skid," *BusinessWeek*, October 14, 2002.

5. Source: Phase Forward Inc.'s Web site and IBM Life Science's Web site.

6. Source: "3D Design Pays Off for Bose Corporation." For more information, read the case study written by EDS, a provider of PLM solutions, which can be found on its Web site, www.eds.com.

7. Source: "Meyer Werft Cruises to Success with IBM RS/6000 and CATIA." This case study is posted on the IBM Web site, www.ibm.com.

8. "Web Smart," *BusinessWeek*, December 2, 2002, p. 68.

9. Jane Black, "Hollywood's Digital Love/Hate Story," BusinessWeek Online, December 24, 2002.

10. Source: "Simon & Schuster, Accenture, and Artesia Implement Digital Asset Management Transformation," joint press release, August 8, 2002.

11. We found this information on the Yahoo! Web site (www.yahoo.com) in an investor relations press release.

12. Source: "Celestica: Keeps Pace with Record Growth." This MatrixOne case study is located on the company's Web site, www.matrixone.com.

13. Karatsu Hajime, "Leading-Edge Technologies and the Future," *Journal of Japanese Trade & Industry (JJTI)*, January 1, 2003.

14. This is based on the VOCAL methodology of E-Business Strategies, www.ebstrategy.com. The technique focuses on assisting companies in listening to the voice of the customer.

15. "No Finish Line," *Footwear News*, November 25, 2002, p. 12.

16. Source: Nike Corporation's 2002 annual report.

17. Stephen Moore, "Software Crunches Mold, Machining Time for Nike," *Modern Plastics*, January 1, 2002, p. 58.

18. Interview with Darcy Winslow, general manager, sustainable business strategies, Nike Inc., U.S., *The Journal of Sustainable Product Design*, Volume 1, Issue 1, 2001.

19. NYTimes.com is a top news and information Web site, with impressive monthly statistics of 350 million page views, 9 million unique visitors, 15 million active registered users, and 750,000 new registered users. It has a much larger national reach than the newspaper.

20. Christopher Saunders, "NYTD Points to 'Surround Session' Benefits," www.internetnews.com, February 7, 2002.

Chapter 9

1. *Encyclopedia Britannica 2001* (Chicago: Encyclopedia Britannica Educational Corp., 2001). Another good reference is "The American Experience: Hoover Dam" found at www.pbs.org/wgbh/amex/hoover/.

2. *Encyclopedia Britannica 2001* (Chicago: Encyclopedia Britannica Educational Corp., 2001). More information is online at "Wonders of the World: Databank," www.pbs.org/wgbh/buildingbig/wonder/structure/akashi_kaikyo.html.

3. Ram Charan and Geoffrey Colvin, "Why CEOs Fail," *Fortune*, June 21, 1999, p. 68–78.

4. Ann Bernasek, "The Economy's Biggest Problem: Tightwad CEOs," *Fortune*, June 10, 2002.

5. Robert Kaplan and David Norton explain how companies can create a strategic management system in *The Balanced Scorecard: Translating Strategy into Action* (Boston: Harvard Business School Press, 1996).

6. For an excellent discussion of the difference between classic strategy—competitive positioning and competitive advantage—and operational strategy, see Michael Porter's article *What Is Strategy?* (Boston: Harvard Business School Press, 2000).

7. Management from Disney addressed this topic at the final Symposium/ITxpo Mastermind Keynote interview held on October 9, 2002, in Orlando, Florida.

8. Source: IBM's press release titled "Nestlé's Landmark Global Business Transformation," March 7, 2002.

9. This information originated from a set of interviews that E-Business Strategies, Inc. conducted with several members of the Eastman Chemical management team—Roger Mowen, senior vice president, developing businesses and corporate strategy; Terry Begley, vice president, global customer supply chain; and Susan Armstrong, supply chain associate. The interviews were conducted on December 7 and 12, 2002.

Chapter 10

1. This is very similar to how religions evolve into multiple factions. The core message might be the same, but the rituals, beliefs, and practices tend to be different.

2. Wesley R. Iversen, "The Six Sigma Shootout; Quality Concept by Motorola," *ASSEMBLY*, June 1993, p. 20.

3. Rob McClusky, "The Rise, Fall, and Revival of Six Sigma Quality," *Measuring Business Excellence*, Second Quarter 2000, vol. 4, no. 2.

4. Del Jones, "Taking the Six Sigma Approach," *USA Today*, October 31, 2002, p. 5B.

5. Tim Studt, "Implementing Six Sigma in R&D," *R&D*, August 1, 2002.

6. Source: General Electric's December quarter investor meeting held on November 21, 2002.

7. Source: Caterpillar's conference call on the company's strategic direction held on November 8, 2002.

8. Source: Merrill Lynch's earnings conference call held on October 16, 2002.

9. Dick Smith and Jerry Blakeslee, "The New Strategic Six Sigma," *T&D* (a magazine published by the American Society for Training and Development), September 1, 2002.

10. Simon London, "When Quality Is Not Quite Enough," *Financial Times*, July 15, 2002.

11. The methods for conducting analysis are discrete, dynamic, and stochastic simulations, experiments, and network flow analysis.

12. Process performance estimation and improvement are often done using techniques or methods from queuing theory, stochastic process theory, and statistical analysis.

13. "Marks' Failed Revolution," *The Economist*, April 14, 2001.

Chapter 11

1. Richard Lefave, "Case Study: Nextel's Big Adventure," *Optimize*, January 2003.

2. It would be interesting to see if companies with CIOs with more than seven years of tenure outperform or have a better ROI than those companies that experience more frequent leadership changes.

3. With the help of Morpheus, Kazaa, BearShare, and other peer-to-peer programs, users can literally download almost any song, movie, or software available.

4. Source: Princeton University case study published by Sun Microsystems, www.sun.com/products-n-solutions/edu/success/SunONE_Princeton.pdf.

5. We describe this model extensively in *e-Business 2.0: Roadmap for Success* (Boston: Addison-Wesley, 2001).

6. Juan Carlos Perez, "Colgate Taps IBM for Hardware Infrastructure," InfoWorld.com, May 17, 2002.

7. Jane Hodges, "Supply Chain CEOs," *Chief Executive* (U.S. edition), January 2002.

8. Earl Cross and J. Sampler, "Transformation of the IT Function at British Petroleum," *MIS Quarterly*, December 1997, p. 401–423.

9. Kristin Krause, "An $800 Million Face-Lift," *Traffic World*, November 11, 2002, p. 34.

10. This information originated from a set of interviews that E-Business Strategies, Inc. conducted with several members of the Eastman Chemical management team—Roger Mowen, senior vice president, developing businesses and corporate strategy; Terry Begley, vice president, global customer supply chain; and Susan Armstrong, supply chain associate. The interviews were conducted on December 7 and 12, 2002.

11. Patti Bond, "Reinventing Ga.-Pacific Is Correll's Big Mission," *The Atlanta Journal and Constitution*, November 4, 2001, p. E1.

12. Source: Georgia-Pacific's press release titled "Georgia-Pacific Announces Plan to Sell Majority Stake in Its Unisource Subsidiary to Bain Capital; Reports Related Charges for 2002," August 14, 2002.

13. Source: Same as note 11.

Chapter 12

1. Stephen A. Rhodes, "Bank Mergers and Banking Structure in the United States, 1980–98," August 2000 Staff Study for the U.S. Federal Reserve Board.

2. Source: AT&T's Web site, www.att.com.

3. Stratford Sherman, "Is He Too Cautious to Save IBM," *Fortune*, October 3, 1994, p. 78.

4. Corinne Bernstein and Nicole Lewis, "Inside IBM's Web-Centric World," *Electronic Buyers News*, June 18, 2001.

5. Source: "IBM: Business Transformation through End-to-End Integration." This IDC e-business case study is located on IBM's Web site, www.ibm.com, and is filed under success stories.

6. Nirmalya Kumar, "The Path to Change," *Financial Times*, December 6, 2002.

7. Source: Same as note 5.

8. PBS developed a "Great Project" series dedicated to some of the most noteworthy engineering projects in history. More information can be found on the PBS Web site, www.pbs.org/greatprojects/about/index.html.

Index

Accenture, 109
Activity Based Management, 267
Adecco, 185
AdminStaff, 185
ADP, 185
Advertising, 89, 92, 235
AdVision, 220
Aetna, 282
Aggregation of processes, 166–167
Agile (company), 229
Agilent Technologies, 29
Air Force (United States), 68, 211
Akashi Kaikyo Bridge, 240–241
Albertsons, 94
Alcatel, 17
Alcoa, 17
Allied Signal, 248, 269
AllState, 46
Amazon.com, 4, 96–97
    disruptive innovation and, 18
    multi-channel blueprint and,
        96–97, 100, 102–105
    service platforms and, 58, 59
American Airlines, 234
American Express, xxi
AOL Time Warner, 235
APAC (company), 96
AppConnect (PeopleSoft), xxiii, 76
Apple Computer, 212
"Architecture of Complexity, The"
    (Simon), 65
Archive packaging, 235
Argentina, 149
Ariba, 126, 133, 139
Armstrong, C. Michael, 19, 318
Armstrong, Susan, 175
Army (United States), 247

ASDA Group PLC, 22
As-Is state, 264, 307
Asset(s)
    management, digital (DAM),
        219
    utilization of, 155–156
AST (company), 15
AT&T (American Telephone &
    Telegraph), 18–19, 247, 329
    divestiture of, 320
    key lessons learned from,
        320–322
    M&A strategies and, 316–322
ATMs (automatic teller
    machines), 35, 87, 92
Auctions, reverse, 126
Audit service platform, 79–80
Autocad, 213
Automation, 8, 9, 91, 128–129,
    297
Aventis Pharma, 217

B2B (business-to-business)
    commerce, 7, 266. See also
    Procurement
    portals, 122, 136
    spend management blueprint
        and, 120–122, 126, 128,
        136–137, 145
Baan, 151
Baby Boom generation, 187–188
Back-end offices, 4, 9, 37–39, 200,
    306
Bain Capital, 311
Balanced Scorecard, 243–247
Bank of America, 94, 185, 248,
    270, 316

Bank One Corporation, 88, 94
Bannister, Roger, 334
BEA Systems, xxiii, 11, 75–76
Begley, Terry, 171
Bell, Alexander Graham, 317
Benchmarks, 247, 298
Benefits management, 185, 188,
    190
Benetton, 149
Benetton, Giuliana, 149
Benetton, Luciano, 149
Best-of-breed approach, 250,
    299–300
Best practices, 229
"Big Dig" (Central Artery/Tunnel
    Project), 330–331
Billing practices, 37, 38–39, 58
Black & Decker, 67
Blueprint(s). See also specific types
    managing enterprise-wide
        execution with, 243–251
    methodology, 239–261
    need for, xxiii–xxv, 13–19
    three categories of, xxvi, 17–18
BMO (blueprint management
    office), 253–259, 281
BMW (Bavarian Motor Works),
    43
Boeing, xxi, 44–45, 131
Boom-bust cycle, 120
Bose, 216
Boston Market, 50
Bowerman, Bill, 230, 231
BP (British Petroleum), 300
    HIVES (Highly Immersive
        Visualization Environments)
        and, 300

BPM (business process management). *See also* Business process management layer
enabling, 69–71
enterprise portals and, 58–59
integration services and, 74
micro-level technology blueprints and, 297
service platforms and, 58–59, 69–71, 74
BPO (business process outsourcing), 42–43, 182, 305–307. *See also* Outsourcing
Brazil, 153
Britain, 8, 282
British Airways, 76, 97, 305
British Telecom, 185, 318
Brochureware Web sites, 91–92
BRS (Blue Ribbon Sports), 230
BTO (build-to-order), 166
Bullwhip effect, 155
Burnham, Dan, 271–272
Business intelligence service platform, 80
Business models, evolving, 49–51
Business process(es). *See also* Business process management layer; Processes
design tools, 230
libraries, 229
mega-trends and, 7
outsourcing (BPO), 42–43, 182, 305–307
re-engineering, 323–324
Business process management layer. *See also* BPM (business process management)
employee-centric blueprint and, 191, 192, 196, 197–198
multi-channel blueprint and, 99, 103, 104–105
product innovation blueprint and, 221, 224–226
spend management blueprint and, 132, 135, 136–137
supply chain blueprint and, 160–161, 165, 166–167
Business transformation blueprint, 18, 31
"Buy versus build" approach, 106
BW (business warehouse), 297

CAD (computer-aided design), 209–210, 212–217, 224
CAE (computer-aided engineering), 210, 213, 215–217
Call centers, 87, 88–91, 96–98
CAM (computer-aided manufacturing), 210, 213, 216–217, 231–232
Canada, 6, 148
CareerBuilder.com, 186
Carrefour, 18
Caterpillar, 18, 248, 271
CATIA, 213
Celestica, 153, 222
Cendian Corporation, 147, 173–175
Central Artery/Tunnel Project, 330–331
Ceridian, 185
CFC (central fulfillment center), 113
Change management, 7, 252, 280–281
Channels. *See also* Multi-channel models
alignment of, 114–115
disruptive innovation and, 18
focal points and, 35–36
integration of, 35–36
service platforms and, 56, 59–61, 81
Chaos
portals and, 62–63
use of the term, 30
Charan, Ram, 241
Charles Schwab (company), 248
Chile, 149
China, 4, 8, 22, 42, 51, 153
Chipotle Mexican Grill, 50
Churchill, Winston, 30, 239
Cigna, 46
Circuit City, 4, 100, 102, 105
Cisco, 18, 55, 248
Citigroup, 94, 333
Clarify (company), 106
Client/server architecture, 89, 151
CNN (Cable News Network), 219
COBRA (Consolidated Omnibus Budget Reconciliation Act), 188
Coca-Cola, 51, 212, 220
Colgate-Palmolive, 299

Collaboration, 155–156, 169–170, 209–210, 213
Columbus, Christopher, 119–120
Colvin, Geoffrey, 241
Compaq, 15
Complexity, managing, 65–66, 68–78
Composite processes. *See also* Composite process layer; Processes
described, 70
employee-centric blueprint and, 191, 195–197
enabling, 101–104, 132–135
multi-channel blueprint and, 99, 101–105
product innovation blueprint and, 221, 222–224, 225
self-service and, 102–104
service platforms and, 59–61, 66–67, 69–71, 76–78
spend management blueprint and, 132–135, 138
supply chain blueprint and, 160, 163–165
translating services into, 104–105
Composite process layer, 59–61, 66–67, 69–71, 76–78. *See also* Composite processes
employee-centric blueprint and, 196
multi-channel blueprint and, 103
spend management blueprint and, 134, 135
Conaway, Charles C., 28
Confederal model, 305
Congress (United States), 149
Consortia, 122
Consultative solution selling, 326–327
Continuous
cost reduction, 123–124
improvement, 61, 167
innovation, 101
Contracts, 129–130, 133, 142, 325. *See also* Service level agreements
Correll, Pete, 309, 311
Cosi, 50
CP&P (company), 311

CPD (collaborative product development), 209–210. *See also* Collaboration

cPDM (collaborative Product Data Management), 213. *See also* Collaboration

CPFR (collaborative planning, forecasting, and replenishment), 152, 163

Creation phase, 214

Credit card industry, 44

CRM (customer relationship management), 7, 252, 265, 266. *See also* Customers
features and functions in, 110
focal points and, 38
IBM and, 324
micro-level technology blueprints and, 297
multi-channel blueprint and, 85, 88–92, 98–99, 104–111, 115–116
process-based, moving to, 107
service platforms and, 58–59, 63, 71, 76, 78–79, 81
spend management blueprint and, 124
supply chain blueprint and, 168

Cross-enterprise processes, 6, 7, 9–10, 59. *See also* Processes

CSRs (customer service representatives), 56, 96

CTI (computer telephony integration), 89

CTQ (Critical to Quality), 249

Currency, 12, 296

Customer(s). *See also* CRM (customer relationship management); Self-service
-Centric Integration focal point, 12, 14, 34, 37–39
changing priorities and, 7, 49–51
different services for different, 97–98
ETDBW projects and, 12–14
evolving expectations of, 36
high visibility of, 142
interactions, synchronized, 93–94
360-degree view of, 97–98

Voice of (VOC), technique, 225–226, 267, 275

Customization, mass, 47–48

CVS, 46

DaimlerChrysler, 52, 153, 220

Daksh (company), 97

DAM (digital asset management), 219

Dassault Systems, 229

Data
collection, 167
models, 295–296
warehouses, 23, 27

Databases, 26–27, 91, 106

Defense Department (United States), 131, 161–162, 211

Dell Computer
direct-to-consumer business model, 16
focal points and, 33, 39–41
IBM and, 327
Low-Cost focal point and, 15, 39–41
operating expense-to-sales ratio, 40
reverse auctions and, 126
service platforms and, 55, 56, 66
spend management blueprint and, 123, 126
strategic improvement and, 18
supply chain blueprint and, 163
three goals of, 41

Delta Airlines, 9, 105

Deming, Edward, 269, 312

Demographics, 184, 187–188

Department of Defense (United States), 131, 161–162, 211

Depression, 93, 239

Deregulation, 8, 86

DHL, 144

DHS (Department of Homeland Security), 265

Differentiation, 13, 16, 59
multi-channel blueprint and, 87, 95–96
product innovation blueprint and, 236
supply chain blueprint and, 156–157, 164
Wal-Mart and, 24–28

Direct mail campaigns, 89

Direct-to-consumer business model, 16

Distribution centers, 25, 26

Divestitures, 186–187, 310–311, 320

DMAIC process, 248, 273

Donatos Pizza, 50

DOS (disk operating system), 91

Dot-com collapse, 14, 16, 53, 334

Double Insulation program, 67

Dow Chemical, 98, 248, 270

Downsizing, 282

DRP (distribution resource planning), 151

DXF (data exchange file) format, 212

EAI (Enterprise Application Integration), 250, 297, 299
multi-channel blueprint and, 108
service platforms and, 73, 74
supply chain blueprint and, 170

Eastman Chemical, 4, 147, 149, 170–175, 253, 304

Eastman Kodak, 17, 170

Easy To Do Business With (ETDBW) focal point, 12–15, 21, 252
described, 15, 34, 35–37
multi-channel blueprint and, 86, 100–101, 103, 109
service platforms and, 56
strategy map for, 100–101
three options yielded by, 35

eBay, 55, 59

Eckerd Corporation, 46, 111

ECNs (electronic communications networks), 58

EDI (electronic data interchange)
purchase orders and, 127
supply chain blueprint and, 149
Wal-Mart and, 23
XML and, 74, 128

EDM (enterprise data model), 295, 296

EDS, 213, 229

EH&S (environmental, health, and safety) regulations, 217–218

80/20 (eighty/twenty) rule, 127

Einstein, Albert, 228
E-learning, 202. *See also* Learning
E-mail, 8, 265, 304
  contacts, outsourcing, 96–97
  employee-centric blueprint
    and, 187
  New York Times Digital and,
    233
  purchase orders and, 127
  spend management blueprint
    and, 127, 133
  supply chain blueprint and, 158
  telesales and, 88
Emerson, Ralph Waldo, 175
Employees. *See also* Employee-
    centric blueprint
  corporate objectives and,
    synchronizing, 189
  Web portals for, 44–46
Employee-centric blueprint
  composite processes and, 191,
    195–197
  described, 177–207
  layers of, 191–193
  long-term trends shaping,
    184–190
  service platforms and, 182–184,
    200–202
EMS (electronic manufacturing
    services), 153
End-to-end supply chain enable-
    ment, 7
Enterprise applications. *See also*
    Enterprise application inte-
    gration layer; Integrated
    enterprise applications layer
  employee-centric blueprint
    and, 191–192, 198–200
  integrating, 137–138, 167–168,
    191–192, 198–200
  micro-level technology blue-
    prints and, 296–301
  multi-channel blueprint and,
    105–106
  spend management blueprint
    and, 132, 134
  supply chain blueprint and,
    167–168
  Wal-Mart and, 23
  Web Services and, 72
Enterprise portals, 58–59, 61–68,
    80. *See also* Portals

Enterprise software providers, 126
E-procurement, 120–123. *See also*
    Procurement
ERM (enterprise resource man-
    agement), 297
ERP (enterprise resource plan-
    ning), 7, 250, 265, 266
  execution issues and, 30
  focal points and, 38
  IBM and, 324
  micro-level technology blue-
    prints and, 297, 302
  Oracle and, 29
  process flexibility and, 8
  service platforms and, 58–59,
    62–63, 71, 76, 81
  spend management blueprint
    and, 124, 134, 137–138
ESA (Enterprise Services Archi-
    tecture), 75
ETDBW (Easy To Do Business
    With) focal point, 12–15, 21,
    252
  described, 15, 34, 35–37
  multi-channel blueprint and,
    86, 100–101, 103, 109
  service platforms and, 56
  strategy map for, 100–101
  three options yielded by, 35
Euro (currency), 12, 296
European Union, 12, 114
Eventra, 170
"Every Day Low Price," 23, 24,
    160. *See also* Prices
Evolving Business Model focal
    point, 35, 49–51
Execution
  blueprint methodologies and,
    239–261
  challenge of, 241–243,
    311–312
  discipline of, 315–334
  enterprise-wide, managing,
    243–251
EXE Technologies, 151
Expedia, 57, 96–97
Expense-to-sales ratios, 40
Express Scripts, 46–47
Extensible Markup Language.
    See XML (Extensible Markup
    Language)
ExxonMobil, 118, 247

Falabella (company), 149
Fast-Service focal point, 11, 34,
    46–47, 148
FDA (Food and Drug Administra-
    tion), 215–216
Feasibility analysis, 278–279
Federal Express, 11, 52, 144, 303
  Cosmos Tracking System, 134
  multi-channel blueprint and,
    95
  process flexibility and, 8
  product innovation blueprint
    and, 212
  spend management blueprint
    and, 134, 144
  third-party logistics and, 43
Federal Reserve (United States), 45
Federated model, 305, 308–312
Fidelity Investments, 182
Field, Marshall, 35
Firewalls, 11
Flextronics, 153
Focal points. *See also specific types*
  blueprint methodology and,
    243, 252
  employee-centric blueprint
    and, 191–194, 203
  identifying, 53
  importance of, 17, 30–31, 34,
    53–54
  list of, 34
  multi-channel blueprint and,
    99, 100–101
  overview of, 15–16, 33–54,
    273–274
  product innovation blueprint
    and, 210, 221, 222
  scope of, 54
  service platforms and, 57–61, 81
  spend management blueprint
    and, 118, 131–132
  supply chain blueprint and,
    148, 160, 161–163, 176
FoodService.com, 125
Ford, Henry, 66, 260
Ford Motor Company, 19, 153,
    333
  employee-centric blueprint
    and, 178
  multi-channel blueprint and, 87
  product innovation blueprint
    and, 212

Foreign languages, 72, 95
Fort James (company), 156, 309, 310
Fortune (magazine), 241
Fortune 500 companies, 203
4PLs (fourth-party logistics providers)
France, 6, 8
FreeMarkets, 126, 139
Frito-Lay, 152
Frontier (company), 17
Fuego (company), 74
Fujitsu (company), 327
Fulfillment, 46–47, 111–113
   service platforms and, 70, 75–76
   spend management blueprint and, 136
   supply chain blueprint and, 148
Future Shock (Toffler), 53

Gartner Group, 242
Gateway, 15, 41, 126
GE (General Electric), xxi, 19–20, 31, 248, 305
   back-office services and, 4
   digitization initiative, 19, 21–22
   focal points and, 34
   meso-level blueprints and, 269, 270
   multi-channel blueprint and, 87
   spend management blueprint and, 123, 141
GENCO, 114
General Electric. *See* GE (General Electric)
General Mills, 156
Generation X, 187–188
Generation Y, 187–188
Georgia-Pacific Corporation, 308–312
Gerber (company), 299
Germany, 22, 114, 273
Gerstner, Louis V., 322, 326
GIGO (garbage in, garbage out), 267
Globalization. *See also* Global sourcing
   AT&T and, 320

employee-centric blueprint and, 177
GE and, 19–21
micro-level technology blueprints and, 306
Global Services (IBM), 95
Global sourcing, 25, 125–127. *See also* Globalization; Sourcing
Global 2000 companies, 14
GLOBE (global business excellence initiative), 250
GM (General Motors), 87, 333
   employee-centric blueprint and, 202–206
   integration services and, 74
   labor productivity and, 205–206
   product innovation blueprint and, 215–216
   service platforms and, 55, 68, 74
Great Depression, 93, 239
Greenspan, Alan, 45, 149
Gyorgi, Albert Szent, 114

Handheld devices, 23, 26, 332
   service platforms and, 62, 81
   spend management blueprint and, 144
   Wal-Mart and, 26
Harley-Davidson, 43
HCM (human capital management), 181–182, 195–197, 200
Hewlett-Packard. *See* HP (Hewlett-Packard)
Hilton Hotels, 247
HIVES (Highly Immersive Visualization Environments), 300
HMOs (health maintenance organizations), 46
Holmes, Oliver Wendell, 145
Home Depot, 148, 248, 309
HomeGrocer.com, 94
Honda, 68, 272
Honeywell, 18, 248
Hong Kong, 4, 51
Hoover Dam, 239
Hora, 65
HotJobs.com, 186

HP (Hewlett-Packard), 29, 327
   consolidation of product lines by, 38
   focal points and, 33, 38
   Project Everest, 29
   reverse auctions and, 126
   service platforms and, 66, 76
   supply chain blueprint and, 153
HR (human resources). *See also* HRMS (human resource management systems)
   employee-centric blueprint and, 177–207
   help desks, 178
   portals, 45, 183, 184, 186, 194, 203–205
   process digitization types, 180–182
   strategic, 180–181, 182, 193–194
   transactional, 180–181, 182
HRMS (human resource management systems), 178, 200. *See also* HR (human resources)
   micro-level technology blueprints and, 297
   service platforms and, 182–184
   transactional HR and, 180
HSBC Holdings PLC, 4
HTML (Hypertext Markup Language), 73, 220
HTTP (Hypertext Transfer Protocol), 73
Humana, 46, 282
Human capital management, 79. *See also* HCM (human capital management)
Human resources. *See* HR (human resources)

IBM (International Business Machines), xxi, xxii, 11, 318, 322–329
   business transformation and, 18, 19
   change of leadership at, 322–323
   cross-channel experiences and, 95
   manufacturing and, 66
   micro-level technology blueprints and, 299

IBM (*continued*)
  multi-channel blueprint and, 95, 109
  OS/2, 212
  outsourcing and, 51
  product innovation blueprint and, 213, 229
  reverse auctions and, 126
  service platforms and, 66, 75
  supply chain blueprint and, 153
  transformational management and, 327–329
  WebSphere, 11, 72, 76
IE (information engineering), 295
IGES format, 212
Immelt, Jeff, 270
Inception phase, 214
India, 4, 8, 97, 119
Industrial Age, 95
Industrial Revolution, 53, 66, 80, 282
Information Age, 95
Ingram, 105
Innovation. *See also* Product innovation blueprint
  "disruptive," 18–19
  focal points and, 15–16, 35, 47–49
  historical perspective on, 7
  piecemeal approach to, 15–16
  process flexibility and, 8
  product innovation blueprint and, 222
  product lifecycles and, 47–49
  senior management and, 29
  service platforms and, 55–56, 59, 64, 69, 72–73, 81
  spend management blueprint and, 120, 123
  supply chain blueprint and, 172–173
"Inside-out/outside-in" views, 6, 12–14, 21, 61
Instill.com, 125
Instinet, 58
Integrated enterprise applications layer, 160–161, 167–168
  employee-centric blueprint and, 191, 192, 198–200
  product innovation blueprint and, 221, 226–228

Integration layer, 59–61, 70–76
  described, 71–76
  employee-centric blueprint and, 196
  multi-channel blueprint and, 103
  product innovation blueprint and, 225
  spend management blueprint and, 134, 135
  supply chain blueprint and, 165
Intel, xxi, 18
  mission of, 4
  servers, used by Dell, 41
  service platforms and, 55
  spend management blueprint and, 123
Interaction Center, 106–107
International Business Machines. *See* IBM (International Business Machines)
International Paper, 185
Internet
  changes set in motion by, 4
  global sourcing and, 126–127
  "is the computer" vision, 71
  process flexibility and, 8
  real-time information flows and, 52
  service platforms and, 59
  spend management blueprint and, 120, 121
Inventories, 70, 102
  "just-in-case," 144
  spend management blueprint and, 143–145
  supply chain blueprint and, 149, 154–155, 157, 170
  Wal-Mart and, 23, 26, 27
Investment Portfolio theory, 250
Iterative development, 296
i2 Technologies, 151, 299

Japan, 23, 224, 272
JC Penney
  multi-channel blueprint and, 85, 93–94, 109–110
  product returns and, 109–114
  synchronized customer inter-actions and, 93–94
J.D. Edwards, 62, 169, 200
JP Morgan, 247

JSF (Joint Strike Fighter), 211
"Just-in-case" inventories, 144. *See also* Inventories
"Just-in-Time" manufacturing, 7, 26

KAIZEN, 244
Kanban, 7
Kenmore, 141
Key performance indicators (KPIs), 129
Kimberly-Clark, 311
Kiosks, 94–95, 100
Kmart, 13, 27–28
Knight, Philip, 159, 230
Kodak, 17, 170
Kozmo.com, 94
KPN (company), 17
Kraft Foods, 17
Kresge, Sebastian, 27
Kresge's, 27. *See also* Kmart
Kroger, 152

Lands' End, 36–37, 56
Languages, foreign, 72, 95
LANs (local area networks), 144
Lao Tzu, 284
lastminute.com, 57
Launch phase, 215
Lean Enterprises, 244, 247, 267, 268–269
Learning
  blueprint methodologies and, 253
  employee-centric blueprint and, 202
  new services meso-level blue-print and, 280–281
Leasing, 299–300
Lexus, 43
Lifecycles, product, 79, 209–236. *See also* PLM (product life-cycle management); Product innovation blueprint
  shrinking, 47–49
  spend management blueprint and, 142
Localization, 125
Lockheed Martin, 211
Logility (company), 299
Logistics
  defense, 161–162

on demand, 161–162
fourth-party (4PL), 155–156
reverse, 156–157
service platforms and, 58, 77
third-party (3PL), 43, 151,
155–156
Wal-Mart and, 23, 24–25
London Business School, 56
Low-Cost focal point
as a continuing challenge, 41
described, 15, 34, 39–41
as a guiding principle, 16–17
spend management blueprint
and, 132–135
Low Price-Always program, 24
Lowe's, 27
Lowest-Overhead focal point, 34,
42–43
Lucent Technologies, 17, 141, 317
Ludd, Ned, 282

M&A (mergers and acquisitions),
8, 77, 184, 186–187, 316–322
MacArthur, Douglas, 80
McDonald's (company), 6, 49–51,
212
McNealy, Scott, 331
Macro-level blueprint, 243,
246–247, 251–253, 258, 260,
316
MADs (mergers, acquisitions, and
divestitures), 186–187
Malcolm Baldridge Award, 269
Manhattan Associates, 134, 151
Manugistics, 151, 169
Marines (United States), 162, 211
Market(s). *See also* Marketing
synchronizing with, 51–52
time to, 216–217, 236
Marketing. *See also* Advertising;
Markets
brochureware and, 92
multi-channel blueprint and,
90, 92
service platforms and, 71
Marks & Spencer, 281
"Mass fighter" models, 162
MASS (manager and associate
self-service), 194
MasterCard, 44
MatrixOne, 213, 222, 229
"Maverick buying" problem, 128

Maytag, 141
Measurement, 22, 275–277
MedcoHealth Solutions, 46
Mega-trends, 5–14, 53
Menlo Logistics, 43
Mercator (company), 170
Mercedes Benz, 272
Merchandising, 23, 24, 27
Merrill Lynch, 271
Meso-level blueprint, 243–244,
247–249, 251–253, 258, 260
Messier, Jean, 19
Mexico, 42, 111, 149
Meyer Werft, 217
Micro-level technology blue-
prints, 249–253, 258, 260
described, 287–314
enterprise application models
and, 296–301
Micron PC, 15
Microprocessors, 66
Microsoft
application integration trends
and, 11
.NET Framework, xxiii, 75, 76
Outlook, 133
PowerPoint, 239
service platforms and, 62,
75, 76
Windows, 89, 91
Modularity, 65–67, 71–72
Monster.com, 186
Morse code, 73
Motorola, 248, 269
Mowen, Roger, 170, 253
MRP (manufacturing resource
planning), 150, 151
MTC (mold and tooling center),
232
Mulally, Alan, 44
Multi-channel blueprint. Multi-
channel models
call centers and, 87, 88–91,
96–98
composite processes and, 99,
101–105
CRM and, 85, 88–92, 98–99,
104–111, 115–116
cross-channel experiences and,
94–96
described, 85–116
differentiation and, 87, 95–96

ETDBW focal point and, 86,
100–101, 103, 109
important questions related to,
114–115
integration problem related to,
87
long-term trends and, 92–98
outsourcing and, 96–97
returns management and,
109–114
synchronized customer interactions and, 93–94
Multi-channel models, 6, 9–10.
See also Multi-channel blueprint; Multi-channel portal
layer
focal points and, 35
government services and,
264–265
service platforms and, 59,
61–62, 69
Multi-channel portal layer, 70,
103, 135, 196. Multi-channel
models
product innovation blueprint
and, 225
supply chain blueprint and, 165
mySAP CRM suite (SAP),
106–107
mySocrates portal (Sun), 203–205

Nasdaq, 58
Nasser, Jacques, 19
Navy (United States), 211
NCR (company), 27, 317
NDP (new product develop-
ment), 209–210
NEC (company), 163, 164
Need-to-have capability, 125–127
Nestlé, 17, 250, 333
GLOBE (global business excel-
lence initiative) and, 250
Netherlands, 287
NetWeaver (SAP), xxiii, 11, 76, 77
New Economics, The (Deming),
312
New York Times, The, 232–235
New York Times Digital (NYTD)
Nextel Communications, 288
Nike, 17, 43, 159, 218, 230–232
Nistevo, 155–156
Nobel Prize for Economics, 65

Nokia, 141, 153, 210
Nordstrom, 4, 100
Nortel Networks, 17, 141
Northrop Grumman, 44
NYTD (New York Times Digital)
NYTimes.com, 232–235

Oberhelman, Doug, 271
Obsolescence, 142, 145
OEMs (original equipment man-
    ufacturers), 153, 326
Office Depot, 4, 100, 105
OHSU (Oregon Health & Sci-
    ences University), 37–38
One Face to the Customer CRM
    strategy, 98
Oracle, 11, 29, 200
    service platforms and, 75
    spend management blueprint
        and, 139
    supply chain blueprint and, 169
Orbitz, 57
Order-to-cash services, 263,
    265–266
OS/2 (IBM), 212
Outlook (Microsoft), 133
"Outside-out/inside-in" views, 6,
    12–14, 21, 61
Outsourcing, 8, 22, 247. *See also*
    Sourcing
    call centers, 96–97
    Dell and, 40
    employee-centric blueprint
        and, 182, 184–186, 190
    focal points and, 40, 42–43, 51
    IBM and, 324
    micro-level technology blue-
        prints and, 299–300, 305–306
    multi-channel blueprint and,
        96–97
    supply chain blueprint and,
        153–154

Packaged applications, 61–62, 106
Packaging, archive, 235
Packard Bell, 15
P&C (property and casualty
    insurance), 42
P&G (Procter & Gamble), 211,
    218
Panera Bread, 50
Parametric, 213, 229

Patrick, Thomas, 271
PBM (Pharmacy Benefits Man-
    agement), 46–47
PDM (product data manage-
    ment), 209–210
PEO (professional employer orga-
    nization), 185–186, 188
PeopleSoft, 11, 169
    AppConnect, xxiii, 76
    call centers, 98
    employee-centric blueprint
        and, 197, 200
    multi-channel blueprint and,
        98, 106
    service platforms and, 62, 75
    spend management blueprint
        and, 134, 139
    Web portals and, 45
Pepsi, 220
Performance service platforms, 80
Pets.com, 94
Philippines, 8, 102
Piggly Wiggly grocery stores, 93
Pipeline, 178
Pliny the Elder, 54
PLM (product lifecycle manage-
    ment). *See also* Innovation;
    Product innovation
    blueprint
    environmental, health, and
        safety regulations and, 217
    evolution of, 212–214
    focal points and, 48
    long-term trends shaping,
        214–220
Plug-and-play model, 71, 72
PMS (project management ser-
    vices), 253
Polaroid, 212
Porsche, 43
Portal(s). *See also* Web portals
    architecture, 302
    B2B, 122, 136
    development of, 80
    enterprise, 58–59, 61–68, 80
    evolution of, 62–63
    fragmented, 68–69
    HR, 45, 183, 184, 186, 194,
        203–205
    infrastructure, 61–68
    integration services and, 74
    investing in, 303–304

micro-level technology blue-
    prints and, 291–292,
    301–304, 307
multi-channel blueprint and,
    87, 92, 103
problems with, 64
product innovation blueprint
    and, 226
productivity rates and, 44–46
service platforms and, 56,
    57–69, 80
spend management blueprint
    and, 122, 134
stovepipe, 63
Wal-Mart and, 26–27
Porter, Michael, 246
Portfolio method, 298, 300–301
PowerPoint (Microsoft), 239
Pret a Manger, 50
Price(s)
    "Every Day Low," 23, 24, 160
    focal points and, 39
    multi-channel blueprint and,
        101
    rapid erosion of, 39
    rollbacks, 24
    service platforms and, 79
    spend management blueprint
        and, 123–125, 129
    supply chain blueprint and, 164
PricewaterhouseCoopers, 326
Princeton University, 289–292
Process(es). *See also* Business
    processes
    aggregation, 166–167
    automation, 8, 9, 128–129
    clarity, 166
    -centric orientation, 12, 13
    cross-enterprise, 6, 7, 9–10, 59
    decomposition, 166–167
    improvement blueprint, 31
    mapping, into applications,
        137–138, 166–168, 198–200
    re-engineering, 7, 267, 268–269
    traditional perspective on,
        13–14
    translating services into,
        104–105, 136–137, 166–167,
        224–226
Processware, 74
Procter & Gamble (P&G), 211,
    218

Procurement. *See also* B2B
(business-to-business)
commerce; Spend manage-
ment blueprint
evolution of, 119–123
as a key part of service management, 144–145
RosettaNet and, 127
self-service and, 128–129
service platforms and, 76
spend management blueprint
and, 118–125, 127–129,
141–145
transparency, 124–125
Product(s). *See also* Product innovation blueprint; Product
lifecycles
custom, 218–219
launches, accelerated, 220
lines, consolidation of, 38
platforms, 66–67
stockouts, 154
Product innovation blueprint.
See also Innovation;
Products
composite processes and, 221,
222–224, 225
custom-configured products
and, 218–219
described, 209–236
layers of,
long-term trends shaping,
service platforms and, 225–226,
228–229
Product Innovation focal point,
34, 47–49
Product lifecycles, 79, 209–236.
See also PLM (product lifecycle management)
product innovation blueprint
and, 219
shrinking, 47–49
spend management blueprint
and, 142
Productivity Multiplier focal
point,
Profits
micro-level technology blueprints and, 294
product innovation blueprint
and, 219, 236
returns management and, 114

spend management blueprint
and, 119, 125–126, 146
Von Siemens on, 332
Project Everest (Hewlett-
Packard), 29
Prototypes
blueprint methodology and,
251
focal points and, 48
product innovation blueprint
and, 223–224, 231–232, 236
Prudential Financial, 185
Puerto Rico, 111

Quality. *See also* TQM (total
quality management)
changing process priorities
and, 7
Critical to (CTQ), 249
focal points and, 36
product innovation blueprint
and, 216–217
Qwest, 17

R&D (research and development),
38, 211, 221, 232
Randstad, 185
Rapid price erosion, 39
Raytheon Corporation, 271–272
RCA, 211
Realization phase, 215
Real-Time Business focal point,
35, 51–52
Reflect.com, 218
Regulations, 185, 188–189,
217–218
Requisition, 133
Résumé management, 186
Return on investment. *See* ROI
(return on investment)
Returns management, 109–115,
156
Revenue service platforms, 79
Reverse auctions, 126
Revolution, use of the term, 30
RFPs (requests for proposals),
133
RFQs (requests for quotes), 133,
136
RJR Nabisco, 322
R-Log (retail reverse logistics)
service, 114

ROI (return on investment), xxiii,
6–7, 240, 261, 333
focal points and, 43
mega-trends and, 5
meso-level blueprints and, 270,
281
micro-level technology blueprints and, 300
multi-channel blueprint and,
108
portals and, 64
spend management blueprint
and, 131, 132
supply chain blueprint and, 176
RosettaNet, 127
Royal Ahold, 193–194
Ryder, 43

Safeway, 94
Samsung, 210
SAP, 249, 324
call centers, 98
employee-centric blueprint
and, 197, 200
micro-level technology blueprints and, 296, 299
multi-channel blueprint and,
98, 106
NetWeaver, xxiii, 11, 76, 77
product innovation blueprint
and, 217
service platforms and, 62, 71,
75–78
spend management blueprint
and, 134, 139, 145
supply chain blueprint and,
151, 169, 171
Web portals and, 45
xApps, xxiii, 11, 71, 76–78, 108
Saunders, Clarence, 93
Savvion, 74
SBUs (single business units), 250,
306
SCC (supply chain council), 259
SCEM (supply chain event management), 152, 158, 170
SCM (supply chain manage-
ment). *See also* SCEM
(supply chain event man-
agement); Supply chain
blueprint
evolution of, 149–152

SCM (*continued*)
features and functions in, 169
meso-level blueprint and, 265,
266
micro-level technology blueprints and, 297
service platforms and, 58–59,
71, 168–170
supply-demand match prob-
lems and, 154–155
trends in, 153–158
Seagate Technology, 158
Sears, Roebuck & Co., 86, 110,
141, 142, 247
Seebeyond (company), 109, 170
Seiyu Ltd., 23
SelectaVision, 211
Self-service
composite processes and,
102–104
employee-centric blueprint
and, 179, 192, 194
multi-channel blueprint and,
92–93
supply chain blueprint and, 168
Service blueprint(s). *See also*
specific types
managing enterprise-wide execution with, 243–251
methodology, 239–261
need for, xxiii–xxv, 13–19
three categories of, xxvi, 17–18
Service level agreements, 102, 119,
142, 158. *See also* Contracts
Service platforms
BPM and, 58–59, 69–71, 74
creating value and, 78–80
CRM and, 58–59, 63, 71, 76,
78–79, 81
elements of, 70
employee-centric blueprint
and, 182–184, 200–202
focal points and, 57–61, 81
high-level view of, 59–61
innovation and, 55–56, 59, 64,
69, 72–73, 81
layers of, 59–61
managing complexity and,
65–66, 68–78
micro-level technology blueprints and, 291–292
modularity and, 65–67, 71–72

moving to applications from, 78
objectives for, 81
portals and, 57–69, 80
product innovation blueprint
and, 225–226, 228–229
reverse auctions and, 126
supply chain blueprint and,
164–165, 168–170
types of, 78–81
Web Services and, 71–76
Services layer, 191, 192, 195–197
described, 23
multi-channel blueprint and,
99, 100–104
product innovation blueprint
and, 221, 222–224
spend management blueprint
and, 132–135
supply chain blueprint and,
160–161, 163–165
Wal-Mart and, 23
Services Oriented Architecture.
See SOA (Services Oriented
Architecture)
SFA (sales force automation), 91,
297
SG&A (sales, general, and administrative) processes, 4, 21
micro-level technology blueprints and, 304
Wal-Mart and, 26
Shewart, Walter, 269
Shopping carts, 133, 136
Siebel, xxi, xxiii
employee-centric blueprint
and, 200
IBM and, 324
multi-channel blueprint and,
98, 106, 108–109
service platforms and, 62
Siemens, 17, 248
Simon, Herb, 65
Simple Mail Transfer Protocol
(SMTP), 73
Simplification, 323–324
Singapore, 51, 56
Single-vendor standardization
Site Sessions, 234–235
Six Sigma, 244–245, 247–249
characteristics of, 268–269
criticism of, 272
cultural change and, 271–272

as the dominant performance
improvement method, 269
initiative (GE), 7, 19–21, 34
meso-level blueprints and,
263–285
micro-level technology blueprints and, 288
momentum of, 270–271
SLAs (service level agreements),
119, 142, 158. *See also*
Contracts; Service level
agreements
SMBs (small- and mid-sized
businesses), 14, 91, 174
Smith, Frederick W., 95
SMTP (Simple Mail Transfer
Protocol), 73
SOA (Services Oriented Architecture), 11–12, 72, 333
business value of, 74
described, 11, 74–77
spend management blueprint
and, 138
Solectron, 153
Sony Electronics, 67, 126, 210
Sourcing. *See also* Outsourcing
employee-centric blueprint
and, 201
spend management blueprint
and, 133, 144
Southwest Airlines, 4, 95
Spar Handels AG, 22
SPD (sustainable product design),
232
Spend analysis, 129–130
Spend management blueprint.
See also Procurement;
Suppliers
composite processes and,
132–135, 138
contracts and, 129–130, 133,
142
defining business problems
and, 143–144
described, 117–146
ERP and, 124, 134, 137–138
the evolution of procurement
and, 119–123
focal points and, 118,
131–132
four categories of spending
used by, 122

global sourcing and, 125–127
long-term trends shaping, 123–130
need-to-have capability and, 125–127
service parts procurement and, 141–145
spend analysis and, 129–130
Spin-offs, 310–311
Standardization, 67, 299–300
Staples, 15
Starbucks, 51
Start-ups, 19, 120
Starwood Hotels, 248
Statistical Process Control, 7
Steam engine, invention of, 80
Stockouts, 154
Store of the Community program, 24
Store-Within-a-Store program, 24
Stovepiped applications, 168
Strategic improvement, 18, 31
Sun Microsystems, xxii–xxiii, 11, 327, 331
    employee-centric blueprint and, 204
    service platforms and, 72, 75, 76
    SUN ONE server, 72, 204
SuperMontage trading platform, 58
Supplier(s). *See also* Spend management blueprint; Supply chains; Vendors
    80/20 rule regarding, 127
    management services, 117–146
    relationship management, 43–44
Supply chain(s), 8, 10. *See also* Suppliers; Supply chain blueprint
    adaptive, 157–158
    BMOs and, 258–259
    changing process priorities and, 7
    focal points and, 39–41, 52
    service platforms and, 58–60, 76, 78, 79
    strategy map, 162–163
    streamlined, 39–41
    visibility, 172
    Wal-Mart and, 23, 24–25, 28

Supply chain blueprint. *See also* Supply chains
    composite processes and, 160, 163–165
    described, 147–176
    the evolution of supply chain management and, 149–152
    layers of, 160–161
    service platforms and, 164–165, 168–170
    supply-demand match problems and, 154–155
Surround Sessions, 233–234
SWOT Analysis, 243–244, 246
Symbiosis, between focal points and portals, 57

Taiwan, 153
Target (company), 4, 86, 100
TCI (Telecommunications, Inc.), 320, 321
TCO (total cost of ownership), 64
TCP/IP (Transmission Control Protocol/Internet Protocol), 73
TD Waterhouse, 36
Technology infrastructure layer, 23, 24
Telecommunications Act (1996), 317
Telesales, 88–91. *See also* Call centers
Telstra, 248
Tempus, 65
Teradata technology, 27
Tesco, 18, 56, 94
Theory of Constraints, 267
ThinkPad (IBM), 66
3M (Minnesota Mining and Manufacturing), 17, 248
3PLs (third-party logistics providers),
Tibco, 74, 109, 170
Tiffany & Co., 43
Time-to-value, 63
To-Be state, 264, 277–279, 307
Toffler, Alvin, 53
Toll-free numbers, 35. *See also* Call centers
TotalHOME (company), 149

Toyota, 15, 43, 52, 272
Toys "R" Us, 4, 100
TPS (Toyota Production System), 244, 267
TQM (Total Quality Management), 7, 247, 248. *See also* Quality
    characteristics of, 268–269
    meso-level blueprints and, 267, 268–269
Transitional plans, 115
Transmission Control Protocol/Internet Protocol. *See* TCP/IP (Transmission Control Protocol/Internet Protocol)
Transora (company), 126
Transparency, procurement, 124–125
Travelocity, 57
Truth, "single version" of the, 226
TSRs (tele-services representatives), 88–89
Tyco, 316

UAN (Universal Application Network), xxiii, 71, 108, 109
Unigraphics, 213
Unisource Worldwide, 310, 311
Unisys, 185
Unitary model, 305
United Kingdom, 22, 281
Universal Studios, 220
UPS (United Parcel Service), xxi, 247
    call centers, 96
    focal points and, 43, 52
    multi-channel blueprint and, 96, 112
    third-party logistics and, 43
Urich Oil station, 93

Value(s). *See also* Value chain
    blueprint methodology and, 246
    focal points and, 13
    service platforms and, 72–73, 78–80
Value chain. *See also* Values
    IBM and, 323, 327
    supply chain blueprint and, 155, 169
    XML Web Services and, 72–73

Vantive (PeopleSoft), 106
Vendors, 7, 23. *See also* Suppliers
    employee-centric blueprint
        and, 200–202
    micro-level technology blue-
        prints and, 299–300
    multi-channel blueprint and,
        108–109
    product innovation blueprint
        and, 228–229
    service platforms and, 168–170
    spend management blueprint
        and, 138–141
    supply chain blueprint and,
        163, 168–170
VF Corporation, 299
Vigilance (company), 158, 170
Vitria (company), 74, 134, 170
Vivendi Universal, 18, 19, 316
VMI (vendor-managed inven-
    tory), 163
vMPF (virtual-Military Personnel
    Flight), 68
VOC (Voice of the Customer)
    technique, 225–226, 267, 275
Volkswagen, 153
Von Siemens, Werner, 332
VPI (Volume Producing Item)
    contest, 24
VSAT networks, 23

Wagoner, Rick, 203
Waitt, Ted, 41

Walgreens, 46
Wall Street Journal, The, 27
Wal-Mart, xxi, 22–28, 31, 52
    cross-channel experiences and,
        94–95
    employee-centric blueprint
        and, 178
    inside-out/outside-in alignment
        problems and, 13
    multi-channel blueprint and,
        94–95
    spend management blueprint
        and, 123
    strategic improvement and, 18
Walt Disney Company, 249–250
Walton, James, 22
Walton, Sam, 22
WebLogic (BEA), xxiii, 76
webMethods, 74, 109, 170, 172
Web portals. *See* Portals
Web Services, 191, 333
    architecture, 71–76, 99
    described, xxii, 11–12, 71
    micro-level technology blue-
        prints and, 299
    modularity and, 71–72
    multi-channel blueprint and, 99
    product innovation blueprint
        and, 221
    service platforms and, 71–76
    spend management blueprint
        and, 132
    supply chain blueprint and, 160

WebSphere (IBM), 11, 72, 76
Webvan (company), 94
Wells Fargo Bank, 247
Wendy's International, 247
Wertkauf hypermarket, 22
Whirlpool (company), 67, 141
Wi-Fi, 144
Windows (Microsoft), 89, 91
Wingspanbank, 94
WMS (warehouse management
    systems), 151, 297
WorldCom, 17
World Trade Center attacks, 27

xApps (SAP), xxiii, 11, 71, 76–78,
    108
Xelus (company), 145
XML (Extensible Markup Lan-
    guage)
    described, 72
    micro-level technology blue-
        prints and, 299
    spend management blueprint
        and, 127–128
    standards, 72–73, 127
    supply chain blueprint and,
        172
    Web Services and, 71–73

Yahoo!, 18, 55, 220

Zero-Defect Quality focal point,
    7, 15–17, 34, 43–44

informIT

YOUR GUIDE TO IT REFERENCE

Articles

Keep your edge with thousands of free articles, in-depth features, interviews, and IT reference recommendations – all written by experts you know and trust.

Online Books

Answers in an instant from **InformIT Online Book's** 600+ fully searchable on line books. For a limited time, you can get your first 14 days **free**.

Catalog

Review online sample chapters, author biographies and customer rankings and choose exactly the right book from a selection of over 5,000 titles.